T0237516

Lecture Notes in Computer Science

Lecture Notes in Computer Science

Edited by G. Goos and J. Hartmanis

143

Operating Systems Engineering

Proceedings of the 14th IBM Computer Science Symposium
Amagi, Japan, October 1980

Edited by M. Maekawa and L.A. Belady

Springer-Verlag
Berlin Heidelberg New York 1982

Editors

Mamoru Maekawa
Associate Professor, University of Tokyo
7-3-1 Hongo Bunkyo-ku, Tokyo, 113, Japan

Laszlo A. Belady
Manager of Software Technology, IBM Corporate Headquarters
Armonk, NY 10504, USA

CR Subject Classifications (1981): 4.35

ISBN 3-540-11604-4 Springer-Verlag Berlin Heidelberg New York
ISBN 0-387-11604-4 Springer-Verlag New York Heidelberg Berlin

Printing and binding: Beltz Offsetdruck, Hemsbach/Bergstr.
2145/3140-543210

PREFACE

Much research and advances in operating systems have been
made since an operating system became one of the largest
pieces of software of a computer system. Operating systems
have been the major driving force for software engineering
research because of performance, delivery and management
problems. Despite of much research and advances, however,
their understanding , construction and maintenance are still
largely based on direct experience. The Working Conference
on Operating Systems Engineering was organized to identify
and discuss major systematic engineering approaches by in-
viting leading specialists in this field. The following eight
topics were identified:

1. Concurrency and access control
2. Program behavior and performance models
3. Operating system evaluation
4. User interfaces
5. Distributed operating systems
6. Network operating systems
7. Development process and tools
8. Data flow machines

The first two topics, concurrency and performance, are tradi-
tionally in the center of operating system research. Here,
new developments are reported in addition to summaries of
past research. The third and fourth topics are concerned with
the dynamics of operating system programs. System evolution
is one of the major software engineering topics and it is
interesting to see how "mammoth" operating systems can be
made soft and flexible. The problem has long been recognized
but relevant systematic research is only recent. The fifth
and sixth topics address the problems in distributed computing systems, which have been in the focus of considerable
interest in recent years. New developments, both theoretical

and practical, are reported. The seventh topic is an important subject in software engineering and is covered by two studies in design methodologies and tools. The eigth and last topic addresses the problems of software development for data flow machines. Both researchers and practitioners should find this book interesting and useful.

The symposium and this book were made possible through the efforts of many people. We would particularly like to acknowledge IBM Japan for sponsoring the symposium.

M. Maekawa   L.A. Belady
University of Tokio   IBM, Armonk

CONTENTS

Part I. Concurrency Control and Access Control

Part II. Program Behavior and Performance Models

Part III. Operating System Evolution

Part IV. User Interfaces

Part V. Distributed Operating Systems

Part VI. Network Operating Systems

Part VII. Development Process and Tools

Part VIII. Data Flow Machines

Part I.

Concurrency Control and Access Control

Concurrency control and access control mechanisms are indispensable facilities to ensure the correctness of operations in multiprocess multiple resource systems. Various research has been carried out to find powerful, efficient and conceptually simple mechanisms. The first three papers discuss problems of concurrency control and the last paper is concerned with access control mechanisms. The first paper by N. Saito surveys major synchronization mechanisms and identifies important research topics. Especially, a classification of these mechanisms is made and properties used in parallel program verification are discussed. The second paper by H. Enomoto, N. Yonezaki, I. Miyamura and S. Sunuma proposes a new parallel programming language and an efficient scheduling algorithm. The algorithm is shown to be easily described in the proposed language. The third paper by K. Wada, K. Hagiwara, T. Araki and N. Tokura discusses new algebraic specification techniques for schedulers. Specifications of schedulers using these techniques are also given. The last paper by Y. Kambayashi is concerned with decentralized dynamic authorization mechanisms. New mechanisms which can specify security levels are presented.

SYNCHRONIZATION MECHANISMS FOR PARALLEL PROCESSING

Nobuo SAITO

Department of Mathematics
Faculty of Engineering
Keio University
3-14-1, Hiyoshi, Kohoku-Ku
Yokohama 223
JAPAN

ABSTRACT

The synchronization mechanism in parallel processing is a very important facility. This paper discusses the recent trends of synchronization mechanisms, especially from the point of general features and program verification.

1. INTRODUCTION

Synchronization mechanisms play an important role in parallel/ concurrent processing. A great varieties of such mechanisms have been proposed so far, and their characteristics have been discussed. This paper gives another discussion about the recent trends of synchronization mechanisms mainly from the points of views of general properties and program verification.

The first general purpose synchronization mechanism is a semaphore system proposed by E. W. Dijkstra. The monitor concept proposed by C. A. R. Hoare is based on the data abstraction technique, and both of these are used in shared resource computer systems. On the other hand, the recent development of microcomputers enabled the realization of distributed computer systems, and new concepts of the synchronization mechanisms for such systems were proposed. Communicating Sequential Processes(CSP), Distributed Processes(DP) and rendezvous mechanism in Ada are much different from rather classical mechanisms. These new mechanisms might rather easily be implemented in distributed computer systems. This paper first discusses the essential differences among these synchronization mechanisms.

It is quite important to develop verification techniques for parallel processing programs since the testing and debugging in such programs are much more difficult and tiresome than in sequential programs. The development of verification techniques is closely related to the investigation of formal semantics. It is very useful to discuss the formal and informal verification techniques for parallel processing programs with synchronization mechanisms. This paper discusses several verification techniques, and points out some difficulties.

2. TYPICAL SYNCHRONIZATION MECHANISMS

The followings are typical synchronization mechanisms proposed so far.

(1) *Semaphore System* [Dijkstra(1968)]

A semaphore system consists of semaphore variables, P operation and V operation. Several variations of this system can be considered.

(2) *Monitor* [Hoare(1974)]

A monitor is an abstract data type for a shared resource in parallel processing. The access to this resource is only allowed through use of the attached monitor procedures. This mechanism is implemented in *concurrent Pascal* and *Modula*, typical higher order languages for operating systems descriptions.

(3) *Path Expression* [Campbell and Habermann(1974)]

This is a specification description method, and it enables us to easily specify the order of executions of given procedures through use of the expressions like regular expressions with several extensions.

(4) *PDR(Process Data Representation)* [Hirose,Saito et al.(1981)]

This is also a specification description technique, and it is based on *Forcing Logic* which enables us to easily specify restriction conditions, e. g. the numbers of objects participated in specific operations in parallel processing.

(5) *CSP(Communicating Sequential Processes)* [Hoare(1978)]

This is the first synchronization mechanisms designed mainly aiming to describe parallel processing in distributed computer systems. There are no shared variables essentially involved in synchronization, and the communication is realized through message passing invoked by input/output commands.

(6) *DP(Distributed Processes)* [Brinch Hansen(1978)]

This also aims to describe parallel processing in distributed computer systems. Processes have no common variables for communication purpose, but they can call any common procedures defined within one process or another. Synchronization can be realized through use of nondeterministic mechanisms called guarded regions.

(7) *Rendezvous Mechanism* [Ada Reference Manual(1979)]

This is proposed in the newly designed higher order language *Ada*. It is much influenced by the above two mechanisms. The basic communication is realized by means of entry calls and their corresponding accept statements.

Let's show the description examples for the 1st readers-writers problem using the above mentioned synchronization mechanisms.

READERS-WRITERS PROBLEM

Ex. 1   semaphore system [Courtois, Heymans and Parnas(1971)]

begin
  readcount:integer;

  mutex,w:semaphore;

  { writecount:integer;}

  readcount:=; mutex:=w:=1; { writecount:=0; }
  parbegin

   .

   .

  reader i:

  begin

  loop

    P(mutex);

    readcount:=readcount+1;

    if readcount=1 **then** P(w);

    V(mutex);

    ——————————————

    reading is performed;

    ——————————————

    P(mutex);

    readcount:=readcount -1;

    if readcount=0 **then** V(w);

    V(mutex);

  end-loop

  end ;

   .

   .

writer j:

begin

loop

  P(w);

  { writecount:=writecount+1;}

  ——————————————

  writing is performed;

  ——————————————

  { writecount:=writecount -1; }

  V(w);

end-loop

end ;

   .

   .

  parend
end ;

Ex. 2   Monitor [Hoare(1974)]

```
class readers and writers: monitor
begin
  readcount:integer;

  busy:Boolean;

  OKtoread,OKtowrite:condition;

  procedure startread;

  begin
    if busy ∨ OKtowrite.queue then OKtoread.wait;

    readcount := readcount + 1 ;

    {rr := rr + 1; }

    OKtoread.signal

  end startread ;
  procedure endread ;

  begin
    readcount := readcount - 1;

    {rr := rr - 1; }

    if readcount = 0 then OKtowrite.signal

  end endread ;
  procedure startwrite ;

  begin
    if readcount ≠ 0 ∨ busy then OKtowrite.wait ;

    busy := true

    {rw := 1; }

  end startwrite ;
  procedure endwrite;

  begin
    busy := false;

    {rw := 0;}

    if OKtoread.queue then OKtoread.signal

            else OKtowrite.signal

  end endwrite;

  readcount :=0; busy := false; {rr := rw := 0;}

end readers and writers ;
```

Ex.3 path expression

> **path** {read} + write **end**

Ex. 4 PDR

$$[< r_1, r_2, r_3 >_0, [\ w_1, w_2\ ]_1]_1 \xrightarrow{\quad\text{ACCESS}\quad} < file >_1$$

> where
>
> r_1, r_2, r_3: readers
>
> w_1, w_2 : writers
>
> ACCESS : file accessing procedure
>
> [   ]: "at most" operator
>
> <   >: "at least" operator

Ex. 5   CSP   [Welsh, Lister and Salzman(1980)]

resource : :

> readers: **set** (n) · int ; readers:=();
>
> {rc,wc:int;   rc := wc := 0; }
>
> * [(i:1..n)   ¬ (i **in** readers); user(i) ? startread()
>
>   ———→   readers.include(i)   {rc:=rc+1; }
>
>   □ (i:1..n) i **in** readers; user(i) ? endread()
>
>   ———→   readers.excluded(i) {rc:=rc -1; }
>
>   □ (i:1..n) readers.empty;   user(i) ? startwrite() {wc:=wc+1; }
>
>   ———→   user(i) ? endwrite()   {wc:=wc -1; }

user(i:1..n)   : :

> * [T ———→   resource ! startread(); reading; resource ! endread()
>
>   □ T   ———→   resource ! startwrite(); writing; resource ! endwrite()
>
>   ]

where include(i) and exclude(i) are operations to add and remove
an element i to a set readers.

Ex. 6   DP   [Brinch Hansen(1978)]

process resource

    s:int

    proc   startread   **when** $s \geq 1$: s:=s+1 **end**

    proc endread   **if** $s > 1$: s:=s -1 **end**

    proc startwrite   **when** $s = 1$: s:=0 **end**

    proc endwrite   **if** $s = 0$: s:=1 **end**

    s:=1

process reader

    do true:

        call resource.startread

        reading

        call resource.endread

    end

process writer

    do true:

    call resource.startwrite

    writing

    call resource.endwrite

    end

Ex. 7 rendezvous

```
task reader-writer is
   entry startread;
   entry endread;
   entry startwrite;
   entry endwrite;
end ;

task body reader-writer is
   readcount: integer :=0;
   begin
     loop
       select
         accept startread;
         readcount := readcount + 1;
       or
         accept endread;
         readcount := readcount - 1;
       or
         when readcount = 0  = >
           accept startwrite;
           accept endwrite;
       end select ;
     end loop ;
   end ;
end reader-writer ;

task body reader is
   begin
     loop
       startread;
       reading;
       endread;
     end loop ;
   end ;
end reader;

task body writer is
   begin
     loop
       startwrite;
       writing;
       endwrite;
     end loop ;
   end ;
end writer ;
```

3. PROBLEMS CONSIDERED

There are many interesting problems about synchronization mechanisms.

(1) *comparison and classification of general features*

It is necessary to classify the features of various synchronization mechanisms.

(2) *descriptive power*

Synchronization mechanisms should be included as basic constructors of certain programming languages for parallel processing. Therefore, it is important for such language constructors to have sufficient power so as to easily describe complex synchronizations and communications among processes.

Descriptive power might be rather a vague sense, but the qualitative and quantitative comparison of CSP and DP reported by J. Welsh et al. [Welsh, Lister and Salzman(1980)] is a very good example of the approach for this problem.

(3) *implementation*

It is very important to efficiently and correctly implement synchronization mechanisms. One problem is what kind of hardware configuration is based on to implement these mechanisms. Whether a shared memory exists or not is one of the essential points. Another problem is to implement synchronization mechanism without causing system deadlocks. It is not required to avoid deadlocks which are caused by a user misuse of synchronization primitives, but it is necessary to avoid deadlocks which are caused by system implementation itself. Especially, synchronization mechanisms based on the message passing should carefully be implemented since the symmetric usage of input/output(read/write) commands can cause intra system deadlocks [Siberschatz(1979)].

(4) *verification of programs*

Verification techniques for parallel programs have been developed so far [Owicki and Gries(1976)]. They are not, however, directly related to synchronization mechanisms. Several essential properties of parallel processing and process synchronization can be represented from the points of particular aspects of process behaviors. For example, for the semaphore system, there is an invariant relation among the times of execution and passing of P and V operations. Such a relation can be utilized to verify several program properties.

Rigorous verification of parallel programs might be done by utilizing both verification techniques for sequential programs(e.g. Floyd-Hoare logic) and of verifictaions of essential properties of parallel programs.

(5) *formal semantics of synchronization mechanisms*

Formal definition of semantics of parallel processing and synchronization mechanisms will contribute to (i) the correct implementation of a language translator and its support operating system, (ii) the establishment of verification rules for parallel programs. The recent development of denotational semantics for parallel processing with message passing synchronization mechanism[Milner(1979)] is one of the examples of such formal semantics.

4. CLASSIFICATION OF GENERAL FEATURES

Various kinds of synchronization mechanisms are classified from the several points of views. The followings are the important points in the classification.

(1) *shared variables/non-shared variables*

The first point is whether a synchronization mechanism is implemented using shared variables or not. If shared variables are used, it is rather easy to realize communication and an indivisible operation. When shared variables are not used, communication is realized using a message passing mechanism. In the case of distributed computer architecture, the non-shared variable mechanism is rather easy to implement. Therefore, the shared variable type is called centralized type, while the non-shared variables type is called distributed type.

(2) *active/passive encapsulated objects*

The second point is whether encapsulated shared resources are active or passive. When a message passing is the basic facility of communication, it is necessary to let all the encapsulated objects active because resource usage requests must be informed through message passing.

(3) *determinism/non-determinism*

When an encapsulated resource is an active object, it is necessary to provide this active object with the capability of describing non-deterministic behaviors. Shared resources should usually accept several kinds of requests simultaneously, and sequentially controlled executions of statements cannot realize the arbitrary order of acceptance of requests.

(4)   *statement/restriction condition*

There are two ways to describe synchronous operations of processes: one is to specify the flow of control through use of statements (synchronization primitives) and the other to specify the behaviors of processes through use of global restriction conditions.

It is easier to understand restriction conditions rather than parallel programs with synchronization primitives . It is, however, more convenient to describe the precise behaviors of processes through use of synchronization primitives rather than through use of restriction conditions.

Table 1 shows the classification of the synchronization mechanisms from these point of views mentioned above.

5. VERIFICATION OF PARALLEL PROGRAMS WITH SYNCHRONIZATION MECHANISMS

The verification of parallel program is a very important and a difficult problem. The verification rules for synchronization mechanisms have not clearly defined yet, and the rigorous formal system for a language with higher order synchronization primitives should be investigated.

Several properties of parallel programs can be defined by means of a certain kinds of higher level concepts(higher level of abstraction), and the informal methods of verification based on higher level concepts would be very convenient. As a higher level concepts, we may consider the number of times of executions of a particular statement, the number of objects participating a certain operation, the timing order of executions of particular statements and so forth.

Some properties generally holding in synchronization mechanisms have been investigated. Let's discuss these properties in the following.

SEMAPHORE   SYSTEM

There is the following invariant relation among the numbers of times P and V operations

Table 1 classification of synchronization mechanisms

	shared variables/ (centralized) non-shared variables (distributed)	active/ passive	determinism/ non-determinism	statement/ restriction condition
semaphore system	shared variables (centralized)	passive	determinism	statement
monitor	shared variables (centralized)	passive	determinism	statement
path expression	shared variables (centralized)	passive	determinism	restrict condition
PDR(Process Data Representation)	shared variables (centralized)	passive	determinism	restrict condition
CSP(Communicating Sequential Processes)	non-shared variables (distributed)	active	non-determinism	statement
DP(Distributed Processes)	non-shared variables (distributed)	active	non-determinism	statement
Rendezvous	non-shared variables (distributed)	active	non-determinism	statement

for one semaphore variables are executed [Habermann(1972)].

$$npp(s) = min[np(s), C(s) + nv(s)] \tag{1}$$

where

s: a semaphore variable

$np(s)$: how many times P(s) was executed;

$nv(s)$: how many times V(s) was executed;

$npp(s)$: how many times P(s) was passed;

$C(s)$: the initial value of s.

From the above invariant, it is possible to introduce several invariant relations among shared variables and control variables.

Consider the semaphore system solution for the readers-writers problem shown in Ex. 1. For a writer process, a control variable writecount is given to count the number of writer processes executing the writing operation. The requirements for this problem are described as follows:

$$\neg(readcount > 0 \wedge writecount > 0) \tag{2}$$

$$0 \leq writecount \leq 1 \tag{3}$$

$$0 \leq readcount \leq n \tag{4}$$

Consider the case when at least one reader is in the reading region and P(w) was passed k times. The value of the readcount is positive. In this case, V(w) was executed (k-1) times, and $npp(s) = 1 + (k - 1) = k$.

If a writer is in the writing region, the writecount becomes positive. However, this is impossible, and the invariant (2) always holds. The other invariants are verified in a similar way.

PATH EXPRESSION

The path expression specifies any number of iterations between **path** and **end**. Therefore, there is an invariant relation among the number of times of executions of the specified procedures during a certain period. For example,

$$\textbf{path} \quad a;b \quad \textbf{end} \quad \Longrightarrow \quad \#(a) \geq \#(b) \geq \#(a) - 1,$$

$$\textbf{path} \quad a + b \quad \textbf{end} \quad \Longrightarrow \quad k \geq \#(a) + \#(b) \geq 0$$

where k is the number of iterations of the path,

$$\textbf{path} \quad (a - b)^n \quad \textbf{end} \quad \Longrightarrow \quad n \geq \#(a) - \#(b) \geq 0$$

$$[n \geq \#(a) \geq \#(b) \geq 0],$$

$$\textbf{path} \quad (a - b - c)^n \quad \textbf{end} \quad \Longrightarrow \quad \#(a) \geq \#(b) \geq \#(c) \geq \#(a) - n,$$

where $\#(p)$ denotes the number of times a procedure p is executed.

These invariants are also useful for verifying the invariants among control variables and some other meaningful variables.

PDR

In PDR, the forcing operators are used to specify the number of objects (processes and data) joining a particular operation at a certain time or period. This representation is considered to be very high level abstraction, and the difficulties of the verification of several properties might be much reduced.

MONITOR

C. A. R. Hoare discussed the verification of monitor procedures in [Hoare(1974)]. The monitor is an abstract data type (an encapsulated object), and the verification method for an abstract data was discussed in [Hoare(1972)]. In this method, a monitor procedure $p_j(a_1, ..., a_{n_j})$ is considered to model the operation f_j in an abstract space. The effect of the monitor procedure statement is represented as an assignment statement

$$t_i := f_j(t_i, a_1, ..., a_{n_j});$$

It is, of course, the case that a certain invariant relation I holds for local variables, and this invariant I holds before and after the monitor procedure call. Moreover, there are several wait and signal operations in monitor procedures, and there is an assertion B corresponding to each of the condition variables b. Using this assertion B, the semantics of the wait and signal for a condition variable b is defined as follows:

$$I\{b.wait\}I \bigwedge B, \tag{5}$$

$$I \bigwedge B\{b.signal\}I. \tag{6}$$

The synchronization primitives in monitor procedures are used only for synchronization of the timings of executions of procedures, and the total effect of the monitor procedure can be defined quite similar to that of the procedure of an abstract data type.

Consider the following monitor procedure:

monitor   M ;
  procedure P_j ;
  begin
    Q_j ;
    b.wait ;
    Q_j'
  end

The semantics of this procedure is defined as follows:

$$\mathcal{A} = t \bigwedge I \bigwedge P_j(t)\{Q_j\}I \bigwedge \mathcal{A} = f_j(t) \tag{7}$$

$$\mathcal{A} = f_j(t) \bigwedge I \bigwedge B\{Q_j'\}I \bigwedge \mathcal{A} = f_j'(f_j(t)) \tag{8}$$

total effect

$$\mathcal{A} = t \bigwedge I \bigwedge P_j(t)\{Q_j; b.wait; Q_j'\}I \bigwedge \mathcal{A} = f_j'(f_j(t)) \tag{9}$$

The semantics of the monitor procedure with signal primitives is also defined in a similar way.

Consider the monitor solution for the readers-writers problem shown in **Ex. 2**. There are four monitor procedures: (1) startread; (2) endread; (3) startwrite; (4) endwrite. The concrete variables are:

readcount:integer;

busy: Boolean;

OKtoread,OKtowrite: condition.

The invariant relation I is

$$busy \supset readcount = 0. \tag{10}$$

And the equivalence relations also hold:

$$OKtoread \equiv \neg busy \tag{11}$$

$$OKtowrite \equiv \neg busy \wedge readcount = 0. \tag{12}$$

The abstract space is represented by the following control variables, and the representation function A is defined as a mapping from the concrete space to the abstract space:

rr: the number of running readers,

rw: the number of running writers.

$$A = (rr = readcount) \wedge (rw = \text{if} \quad busy \quad \text{then} \quad 1 \quad \text{else} \quad 0). \tag{13}$$

The effects of the operations on the abstract space are required to satisfy the following definition:

(1)   startread: $rr := \textbf{if} \quad rw = 0 \quad \textbf{then} \quad rr + 1;$

(2)   endread: $rr := rr - 1;$

(3)   startwrite: $rw := \textbf{if} \quad rr = 0 \wedge rw = 0 \quad \textbf{then} \quad 1;$

(4)   endwrite: $rw := 0.$

It is necessary to verify that the concrete monitor procedures will model the above abstract operations. For example, in the startread procedure, there is a synchronization primitives OKtoread.wait. Using the semantics of wait in (5), the equivalence relation (11) and the representation function A in (13), the effect of the startread procedure is given by the following:

$$rr := \textbf{if} \quad rw = 0 \quad \textbf{then} \quad rr + 1.$$

The verification for other procedures can also be done in a similar way.

CSP

In CSP, there are no shared variables among processes, and interactions are only done by message passing through input/output commands.

Consider the two processes X and Y as shown in **Fig. 1**. In the process Y, the input command X?F is considered to be an assignment statement $F := E$. Of course, the input/output commands synchronize the progress of execution, and the following ordering of the program section should be observed:

$$X1 \quad \text{precedes} \quad X2 \quad \text{and} \quad Y2;$$
$$Y1 \quad \text{precedes} \quad Y2 \quad \text{and} \quad X2.$$

Moreover, when these processes iterate forever, the corresponding input/output com-

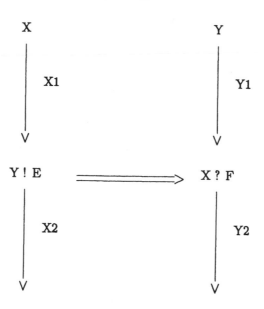

Figure 1   Process Interaction in CSP

mands match the same number of times. Therefore, the following restriction holds:

$$np(!) = np(?) \tag{14}$$

$$np(?) \le n(!) \le np(?) + 1 \tag{15}$$

$$np(!) \le n(?) \le np(!) + 1 \tag{16}$$

    where

$np(\ )$: the number of passing of the corresponding commands;

$n(\ )$: the number of issuing of the corresponding commands.

The sequential control part in each of the processes can be verified by means of the conventional methods(e.g. Floyd-Hoare logic).

The fundamental method of the verification for CSP is summarized as follows:

(1)   For each process, define program sections which are separated by input/output com-

mands.

(2) Make all the possible arrangements of the program sections preserving ordering relations defined by input/output commands and other conditions.

(3) Verify that specified assertions are satisfied for each of the possible arrangements of the program sections.

The arrangement of the program sections corresponds to the introduction of power domain in denotational semantics of parallel processing[Milner(1979) and Plotkin(1976)].

This method, however, looks very messy, and we need some devices to reduce the number of arrangements of program sections. For example, the restriction on passing of input/output commands, the ordering of issuing of input/output commands, the Boolean guards in guarded commands, the sequential control flow in a process and so forth might be useful and convenient tools for this purpose.

6. CONCLUSION

This paper surveyed and discussed the synchronization mechanisms for parallel processing. Newly proposed synchronization mechanisms aim to handle distributed computer systems.

Verification methods for these synchronization mechanisms were also discussed, and it is necessary to investigate a good method for CSP,DP and rendezvous. One approach is to analyse several practical examples so as to find out several convenient rules for verification. This might be called an informal approach. Another one is to establish the formal semantics for the above mentioned new mechanisms so that rigorous verification rules can be obtained. Since interactions among processes are very simple, it is quite hopeful to get a good result. Several works on denotational semantics for distributed processing would stimulate this investigation. This might be called a formal approach. In addition, the cooperation of these two approaches will enhance the development of the verification method so much.

REFERENCES

Brinch Hansen, Per (1978).   Distributed Processes: A Concurrent Programming Concept, CACM, Vol. 21, No.11, Nov. 1978, pp.934-941

Campbell, R. H. and Habermann, A. N. (1974).   The Specification of Process Synchronization by Path Expressions, Lecture Notes in Computer Science, Vol.16, Springer Verlag, 1974, pp.89-102

Courtois, P. J., Heymans, F. and Parnas, D. L. (1971). Concurrent Control with "Readers" and "Writers",   CACM , Vol.14, No.10, Oct. 1971, pp.667-668

Dijkstra, E. W. (1968). Cooperating Sequential Processes,   Programming Languages (ed. Genuys, F.), Academic Press, New York, 1968, pp.43-112

Habermann, A. N. (1972).   Synchronization of Communicating Sequential Processes, CACM, Vol.15, No.3, March 1972, pp.171-176

Hirose, K. Saito, N. Doi, N. et al. (1981). Specification Technique for Parallel Processing: Process-Data Representation, AFIPS Conference Proceedings NCC, Vol.50, May 1981 , pp.407-413

Hoare, C.A.R. (1972). Proof of Correctness of Data Representations,   Acta Informatica, Vol. 1, 1972, pp.271-281

Hoare, C.A.R. (1974). Monitors: An Operating System Structuring Concept,   CACM, Vol.17, No.10, Oct. 1974, pp.549-557

Hoare, C.A.R. (1978). Communicating Sequential Processes,   CACM, Vol.21, No.8, Aug. 1978, pp.666-677

Milner, R. (1979). Flowgraphs and Flow Algebras,   JACM, Vol. 26, No.4, Oct. 1979, pp.794-818

Owicki, S. and Gries, D. (1976). Verifying Properties of Parallel Programs: An Axiomatic Approach,   CACM, Vol. 19, No.5, May 1976, pp.280-285

Plotkin, G. (1976). A Powerdomain Construction,   SIAM Journal on Computing, Vol.5,

No.3, 1976, pp.452-487

Siberschatz, A. (1979). Communication and Synchronization in Distributed Systems, IEEE Trans. on Software Engineering, Vol. SE-5, No. 6, Nov. 1979, pp.542-546

SIGPLAN Notices (1979). Preliminary Ada Reference Manual, SIGPLAN Notices, Vol.14, No.6, Part A, June 1979

Welsh, J., Lister, A. and Salzman, E.J. (1980). A Comparison of Two Notations for Process Communication, Lecture Notes in Computer Science, Vol. 79, Springer Verlag, 1980, pp.225-254

A PARALLEL PROGRAMMING LANGUAGE

AND

DESCRIPTION OF SCHEDULER

Hajime Enomoto[*], Naoki Yonezaki[*],
Isao Miyamura[**], Masayuki Sunuma[*]

[*] Tokyo Institute of Technology
[**] Niigata University

ABSTRACT

A new parallel processing language and a scheduling algorithm for parallel processing systems are introduced. The design objectives of the language are clarity, understandability and modifiability. Considering these objectives, we give frameworks of the language. In this language, an algorithm and its constraints are described separately, and hierarchical structure of a problem decomposition is described explicitly. We also give a scheduling algorithm in which processing states are considered. As the state change incurs overheads, the scheduler makes trade-off between wating time of tasks and total loss. Finally, we describe the outline of the scheduler in this language for comprehension of both the language and the scheduler.

1. INTRODUCTION

We are now confronting software crisis, and we need a new programming language which has such characteristics as simplicity of description, program understandability, modifiability and computational efficiency. In order to overcome these problems, many researches have been carried out: hierarchical design by stepwise refinement, structured programming, modularization, abstraction, information hiding and localization. But almost all of currently used programming languages have a fatal drawback, that is, a procedure is a mixture of the algorithm and its constraints for execution. As the constraints are mixed with the algorithm, it is difficult to understand them without tracing the program.

Until now, many parallel programming languages are proposed. They can express parallel operations so that they can be executed efficiently. Besides this merit, they also have a demerit. As the components are executed concurrently, it is difficult to understand the total behavior and even a little error can cause enormous damages.

Considering these points, we propose a new parallel programming language. It can describe parallel operation among modules and constraints are described separately from the respective module actions. So the mutual relationship among modules is very clear and explicit. We allow processes to be nested arbitrarily to leave the steps of hierarchical design explicitly in the program text. This increases the program understandability and modifiability.

Next, we give a scheduling algorithm for the parallel processing system which executes a program written in this language. We introduce a concept of processing state for a processing unit. A processing unit changes its state in accordance with the task it executes. Each task requires a processing unit to take some state. Under this model, we give the optimal scheduling algorithm which trades-off the average waiting time of tasks and the state changes.

2. DESIGN PHILOSOPHY

Many parallel programming languages have been developed or proposed. As all of them have some defects, we propose a new parallel programming language which lessens these defects.

Before the detailed language specification, we explain the design philosophy of this language. A language is not only a tool to describe an algorithm but it also models human thought. A parallel programming language can express parallel operations and it isn't necessary to serialize the parallel actions. This reduces the artificial restrictions. In this way, a parallel programming language is superior to sequential one in efficiency and in conceptual clarity.

Besides above mentioned merits, it also has many demerits. As each component of the algorithm is executed concurrently, problems of synchronization and mutual exclusion between components arise, and it is difficult to understand the total behavior. Even a little carelessness often results in enormous confusion. To avoid these defects, we establish the following design philosophies.

2.1 HIERARCHICAL DECOMPOSITION

We need facilities to hierarchically decompose a problem and to express its step explicitly in the program text. Even if the total problem is complex and beyond our comprehension, each decomposed module is simple and comprehensive. This makes both software development and modification more easy.

We introduce four kinds of modules: process, resource, procedure and function. They can be arbitrarily nested to express the hierarchical structure.

2.2 DESCRIPTION OF PARALLELISM

A parallel programming language must be able to express parallel actions, but extra description of parallelism makes a program much complicated. We must decide what parallelism should be described and what parallelism shouldn't.

We can distinguish two levels of parallelism. One is at the statement level, and the other is at the module level. Parallelism at the statement level can be detected automatically by elaborate compilers, so the description of this level only complicates the program. We don't provide primitives to describe parallelism at this level. On the other hand, it is difficult to automatically detect parallelism among modules which interact with each other.

Considering these points, major efforts should be devoted to the description of parallelism among modules. This parallelism enables decomposition based on the functions which modules perform rather than based on the control flow.

As for parallelism, two types of implementation are possible. One is that parallelism is only the possibility declaration of parallel processing and nothing is assumed about whether or not parallel processing is actually done.

The other is that it requires actual parallel processing. That is, if a module is declared to be executed in parallel and it doesn't await an event, it obtains processor control within a finite time regardless of the other modules.

The second assumption is stronger and more useful than the first one, and we adopt the second implementation in our language.

2.3 SEPARATION OF ALGORITHM FROM ITS CONSTRAINTS

Synchronization and mutual exclusion among modules are needed only for parallel processing. They are not essential parts of the algorithm and they should be described separately from the program body.

If the constraints of the algorithm are dynamically expressed in the program body, readability and understandability of the program will be lost. Program modification and error detection also become more difficult. We describe static constraints in the program text to be able to understand them without tracing the behavior of the program.

2.4 MODULE INTERACTION

Modules which constitute a program can't be completely independent and they interact with each other. Former parallel programming languages allow shared variables among multiple modules. This requires primitives such as SEMAPHORE to synchronize or to control mutual exclusion. These primitives are major cause of errors.

Module interaction is implemented in two ways.

1) Shared objects. A module which shares objects with other modules can access them

freely.

2) Shared values. A module only shares values with particular modules. That is, a module receives values from another module. After that, two modules can't affect each other concerning to the values.

These two types of module interactions are different in nature. They are just like call-by-reference and call-by-value in parameter passing. We provide two primitives for respective types. The first type of module interaction is implemented by a resource. A resource controls the access to the shared variables. The second type is implemented by message communication. All the former parallel programming languages which don't allow direct sharing of variables provide only one primitive.

A module can interact with other modules by means of two primitives, but it should have the minimum facilities to perform its function. If it has more than the minimum, its error can give enormous damages to other modules. The facilities of a module are restricted in both static and dynamic manners.

2.5 NON-DETERMINACY

Non-determinacy means that there exist multiple possible sequences of operations. It has two different interpretations.

1) If there exists a sequence of operations that produces a result which satisfies specified conditions, its result becomes that of the total operation. If all the sequences produce unsatisfactory results, the total result is undefined. This is just like one in case of automata theory.

2) The result of the total operation is any one of the results obtained by respective sequences. Usually all the sequences produce the same result.

The first interpretation is difficult to understand and to implement. On the other hand, the second interpretation is easy to implement. We usually use non-determinacy in the second sense.

3. LANGUAGE SPECIFICATION

In this language, we introduce four types of modules: process, resource, procedure and function. They can be nested arbitrarily so as to describe hierarchical decomposition of a given problem. Procedure and function are not so different from those in other languages, thus we don't explain them in detail.

A program is constructed from declarations of processes, procedures, functions and types. The processes declared here are initiated automatically when the program starts, the other objects declared here can be accessed by all the modules.

3.1 PROCESS

A process is a module and is executed concurrently. A process is composed of declaration part and execution part. Each process has its name. Process name is a character string or a string with subscripts. Sometimes it is necessary to initiate many processes which perform the same function with different parameters. Subscripts are introduced to discriminate respective occurrences. Such a process is identified by a character string with subscripts. Each subscript can take only a discrete value and its range must be declared explicitly.

```
p_name [subscripts] = PROCESS (parameters) ;
      { process declarations }
      { type declarations }
        variable declarations
      { procedure declarations }
      { function declarations }
      { constant declarations }
      { exception definition }
        statement list
END
```

The outermost processes are initiated automatically, and the other processes are initiated by initiate statements as below. The modules which can execute an initiate statement of a process are bounded to its father or brother modules.

```
INIT process_name ( parameters ) ;
```

When a process is initiated, it can receive value parameters, process names, procedure names and function names.

A process can declare processes, types, variables, procedures, functions and constants in any order. The scope of types, procedures, functions and constants obeys the general scope rule in ALGOL 60. But the variables declared here can be accessed only here. Besides the objects declared here, any types, procedures, functions and constants declared in ancestor modules can also be accessed here.

The process body which describes the action can include an exception definition and a statement list. An exception definition describes the action in exceptional cases. In ordinary case, the statement list is being executed. Further details of an exception definition will be explained later.

A process normally terminates when it executes TERMINATE statement or when it reaches END statement, and abnormally terminates when its father module terminates before it normally terminates.

3.2 MESSAGE COMMUNICATION

Message communication is one type of module interactions. It directly transmits a message from one module to another. Message communication is categorized to two types according to the participants.

type 1. between processes

type 2. between father module and its child process

In case of type 1, a target process is either 1) its father, 2) its brother, 3) its child or 4) a process whose name is informed of by another module as a parameter.

In case of type 2, the father module can be a resource, a procedure or a function which includes the declaration of the target process.

To exchange a message, one module executes an INPUT statement and another module executes an OUTPUT statement. An INPUT statement receives data from the sender and assigns them to the variables. An OUTPUT statement sends data evaluated from the expressions to the receiver. A label is used to identify the message, but it can be omitted.

```
INPUT   {label:} variable_list FROM sender
OUTPUT  {label:} expression_list TO receiver
```

Sender and receiver specify the destination processes. A destination is either a process name or 'PARENT'. If the destination process has subscripts, some of them may not be specified explicitly. To indicate this, don't care symbol '?' is used before the identifier.

```
identifier (sub1, sub2, ?id3, sub4,... )
```

When a message is transmitted, the identifier preceded by don't care symbol '?' takes the corresponding value. Its value can be referenced after that, but it can't be modified. If 'PARENT' is specified as destination, it means that the destination module is its father.

An INPUT statement and an OUTPUT statement are said to match if the following conditions hold.

1. Both labels are equal or both labels are omitted.

2. Sender of the INPUT statement specifies the module which executes the OUTPUT statement.

3. Receiver of the OUTPUT statement specifies the module which executes the INPUT statement.

A message is actually transmitted when an INPUT statement and an OUTPUT statement match. That is, automatic buffering isn't supported.

In this way, we statically restrict the destination module because of the following reasons. In other languages, message communication is allowed between any pair of modules. This increases danger of deadlocks and damages in case of errors. To avoid them, we restrict the message communication as statically as possible. This is based on the principle that a module should have the minimum rights to perform its function.

3.3 EXCEPTION HANDLING

The action of a process is determined by the program text, including non-determinacy. A process is not affected by other modules unless it executes an I/O statement. There remains a problem how to describe the actions to respond to exceptional events.

As such an event seldom happens, embedding exception handling in normal actions makes the program text more difficult to understand. Considering these points, we describe exception handling separately from the normal control flow as an EXCEPTION statement.

```
EXCEPTION
        {P=i_1 :} input statement_1 -> statement list_1 ,
        {P=i_2 :} input statement_2 -> statement list_2 ,
                    .
                    .
                    .
        {P=i_n :} input statement_n -> statement list_n
    END ;
```

An exceptional event is reception of an urgent message. Where i_1, i_2 and so on are integer values and specify priority of respective exception handling. Small number means high priority. If 'P=i' is omitted, the lowest priority is assumed.

If the control is on the normal action or on the exception handling with lower priority and if another module executes an OUTPUT statement which matches with input statement$_j$, its processing is interrupted and the control transfers to statement list$_j$. At the end of statement list$_j$, the control returns to the point interrupted before.

As a restriction, the INPUT statement in a guard of EXCEPTION statement is not allowed to appear elsewhere. Multiple occurrences make it impossible to decide which occurrence should receive a message. To avoid this problem, multiple occurrences of such an INPUT statement are inhibited.

A message receiver can decide whether it receives a message in exceptional mode or normal mode. The sender can't specify the message mode. This separate description increases clarity and understandability of a program.

3.4 RESOURCE

A resource consists of global variables and global procedures. It controls the access to the shared variables.

```
TYPE r_name = RESOURCE  (parameters) ;
                { process declarations }
                { type declarations }
                  variable declarations
                { constant declarations }
                  global procedure declarations
                { procedure declarations }
                { function declarations }
                { parallel definition }
                { initialization statement list }
        END;
```

This declares a type and names it r_name. An instance of this resource is created by a CREATE statement and the area for global variables are reserved.

```
VAR xx: r_name ;      CREATE ( xx: actual_parameters );
```

When an instance is created, its initialization statement list is executed and its global variables exist until it lapses.

An instance of a resource is accessed by a variable called capability. A capability consists of access rights and a pointer to an instance of the declared type. Access right is the right to invoke respective global procedures or to copy the capability.

A global procedure in an instance pointed by capability xx is accessed like a procedure call.

```
CALL proc_name ( xx: actual_parameters );

GLOBAL PROCEDURE proc_name ( parameters );
                variable declarations
                {CONDITION : p(x) ;}
                statement list
        END;
```

There is a case in which a global procedure can't be executed until some conditions become true. In such case, the conditions are separated from the procedure body and are represented as condition statement. For example, pop

operation for a stack can be applied only if the stack isn't empty. Emptiness of
the stack must be checked before pop operation. Even if the procedure is called, it
must wait until the condition holds. It is similar to AWAIT primitive proposed by
HANSEN[1973].

A resource can only access the variables declared in it and the variables
passed as parameters. A module which wants to access the shared variables calls the
global procedure and accesses them indirectly.

Global procedures in a resource are usually called by multiple modules. Some
combinations of procedures can be executed concurrently and the others can't. In
MONITOR, all the procedures are executed exclusively and this restriction is too
severe. The specification of parallel execution by means of SEMAPHORE or PATH
EXPRESSION makes a program more complex and difficult to understand. We decide to
specify parallelism statically in parallel definition as follows.

PARALLEL
$$p_1(x) \;-\!\!>\! proc_{11}, proc_{12}, \ldots, process_{1m_1};$$
$$p_2(x) \;-\!\!>\! proc_{21}, proc_{22}, \ldots, process_{2m_2};$$
$$\cdot$$
$$\cdot$$
$$\cdot$$
$$p_n(x) \;-\!\!>\! proc_{n1}, proc_{n2}, \ldots, process_{nm_n}$$
END;

If condition $p_i(x)$ holds, procedures $proc_{i1}$, $proc_{i2}$ and so on can be executed
concurrently. If procedure yyy can be called concurrently by multiple modules, it
is described as follows.

$$p(x) \;-\!\!>\! yyy;$$

Condition $p_i(x)$ can only include global variables. Instead of specifying the
conditions for exclusive execution, we decide to specify the condition to execute
multiple procedures concurrently. Even if we forget to describe the parallelism, it
causes no vital errors. However, in the opposite case, vital errors may occur.

A resource can access the local procedures and resources declared in it. It
can also communicate with its child processes.

A variable of a resource type is different from variables of the other types.
Access control such as all or nothing is so coarse that more detailed control is
needed. To achive this control, we adopted the concept of capability. A global
procedure pointed by capability yyy is called only if capability yyy has right to
call it.

A capability is copied to another capability if the former capability has the right to copy.

$$x := y \ [\ a_1, \ a_2, ..., a_n \ ] \ ; \qquad \text{or } x := y \ ;$$

where x and y are the same resource type, and y has the access rights of copy, a_1, a_2 and so on. This statement means that x points to an instance pointed by y and the access rights of x are equal to $[\ a_1, \ a_2, ..., a_n \ ]$. If the access right list is omitted, x has the same access rights as y has.

To nullify a capability, NULL value is assigned to it.

$$x := NULL \ ;$$

After this statement, capability x does't point to any instance. If there are no capabilities which point to an instance, it lapses.

If a resource is declared as a type, its many instances can be created. If only one instance is created, we can join type declaration and variable declaration as follows.

```
VAR xx : RESOURCE ( parameters ) ;
            .
            .
            .
        END;
```

In this case, the resource is automatically created at the beginning.

A resource bounds the implementation details within it and makes barrier to the access of shared variables. This prevents an error from damaging the total behavior.

As an example, we show programs of READERS'/WRITERS' problem. A writer puts a data in a buffer and a reader reads it. Multiple readers can execute concurrently, but writers execute exclusively. In such a situation, we describe two cases, 1) reader's priority and 2) writer's priority.

```
1. READER'S PRIORITY
        TYPE buffer = RESOURCE;
                VAR content : t ;
                GLOBAL PROCEDURE read(d);
                        VAR d : t ;
                        d:=content
                END;
                GLOBAL PROCEDURE write(d);
                        VAR d : t ;
                        content:=d
                END;
                PARALLEL
                        -> read
                END;
                content:=NULL
        END;


2. WRITER'S PRIORITY
        TYPE buffer = RESOURCE;
                VAR content : t ;
                    nw : INTEGER ;
                GLOBAL PROCEDURE read(d);
                        VAR d : t ;
                        CONDITION : nw=0 ;
                        d:=content
                END;
                GLOBAL PROCEDURE write(d);
                        VAR d : t ;
                        nw := nw + 1 ;
                        CALL wwrite(d) ;
                        nw :=nw - 1
                END;
                PROCEDURE wwrite(d);
                        VAR d : t ;
                        content := d
                END;
                PARALLEL
                        -> read, write;
                        -> read;
                        -> write
                END;
                content:=NULL;
                nw := 0
        END
```

3.5 PRIMITIVES FOR NON-DETERMINACY

To express non-deterministic behavior, we provide three primitives, IF statement, DO statement and WHILE statement. They are all based on the guarded command proposed by DIJKSTRA[1976].

1. IF statement

```
        IF p₁(x) -> statement list₁,
           p₂(x) -> statement list₂,
                 .
                 .
                 .
           pₙ(x) -> statement listₙ

        FI;
```

'$p_i(x)$ -> statement list$_i$' is called guarded command, and '$p_i(x)$' is called its guard. A guard is either a sequence of logical expressions separated by comma or an INPUT/OUTPUT statement preceded by a sequence of logical expressions. A sequence of logical expressions can be empty sequence.

$$le_1, le_2, \ldots, le_n\{, I/O \text{ statement}\}$$

Truth value of logical expression is evaluated in an ordinary sense and that of an I/O statement is evaluated as follows. If the I/O statement which matches with this I/O statement is ready to be executed, the I/O guard is said to be true. If the target module of this I/O statement has already terminated, the value is false. In neither case, the value is undefined.

The meaning of IF statement is that if there exists a guard whose components are all true, the corresponding statement list is executed. If multiple guards become true, one of them is selected in non-deterministic way and the corresponding statement list is executed. If all the guards become false, no statement list is executed and IF statement is skipped.

If values of some guards are undefined and those of the other guards are false, execution of IF statement is delayed until either all the guards become false or some guards become true.

If a guard which includes an I/O statement is selected, the I/O statement is executed before the statement list.

2. DO statement

```
DO  {IN PARALLEL}
   p_1(x) -> statement list_1,
              .
              .
              .
   p_n(x) -> statement list_n
OD;
```

DO statement means that at each time, one of the statement lists whose guard is true and which has not been executed is executed. This continues until any statements can't be executed.

Selection of a statement list is done in non-deterministic way like IF statement. If 'IN PARALLEL' phrase is specified, multiple statement lists can be executed concurrently.

3. WHILE statement

```
WHILE DO  {IN PARALLEL}
   p_1(x) -> statement list_1,
              .
              .
              .
   p_n(x) -> statement list_n
OD;
```

In WHILE statement, as far as there exists a guard whose value is true, the corresponding statement list is executed many times. After this WHILE statement, all the guards are false. If 'IN PARALLEL' phrase is specified, multiple statement lists can be executed concurrently like DO statement.

To exit loops, EXIT statement is used.

```
EXIT n ;
```

where n specifies an integer which is the depth of the loop to be exited. If n=1, n may be omitted. If n is greater than the maximum depth, the control exits from the outermost loop.

These three primitives can express non-determinacy because guards aren't necessarily exclusive. Non-determinacy can be resolved in two different ways. In the first case, a guard consists only of logical expressions and non-determinacy is resolved internally. In the other case, a guard includes an I/O statement and nondeterminacy is resolved in relative to other modules. It is difficult to implement the second case, but it enables a module to change its action according to other modules. This decreases the danger of deadlocks concerning message communications.

4. SCHEDULING ALGORITHM

A program written in this language is executed on a parellel processing system. We give the optimal scheduling algorithm to execute the program efficiently.

The computing system is assumed to consist of a supervisory processor and several processing units with identical facilities. As the application of computer systems is becoming broader and more complex, it is necessary to introduce the concept of processing states for prccessing units. A processing unit changes its state according to the task executed on it.

We can consider many things as candidates for processing states. In a distributed database system, a state is a data set each processing unit has in its local memory. In a functionally distributed system, a state is a function each processing unit performs at that time if the function can be changed dynamically.

In every case, the state change of a processing unit always incurs overheads. The overheads incurred by a state change are quantified as loss Ls. The set of states is assumed to be $\{S_1, S_2, ..., S_N\}$. Tasks are classified by the states which processing units take to execute them.

A quantity k called loss coefficient is assigned to each task. In the time interval [t,t+dt], a task which is kept waiting at that time and whose loss coefficient is k incurs loss k·dt. Let L(t)dt denote the total loss incurred by both waiting tasks and state changes. The loss caused by waiting tasks is the sum of the loss coefficients of the tasks waiting then. The loss of state changes is Ls multiplied by the number of state changes occurred then.

We adopt the objective function P of the following form.

$$P = \int_0^\infty L(t) e^{-at} dt \qquad (4.1)$$

, where $a > 0$ is called discounting factor. The loss that will be caused in the future is discounted by the definite ratio. In stead of simple average, discounting is introduced to reduce the effect of uncertainty in the future.

The task arrival is assumed to obey the Poisson process and the ratio of each category is fixed. The processing time of a task is assumed to be definite and known to the scheduler. Ignoring state changes, the ratio of the loss coefficient k to the processing time t specifies the processing order of tasks, that is, a task with higher ratio precedes to a task with lower ratio. We call the ratio its priority. Tasks in each category form a queue in order of priority.

If the number of processing units of each state is determined at every time, a task which each processing unit should execute is determined naturally. What the scheduler should do is to determine the number of processing units of each state, that is, to determine the state change of each processing unit.

The optimal time t when a processing unit changes its state from state S_i to state S_j is the solution t^* of the following equation.

$$\beta_j^{(+)}(t) - \alpha \cdot Ls = \beta_i^{(-)}(t) \ , \tag{4.2}$$

, where $\beta_j^{(+)}(t)$ denotes the increase rate of losses caused by the tasks belonging to category j if the state change from state S_i to state S_j is delayed from time t. $\beta_i^{(-)}(t)$ denotes the decrease rate of losses caused by the tasks belonging to category i if the state change is delayed.

Let $C_n(\tau,t)$ (n=i or j) denote the maximum priority of the tasks which belong to category n and are kept waiting at time τ. If the state change occurs at time t, then $C_n(\tau,t)$ can be estimated from such informations obtained at time 0 as 1) the number of processing units in state S_n, 2) tasks which are in category n and are kept waiting and 3) the statistics of task arrival.

$\beta_j^{(+)}(t)$ and $\beta_i^{(-)}(t)$ are represented as follows.

$$\beta_j^{(+)}(t) = \int_t^\infty C_j(\tau,t) \cdot e^{-\alpha(\tau-t)} d\tau \tag{4.3}$$

$$\beta_i^{(-)}(t) = \int_t^\infty C_i(\tau,t) \cdot e^{-\alpha(\tau-t)} d\tau \tag{4.4}$$

The derivation of each equation is omitted in this paper.

From the above discussion, the optimal scheduling algorithm becomes as follows.

[ALGORITHM]
1. For all i, compute $\beta_i^{(+)}$ and $\beta_i^{(-)}$ at t=0.
2. If there exists a pair (i,j) of categories which satisfies eq(4.2), select one processing unit in state S_i and change its state to state S_j.
3. Repeat this step unitl any pair of categories doesn't satisfy eq(4.2).

This algorithm seems complex and time-consuming, however simulation results show that the computation time of this algorithm is only two or three times as much as that of the simple priority scheduling. As the algorithm is strictly applied in these simulations, the computation time will become shorter if the algorithm is revised or simplified.

This scheduler makes trade-off between waiting time of tasks and state changes of the processing units, and selects the optimal action in order to lessen the total losses. Usefulness of this scheduler is shown in Fig.1, where ρ is the utilization factor of the system, i.e. the ratio of non—idling time of processors to the whole processing time. As the number of states becomes more than the number of the processing units, the effect of this scheduler becomes more vivid.

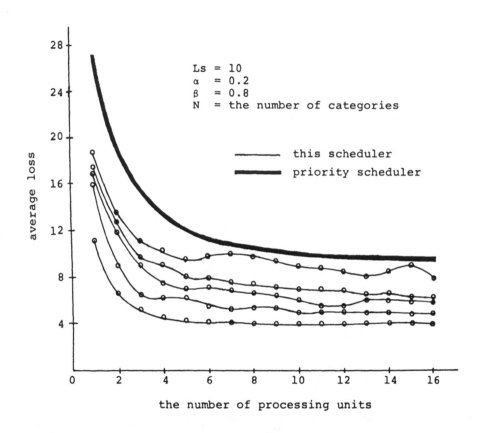

Fig.1 Average Loss as a Function of
the number of processing units

5. PROGRAMMING EXAMPLE OF THE SCHEDULING ALGORITHM

As an example, we show the outline of the program which implements the scheduling algorithm. It isn't necessary to describe full details in this language, thus we use English—like statements.

The program consists of three kinds of processes and two resources. Process SCHEDULER controls state changes. If it receives a request for state change, it investigates whether it had better change a state. If so, it orders MANAGER to change the state of a processor.

```
SCHEDULER = PROCESS;
   VAR CALCULATE : COEFFICIENT ;
   CREATE (CALCULATE) ;
   FOR [I:1..N] IN PARALLEL
      OUTPUT CALCULATE TO MANAGER [I]
   ROF;
   WHILE DO
      INPUT 'GET':β^(+) FROM MANAGER[?J] ->
          CALL RELEASE(CALCULATE: J,β^(+): K);
          IF K≠NULL->OUTPUT'DECREMENT': J TO MANAGER[K]
          FI;
      INPUT 'RELEASE': β^(-) FROM MANAGER[?J] ->
          CALL OBTAIN(CALCULATE: J, β^(-): K);
          IF K ≠ NULL -> OUTPUT 'DECREMENT': K TO MANAGER[J]
          FI
   OD
END;
```

There exists a process MANAGER for each category. MANAGER[i] controls category i. It deals with task arrival, task termination and state changes. If $\beta^{(+)}$ is greater than the value VAL0, MANAGER[i] requests SCHEDULER to command state change. If $\beta^{(-)}$ is less than the value VAL1, MANAGER[i] declares it to SCHEDULER. If MANAGER[i] is ordered to change a state by SCHEDULER, MANAGER[i] selects an idling processor and changes the processor's state.

```
MANAGER[ I : 1..N ] = PROCESS;
   VAR BUF : QUEUE, CALCULATE : COEFFICIENT;
   EXCEPTION
      INPUT 'ARRIVE' : TASK FROM ACCEPTOR ->
          CALL PUT ( BUF::TASK ) ;
          IF idle processor ? ->assign TASK to it FI,
      INPUT 'END': FROM PROCESSOR[?J]  ->
          CALL GET ( BUF::TASK );
          IF TASK ≠ NULL -> assign TASK to PROCESSOR[J],
             TASK = NULL -> register PROCESSOR[J] as idle processor
          FI
      INPUT 'INCREMENT' : L FROM MANAGER[?J] ->
          register PROCESSOR[L] ;
          CALL GET ( BUF::TASK );
          IF TASK ≠ NULL -> assign TASK to PROCESSOR[L],
```

```
              TASK = NULL -> register PROCESSOR[L] as idle processor
        FI,
   INPUT 'DECREMENT' : J FROM SCHEDULER ->
        select idle PROCESSOR[L];
        erase it;
        OUTPUT 'INCREMENT' : L TO MANAGER[J]
END;


CREATE ( BUF );


INPUT CALCULATE FROM SCHEDULER;


WHILE DO
```

$$-> \text{compute } \beta^{(+)} \text{ and } \beta^{(-)} \text{ ; inform them to CALCULATE;}$$

```
        IF β(+) > VAR0 -> OUTPUT 'GET':β(+) TO SCHEDULER,
           β(-) < VAR1 -> OUTPUT 'RELEASE': β(-) TO SCHEDULER
        FI
   OD
END;
```

The other process receives an arrived task and delivers it to MANAGER[i] according to its category. Resource QUEUE controls task queues of respective categories. Resource COEFFICIENT collects $\beta^{(+)}$ and $\beta^{(-)}$ from each MANAGER, and investigates whether there exists a pair of categories which satisfies eq(4.2).

```
TYPE QUEUE = RESOURCE ;
   VAR BUFFER : the buffer to memorize the task queue ;
   GLOBAL PROCEDURE PUT(TASK) ;
        CONST TASK : PROCESS ;
        put TASK into BUFFER in order of priority
        END;
   GLOBAL PROCEDURE GET(:TASK) ;
        CONST TASK : PROCESS ;
        get the task with the highest priority from BUFFER;
        assign it to TASK;
        delete it from BUFFER
        END;
   global procedures to compute β(+) and β(-).
   END.
```

6. CONCLUSION

We have presented fundamental frameworks of our parallel processing language in which algorithms and their constraints are described separately. Since static description has such good features as understandability and modifiability of programs, these constraints are described as statically as possible.

We have also given the efficient scheduling algorithm for parallel processing systems. In the algorithm, processing states play an important role.

We believe we have resolved many difficulties which existing languages are confronted with. We are now implementing the language, and some parts of the specification may altered after the experiments. Furthermore, we are now studying the computer architecture fit for both the language and the scheduler.

REFERENCES

HANSEN P.B. (1974). Concurrent Pascal: A Programming Language for Operating System Design. Information Science Technical Report, no.10. April 1974.

HOARE C.A.R. (1974). An Operating System Structuring Concept. Comm. ACM, Vol.17, no.10. October 1974.

HANSEN P.B. (1973). Operating System Principles. Prentice-Hall 1973.

HANSEN P.B. (1975). The Programming Language Concurrent Pascal. IEEE Tras. on Software Engineering, Vol.SE-1,No.2. June 1975.

HANSEN P.B. (1976). The Solo Operating System. Software-Practice and Experience, Vol.7, No.2. 1976.

WIRTH N. (1977). Modula: A Language for Modular Multiprogramming. Software-Practice and Experience, Vol.7, No.1. 1977.

HOARE C.A.R. (1978) Communicating Sequential Processes. Comm. ACM, Vol.21, No.8. August 1978.

DIJKSTRA E.W. (1976). A Discipline of Programming. Prentice-Hall, Series in Automatic Computation, 1976.

HANSEN P.B. (1978). Distributed Processes - A Concurrent Programming Concept. Comm. ACM, Vol.21,No.11. 1978.

ANDREWS G.R., and MCGRAW J.R. (1977). Language Features for Process Interaction. Proc. of an ACM Conf. on Language Design for Reliable Software. 1977.

SPECIFICATION OF SCHEDULERS
WITH ALGEBRAIC SPECIFICATION TECHNIQUES

Kouichi WADA   Kenichi HAGIHARA
Toshiro ARAKI   Nobuki TOKURA

Department of Information and Computer Sciences
Faculty of Engineering Science
Osaka University
Toyonaka, Osaka 560 Japan

ABSTRACT

The specification of a class of single resource schedulers is presented. A class of these schedulers is regarded as a parameterized data type whose formal parameter is a scheduling strategy. The specification is given by using the concept of parameterization in algebraic techniques. The specification of each scheduler instance can be directly obtained only by replacing the formal parameter with a concrete scheduling strategy. The assignment of an actual parameter to a formal parameter is given by a mechanism called extended parameter morphisms. This specification technique is applicable to many other objects.

I. INTRODUCTION

To specify an operating system (for short OS) formally is a very important problem both in practice and in theory. But there has been few works on specifying the total OS formally. Because OS is too complex and has many machine-dependent parts, and we do not have a framework of formal specification enough to describe large objects such as OS.

An algebraic specification technique has been investigated by many researchers, Guttag (1975), ADJ (1976,1979), Ehrig (1977) and Ehrich (1979). This technique is considered a promising method for formal specification. However, this method has been also lack of a framework to treat large objects. Recently by ADJ (1979) and Ehrig (1979) the concept of parameterization in algebraic specification is presented. In those papers a precise mathematical treatment is shown. This concept is considered to be the one step specifying large objects.

In the part, with the algebraic technique a specification for a file management system is presented (Kasami et al (1978)). In this paper by using the concept of parameterization in an algebraic specification technique , some specifications of schedulers are described. A scheduler is a kernel of a process management system, which is one of the most significant parts in OS . To specify schedulers advances works on specifying total OS formally.

In section 2 we summarize some definitions in algebraic specification needed in this paper. In section 3 we specify a class of single resource schedulers as a parameterized data type, i.e., a scheduler with scheduling strategy as a formal parameter, and show that the specification is correct. If we consider a scheduler as a parameterized data type and we assign a concrete scheduling strategy to the scheduler, we can obtain a correct specification of the scheduler with the concrete schedulng strategy. In section 4 we give a specification of schedulers with a concrete scheduling strategy and we give a mechanism called extended parameter morphisms in order that we can get a specification of schedulers with more complex scheduling strategy without changing the specification given in section 3. And in section 5 as an example of an extended parameter morphism, the specification of schedulers with a more complex scheduling strategy is presented.

2. PRELIMINARIES

we shall assume the algebraic and categorical background of ADJ (1973,1976) or of Ehrig and Kreowski (1977). Some definitions from category theory will be found in Appendix. The basic algebraic background is as follows. We start with a set S of names of data types (S is called <u>sort set</u>).

<u>Definition 2.1.</u> An <u>S-sorted signature</u> Σ is a family $\Sigma_{w,s}$ of sets, for $s \in S$ and $w \in S^*$. Call $\sigma \in \Sigma_{w,s}$ an <u>operation symbol</u> and w is its source and s is its target.

<u>Definition 2.2.</u> Let Σ be an S-sorted signature. Then an $<S,\Sigma>$-algebra A consists of a set A_s for each $s \in S$ (called the <u>carrier of A of sort S</u>) and a function
$$\sigma_A: A_{s_1} \times A_{s_2} \times \cdots \times A_{s_n} \rightarrow A_s$$
for each $\sigma \in \Sigma_{w,s}$ with $w = s_1 s_2 \cdots s_n$ (called the <u>operation of A named by σ</u>). For $\sigma \in \Sigma_{\lambda,s}$ we have $\sigma_A \in A_s$ (also written $\sigma_A: \rightarrow A_s$), that is, $\Sigma_{\lambda,s}$ is the set of (names of) constants of A of sort S.

<u>Definition 2.3.</u> Let A and B be $<S,\Sigma>$-algebras, A Σ-<u>homomorphism</u> h: A $\rightarrow$ B is a family of functions $<h_s: A_s \rightarrow B_s>_{s \in S}$ that preserve the operations, i.e., that satisfy
(h0) if $\sigma \in \Sigma_{\lambda,s}$ then $h_s(\sigma_A) = \sigma_B$;
(h1) if $\sigma \in \Sigma_{s_1 \cdots s_n,s}$ and $<a_1, \cdots, a_n> \in A_{s_1} \times \cdots \times A_{s_n}$ then
$$h_s(\sigma_A(a_1, \cdots, a_n)) = \sigma_B(h_{s_1}(a_1), \cdots, h_{s_n}(a_n)).$$

A <u>data type</u> is regarded as (the isomorphism class of) a minimal $<S,\Sigma>$-algebra (an algebra A is <u>minimal</u> iff the only subalgebra of A is A itself). The pair $<S,\Sigma>$ determines the category $\underline{Alg}_{<S,\Sigma>}$ of all S-sorted Σ-algebras with Σ-homomorphisms between them.

A signature describes the syntactic part of a specification. And the semantic part of the specification is described by Σ-<u>axioms</u> (for short axioms) which in the most general case are universally quantified implication:
(a-1) $e_1 \& e_2 \& \cdots \& e_n ==> e_{n+1}$,
where each e_i is an equation or inequation between Σ-<u>terms</u> (expressions over Σ with variables). When all the antecedents of (a-1) are equations and the consequent is either an equation or an inequation, the axiom is called <u>universal Horn</u>. For Universal

Horn axioms, standard algebraic results (e.g., Proposition 2.5.) hold for classes of algebras characterized by such axioms, and it is sufficient to specify formal parameters in dealing with a parameterized data type.

Definition 2.4. A __specification__ SPEC = <S,Σ,E> is a triple, where S is a sort set, Σ is an S-sorted signature and E is a set of universal Horn axioms. __Alg__ $_{SPEC}$ denotes the category of all SPEC-algebra (SPEC-algebra is an <S,Σ>-algebra satisfying the axioms E). When we write the __combination__ SPEC' = SPEC + <S',Σ',E'> we mean that

(1) S and S' are disjoint,

(2) Σ' is an S∪S'-sorted signature and Σ and Σ' are disjoint,

     and

(3) E' is a set of axioms over <S∪S', Σ∪Σ'>.

In algebraic specification, the semantics of a specification SPEC is given by the (isomorphism class of the) initial algebra T_{SPEC} in $\underline{Alg}_{SPEC}$. When all axioms in a specification are universal Horn, the next result holds for the existence of an initial algebra in $\underline{Alg}_{SPEC}$.

Proposition 2.5. Let SPEC be a specification. If $\underline{Alg}_{SPEC}$ is non-empty then there exists an initial algebra T_{SPEC} in $\underline{Alg}_{SPEC}$ (Ehrig (1979)).

We repeat the definition of correctness as given in Ehrig and Kreowski (1977), which allows for "hidden functions".

Definition 2.6. Let A be an <S,Σ>-algebra and SPEC'=<S',Σ',E'> be a specification. The specification SPEC' is correct with respect to the <S,Σ>-algebra A iff

(1) S ⊆ S' and for all w ∈ S*, s ∈ S; $\Sigma_{w,s} \subseteq \Sigma'_{w,s}$ (for short Σ ⊆ Σ'),
     and

(2) the <S,Σ>-reduct[†] of $T_{SPEC'}$ is isomorphic to A.

In section 3 this definition will be extended for parameterized data types, and the concept of "reduct" will basically play a significant role.

Example 2.1. MODEL (SPEC = <S,Σ>): __Nat__

        sorts(S) : __nat__ , __bool__

        opns(Σ) : T , F : → __bool__

                    0 : → __nat__

                    PRED , SUCC : __nat__ → __nat__

                    NATEQ , LE : __nat__ __nat__ → __bool__

---

† See Appendix.

The $\langle S, \Sigma \rangle$-algebra A has $A_{nat} = \mathbb{N}$ (the natural numbers) and $A_{bool} = \{true, false\}$, with the obvious definition of the operations. In particular $NATEQ_A$ is the identity relation (actually Boolean-valued function) on $\mathbb{N}$.

SPECIFICATION (SPEC' = SPEC + $\langle \Sigma'$, E'$\rangle$): Nat' = Nat +

      opns(Σ'): $^\wedge$: bool bool $\rightarrow$ bool

      axioms(E'):

          F $^\wedge$ x = F

          x $^\wedge$ F = F

          T $^\wedge$ T = T

          PRED(0) = 0

          PRED(SUCC(n)) = n

          LE(0 , n) = T

          LE(SUCC(n) , 0) = F

          LE(SUCC(n) , SUCC(n')) = LE(n , n')

          NATEQ(n , n') = LE(n , n') $^\wedge$ LE(n' , n)

we can see the specification Nat' is correct relative to the Nat-algebra.

3. SCHEDULER AS A PARAMETERIZED DATA TYPE

In this section a class of single resource schedulers is described by using an algebraic specification technique (Wada et al (1980)).

INFORMAL DESCRIPTION OF A SCHEDULER

To begin with, an informal description of a single resource scheduler is given bellow:

(1) Each process can perform two kinds of operations A (acquire) and R (release). An operation A is to notify to the scheduler that the process wants to acquire the resource and the process will be in wait state until the scheduler assigns the resource to the process. An operation R is to notify to the scheduler that the process abandons the resource assigned by the scheduler.

(2) The scheduler assigns the resource in turn to each process in the following ways:

Case-1.) The scheduler receives an A from a process. If there is no process occupying the resource the scheduler passes the right to the process, otherwise there is no change except that the scheduler accepts the request.

Case-2.) The scheduler receives an R from the process currently having the resource. There are three cases:

Case-2.1.) If there is no process being in wait state, the scheduler makes the resource unoccupied state by any process.

Case-2.2.) If there is one process being in wait state, the scheduler allows the process to acquire the resource.

Case-2.3.) If there is more than one process being in wait state the schduler selects one process from among waiting processes by a proper scheduling strategy, and assigns the resource to the process.

(3) In the following cases the scheduler returns error message.

Case-1.) An operation A is performed by the process currently having the resource or being in wait state.

Case-2.) An operation R is performed by the process currently not having the resource.

In the above description the concrete scheduling strategy is not specified, so it is not a complete descriprion of a scheduler. However it is considered to be the description of a class of single resource schedulers, that is to say, the fundamental structure of schedulers is given although it is not specified how to schedule the resource. As is shown with this example, the descriptions having some parts left unspecified are often encountered in practical case. For example, in top down design we only define operation names and their properties having to be satisfied. And how to refine it or how to implement it is put off to the later stage. In these cases the description has unspecified parts. These specifications at that level would be interesting and useful. In the following how to treat these cases will be mentioned.

When we specify the scheduler above, the concept of parameterization is applicable. In other words we can specify the scheduler as an object with unspecified parts as formal parameters. When we consider a class of single resource schedulers as a parameterized object, the formal parameter corresponds to scheduling strategy and (resultant) parameterized object corresponds to the fundamental structure of the scheduler. Moreover in this treatment, if we could specify a class of schedulers as a parameterized object, a concrete scheduler could be obtained by substituting a concrete scheduling strategy to the formal parameter.

ALGEBRAIC SPECIFICATION OF THE SCHEDULER

We repeat the definition of parameterized data type as given in ADJ (1979) and Ehrig (1979). The notation is due to Ehrig (1979).

Definition 3.1. A parameterized data type PDT = <SPEC , SPEC1 , T> consists of the following data:

PARAMETER DECLARATION   SPEC = $<S,\Sigma,E>$

TARGET SPECIFICATION   SPEC1 = SPEC + $<S1 , \Sigma1 , E1>$

and a functor T: $\underline{Alg}_{SPEC} \to \underline{Alg}_{SPEC1}$, equipped with a natural family of homomorphisms $<I_A: A \to U(T(A))>_{A \in \underline{Alg}_{SPEC}}$ where U is the forgetful functor[+] from $\underline{Alg}_{SPEC1}$ to $\underline{Alg}_{SPEC}$

[+] See Appendix.

This data is subject to the condition that T(A) is generated by the image of I_A.
PDT is called <u>persistent</u> (<u>strongly persistent</u>) if T is, i.e., for every SPEC-algebra A, I_A is an isomorphism (I_A is the identity).

By using Definition 3.1., we define the scheduler as a parameterized data type formally.

<u>PDT-1</u> (parameterized data type: <u>Scheduler</u>)

PARAMETER DECLARATION (SPEC = <S,Σ,E>): <u>Scheduling-strategy</u>

   sorts(S) : <u>pn</u>, <u>pn'</u>, <u>bool</u>, <u>future</u>, <u>sfactor</u>

   opns(Σ) : T , F : → <u>bool</u>

   $\perp$, $*_p$: → <u>pn'</u>
   PEQ : <u>pn' pn'</u> → <u>bool</u>

   λ_f , $*_f$: → <u>future</u>
   CON_f , DLT_f : <u>future pn</u> → <u>future</u>
   FEQ : <u>future future</u> → <u>bool</u>
   ISNT? : <u>future pn</u> → <u>bool</u>

   INIT , $*_{sf}$: → <u>sfactor</u>
   UPDATE : <u>sfactor pn</u> → <u>sfactor</u>
   SEQ : <u>sfactor sfactor</u> → <u>bool</u>

   SF : <u>future sfactor</u> → <u>pn'</u>

   axioms(E) :

(E.1) T ≠ F

(E.2) PEQ(i , i) = T
(E.3) PEQ(i , j) = PEQ(j ; i)
(E.4) PEQ(i , j) = T & PEQ(j , k) = T ==> PEQ(i , k) = T

(E.5) ISNT?(λ_f , i) = T
(E.6) ISNT?($*_f$, i) = F
(E.7) ISNT?(CON_f(x , i) , i) = F
(E.8) PEQ(i , j) = F & ISNT?(x , i) = T ==> ISNT?(CON_f(x , i) , j) = ISNT?(x , j)
(E.9) ISNT?(x , i) = F ==> CON_f(x,i) = $*_f$
(E.10) DLT_f(λ_f , i) = λ_f
(E.11) DLT_f($*_f$, i) = $*_f$
(E.12) ISNT?(x , i) = T ==> DLT_f(CON_f(x,i) , i) = x
(E.13) PEQ(i,j) = F & ISNT?(x,i) = T ==> DLT_f(CON_f(x,i),j) = CON_f(DLT_f(x,j),i)

(E.14) $FEQ(x,x) = T$

(E.15) $FEQ(x,y) = FEQ(y,x)$

(E.16) $FEQ(x,y) = T \& FEQ(y,z) = T ==> FEQ(x,z) = T$

(E.17) $SEQ(u,u) = T$

(E.18) $SEQ(u,v) = SEQ(v,u)$

(E.19) $SEQ(u,v) = T \& SEQ(v,w) = T ==> SEQ(u,w) = T$

(E.20) $SEQ(u,*_{sf}) = F ==> SF(\lambda_f,u) = \perp$

(E.21) $SEQ(u,*_{sf}) = F ==> SF(CON_f(\lambda_f,i),u) = i$

(E.22) $SF(*_f,u) = *_p$

(E.23) $SF(x,*_{sf}) = *_p$

(E.24) $ISNT?(x,i) = T \& PEQ(i,\perp) = F ==> SF(x,u) \neq i$

In this description only the property that has to be satisfied is described for
each operation. For example PEQ, FEQ and SEQ are required to be equivalence relations
(by E.2 — E.4, E.14 — E.16 and E.17 — E.19 respectively). For a scheduling function
(SF): (a) when there is no waiting process, the value of SF must be $\perp$ (by E.20);
(b) the processes which are not waiting must not be selected (by E.24), and so on.
If a concrete scheduling strategy satisfies this property, we can assign it to this
Scheduling-strategy. In section 4 we will mention relationship between a formal parameter (Scheduling-strategy) and an actual parameter (a concrete scheduling strategy),
and show an example of an assignment of an actual parameter.

Next we give a fundamental structure of the scheduler using the formal parameter.
TARGET SPECIFICATION (SPEC1 = SPEC + <S1,Σ1>) :

Scheduler = Scheduling-strategy +

     sorts(S1) :   scheduler

     opns(Σ1) : $E,*_S$:   → scheduler

                A , R :   scheduler pn → scheduler

                Am , Rm :   scheduler pn → bool

                Ap , Rp :   scheduler pn → pn'

The functor SCHD : $\underline{Alg}_{SPEC} \to \underline{Alg}_{SPEC1}$ is defined as follows : For a
SPEC-algebra B, SCHD(B) determines the SPEC1-algebra (denoted B') with

$B'_{scheduler} = B_{pn'}$ / PEQ × B_{future} / FEQ × $B_{sfactor}$ / SEQ

$-\{<[i],[x],[u]>|[i] \in B_{pn'}$ / PEQ , $[x] \in B_{future}$ / FEQ ,

$[u] \in B_{sfactor}$ / SEQ such that

$[i] = [*_p] , [x] = [*_f] , [u] = [*_{sf}] , \neg([i] = [\perp] \wedge [x] = [\lambda_f])$ or

$ISNT?_B ([x] , [i]) = T\} \cup \{\circledast\}$,

and other carriers are the same as those of SPEC-algebra.

The operations in SCHD(B) are defined by S1 — S10 (note that S1 — S10 are not axioms).

(S1) $E_{B'} = <[\perp_{B'}], [\lambda_{f_{B'}}], [INIT_{B'}]>$

(S2) $*_{S_{B'}} = \circledast$

(S3) $A_{B'}(<[i], [x], [u]>, j)$

$\quad = \underline{if}\ ([i] = [\perp_{B'}]) \wedge ([x] = [\lambda_{f_{B'}}])\ \underline{then}\ <[j], [CON_{f_{B'}}(\lambda_{f_{B'}}, j)], [u]>$

$\quad\quad \underline{elif}\ ISNT?_{B'}([x], [j]) \qquad\qquad \underline{then}\ <[i], [CON_{f_{B'}}(x,j)], [u]>$

$\quad\quad\quad\quad\quad\quad\quad\quad\quad\quad\quad\quad\quad\quad\quad\quad \underline{else}\ *_{S_{B'}}$

(S4) $A_{B'}(\circledast) = \circledast$

(S5) $R_{B'}(<[i], [x], [u]>, j)$

$\quad = \underline{if}\ [i] = [j]$

$\quad\quad\quad \underline{then}\ <[SF_{B'}(DLT_{f_{B'}}(x,i), u], [DLT_{f_{B}}(x,i)], [UPDATE_{B'}(u,i)]>$

$\quad\quad\quad \underline{else}\ *_{S_{B'}}$

(S6) $R_{B'}(\circledast) = \circledast$

(S7) $Am_{B'}(<[i], [x], [u]>, j)$

$\quad = \underline{if}\ ([i] = [\perp_{B'}] \wedge [x] = [\lambda_{f_{B'}}]) \vee ISNT?([x],j)\ \underline{then}\ T_{B'}$

$\quad\quad\quad\quad\quad\quad\quad\quad\quad\quad\quad\quad\quad\quad\quad\quad \underline{else}\ F_{B'}$

(S8) $Rm_{B'}(<[i], [x], [u]>, j) = \underline{if}\ [i] = [j]\ \underline{then}\ T_{B'}$

$\quad\quad\quad\quad\quad\quad\quad\quad\quad\quad\quad\quad\quad\quad\quad\quad \underline{else}\ F_{B'}$

(S9) $Ap_{B'}(<[i], [x], [u]>, j)$

$\quad = \underline{if}\ [i] = [\perp_{B'}] \wedge [x] = [\lambda_{f_{B}}]\ \underline{then}\ j$

$\quad\quad \underline{elif}\ ISNT?_{B'}([x], [j]) \qquad \underline{then}\ \perp_{B'}$

$\quad\quad\quad\quad\quad\quad\quad\quad\quad\quad\quad\quad \underline{else}\ *_{P_{B'}}$

(S10) $Rp_{B'}(<[i], [x], [u]>, j)$

$\quad = \underline{if}\ [i] = [j]\ \underline{then}\ SF_{B'}([DLT_{f_{B'}}(x,i)], [u])\ \underline{else}\ *_{P_{B'}}$

We can consider this <u>Scheduler</u> to be a generalized or abstract scheduler. The scheduler selects a process with abstract scheduling factor (<u>sfactor</u>) from among waiting processes (<u>future</u>). The scheduler having a concrete scheduling strategy is obtained by substituting a concrete scheduling factor into this <u>sfactor</u>. For <u>Scheduler</u> as a parameterized data type, the specification must be given next. A parameterized specification for a parameterized data type is defined as follows.

<u>Definition 3.2.</u> A <u>parameterized specification</u> consists of the following data:

PARAMETER DECLARATION SPEC = $<S, \Sigma, E>$

TARGET SPECIFICATION SPEC1 = SPEC + $<S1, \Sigma1, E1>$

The semantics of the specification is the free construction (ADJ (1979)), T: $\underline{Alg}_{SPEC} \rightarrow \underline{Alg}_{SPEC1}$, i.e., the parameterized data type PDT = $<SPEC, SPEC1, T>$.

In <u>PDT-1.</u> we have the parameterized object <u>Scheduler</u> as a parameterized type, now we want to describe a parameterized specification for <u>Scheduler</u>. We expressed <u>Scheduling-strategy</u>, <u>Scheduler</u>, SCHD> for the type. For the specification we will

use the notation <u>Scheduling-strategy'</u> , <u>Scheduler'</u>>. Now let <SPEC , SPEC1 , T>
and <SPEC' , SPEC1'> be a parameterized data type and a parameterized specification
respectively. Generally in specifying a type we will have SPEC ⊆ SPEC'[†] and SPEC1 ⊆
SPEC1', and SPEC1' will be expressed by SPEC' $\cup$ SPEC1 + <S1' , Σ1' , E1'>; the S1' and
Σ1' being "hidden" sorts and operations and E1' being the real essential parts of
specification. In the specification of <u>Scheduler</u>, we describe only S1' , Σ1' , E1'
and do not rewrite all the sorts and operations of SPEC1.

    <u>PS-2.</u> (parameterized specification: <u>Scheduler'</u>)

PARAMETER DECLARATION (SPEC' = SPEC):

<u>Scheduling-strategy'</u> = <u>Scheduling-strategy</u>

TARGET SPECIFICATION (SPEC1' = SPEC' $\cup$ SPEC1 + <Σ1', E1'>):

<u>Scheduler'</u> = <u>Scheduling-strategy</u> $\cup$ <u>Scheduler</u> +

      opns(Σ1'):   FUT: <u>scheduler</u> → <u>future</u>

                GETS: <u>scheduler</u> → <u>sfactor</u>

      axioms(E1'): $FUT(E) = \lambda_f$

           $FUT(*_S) = *_f$

           $Am(t,i) = T ==> FUT(A(t,i)) = CON_f(FUT(t),i)$

           $Rm(t,i) = T ==> FUT(R(t,i)) = DLT_f(FUT(t),i)$

           $GETS(E) = INIT$

           $GETS(*_S) = *_{sf}$

           $Am(t,i) = T ==> GETS(A(t,i)) = GETS(t)$

           $Rm(t,i) = T ==> GETS(R(t,i)) = UPDATE(GETS(t),i)$

           $ISNT?(FUT(t),i) = T ==> Am(t,i) = T$

           $ISNT?(FUT(t),i) = F ==> Am(t,i) = F$

           $FEQ(FUT(t),*_f) = T ==> Rm(t,i) = F$

           $ISNT?(FUT(t),i) = T ==> Rm(t,i) = F$

           $PEQ(Ap(t,i),i) = T ==> Rm(A(t,i),i) = T$

           $PEQ(Ap(t,i),\lambda) = T ==> Rm(A(t,i),i) = F$

[†] This means that sort set, signature and set of axioms in SPEC are included by those
in SPEC' respectively.

PEQ(Ap(t,j) ,⊥) = T & PEQ(i,j) = F ==> Rm(A(t,j) , i) = Rm(t,i)

PEQ(Ap(t,j) , j) = T & PEQ(i,j) = F ==> Rm(A(t,j) , i) = F

ISNT?(FUT(R(t,j) , i) = F & PEQ(Rp(t,j) , i) = T ==> Rm(R(t,j) , i) = T

ISNT?(FUT(R(t,j) , i) = F & PEQ(Rp(t,j) , i) = F ==> Rm(R(t,j) , i) = F

FEQ(FUT(t) , λ_f) = T ==> Ap(t,i) = i

FEQ(FUT(t) , $*_f$) = T ==> Ap(t,i) = $*_p$

FEQ(FUT(A(t,i)) , $*_f$) = F & FEQ(FUT(A(t,i)) , λ_f) = F ==> Ap(t,i) = ⊥

Rp(t,i) = SF(FUT(R(t,i)) , GETS(R(t,i)))

Am(t,i) - F ==> A(t,i) = $*_S$

Rm(t,i) = F ==> R(t,i) = $*_S$

FEQ(FUT(t) , FUT(s)) = T & SEQ(GETS(t) , GETS(s)) = T

         & Rm(t,i) = T & Rm(s,i) = T ==> t = s

FEQ(FUT(t) , λ_f) = T & FEQ(FUT(s) , λ_f) = T

         & SEQ(GETS(t) , GETS(s)) = T ==> t = s

We will want to show correctness of the parameterized specification <u>Scheduler'</u> relative to the parameterized data type <u>Scheduler</u>. Definition 2.6. is extended to the case for correctness of parameterized data types.

<u>Definition 3.3.</u> Let PDT = <SPEC , SPEC1 , T> be a parameterized data type and let PDT' = <SPEC' , SPEC1'> be a parameterized specification. Then PDT' is correct with respect to PDT if SPEC ⊆ SPEC', SPEC1 ⊆ SPEC1' and the diagram

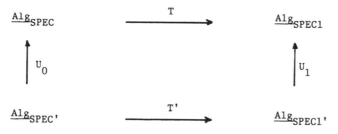

commutes up to isomorphism where U_0 and U_1 are the forgetful functors and T' is the functor obtained as the semantics of the specification.

<u>Theorem 3.4.</u> The parameterized specification

          < <u>Scheduling-strategy'</u> , <u>Scheduler'</u>>   (PS-2)

is correct with respect to the parameterized data type

          < <u>Scheduling-strategy</u> , <u>Scheduler</u> , SCHD>   (<u>PDT-1</u>).

    (proof) We can prove it using Theorem 10., Lemma 11. and Lemma 12. in ADJ(1979).

We have obtained the formal specification of a class of single resource schedulers and shown it to be correct by Theorem 3.4. By using this specification, we can get the correct specification of schedulers with each concrete scheduling strategy. This is accomplished by assigning each concrete scheduling strategy to the formal parameter of Scheduler', i.e., Scheduling-strategy'. But there are some problems of the parameter passing in algebraic specification. In order to resolve the problems we need the "parameter morphisms" by Ehrig (1979). (A parameter morphism is, intuitively, the morphism which shows correspondence of sorts and operations between a formal parameter and an actual parameter.) So we defer the example of the scheduler with a concrete scheduling strategy in section 4, and there we will extend the concept of parameter morphisms and give a mechanism which we can apply to a broad class of actual parameters.

4. EXTENDED PARAMETER MORPHISMS

To begin with, we mention the concept of a parameter morphism by Ehrig (1979).
Let   PDT = <SPEC , SPEC1 , T>,

SPEC = <S , Σ , E>

$\overline{\text{SPEC}}$ = <$\overline{S}$, $\overline{\Sigma}$, $\overline{E}$> be a parameterized data type , a formal parameter specification and an actual parameter specification respectively. The parameter morphism from a formal parameter (SPEC) to an actual paramater ($\overline{\text{SPEC}}$) identifies each sort in S (a formal parameter sort, for short FPS) with the sort in $\overline{S}$ (an actual parameter sort, for short APS), and each operation in Σ (a formal parameter operation, for short FPO) with the operation in $\overline{\Sigma}$ (an actual parameter operation, for short APO). And the initial $\overline{\text{SPEC}}$-algebra satisfies the axioms E translated by the parameter morphism. We can see that there is a SPEC-algebra A obtained from that initial $\overline{\text{SPEC}}$-algebra by renaming and/or forgetting the SPEC operations. (This is shown by the existence of the forgetful functor U: $\underline{\text{Alg}}_{\overline{\text{SPEC}}}$ → $\underline{\text{Alg}}_{\text{SPEC}}$ (Ehrig (1979)).) By the parameter morphism we can get a SPEC1-algebra whose parameter part is replaced by APS and APO. Also using the main theorem in Ehrig (1979) the parameterized specification whose parameter part is replaced by $\overline{\text{SPEC}}$ can be shown to be correct. An example of a parameter morphism is shown in Example 4.1.

The concept of parameter morphisms plays a significant role in a parameterized data type or specification. However in the framework of Ehrig (1979), the form of the actual parameter is limited, which is assigned in a parameterized data type. The parameter morphism of Ehrig (1979) takes an FPS and an FPO to the single APS and APO. So we can not assign the actual parameter in which each FPS corresponds to more than one APS and each FPO corresponds to a compound APO. In this paper, we extend the parameter morphism in Ehrig (1979) (the extended version is called an extended parameter morphism). As an extended parameter morphism can take each FPS to more than one APS and each FPO to a compound APO, we can extend the form of actual parameter assigned in a parameterized data type. In section 5 we will show the example using an extended parameter morphism. Although we extend the parameter morphism in this way we can show that the result corresponding to the main theorem in Ehrig (1979) does hold (see Theorem 4.5.).

Now an extended parameter morphism is defined . To begin with , an extended specification morphism is shown.

<u>Definition 4.1.</u> An <u>extended specification morphism</u> f: $<S , \Sigma , E> \rightarrow <S' , \Sigma' , E'>$ consists of a mapping f_S: $S \rightarrow S'^*$ and a family of mappings $d_{w,s}$: $\Sigma_{w,s} \rightarrow (T_{\Sigma'})_{f_S(w),f_S(s)}$, where $f_S(s_1,..,s_n) = f_S(s_1) \cdots f_S(s_n)$, and where $(T_{\Sigma'})_{f_S(w),f_S(s)}$ denotes the set of all Σ'-terms of sort $f_S(s)$ using variables $\{y_1,...,y_n\}$ with y_i of sort $f_S(s_i)$. This data is subject to the condition that every axiom of E translated by f is true of every $<S' , \Sigma' , E'>$-algebra.

In Ehrig (1979) a specification morphism h: $<S , \Sigma , E> \rightarrow <S' , \Sigma' , E'>$ is defined by a mapping h_S: $S \rightarrow S'$ and a family of mappings h_Σ: $\Sigma \rightarrow \Sigma'$, and there is a forgetful functor V_h: $\underline{Alg}_{<S' , \Sigma' , E'>} \rightarrow \underline{Alg}_{<S , \Sigma , E>}$, which plays a significant role for the main theorem. For an extended specification morphism, next lemma holds.

<u>Lemma 4.2.</u> Let f: $<S , \Sigma , E> \rightarrow <S' , \Sigma' , E'>$ be an extended specification **morphism**. For the extended specification morphism f, the specification $<\bar{S} , \bar{\Sigma} , \bar{E}>$ is determined where $\bar{S} = S' \cup \{sort_{f_S(s)} | s \in S$ and $f_S(s) \notin S'\}$, $\bar{\Sigma} = \Sigma' \cup \{OP_{d_{w,s}(\sigma)} | \sigma \in \Sigma_{w,s}$ $(w \in S^*, s \in S)$ and $d_{w,s}(\sigma) \notin \Sigma'\}$ and $\bar{E}$ is E' and all axioms E translated by f. Then there is a functor V_f: $\underline{Alg}_{<S' , \Sigma' , E'>} \rightarrow \underline{Alg}_{<S , \Sigma , E>}$ such that $V_f = U_f \cdot W_f$, where W_f: $\underline{Alg}_{<S' , \Sigma' , E'>} \rightarrow \underline{Alg}_{<\bar{S} , \bar{\Sigma} , \bar{E}>}$ is a functor determined by f, and where U_f: $\underline{Alg}_{<\bar{S} , \bar{\Sigma} , \bar{E}>} \rightarrow \underline{Alg}_{<S , \Sigma , E>}$ is a forgetful functor.

In Lemma 4.2., the functor U_f corresponds to the forgetful functor V_h in Ehrig (1979). And for each $A' \in \underline{Alg}_{<S' , \Sigma' , E'>}$, $W_f(A')$ includes new carrier $A_{sort_{f_S(s)}}$ and new opration $OP_{d_{w,s}}(\sigma)$ in addition to all carriers and operations in A'.

Next by using the extended specification morphism, an extended parameter morphism is defined as follows.

<u>Definition 4.3.</u> Given a parameterized data type PSPEC = $<SPEC , SPEC1 , G>$ with SPEC = $<S , \Sigma , E>$ and SPEC1 = SPEC + $<S1 , \Sigma1 , E1>$, the <u>body specification</u> of PSPEC is defined to be

BODY = $<S , \Sigma>$ + $<S1 , \Sigma1 , E1>$.

(Parameterized data type PSPEC is also represented by $<SPEC , BODY , SPEC1 , G>$ using the body specification).

<u>Definition 4.4.</u> Let PSPEC = $<SPEC,BODY,PSPEC1,G>$ and PSPEC' = $<SPEC',BODY',SPEC1',G'>$ be parameterized data types. An <u>extended parameter morphism</u> f: PSPEC $\rightarrow$ PSPEC' is an extended specification morphism f: BODY $\rightarrow$ BODY' with the <u>preservation property</u> that for every (actual) parameter algebra $A' \in \underline{Alg}_{SPEC'}$, there exists a (formal) parameter algebra $A \in \underline{Alg}_{SPEC}$ such that $V_f(G'(A')) = A$. (Note: $\underline{Alg}_{SPEC1} \subseteq \underline{Alg}_{BODY}$ and

$\underline{Alg}_{SPEC1'} \subseteq \underline{Alg}_{BODY'}$, so we do not explicitly mention inclusion functor $\underline{Alg}_{SPEC1} \to$ $\underline{Alg}_{BODY}$ and $\underline{Alg}_{SPEC1'} \to \underline{Alg}_{BODY'}$.) The extended parameter morphism f is <u>simple</u> if SPEC = SPEC' and SPEC1 $\subseteq$ SPEC1' so that the extended specification morphism is given by the inclusions of sorts and operation symbols.

The main theorem in Ehrig (1979) is sufficiently general that it provides the necessary apparatus for approaching many related problems, e.g., the inserting of non-parameterized specification into parameterized specification, the composition of parameterized types or specifications, the compatibility of different "call by name" strategies, compatibility of "call by name" and "call by value", proof of correctness (e.g., that if we have correct specifications for <u>int</u> and <u>set</u>( ), then this implies the correctness of the specification <u>set(int)</u>), etc. And in the main theorem everything is pushed up to the level of parameterized types (viewing a non-parameterized type as a parameterized type with trivial parameter). The advantage of this is that it allows us to put the necessary condition on the morphism in a very clean and uniform way and state all results within the category of parameterized types (Ehrig (1979)).

Now we show that the similar result as the main theorem also holds for the extended version in this paper. Therefore we can treat many problems mentioned above in parameterized data types for the extended version.

In a data type <SPEC , BODY , SPEC1 , G>, G was defined as a functor from $\underline{Alg}_{SPEC}$ to $\underline{Alg}_{SPEC1'}$ and also have a forgetful functor V: $\underline{Alg}_{SPEC1} \to \underline{Alg}_{BODY}$. Let $\overline{G}$ be the functor such that $\overline{G}(A) = V(G(A))$ for each $A \in \underline{Alg}_{SPEC}$.

<u>Theorem 4.5.</u> Let $PSPEC_i = <SPEC_i , BODY_i , SPEC1_i , G_i>$ i = 1 , 2 , 3 , be given parameterized data types; $PSPEC_4$ will be constructed:
$$PSPEC_i = <SPEC , SPEC1_i , G_i> \text{ for } i = 1 , 2 ,$$
$$PSPEC_i = <SPEC' , SPEC1_i , G_i> \text{ for } i = 3 , 4 .$$
Let s: $PSPEC_1 \to PSPEC_2$ be a simple parameter morphism and f: $PSPEC_1 \to PSPEC_3$ be an extended parameter morphism.

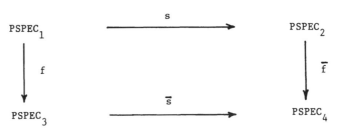

Further let F: $\underline{Alg}_{BODY_1} \to \underline{Alg}_{BODY_2}$ be strongly persistent with respect to forgetful functor V_s and having the property that $F(\overline{G}_1(A)) = \overline{G}_2(A)$ for all SPEC-algebra A.

Then there exists a persistent parameterized data type $PSPEC_4$, a functor F': $\underline{Alg}_{BODY_3} \to \underline{Alg}_{BODY_4}$ with $\overline{G}_4 = F' \cdot \overline{G}_3$, and a simple parameter morphism $\overline{s}$: $PSPEC_3 \to PSPEC_4$ and an extended parameter morphism $\overline{f}$: $PAPEC_2 \to PSPEC_4$ such that

(1) $<\overline{f}, \overline{s}>$ is a pushout for $<f, s>$.

(2) $\bar{s}$ is injective.

(3) $V_{\bar{f}} \cdot F' = F \cdot V_f : \underline{Alg}_{BODY_3} \to \underline{Alg}_{BODY_2}$.

(4) $V_{\bar{s}} \cdot F' = 1$, (the identity on $\underline{Alg}_{BODY_3}$).

In section 3, we have shown that the specification of a class of single resource schedulers is correct. We assign a specification of a concrete scheduling strategy to Scheduling-strategy' in Scheduler' in section 3, (this is done by extended parameter morphisms), and show that the specification of the scheduler that has the concrete scheduling strategy is correct, (this is shown by Theorem 4.5.).

In Theorem 4.5., everything is pushed up to the level of a parameterized type, as is the same in the main theorem of Ehrig (1979). So we must consider non-parameterized data types as parameterized data types. In order to do so there are two ways as follows:

(1) A non-parameterized data type SPEC is considered as a parameterized data type having an empty parameter declaration; Let ϕ denote the empty parameter declaration ($<\phi , \phi , \phi>$). SPEC is a parameterized data type expressed by $<\phi , SPEC , G>$, where G is a functor from the one point category $\underline{OPC}$ to the category of SPEC-algebras and where the image of G is required by Definition 3.1. to be a minimal algebra, i.e., a data type. This type of the non-parameterized data type will be represented by $\phi \subseteq SPEC$.

(2) A non-parameterized data type SPEC is considered as a parameterized data type having itself as a parameter declaration; SPEC is a parameterized data type expressed by $<SPEC , SPEC , G>$, where G is the identity functor on the category of SPEC-algebras. This type will be represented by $SPEC \subseteq SPEC$.

Next an example of an extended parameter morphism is shown using the specification of Scheduler.

Example 4.1. We consider the following scheduling strategy:
As the scheduling factor, the service count will be taken into account, where the service count of each process is how many times the process acquired the resource up to the time. The scheduler selects the process with the least service count among the waiting processes, and assigns the resource to the process. If there is more than one process with the least service count, the scheduler selects the process performing an operation A at the earliest time.

This scheduling strategy is called $\text{Scheduling-strategy}_A$ (the actual parameter of Scheduling-strategy'). The specification of $\text{Scheduling-strategy}_A$ $<S_A , \Sigma_A , E_A>$ is shown below:

SPECIFICATION ($SPEC_A = <S_A , \Sigma_A , E_A>$)
: $\underline{\text{Scheduling-strategy}}_A$ = $\underline{Nat}'$ +
sorts(S_A): pn, pn', bool, future, history
opns(Σ_A): T , F : $\to$ bool

$\perp$, $*_p$: $\to$ pn'
PEQ: pn' pn' $\to$ bool

λ_f, $*_f$: $\rightarrow$ <u>future</u>

CON_f, DLT_f: <u>future</u> <u>pn</u> $\rightarrow$ <u>future</u>

ISNT? : <u>future</u> <u>pn</u> $\rightarrow$ <u>bool</u>

FEQ: <u>future</u> <u>future</u> $\rightarrow$ <u>bool</u>

λ_h : $\rightarrow$ <u>history</u>

CON_h : <u>history</u> <u>pn</u> $\rightarrow$ <u>history</u>

HEQ: <u>history</u> <u>history</u> $\rightarrow$ <u>bool</u>

SF: <u>future</u> <u>history</u> $\rightarrow$ <u>pn'</u>

NUM: <u>history</u> <u>pn</u> $\rightarrow$ <u>nat</u>

axioms(E_A):

  {Include E.1 — E.16 in <u>PDT-1</u>}

  $FEQ(\lambda_f , *_f) = F$

  $FEQ(CON_f(x,i) , \lambda_f) = F$

  $ISNT?(x,i) = T$ & $ISNT?(y,i) = T ==> FEQ(CON_f(x,i) , CON_f(y,i)) = FEQ(x,y)$

  $ISNT?(x,i) = T ==> FEQ(CON_f(x,i) , *_f) = FEQ(x,*_f)$

  $PEQ(i,j) = F$ & $FEQ(CON_f(x,i) , *_f) = F$ & $FEQ(CON_f(y,j) , *_f) = F$

                  $==> FEQ(CON_f(x,i) , CON_f(y,j)) = F$

  $HEQ(h,h) = T$

  $HEQ(h,h') = HEQ(h',h)$

  $HEQ(h,h') = T$ & $HEQ(h',h'') = T ==> HEQ(h,h'') = T$

  $HEQ(CON_h(h,i) , CON_h(h',i)) = HEQ(h,h')$

  $HEQ(CON_h(h,i) , \lambda_h) = F$

  $NATEQ(NUM(h',i) , 0) = T ==> HEQ(CON_h(h,i) , h') = F$

  $CON_h(CON_h(h,i) , j) = CON_h(CON_h(h,j) , i)$

  $NUM(\lambda_h,i) = 0$

  $NUM(CON_h(h,i) , i) = SUCC(NUM(h,i))$

  $PEQ(i,j) = F ==> NUM(CON_h(h,i) , j) = NUM(h,j)$

  {Include E.20 — E.22 in <u>PDT-1</u>}

  $ISNT?(x,i) = T$ & $ISNT?(x,j) = T$ & $LE(NUM(h,i) , NUM(h,j)) = T$

                $==> SF(CON_f(CON_f(x,i) , j) , h) = SF(CON_f(x,i) , h)$

  $ISNT?(x,i) = T$ & $ISNT?(x,j) = T$ & $LE(NUM(h,i) , NUM(h,j)) = F$

                $==> SF(CON_f(CON_f(x,i) , j) , h) = SF(CON_f(x,j) , h)$

We assign this <u>Scheduling-strategy</u>$_A$ to the formal parameter of <u>Scheduler'</u>

in PS-2. Let $\underline{\text{Scheduling-strategy}}' = <\text{SPEC}', \text{SPEC}', I>$, $\underline{\text{Scheduler}}' = <\text{SPEC}', \text{SPEC1}'$,

SCHD> and $\underline{\text{Scheduling-strategy}}_A = <\phi, \text{SPEC}_A, \text{FOPC}>$, where I is the identity functor on $\underline{\text{Alg}}_{\text{SPEC}'}$, and where FOPC is the functor from one point category $\underline{\text{OPC}}$ to $\underline{\text{Alg}}_{\text{SPEC}_A}$. In

this case the extended parameter morphism

f: $\underline{\text{Scheduling-strategy}}' \subseteq \underline{\text{Scheduling-strategy}}'$

$\rightarrow \phi \subseteq \underline{\text{Scheduling-strategy}}_A$ is as follows:

definition of $f_{S'}: S' \rightarrow S_A$

$f_{S'}(\underline{\text{sfactor}}) = \underline{\text{history}}$

$f_{S'}(s) = s$ for other sort $s \in S'$.

definition of $d_{w,s}: \Sigma' \rightarrow (T_{\Sigma_A})_{f_{S'}(w), f_{S'}(s)}$

$d_{\lambda, \underline{\text{sfactor}}}(\text{INIT}) = \lambda_h;$

$d_{\underline{\text{sfactor pn}}, \underline{\text{sfactor}}}(\text{UPDATE}) = \text{CON}_h(h, i)$

$d_{\underline{\text{sfactor sfactor}}, \underline{\text{bool}}}(\text{SEQ}) = \text{HEQ}(h, h');$

$d_{w,s}(\sigma) = \sigma$ for other operation $\sigma \in \Sigma'$.

(Note: in this case the extended parameter morphism f coincides the parameter
morphism of Ehrig (1979).)

As we can see the conditions in Theorem 4.5. are all satisfied, the specification
of the scheduler with $\underline{\text{Scheduling-strategy}}_A$ can be obtained. This situation is shown
below:

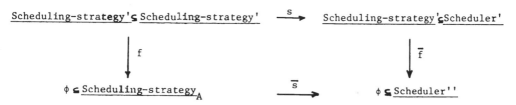

The $\underline{\text{Scheduler}}''$ is the specification of the scheduler with $\underline{\text{Scheduling-strategy}}_A$
and is shown to be correct by Theorem 4.5.

5. AN EXTENDED VERSION OF THE SCHEDULER

In this section by using the concept of an extended parameter morphism, we show
a scheduler specification with a more complex scheduling strategy than that of Example
4.1. Here remarkable point is that a correct specification of schedulers can be directly derived from $\underline{\text{Scheduler}}'$ (PS-2) only by replacing the formal parameter with a more
complex scheduling strategy.

The next scheduling strategy is considered (it is the actual parameter to be
assigned later).

(1) It is assumed that each process has an initial priority, and its priority
can be changed by each process.

(2) Among waiting processes the scheduler selects the process with the maximum
priority currently, and assigns the resource to the process. If there is more than

one process with the maximum priority the scheduler selects the process with the least service count (see Example 4.1.). Further if there is more than one process with the least service count, the scheduler selects the process performing an operation A at the earliest time.

This scheduling strategy is the same as that in Example 4.1. except each process priority is taken into account. To specify this scheduling strategy (being denoted by Scheduling-strategy$_{NA}$: $<S_{NA}, \Sigma_{NA}, E_{NA}>$), new sorts priority[†] (priority value) and pri-entry (priority entry table for each process) are introduced and new operations shown below below are introduced:

    INITPRI : initial priority value for each process;

    CRT : current priority value of a process;

    CHNG : change of priority value of a process;

    PRIEQ : equality predicate on pri-entry.

Further the source of the scheduling function SF is changed. The specification of Scheduling-strategy$_{NA}$ is given as follows:

    SPECIFICATION($<S_{NA}, \Sigma_{NA}, E_{NA}> = <S_A, \Sigma_A, -\{SF: \underline{future}\ \underline{history} \rightarrow \underline{pn}'\}, E_A>$
$+ <S'_{NA}, \Sigma'_{NA}, E_{NA}>$):

    Scheduling-strategy$_{NA}$ = Scheduling-strategy$_A$ +

      sorts(S'$_{NA}$): priority, pri-entry

      opns(Σ'_{NA}): INITPRI: → pri-entry

        CRT : pri-entry pn → priority

        CHNG : pri-entry pn priority → pri-entry

        PDLT : pri-entry pn → pri-entry

        PRIEQ : pri-entry pri-entry → bool

        SF : future pri-entry history → pn'

      axioms(E'$_{NA}$) :

        CRT(CHNG(e , i , p) , i) = p

        PEQ(i , j) = F ==> CRT(CHNG(e , i , p) , j) = CRT(e , j)

        CHNG(CHNG(e , i , p) , i , q) = CHNG(e , i , q)

        PEQ(i , j) = F ==> CHNG(CHNG(e , i , p) , j , q) = CHNG(CHNG(e , j , q) , i , p)

        PDLT(INITPRI , i) = INITPRI

        PDLT (CHNG(e , i , p) , i) = PDLT(e , i)

        PEQ(i , j) = F ==> PDLT(CHNG(e , i , p) , j) = CHNG(PDLT(e , j) , i , p)

[†] In this case priority is denoted by nat and each operation on nat is assumed.

```
PRIEQ(p , p) = T
PRIEQ(p , q) = PRIEQ(q , p)
PRIEQ(p , q) = T & PRIEQ(q , r) = T ==> PRIEQ(p , r) = T

NATEQ(CRT(CHNG(e , i , p) , i) , CRT(e' , i)) = T
    ==> PRIEQ(CHNG(e , i , p) , e') = PRIEQ(PDLT(e , i) , PDLT(e' , i))
NATEQ(CRT(CHNG(e , i , p) , i) , CRT(e' , i)) = F
    ==> PRIEQ(CHNG(e , i , p) , e') = F
```

$$SF(\lambda_f , e , h) = \bot$$
$$SF(CON_f(\lambda_f , i) , e , h) = i$$

```
ISNT?(x , i) = T & ISNT?(x , j) =T & LE(CRT(e , j) , CRT(e , i)) = F
    ==> SF(CON_f(CON_f(x , i) , j) , e , h) = SF(CON_f(x , j) , e , h)
ISNT?(x , i) = T & ISNT?(x , j) = T &
        NATEQ(CRT(e , i) , CRT(e , j)) = T & LE(NUM(h , i) , NUM(h , j)) = T
    ==> SF(CON_f(CON_f(x , i) , j) , e , h) = SF(CON_f(x , i) , e , h)
ISNT?(x , i) = T & ISNT?(x , j) = T &
        NATEQ(CRT(e , i) , CRT(e , j)) = T & LE(NUM(h , i) , NUM(h , j)) = F
    ==> SF(CON_f(CON_f(x , i) , j) , e , h) = SF(CON_f(x , j) , e , h)
ISNT?(x , i) = T & ISNT?(x , j) = T & LE(CRT(e , i) , CRT(e , j)) = F
    ==> SF(CON_f(CON_f(x , i) , j) , e , h) = SF(CON_f(x , i) , e , h)
```

Now we substitute this <u>Scheduling-strategy</u>$_{NA}$ for the formal parameter in <u>Scheduler'</u> by using the extended parameter morphism f. In this case sort <u>sfactor</u> corresponds to the two sorts <u>pri-entry</u> and <u>history</u>, and each operation on <u>sfactor</u> corresponds to a compound operation on <u>pri-entry</u> and <u>history</u>. This correspondence between these parameters can be well obtained by the extended parameter morphism. We define the extended parameter morphism

f: <u>Scheduling-strategy'</u> $\subseteq$ <u>Scheduling-strategy'</u> $\rightarrow$ $\phi \subseteq$ <u>Scheduling-strategy</u>$_{NA}$ as follows:

definition of $f_{S'}$: $S' \rightarrow S_{NA}^{*}$
$\quad f_{S'}(\text{sfactor}) = \underline{pri\text{-}entry}\ \underline{history}$;
$\quad f_{S'}(s) = s$ for other sort $s \in S'$.

definition of $d_{w,s}$: $\colon\Sigma'_{w,s} \rightarrow (T_{\Sigma_{NA}})_{f_{S'}(w) , f_{S'}(s)}$
$\quad d_{\lambda , \text{sfactor}}(\text{INIT}) = <\text{INITPRI} , \lambda_h>$;
$\quad d_{\text{sfactor sfactor} , \text{bool}}(\text{SEQ}) = \text{PRIEQ}(e , e') \wedge \text{HEQ}(h , h')$;
$\quad d_{\text{sfactor pn} , \text{sfactor}}(\text{UPDATE}) = <e , CON_h(h , i)>$;
$\quad d_{w,s}(\sigma) = \sigma$ for other operation $\sigma \in \Sigma'_{w,s}$.

By means of this definition,

W_f: $\dfrac{\text{Alg}}{<S'_{NA} , \Sigma'_{NA} , E'_{NA}>} \rightarrow \dfrac{\text{Alg}}{<\bar{S}_{NA} , \bar{\Sigma}_{NA} , \bar{E}_{NA}>}$ in Lemma 4.2. is constructed:

For every $<S'_{NA} , \Sigma'_{NA} , E'_{NA}>$-algebra A,

$W_f(A)$ includes new carrier $A_{sort\ \underline{pri-entry}\ \underline{history}}$ (for short $A_{\underline{ph}}$) and the next operation:

$$op_{d_{\lambda,\underline{sfactor}}} \text{(INIT)} : \rightarrow A_{\underline{ph}} ;$$

$$op_{d_{\underline{sfactor}\ \underline{sfactor},\underline{bool}}} \text{(SEQ)} : A_{\underline{ph}} \times A_{\underline{ph}} \rightarrow A_{\underline{bool}} ; \text{ and}$$

$$op_{d_{\underline{sfactor}\ \underline{pn},\underline{sfactor}}} \text{(UPDATE)} : A_{\underline{ph}} \times A_{\underline{ph}} \rightarrow A_{\underline{pn}}.$$

(Of course $W_f(A)$ includes all carriers an operations in A.)

By the definition of f, $A_{\underline{ph}}$ is equal to $A_{\underline{pri-entry}} \times A_{\underline{history}}$ and each operation on $A_{\underline{ph}}$ is defined by the product of corresponding operation on $A_{\underline{pri-entry}}$ and $A_{\underline{history}}$.

In this way the specification of the scheduler with $\underline{Scheduling-strategy}_{NA}$ can be given and shown to be correct by Theorem 4.5. after the same manner as Example 4.1.

6. CONCLUSION

In this paper we have described two kinds of specifications of schedulers with the algebraic specification technique. One is the specification of the scheduler selecting the process by using only service counts of processes. Another is that of the scheduler selecting the process by using the priority of each process in addition to service counts of processes. Both specifications can be constructed from that of the scheduler having the abstract scheduling strategy as the formal parameter. We simply replace one scheduling strategy by another, then we can obtain each specification of scheduler with the scheduling strategy. Here the extended parameter morphism introduced in this paper has played an important role. Further if both the specification of schedulers and that of a scheduling strategy are correct then the specification of the scheduler to which the scheduling strategy is inserted can be guaranteed to be correct by Theorem 4.5.

When we want to specify large objects such as OS with the algebraic technique, the concept of parameterization in an algebraic framework works as strong mechanism. In this paper we have specified the scheduler having a scheduling strategy as a parameter . As an example of large objects a process management system with a scheduler as a parameter could also be constructed. In these situation the role of extended parameter morphisms seems to be more significant. This extended parameter morphism is useful for not only the assignment of an actual parameter to a formal parameter but the implementation of parameterized data types in further development.

REFERENCES

ADJ (Authors: Goguen J.A., Thatcher J.W., Wagner E.G. and Wright J.B.). (1973). A junction between computer science and category theory: I, Basic definitions and examples, part 1. <u>IBM Research Report</u> RC4526, September 1973.

ADJ (GJA, TJW, WEG). (1976). An initial algebra approach to the specification, correctness, and implementation of abstract data types. IBM Research Report RC6487, October 1976.

ADJ (TJW, WEG, WJB). (1979). Data Type specification: parameterization and the power of specification technique. IBM Research Report RC7757, July 1979.

Ehrich H.-D. (1978). On the theory of specification, implementation and parameter-ization of abstract data types. Research Report, Dortmunt, 1978.

Ehrig H. and Kreowski H.-J. (1977). Some remarks concerning correct specification and implementation of abstract data types. Technical University of Berlin Report Berich-Nr. 77-13, August 1977.

Ehrig H., Kreowski H.-J., Thatcher J.W., Wagner E.G. and Wright J.B. (1979). Para-meterized data types in algebraic specification languages (summary). The Seventh International Colloquium on Automata Language and Programming, 1-19, November 1979.

Guttag J.V. (1975). The specification and application to programming of abstract data types. University of Toronto Computer Systems Research Group Technical Report, CSRG59, September 1975.

Kasami T., Taniguchi K., Sugiyama Y., Hagihara K., Suzuki I. and Okui J. (1978). On algebraic techniques for program specification. Paper of Technical Group on Automata and Languages, AL78-5, IECE Japan, May 1978 (In Japanese).

Wada K., Hagihara K., Araki T. and Tokura N. (1980). Algebraic specifications with function parameters. Paper of Technical Group on Automata and Languages, AL79-111, IECE Japan, February 1980 (In Japanese).

Appendix-SOME DEFINITIONS FROM CATEGORY THEORY

Definition A.1. A category C consists of:
(1) a class $|C|$, whose elements are called objects;
(2) a class C, whose elements are called morphisms;
(3) a pair of function ∂_0, ∂_1: $C \to |C|$, called source and target respectively;
(4) a function 1: $|C| \to C$ called the identity function;
(5) a partial binary operation o: $C \times C \to C$ called composition (we shall write f o g for o (f , g))

such that the following axioms hold for f , g , h $\in$ C and A $\in$ $|C|$:
(1) $A1\partial_0 = A1\partial_1 = A$;
(2) $(f\partial_0 1) \circ f = f \circ (f\partial_1 1) = f$;
(3) f o g is defined iff $f\partial_1 = g\partial_0$;
(4) if f o g and g o h are defined, then both (f o g) o h and f o (g o h) are defined, and they are equal;
(5) if f o g is defined, then $(f \circ g)\partial_0 = f\partial_0$ and $(f \circ g)\partial_1 = g\partial_1$.

The most familiar category is that of sets denoted <u>Set</u>. Its objects are sets, and its morphisms are functions from sets to sets. In an algebraic specification, we consider the category denoted $\underline{Alg}_{<S,\Sigma>}$. Its objects are $<S,\Sigma>$-algebras and its morphisms are Σ-homomorphisms.

<u>Definition A.2.</u> An $<S,\Sigma>$-algebra A is <u>initial</u> in a category of $<S,\Sigma>$-algebras $\underline{Alg}_{<S,\Sigma>}$ iff for every $<S,\Sigma>$-algebra B in $\underline{Alg}_{<S,\Sigma>}$ there exists a unique Σ-homomorphism h: A $\rightarrow$ B.

<u>Definition A.3.</u> A <u>functor</u> from a category $\underline{A}$ to a category $\underline{B}$ is a quadruple $<\underline{A},$ $|F|, F, \underline{B}>$, where $|F|: |\underline{A}| \rightarrow |\underline{B}|$ and F: $\underline{A} \rightarrow \underline{B}$ are functions, such that:

(1) if f: A $\rightarrow$ A' in $\underline{A}$, then fF: $A|F| \rightarrow A'|F|$ in $\underline{B}$

(2) (f o g)F = (fF) o (gF) whenever the composition f o g is defined in A; and

(3) $1_A F = 1_{A|F|}$ for $A \in |\underline{A}|$.

Let $<S, \Sigma, E>$ be a specification. A category of $<S,\Sigma>$-algebras satisfying the axioms E is denoted by $\underline{Alg}_{<S,\Sigma,E>}$.

<u>Definition A.4.</u> Let $<S, \Sigma, E>$ and $<S', \Sigma', E'>$ be specifications, and let $S \subseteq S'$, $\Sigma \subseteq \Sigma'$ and $E \subseteq E'$. A <u>forgetful functor</u> U: $\underline{Alg}_{<S',\Sigma',E'>} \rightarrow \underline{Alg}_{<S,\Sigma,E>}$ is the functor which takes each $<S', \Sigma', E'>$-algebra A' to the $<S, \Sigma, E>$-algebra A such that for each $s \in S$, $A_s = A'_s$ and for each $\sigma \in \Sigma$, $\sigma_A = \sigma_{A'}$. (The carriers in S'-S, and the operations in $\Sigma'-\Sigma$ are "forgotten"). A is called the Σ-<u>reduct</u> of A', A' is a Σ'-<u>expansion</u> of A. A functor F: $\underline{Alg}_{<S,\Sigma,E>} \rightarrow \underline{Alg}_{<S',\Sigma',E'>}$ is called <u>persistent</u> (or <u>strongly persistent</u>, respectively) if A is isomorphic (or equal, respectively) to U(F(A)) for all A in $\underline{Alg}_{<S,\Sigma,E>}$.

<u>Definition A.5.</u> Let $\underline{C}$ be a category, and let $A, B, D, E \in |\underline{C}|$, f: A $\rightarrow$ B, g: A $\rightarrow$ D. f': B $\rightarrow$ E, g': D $\rightarrow$ E $\in \underline{C}$. The morphism pair $<f', g'>$ is a <u>pushout</u> for $<f, g>$ iff

(p-1) f o f' = g o g'; and

(p-2) for every X $\in |\underline{C}|$ and every h: D $\rightarrow$ X, k: B $\rightarrow$ X $\in \underline{C}$, there exists a unique morphism c: E $\rightarrow$ X ($\in \underline{C}$) such that h = g' o c and k = f' o c.

GENERALIZED DYNAMIC AUTHORIZATION MECHANISMS

Yahiko Kambayashi

Department of Information Science
Kyoto University
Sakyo, Kyoto, 606, JAPAN

In this paper powerful authorization (acess right checking) mechanisms are presented, which can be used to realize secure multi-user systems. Most currently used authorization mechanisms are not suitable for systems, such that the user set and the usage of files will change according as the contents of the files change. The mechanism developed by Griffiths, Wade and Fagin (the GWF mechanism) is the most advanced one used in such systems. There are, however, still problems in the GWF mechanism which will be discussed in this paper. New decentralized dynamic authorization mechanisms are presented. The Simple Threshold Authorization Mechanism with Time Stamps (STAMT) is a generalization of the GWF mechanism. According to the security levels required for files, different levels of authorization mechanisms are realized by determining threshold values appropriately. An efficient algorithm to calculate the effect of a revoke command is given. As a further generalization, the Threshold Authorization Mechanism (TAM) is also given, which seems to match the users' world, since it is similar to the security mechanism of the human society.

1. INTRODUCTION

The security problem is one of the key factors of multiuser system development. In order to handle the problem, procedures for authentication (user identification), authorization (access right checking), secure communication and auditing of data usage are required to be developed (Wood and Kimbleton(1979)). This paper will present flexible authorization mechanisms.

Authorization mechanism assigns the right to access an object to each user. Fixed and dynamic ones are known. In a fixed one, the right for each user does not change after its first assignment, which was made

when the object was created. It is suitable for the object which does
not change, since it is simple. In many multiuser systems, however,
system users, system usages and objects themselves are permitted to
change. In such cases dynamic authorization mechanisms are suitable,
since the assignment of access rights can be altered according to these
changes. There is another classification of the mechanisms; centralized and decentralized. If access rights are assigned by a predetermined
set of persons such as creators, system security officers or database
administrators, it is called centralized, otherwise it is called decentralized. Decentralized dynamic authorization mechanisms are considered to be the highest level among all these mechanisms. Fig. 1 summari
the above discussion.

$$\begin{cases} \text{AUTHENTICATION} \\ \text{AUTHORIZATION} \quad \begin{cases} \text{centralized fixed} \\ \text{centralized dynamic} \\ \text{decentralized dynamic} \end{cases} \\ \text{SECURE COMMUNICATION} \\ \text{AUDITING OF DATA USAGE} \end{cases}$$

Fig. 1 - System Security Mechanisms

Griffiths and Wade (1976) proposed a decentralized dynamic authorization mechanism, and Fagin (1978) showed a correct algorithm for this
mechanism. In this paper their mechanism is called the GWF (authorization) mechanism for short. The GWF mechanism permits a user to transfer
the right to grant privileges to other users. Such flexibility is realized by the introduction of the concept of the time stamp. Although
the GWF mechanism provides a decentralized dynamic authorization procedure, there are the following problems.
(1) The mechanism permits unlimited number of privilege transfer betwee
any pair of users. As a result, the graph to analyze the effect of one
revoke command will have a large number of edges, which will make the
analysis difficult.
(2) Usually older users have more power than newer ones, due to the
history sensitive nature of the time stamp. For example, if the creator
of the file withdraws all privileges and grant transfer rights which he
has given, then all users except the creator will lose these rights.
     For the problem (1), conditions to find redundant privilege trans-
fer are given. Furthermore, in order to limit the number of privilege

transfer, a modification is made on the GWF mechanism. Some other modifications to solve the problem (2) are also presented.

According to the security levels defined for files, several levels of authorization will be required. The Simple Threshold Authorization Mechanism with Time Stamp(STAMT) discussed in Section 3 is a generalization of the GWF mechanism, which can be used to define a hierarchy of security levels. By utilizing the similarity between granting operations and functional dependencies of the relational data model, an efficient procedure is derived to calculate the effect of one revoke command.

Further generalization is made because of the requirements of (1) veto, (2) reflection of weighted voting rights, (3) permitting 'pass' as well as 'yes' and 'no' in the decision process. The Threshold Authorization Mechanism (TAM) is introduced for this purpose, which is similar to the security system in the human society. For example, by the decision of over half of the authorized users, a new user gets the right or some user loses the right. To change the threshold value (in this case 1/2), support of, say, over two-thirds of the authorized users is required. In order to change the contents of the shared file, at least two (for example) users must agree.

By this mechanism, the user set can be changed as flexible as the data (for example, the creator of the file may lose his rights). It is especially suitable for the case when a group of people develops database cooperatively. The creator of the file is not necessarily most active in the group and due to the change of data contents, data usage and the user set will change. Realization of each decision function by a combination of two monotonic binary threshold functions is shortly discussed.

2. THE GWF AUTHORIZATION MECHANISM AND ITS GENERALIZATION

In System R an advanced dynamic authorization mechanism is used, which was proposed by Griffiths and Wade (1976) and modified by Fagin (1978). Key ideas of this GWF mechanism are as follows.
(1) Any user may be authorized to create a new file.
(2) If the user wishes to share his file with other users, he may use the GRANT command to give various privileges on that file to various users. Examples of these privileges are READ, INSERT, DELETE, UPDATA and DROP.
(3) The user may grant a set of privileges with the grant option, which permits the grantee to further grant his acquired rights to other users.
(4) Any user who has granted a privilege may subsequently withdraw it

by issuing the REVOKE command.

One important problem is to calculate all users who will lose the privilege by a given revoke command, since if user i loses the privilege all the users who have gotten the privilege from i will also lose the privilege unless they got the same privilege from other users. This problem is not simple because of its recursive nature.

Definition 1: The GWF graph is represented by $G_{GWF} = (V, E, v_1)$. $V = \{v_1, v_2, \ldots, v_m\}$ is a set of vertices, $E = \{e_{ij}(t)\}$ is a set of weighted directed edges, where e_{ij} corresponds to an edge from v_i to v_j and t is a weight (positive integer) of the edge, and $v_1 \varepsilon V$ is called the initial vertex.

For simplicity we assume that one GWF graph is prepared for each combination of a file and a privilege, althouth merging of several GWF graphs is possible. Since it is simple to handle the grant transfers without grant options, we will treat only grant transfer with grant options. Each vertex of the graph corresponds to a user who can have the privilege on the file and the right to issue the grant command with the grant option. v_1 corresponds to the creator of the file. If at time t, user i grants the privilege to user j with grant option, there exists an edge $e_{ij}(t)$, which is called an grant transfer edge. The weight t is called the time stamp, which is used in common for all GWF graphs in the system and increased by 1 whenever necessary. We assume that if a user get the privilege at time t, he can transfer the privilege at time t', satisfying $t' \geq t+1$. If user i revokes the privilege from j, all edges from i to j are removed by this command, that is, user i cannot remove one of the edges from i to j by specifying a particular time stamp. If a revoke command is issued, the edges corresponding to the command must be removed. Furthermore, an edge $e_{pq}(t)$ must be removed if there does not exist any path $e_{k_1 k_2}(t_1)$ $e_{k_2 k_3}(t_2) \ldots e_{k_h p}(t_h)$ satisfying $v_{k_1} = v_1$ and $t_1 < t_2 < \ldots < t_h < t$.

Fagin showed that for correct calculation, grants which were issue from the same grantor to the same recipient at different time must be recorded. His example is shown in Fig. 2. If user 2 revokes the privilege from user 3, only edges shown by bold lines will remain. He showe that if one of the two edges from user 3 to user 4 is omitted, the proce dure does not work correctly.

This property of the GWF mechanism causes a problem because the number of edges is unlimited even for a finite number of users. The

following propositions
show conditions for
redundant edges.

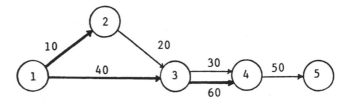

Fig. 2 - Fagin's Example

Proposition 1: An edge $e_{ij}(t)$ is redundant if the following condition A or B is satisfied.

A: (1)   There exists $e_{ij}(t_1)$ satisfying $t_1 < t$.

      (2)   There does not exist any edge $e_{hi}(t_2)$ for some h such that $t_1 \leq t_2 < t$.

B: j=1.

Proof: A.   If i does not get any grant transfer after issuing $e_{ij}(t_1)$, $e_{ij}(t)$ for $t_1 < t$ will not change the possible set of users for any revoke command.   B.   It is obvious since v_1 always has the right.   Q.E.D.

Proposition 2:   If there exist $e_{ij}(t_1)$ and $e_{ij}(t_2)$ such that $t_1 < t_2$,

(1) $e_{ij}(t_2)$ is redundant if i=1,

(2) $e_{ij}(t_1)$ is redundant if $i \neq 1$ and there exists no $e_{jk}(t_3)$ for any k satisfying $t_1 < t_3 \leq t_2$.

Proof: (1) is obvious.   In the GWF mechanism, a revoke command cannot specify the time stamp, so if user i revokes a privilege transfer to user j both $e_{ij}(t_1)$ and $e_{ij}(t_2)$ will be removed.   When both edges exist $e_{ij}(t)$ is always redundant for $i \neq 1$ Q.E.D.

Even if we create edges which do not satisfy the redundancy condition of the above propositions, the number of edges is unlimited by the existence of cycles. A stronger condition is given below.

Definition 2:   In a GWF graph, a path $e_{k_1 k_2}(t_1) \; e_{k_2 k_3}(t_2) \ldots e_{k_{p-1} k_p}(t_{p-1})$ from v_{k_1} to v_{k_p} is critical if the following conditions are satisfied.

(1) $k_1 = 1$

(2) $t_1 < t_2 < \ldots < t_{k+1}$.

(3)   If there is more than one edge from k_i to k_{i+1}, select $e_{k_{i+1} k_{i+2}}(t_{i+1})$ such that t_{i+1} is the minimum satisfying $t_i < t_{i+1}$.

(4)   For any $i \neq j$, $k_i \neq k_j$.

<u>Proposition 3</u>: An edge $e_{ij}(t)$ is redundant if it is not contained in any critical path from v_1 to some v_i in the GWF graph at a certain instance.

<u>Proof</u>: If at a certain instance an edge is not contained in any critica path, it is redundant at this instance. We need to prove that such an edge will never contained in any critical path. If no revoke commands are involved, the proof is easy, since the time stamps of the edges adde after the generation of such edge $e_{ij}(t)$ is at least t and thus these edges will not contribute to make $e_{ij}(t)$ a part of a critical path.

Next, we will show that any revoke command does not make $e_{ij}(t)$ be a part of a critical path. There are the following cases.
(1) Any revoke command which removes only edges whose labels are greater than t does not make $e_{ij}(t)$ be critical.
(2) Assume that there exists another edge $e_{ij}(t')$ from v_i to v_j, which is contained in a critical path P.
(2-1) A revoke command for an edge in P cuts P and thus $e_{ij}(t')$ may not be in a critical path after this operation, but it does not make $e_{ij}(t)$ be in a critical path. A revoke command for edges not contained in any critical path passing $e_{ij}(t')$ does not give any effect to $e_{ij}(t)$.
(2-2) If we can remove $e_{ij}(t')$ alone, $e_{ij}(t)$ will be contained in a critical path. It is not possible, however, since the revoke command to remove $e_{ij}(t')$ will also remove $e_{ij}(t)$.
(3) Assume that $e_{ij}(t)$ is the only one edge from v_i to v_j. Since this edge is not contained in a critical path, any critical path from v_1 to v_2 through v_i,v_j reaches v_j before v_i (see Fig. 3). If $e_{ij}(t)$ becomes a part of a critical path P after revoke commands, there exists a critical path from v_1 to v_i not passing through v_j. Existence of such a path contradicts the above fact.

Q.E.D.

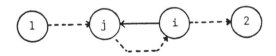

Fig. 3 - An Edge not in a
Critical Path

Fig. 4 shows an example of a redundant edge detected by Proposition 3 but not by Propositions 1 and 2.
(1) There are two critical paths $v_{12}(1)v_{23}(2)v_{34}(3)$ and $v_{15}(5)v_{53}(6)$ $v_{34}(7)$ from v_1 to v_4, and there exist two different revoke commands to eliminate these paths. Both $e_{34}(3)$ and $e_{34}(7)$ are not redundant.
(2) There are two critical paths from v_1 to v_5; $e_{15}(5)$ and $e_{12}(1)$ $e_{23}(2)e_{34}(3)e_{45}(4)$. $e_{45}(8)$ is not contained in these paths, so it is

redundant. Since both $e_{34}(3)$
and $e_{34}(7)$ are not redundant,
redundancy of $e_{45}(8)$ cannot
be detected by Propositions
1 and 2.

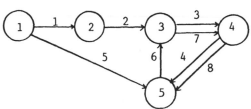

In order to calculate
all critical paths efficiently,
an efficient procedure to
calculate all regular expressions

Fig. 4 - Example of Proposition 3

between states for an automata (see Aho, Hopcroft and Ullman (1974))
can be used.

Since usually an edge which is contained in a critical path cannot
be removed without side effects, Proposition 3 is the best possible
redundancy condition for the GWF mechanism. The following proposition
shows that the number of edges is exponential even if we only permit
edges in critical paths.

Proposition 4: If there are n users, the upper bound of the number of
edges in critical paths is $\sum\limits_{k=1}^{n-1} \dfrac{(n-1)!}{k!}$. There exists such a GWF graph
for any $n \geq 1$.

Proof: Each critical path starts from v_1 and its length is at most n-1.
The upper bound of the number of edges can be obtained by the tree shown
as Fig. 5. Let f(n) be the number of edges for each tree. Obviously,
$f(n)=(n-1)+(n-1)f(n-1)$ and $f(2)=1$, $f(1)=0$,
We have,
$$f(n) = \sum_{k=1}^{n-2} \frac{(n-1)!}{k!}$$

As shown in Fig. 5,
the labeling on edges
is done by the depth-
first ordering. The
GWF graph corresponding
to the tree is formed
by merging vertices
of identical names.
This example for n=4
can be generalized
for any n. Q.E.D.

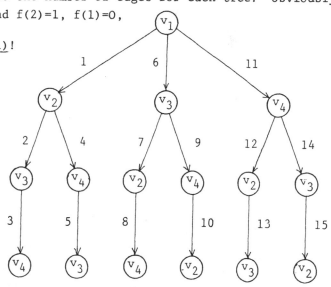

Fig. 5 - The Upper Bound of the Edge Count
in Critical Paths

One possible approach to prevent the increase of edges is to permit only one edge from v_i to v_j for any ordered pair (i,j).

Fig. 6 shows a problem caused by this method. When we want to replace $e_{23}(10)$ by $e_{23}(20)$, relabeling of other edges is required. In Fig. 6 (a) without $e_{23}(20)$, there are two critical paths from 2 (2-3-5 and 2-3-4-6-7). In order to preserve the critical paths we have to relabel some of the edges as shown in Fig. 6 (b).

For relabeling, we will modify the definition of a critical path such that (1) in Definition 1 is $t_1 \leq t_2 \ldots \leq t_{k+1}$, since the labeled value may exceed current time value if we require $t_1 < t_2 < \ldots$ in the critical path, when the path is long.

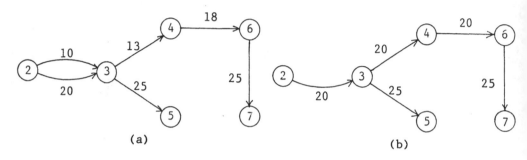

(a)   (b)

Fig. 6 - Relabeling of Edges

Since in the above method we have to keep all critical paths, we will introduce the following practical method.

The Modified GWF Mechanism

Grants which are issued from the same grantor to the same recipient at different time are usually required when the grantor wants to make sure that the recipient has the privilege whenever the grantor has it. In order to represent it, we will introduce a new label * for edges. If $e_{ij}(t)$ is labeled by *, it is regarded as $e_{ij}(t')$ for any $t' \geq t$. For convenience, in the GWF graph an edge $e_{ij}(t)$ with * is represented by an edge from i to j labeled by *t. By introducing this new kind of edges, we will permit at most one edge from i to j for any pair i and j. The modified GWF graph for the graph shown in Fig. 4 is given in Fig. 7.

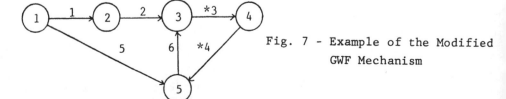

Fig. 7 - Example of the Modified GWF Mechanism

The procedure for the modified GWF authorization mechanism is almost same as the procedure for the GWF mechanism (Fagin (1978)), except for handling edges with *'s.

(1) If user k issues a revoke command to $e_{kj}(t)$ with *, the edge is eliminated.

(2) If (a) user i loses the privilege by a revoke command issued at time t and (b) there exists an edge $e_{ij}(t_1)$ with *, then it is replaced by $e_{ij}(t)$ with *. This operation makes the edge ineffective for the current privilege calculation, but whenever user i gets the privilege again user j will get it by the existence of this edge.

Another problem of the GWF mechanism is caused by the history sensitive nature of the time stamps. In Fig. 2, if user 1 revokes the privileges from users 2 and 3, all the users except user 1 will lose the privilege. Because of the time stamp, older users are usually more influential than new users. Contents of a file can change without such a restriction (i.e., the oldest data may be erased), so a more flexible dynamic mechanism is required. Simple extentions are (1) to permit to transfer the ownership of a file to another user, and (2) to permit co-ownership of a file.

3.   THE SIMPLE THRESHOLD AUTHORIZATION MECHANISM

In computer systems, usually several security levels are required, such as 'top secret', 'secret', 'confidential' and 'public'. According to the security levels of files, we should have different levels of authorization mechanisms. In order to handle this problem, a simple threshold authorization mechanism will be introduced in this section.

The mechanism has the same problems as the GWF mechanism for the number of privilege transfers and for the history sensitive nature of time stamps. For the first problem, the approach used in the modified GWF mechanism is used, although we can modify the procedure to use the relabeling procedure. Modification for the second problem is not mentioned in this section, since it is rather easy.

<u>Definition 3</u>: A simple threshold authorization mechanism with time stamps (STAMT for short) is defined as follows.

$$A_{ST}(F,P)=(U,\ G,\ U_o,\ Q)$$

It is defined for each combination of F (a set of files with which the mechanism is concerned) and P (a set of privileges). $U=\{u_1,u_2,\ldots,u_n\}$

is a set of users. $G=\{g_1, g_2, \ldots, g_m\}$ is a set of granting operations, where $g_i: U_i \to u[t,w]$ and U_i is a set of users ($U_i \subseteq U$), $u \in U$, t is a time stamp for this granting operation, and $w \in \{r, g, r^*, g^*\}$ shows the type. r and g are granting privileges and granting privileges with grant options repectively. * shows the grant transfer such that the grantor wants to make sure that the recipient has the privilege whenever the grantor has it. U_o is the set of users called the co-owners of F. $Q=\{q_r, q_g\}$ is a set of threshold values. q_r and q_g correspond to these of the granting privileges and the granting privileges with grant options, respectively.

For example, $g_1: \{u_1, u_2\} \to u_3[t, r(\text{or } r^*)]$ $(u_3[t, g(\text{or } g^*)])$ shows that users u_1 and u_2 together grant privileges P (with grant options, respectively) to u_3 at time t. The number of users in the left side of $\to$ is determined by min $(q_r, |U_g|)$ $(\min(q_g, |U_g|)$, respectively). Here, U_p, U_g and U_n are subsets of U, each of which corresponds to a set of users with the privileges, a set of users with the privileges and grant transfer rights or a set of users without any rights at all, respectivel Since users in U_g have the privileges, $U_g \subseteq U_p$ and $U=U_p \cup U_n$.

The modified GWF mechanism introduced in Section 2 corresponds to the case when $q_r=q_g=1$ in Definition 3. We assume that $q_r \leq q_g$, since to obtain the privileges with grant option should not be easier than to obtain the privileges without grant option. The larger values of q_r and q_g correspond to the higher security levels.

For example, let $U=\{u_1, u_2, u_3, u_4, u_5\}$, $G=\{g_1, g_2, g_3\}$ and $U_o = \{u_1, u_2\}$ and $Q=\{2, 2\}$. Granting operations are assumed to be as follows

$g_1: u_1 u_2 \to u_3[10,g]$

$g_2: u_1 u_2 \to u_4[10,r]$

$g_3: u_2 u_3 \to u_4[20,g]$

The sets U_p, U_g and U_n are as follows

	U_p	U_g	U_n
At time 5	$u_1 u_2$	$u_1 u_2$	$u_3 u_4 u_5$
At time 10	$u_1 u_2 u_3 u_4$	$u_1 u_2 u_3$	u_5
At time 20	$u_1 u_2 u_3 u_4$	$u_1 u_2 u_3 u_4$	u_5

At least one user in the left set of g_i can revoke the granting operation g_i (i=1,2,3). If u_2 revokes g_3 at time 30, u_4 will lose the grant transfer right. If, however, u_2 revoke g_1 at time 30, u_3 will lose the privilege as well as the grant transfer right. Because of this g_3 becomes ineffective and u_4 will lose the grant transfer right.

Because of the generalization, the calculation to compute an effect of one revoke command becomes complicated. We have the following efficient algorithm for the calculation, which utilizes the similarity between the granting operations and the functional dependencies in the relational database model.

Algorithm 1: An algorithm to compute the effect of one revoke command in STAMT.

(1) Let t_{ri} and t_{gi} be the time when u_i first obtained the privileges and the privileges with grant option, respectively. If not defined, a sufficiently large number is assigned.

(2) Assume that user u_i revokes g_j: $U_j \rightarrow u_{gj}[t_j,w]$ satisfying $u_i \epsilon U_j$, remove g_j from the set G.

(3) Let U_{go} be the set of users whose t_{gi} is less than t_j. Users in U_{go} have the privilege as well as the grant transfer right and are not influenced by the revocation of g_j.

(4) If there exists g_k: $U_k \rightarrow u_{gk}[t_k,g]$ (or $[t_k,g*]$) such that $U_k \subseteq U_{go}$ and for any $u_{ki} \epsilon U_k$, $t_{g_{ki}} < t_k$ (the condition is not required for $g*$), then u_{gk} is added to U_{go} and $t_{g_{gk}}$ is defined to be t_k (for $g*$, $\max(t_k, t_{g_{ki}})$ for $u_{ki} \epsilon U_k)$).

(5) Repeat step (4) until no new user is added to U_{go}.

(6) After calculating U_{go}, calculate U_{ro} as follows. U_{ro} is initially U_{go}. If there exists g_h: $U_h \rightarrow u_{gh}[t_h,r(or r*)]$ such that $U_h \subseteq U_{go}$ and for any $u_{hi} \epsilon U_h$, $t_{g_{hi}} < t_h$ (the condition is not required for $r*$), then u_{gh} is added to U_{ro} and $t_{r_{gh}}$ is defined to be t_h (for $r*$, $\max(t_h, t_{g_{hi}})$ for $u_{hi} \epsilon U_k)$). Repeat this process until no increase of U_{ro} occurs.

(7) If there exist g's with w=r or g which are not used in steps (4) and (6), remove them from G. Granting operations with w=r* or g* which are not used in these steps, need not be modified.

The granting operation g_i:$U_i \rightarrow u[t_i,w]$ can be regarded as a functional dependency with a label. There is an efficient algorithm to calculate all attributes which depend on the given set of attributes

(Beeri, Bernstein (1979)). If we sort g's by the value t, then we only need to test g's according to the increasing order of t. For g's with the same t, the functional dependency calculation procedure can be used.

When q is expressed by the function of $|U_q|$ (for example $|U_q|/2$), the value changes according as $|U_q|$ changes.

In order to change the security level (values in Q), a similar machanism can be used.

4. THRESHOLD AUTHORIZATION MECHANISM

Further generalization of the authorization mechanism is preferable by the following requirements.
(1) There can be users who have right to veto the decision.
(2) There can be users whose opinion corresponds to several users.
(3) For some decision, each user can express 'pass' as well as 'yes' and 'no'.
(4) Threshold values for revocation are required to be more than 1.

(1) and (2) are required, since in many organizations some executive members want to control their authorization mechanism. By a simple modification, (2) can be realized by STAMT. The threshold values for revocation are regarded as 1 in STAMT.

Definition 4: A general authorization mechanism is given by
$$A_G(F,P)=(U, Q, M_1, M_2, C, R).$$
It is defined for each combination of F(a set of files with which the mechanism is concerned) and P(a set of privileges). U is a set of users and $Q=\{Q_1, Q_2\}$ is a set of mappings such that $Q_1:U\rightarrow\{0,1,2\}$ and $Q_2:U\rightarrow 2^P$. Let U_i be $\{u|Q_1(u)=i\}$ for i=0,1,2. $|U|=n$, $|U_i|=n_i$ for i=0,1,2, where $|U|$ denotes the number of elements in set U. User u has privileges in $Q_2(u)$. Each user in U_1 and U_2 has some privileges in P and for a user u in U_o, $Q_2(u)=\phi$. Furthermore, users in U_2 can contribute to change Q, M_1, M_2, C and R. M_1 and M_2 define the procedures to change Q. M_i defines the membership procedure for U_i as well as the privilege assignment procedure for U_i, i=1,2. C defines the procedure to change the contents of files in F. R defines the procedure for changing M_1, M_2, C and R itself.

Interpretation of the above mechanism is as follows. First a set U_I of users (possibly one user) create a set F of files. P is normally a set of all possible operations on the files. Users in U_I can determi procedures to add or delete users who can use F. For each user his

privilege must be determined. $Q_2(u)$ defines the set of all operations
which u can use. Another privilege is the right to change the procedures.
Usually a part of users (users in U_2) have this right. Procedures to
select users in U_1 and U_2 could be different, since the users in U_2 have
more privileges. These procedures are defined by M_1 and M_2, respectively.
Since the data in F is shared, we impose a restriction represented
by C on changing data in F. R defines the rules to change all these
procedures including R itself.

   Initially for any u in U_I, $u \varepsilon U_2$, $Q_2(u)=P$. All the procedures are
determined by users in U_I. By membership procedures M_1 and M_2, new
members can be added to U_1 and U_2. It is possible that a user in U_I
loses his privileges sometime. The procedures can be changed by users
in U_2 if R is satisfied.

   This mechanism is especially suitable when a group of people develops a database cooperatively. The creator of the file is not necessarily
most active in collecting data and due to the change of data contents
the user set should change.

   Procedures determined by Q, M_1, M_2, C and R must be defined for
arbitrary set U_2, since U_2 changes dynamically. The threshold authorization mechanism uses simple procedures and is a special case of the
general authorization mechanism.

<u>Definition 5</u>: The threshold authorization mechanism (TAM, is given by

   $A_T(F,P)=(U, Q, M_{1T}, M_{2T}, C_T, R_T)$.

which is a special case of the GAM. M_{iT}, M_{2T}, C_T and R_T are defined by
sets of ternary threshold functions.

   For each user u_i a ternary variable x_i is assigned. According to
the user's opinion, 'yes', 'no' or 'pass', x_i is 1, 0 or *, respectively.
For example, let $f(x_1, x_2,..., x_n)$ be a ternary function and values of
x_i's are given. According to the value of f, 1, 0 or *, the corresponding decision is supported, rejected or undetermined (in the last case
no change occurs). Let M_{iT} be $\{f_i,g_i\}$ for i=1, 2. A new user can be
added to U_i if $f_i(X)=1$ and a user loses the position if $g_i(X)=1$ $(X=(x_1,...,$
$x_n)$, value x_i can be 1,*,0 if x_i corresponds to a user in U_2). $C_T=\{c\}$
and according to the value of $c(X)$, the proposed update operation is
admitted or rejected. $R_T=\{r\}$ and if $r(X)=1$, all the above ternary
functions can be modified.

   The function should be monotonic by the following reasons. We
define 1>*>0. For two vectors $X_1=\{x_{11}, x_{12}, ..., x_{1i}\}$ and

$X_2 = \{x_{21}, x_{22}, \ldots, x_{2n}\}$, $X_1 \geq X_2$ iff $x_{1i} \geq x_{2i}$ for all $i (1 \leq i \leq n)$. A ternary logic function f is monotonic if for any $X_1 \geq X_2$, $f(X_1) \geq f(X_2)$. Assume tha f is not monotonic, then there exist X_1 and X_2 such that $X_1 > X_2$ and $f(X_1) < f(X_2)$. For example, $X_1 = (1,0,1,*)$ and $X_2 = (1,0,0,*)$ satisfy $X_1 > X_2$. If $f(X_1) = 0$ and $f(X_2) = 1$, then the third users opinion has negative effect (the decision is approved when he says 'no' while it is rejected when he says 'yes'). Such a situation can be avoided if we assume that f is monotonic. Threshold functions with positive weights are monotonic. A ternary threshold function can be realized by two binary threshold functions h_1 and h_2, by assigning '1' = (1,0), '*' = (0,0) and '0' = (0,1) or (1,1).

A binary threshold function h_i is defined by $(T_i, w_{i1}, w_{i2}, \ldots, w_{i}$ and if $\sum_j w_{ij} x_j \geq T_i$, $h_i = 1$ otherwise $h_i = 0$.

The weights for users' opinion can be expressed by w_{1j}'s. The righ to veto the proposal can be expressed by w_{2j}'s. For example, assume that it is required to make an authorization mechanism by which a pro-posal is rejected if at least two of the five executive members $(u_1, u_2, \ldots, u_s)$ say 'NO'. The definition of h_2 is $(2,1,1,1,1,1,0, \ldots, 0)$ that is, the threshold value is 2 and the weights for the five users are 1 and the other weights are 0.

5. CONCLUDING REMARKS

In this paper several dynamic authorization mechanisms are proposed These mechanisms can be used in various areas, such as view handling problems, but details of implementation techniques are omitted. The threshold authorization mechanism can be generalized further by adding time-stamp handing function.

This work was started in 1979 while the author was with the Department c Computer Science, McGill University, Montreal, Canada.

REFERENCES

Aho A.V., Hopcroft J.E. and Ullman J.D. (1974). The Design and Analysis of Computer Algorithm. Addison-Wesley, Reading Mass.

Armstrong W.W. (1974). Dependency structures of data base relationships. Proc. IFIP Congress, 1974, pp 580-583.

Beeri C. and Bernstein P.A. (1979). Computational problems related to the design of normal form relation schemes. ACM Trans. on Database Systems, Vol 4, No 2, March 1979, pp 30-59.

Fagin R. (1978). On an authorization mechanism. ACM Trans. on Database Systems, Vol 3, No 3. Sept. 1978, pp 310-319.

Graham G.S. and Denning P.J. (1972). Protection-Principles and practice. AFIPS SJCC, 1972, pp 417-429.

Griffiths P.P. and Wade B.W. (1976). An authorization mechanism for a relational database system. ACM Trans. on Database Systems. Vol 1, No 3. Sept. 1976, pp 242-255.

Harrison M.A., Ruzzo W.L. and Ullman J.D. (1976). Protection in operating system. Communications of the ACM, Vol 19, No 8. August 1976, pp 461-471.

Thomas R.H. (1979). A majority consensus approach to concurrency control for multiple copy databases. ACM Trans. on Database Systems, Vol 4, No 2. June 1979, pp 180-209.

Wood H.M. and Kimbleton S.R. (1979). Access control mechanisms for network operating system. AFIPS NCC, 1979, pp 821-829.

Part II.

Program Behavior and Performance Models

Performance modelling and evaluation has been a focus of
active and continuing research on operating systems, and
significant results have been obtained. The first paper by
T. Masuda and T. H. Fin summarizes the program behavior
models developed so far and then proposes a new program
behavior model which is based not only on the information in
the reference string generated by the program during its
execution but also on the information in the source program.
The authors suggest that the approach lead to a new locality
concept. The second paper by H. Kameda investigates the
effectiveness of the CPU scheduling discipline that gives
higher preemptive priority to I/O bound jobs than compute
bound jobs. This scheduling discipline was empirically
claimed by Ryder to give higher throughput than any other
discipline. The author analytically shows that this claim
holds for a variety of queuing models. The third paper by
C. Ishikawa, K. Sakamura and M. Maekawa addresses the
problem of dynamic tuning of computer systems. The paper
categorizes dynamic tuning methods and then discusses their
individual and combined effects. The last paper by M.
Miyazaki, S. Matsuzawa, S. Obata and S. Noguchi is concerned
with the performance evaluation of an actual time-sharing
system. The authors point out the need of a standard
workload for the effective measurement of system performance.
The authors then propose and discuss a method to create a
simulated workload. Also included are several case studies.

PROGRAM BEHAVIOR AND ITS MODELS

Takashi Masuda*
Tong-Haing Fin**

* Institute of Information Sciences
   and Electronics
   University of Tsukuba
   Sakuramura, Niiharigun
   Ibaraki 305
   Japan

** Department of System Science
   Tokyo Institute of Technology
   O-okayama, Meguroku
   Tokyo 152
   Japan

ABSTRACT

This paper first discusses the program behavior models developed until now. It includes non-locality models, locality models and phase/ transition models. Then a new model of program behavior is proposed. The previous models are based only on the information in the reference string generated by the program during its execution. Our approach is to utilize the information in the source programs as well as the one in the program's reference string. It seems to be useful not only for modeling of program behavior, but also it suggests a new locality concep

1. INTRODUCTION

In virtual storage systems memory management strategies have a profound effect on total system performance. The role of memory management strategies includes the decisions of the optimal multiprogramming degree, memory allocation among active processes, pages to be kept in main memory, and so on.

A number of memory management strategies have been proposed and implemented in actual systems. At the same time the analysis of these strategies have been performed by theoretical approaches, simulation techniques and monitoring methods. For these analysis we must, as the first step, construct an accurate model of the programs executing within the system. Several program behavior models based on the program reference strings have been developed. These models can be classified into some categories.

In this paper, first, we discuss these program models, and, secondly, we propose a new model of program behavior, which uses information of source programs. The program behavior model or program locality concept developed until now is based only on the information in the reference string generated by the program during its execution. Our approach is to utilize the information in the source programs as well as the one in the program's reference strings. This approach seems to be very useful not only for modeling of program behavior, but also it suggests a new locality concept and must be useful in the choice of parameters of memory management strategies.

2. PROGRAM BEHAVIOR

PAGE REPLACEMENT ALGORITHMS

We consider an n-page program whose pages constitute the set $N = \{1, 2, \cdots, n\}$. The program will generate a sequence of references, called an *address trace*, in its virtual address space during its execution. The *reference string* of the program is a sequence

$$R = r_1 \, r_2 \, \cdots \, r_t \, \cdots$$

where r_t is the page number containing the virtual address referenced at time t.

A page fault occurs at virtual time t if r_t is not in main memory. If there is no available page frame when a page fault occurs, a page of the program in main memory must be replaced.

Commonly referred examples of page replacement algorithms for fixed memory allocation policy include:

(1) FIFO (First In First Out): replaces the page of the program which is in main memory for the longest time.

(2) LRU (Least Recently Used): replaces the least recently used page of the program in main memory.

(3) RANDOM: replaces a randomly selected page of the program in main memory.

(4) OPT (Optimum): replaces the page of the program in main memory which will not be referenced for the longest time.

The advantage of FIFO algorithm is that it is very easy to implement in the actual system. The LRU algorithm is based on the properties of program behavior; there is a high correlation between the pages which have been referenced in the near past and those pages which will be referenced in the near future. Though OPT algorithm cannot be implemented in the actual system because it is based on the future page references, it is possible to calculate the page fault rate of the algorithm when a program's address trace is given. Since OPT is the optimal replacement algorithm among fixed space policies, it is useful to compare the paging efficiency of other replacement algorithms with the one of the OPT algorithm.

The LRU and OPT replacement algorithms described above belong to a class of paging algorithms, called stack algorithms [Mattson (1970)]. In stack algorithms, it is known that page fault rate is monotone decreasing for every reference string as the allocated page frame increases.

To compare the efficiency of these algorithms, the page-fault rate function or the lifetime function is commonly used. The lifetime is the mean virtual time interval between page faults when a reference string is processed. An example is given in Fig. 1, which shows the relationship between the lifetime and the allocated main memory space for the four replacement algorithms described above. The sample program of Fig. 1 is a BASIC compiler. This pattern does not change in most programs. The LRU replacement policy tends to show the maximum lifetime, with the exception of the OPT policy.

CHARACTERISTICS OF PROGRAM LOCALITIES

The fact that the LRU algorithm is superior to other algorithms shows that those pages which have been referenced in the near past tend to be referenced again in the near future. In order to investigate the more general characteristics of program behavior, it is very useful to figure the address reference patterns of a program. Fig. 2a shows an example of program address reference pattern. The figure shows the behavior of FORTRAN compiler. In the figure the vertical scale is address space measured by 4K bytes, and the horizontal scale is time measured in instructions executed. Fig. 2b corresponds to the third phase of Fig. 2a. A solid dark area indicates concentrated references to a set of contiguous addresses. A dot or thin vertical line indicates a single or very small number of references to some location.

From the analysis of the address reference patterns of some commonly used programs, it can be said that most programs exhibit the following properties to varying degrees [Denning (1972)]:

(1) A program distributes its references nonuniformly over its pages, some pages being favored over others.

(2) The density of references to a given page tends to change slowly in time.

(3) Two reference string segments are highly correlated when the interval between them is small, and tend to become uncorrelated as the interval between them becomes large.

These properties are known as the concept of *locality of references* (or simply *locality*). We speak of programs as having *good locality* when they reference small subsets of their space for relatively long periods of time. Programs having good locality perform well on virtual storage systems even in small allocation of main memory. Program structures with good locality of references are investigated from several viewpoints [Hatfield (1971), Ferrari (1974), Masuda (1974)].

WORKING SET

To execute a program efficiently in a phase, it is necessary to keep the locality set corresponding to the phase in main memory. Fixed allocation policies cannot take into account the transitions of program locality. Then variable allocation policies are necessary which try to keep the correct locality set in main memory during program execution. The best known locality estimation method is the working set [Denning (1968)]. The *working set* at time t is the collection of pages referenced by that program between virtual times t-T and t, and is denoted as W(t,T). Parameter T is called the *window size*. The number of different pages in the working set W(t,T) is called the *working set size* and is denoted as w(t, T).

When the concept of working set is applied to page replacement policy, working set policy removes a page from main memory at time t whenever it does not belong to the working set W(t,T). There are a number of researches about the properties and the usefulness of working set.

3. NON-LOCALITY MODELS

INDEPENDENT REFERENCE MODEL (IRM) [Aho (1971)]

This model assumes that the reference string is a sequence of independent random variable with a common stationary reference distribution:
$$Pr[r_t=i] = a_i \quad \text{for all t and } 1 \le i \le n.$$
This model has the best mathematical tractability and is frequently used for the analysis of page replacement algorithms. However, the IRM does not reflect actual program behavior and does not provide a realistic definition for the program localities. Because it fails to capture phase/transition behavior, the mean working set size calculated from this model is far greater than the mean size measured on the real program when the a_i are the observed reference densities of the program's pages [Spirn (1972)].

A recent study by Baskett and Rafii [Baskett (1976)] has shown that if the IRM's a_i are chosen so that the fault rate of the optimal A_0 policy [Aho (1971)] (A_0 is the optimal replacement algorithm for the IRM) matches that of the MIN policy [Belady (1966)] on the real program the IRM formulae for other policies (FIFO, LRU, WS, etc, ···) will estimate the actual fault rate surprisingly well.

MARKOVIAN REFERENCE MODEL (MRM) [Aho (1971)]

The MRM is based on the knowledge of a transition matrix $P = \{p_{ij}\}$ where p_{ij} represents the probability that page j is referenced following page i. This model is much more adequate than the IRM. More recently,

this model has been used as a model of program behavior by Franklin and
Gupta [Franklin (1974)] to calculate the page fault probability of certain replacement algorithms, by Hofri and Tzelnic [Hofri (1979)] and by
Kobayashi [Kobayashi (1979)] to calculate the exact distribution of the
working set size. However, it is difficult to use this model for program consisting of large number of pages since the number of parameters
of the MRM is n^2 (n is the total number of program's pages).

4. LOCALITY MODELS

VERY SIMPLE LOCALITY MODEL (VSLM) [Spirn (1972)]

In this model, the locality set has a fixed size of l pages, where
$1 \le l < n$. Pages in the locality set are independently referenced at the
same probability $(1-\lambda)$. All non-locality pages are likewise equally
probable of reference with probability λ (See Fig. 3). If a page in
the locality is referenced, the locality set membership does not change.
If a non-locality page is referenced, it enters the locality set, replacing a randomly chosen locality page. This model is characterized
completely by only two parameters —— the locality size l and the transition probability λ. Spirn and Denning [Spirn (1972)] compare the performance of IRM and the VSLM and they observe that the VSLM produces a
better approximation to the real world bahavior of program.

SIMPLE LEAST RECENTLY USED STACK MODEL (SLRUSM) [Spirn (1972, 1976, 1977)]

This model was based on the fact that LRU replacement algorithm
seems to perform well as a locality estimator. Note that with the LRU
stack algorithm there is a distance string d_1, d_2, $\cdots$, d_t associated
with any reference string r_1, r_2, $\cdots$, r_t. Since knowledge of the initial stack and of the distance string is sufficient to determine LRU
stack at each time, and since the top of the stack is the currently referenced page, the reference string and the distance string are equivalent information.

In the SLRUSM, a fixed probability is assigned to each stack distance
(called stack distance probability):

$$P_r[d_t=i] = b_i \quad \text{for all t and } 1 \le i \le n.$$

A stack distance string is generated as a series of independent random variables. One major characteristic of the SLRUSM is that if a page is referenced, it moves to the top of the stack, where its probability of reference will be different (See Fig. 4). With proper choice of the b_i, experiments [Spirn (1972, 1977)] have shown that the SLRUSM produces good predictions of the average working set size and page fault rate of some real programs.

However, this model does not accurately predict all aspects of realistic program behavior. For example, the page fault probability, under LRU replacement algorithm, calculated from this model is constant for all time. This is not an accurate characterization of page faults, which tend in real program to occur in bursts, during transition between disjoint localities. Another kind of inaccuracy is that if the distance probability b_i satisfies the following condition (*locality condition*):

$$\min\{b_1, \cdots, b_l\} \geq \max\{b_{l+1}, \cdots, b_n\}$$

it can be shown that for SLRUSM, the page fault rate under fixed LRU replacement algorithm is better than that for a dynamic algorithm with the same average size l [Spirn (1977)]. This is in contradiction with the experimental evidence available in literature that, for example, the working set algorithm performs better than LRU [Graham (1976), Spirn (1977)].

MULTIPLE DISTANCE DISTRIBUTION MODEL

There have been several attempts to improve the simple LRU stack model. To account for clustering of page faults during phase transitions, the distance probabilities must be allowed to vary in time. In a simplified analysis one would assume that there are two distributions of the distance probabilities [Spirn (1972)]. One represents the intraphase behavior and is biased toward the top of the stacks. The second corresponds to phase transition behavior and is biased toward larger stack distances. A two-state Markov chain can be used to choose between the distance distributions (See Fig. 5). The labels on the edges between the states in Fig. 5 are the transition probabilities of the two-state Markov chain. In state 1, the intraphase distribution is used. In state 2, the phase transition distribution is used. Although this two-distribution model exhibits the clustering of page faults and phase transition phenomenon, it does not allow for changes in a program's locality set size. This method can clearly be extended to more than two distributions [Arvind (1973)]. Such a multiple-distribution model can become very complicated and it also becomes impractical if there are many distributions, since we must choose the distance probabilities of each distribution, as well as the transition probabilities of the Markov chain to choose among the distributions.

Validation experiments of this multiple distribution model [Arvind (1973), Gupta (1974), Spirn (1972)] have shown no significant improvement over the simple LRU stack model.

MARKOVIAN LRU STACK MODEL [Spirn (1972, 1976, 1977)]

Another approach to improve the simple LRU stack model is to generate successive stack distances from a Markov model, instead of as independent trials. In this model, there are n^2 conditional distance probabilities b_{ij}, where
$$b_{ij} = Pr[d_t=j \mid d_{t-1}=i] \quad \text{for all t and } 1 \le i, j \le n.$$
The large number of parameters make this model complicated and difficult to analyze. Shedler and Tung [Shedler (1972)] proposed a simpler model of this kind by assuming certain properties of the distance string that would cause many of the parameters b_{ij} to be zero. This model has not yet been validated for real program.

The models mentioned above have the common ability to describe the stable behavior within phases. None of these models contains an explicit concept of phase/transition behavior. None is considered accurate enough to be a model of long term program behavior. A realistic model must account for multiple program phases over locality sets of significantly different sizes.

5. PHASE/TRANSITION MODELS

In this section, we will review several studies that address the problem of modeling intraphase and phase transition behavior more directly.

A useful approach to modeling phase/transition behavior derives from the principle of decomposability for systems studied by Courtois and Vantilborgh [Courtois (1976)]. The central observation is that if the rate of interactions within a given system is high compared with the rate of interactions between that system and its environment, then transient behavior of the system has no significant influence on the long-run dynamics of the environment. Under this assumption we can

approximate the true behavior by assuming that system is in equilibrium
for the full duration of each interval between interactions with the
environment. In other words, we can decompose the problem, studying
first the system in its own right and then using just its equilibria
to study the environment.

DECOMPOSABLE MODEL [Courtois (1976, 1977)]

This model assumes that all localities are strictly disjoint and
that the page reference string behavior is generated by the Markovian
Reference Model as described in section 3. Let P be the MRM's page
transition matrix. Its rows and columns are arranged so that pages of
a same locality have consecutive entries. Then by the definition of
locality, the matrix P will have along the main diagonal a string of
square submatrices of large elements. And, since the localities are
supposed strictly disjoint these submatrices will be principal matrices
of P; outside these submatrices all elements will be comparatively small
since they are the probabilities of referencing a page which does not
belong to the current locality. P is then said to be *nearly completely
decomposable* [Courtois (1976, 1977)], i.e. takes the form:

$$P = P^* + \varepsilon C$$

where C is a square matrix of the same order as P, which has the propert
of keeping both P and P* stochastic, ε is a real positive number, small
compared to the elements of P*, and

$$P^* = \begin{bmatrix} P_1^* & & & & \\ & P_2^* & & & \\ & & \ddots & & \\ & & & & P_N^* \end{bmatrix}$$

with the elements not displayed being equal to zero. P*, also of order
n, is a stochastic matrix completely decomposable into the stochastic
submatrices P_I^*, $1 \leq I \leq N$, of order n(I), if N is the number of strictly
disjoint localities and n(I) the size of locality I ($\sum_{I=1}^{N} n(I) = n$).
Clearly, in this model, each submatrix P_I^* is a separate MRM of program
behavior within locality I, and ε is the maximum probability of leaving
a locality. Under these assumptions, Courtois showed that the principa
of near-complete decomposability can be used to partition the program's
time behavior into short and long-run dynamics with the following prope
ties;
(i) during the short-term period, each locality's interval characteristics (such as its mean size, paging rate, and estimate of the working
set size) can be separately analysed in function of the distribution of

reference over its pages only; and

(ii) during the long-term period, the global characteristics of the whole program can be determined in terms of the equilibrium values of the locality interval characteristics.

This distinction leads to the use of two types of models. A model of program global behavior, viz. a Markov chain model of the transitions between localities; and separate models for the locality interval behavior. Note that no specific model is in principle required by this approach to determine the internal characteristics of each locality. It is not even necessary to use one same model for all the localities of a same program.

MACRO/MICRO MODEL [Kahn (1975)]

To employ the principle of decomposability in program modeling, Kahn and Denning [Kahn (1975)] use a *macro model* to generate the phase transition behavior between locality sets and a *micro model* to generate the reference patterns within each phase determined by the macro model.

Kahn and Denning [Kahn (1975)] stated that to quantify program's phase/transition behavior, there are four factors to specify:

(i) The distribution of holding time in each locality set - i.e., the duration of phases;

(ii) The process by which program chooses new locality sets at phase transitions;

(iii) The extent to which locality sets of adjacent phases overlap;

(iv) The process by which the program generates references from within a given locality set.

Factors (i) - (iii) are associated with the phase transition behavior and will be described by a *macro model*. Factor (iv) is associated with the reference pattern within phases and will be described by a *micro model*.

A semi-markov chain can be used to describe the macro model over a given collection of locality sets S_1, S_2, $\cdots$, S_N. When the program is in the locality set S_i, the state of the chain is i. The probability that a phase over S_i lasts for t references is described by a holding time distribution $h_i(t)$ with mean $\bar{h}_i$. A transition matrix $[q_{ij}]$ gives the probability that S_j is the next locality set after S_i.

Kahn and Denning have tried this approach and had the limited objective to test the ability of simple phase/transition models to reproduce known properties of empirical lifetime functions. For this purpose, they chose to specify the above general semi-markov chain macro model

with as few parameters as possible:
1. The holding time distribution was state independent, i.e., $h_i(t) = h(t)$ for all t, with mean $\bar{h}$;
2. The type of the observed locality distribution $\{P_i\}$, where P_i denotes the fraction of time that S_i is the locality set, together with its mean m and standard distribution σ, were given. This was used to derive a distribution $\{P_i\}$ over locality set sizes $\{I_i\}$, which in turn was used to determine the locality sets $\{S_i\}$. The locality sets S_i are assumed to be mutually disjoint locality sets;
3. At the phase transition, S_i is entered with probability P_i. In other words, $q_{ij} = P_j$ for all i.

This simple model requires only 2n + 1 parameters ($\bar{h}$, P_1, $\cdots$, P_n, S_1, $\cdots$, S_n) rather than at least 2n + n for the full semi-markov chain. For micro models, they chose cyclic, sawtooth, and random reference patterns.

From experiments, Kahn and Denning observed that the choice of micro model affected primarily the convex region of the simulated lifetime functions, these effects being small for the working set lifetime. The concave or tail-off region of the curve was significantly affected by the choice of macro model. Note that no experiments with LRU stack micro model were conducted. Behavior other than that lifetime function was not investigated.

BOUNDED LOCALITY INTERVAL MODEL [Madison (1975, 1976), Batson (1976a, 1976b)]

Even though the property of locality of reference is commonly referred to and used in the description of program behavior, no study up until recently has provided a precise definition of what constitutes an interval of localized reference behavior. Without such a definition, the true nature of this property in actual program cannot be accurately measured, and models of program reference behavior that are based upon this property, cannot be easily developped and verified.

In 1975, the work of Madison and Batson [Madison (1975, 1976)] on Bounded Locality Intervals is the only attempt found in the literature to date to provide a formal definition of a locality set and a method to partition an arbitrary reference string into phases and transitions. Their definition of phases and transitions uses an LRU stack vector of program segment names. They defined the concepts of *Activity Set and Bounded Locality Interval*. The starting point of the development of these concepts is the observation by Spirn and Denning [Spirn (1972)] that the LRU stack may be used to construct a hierarchy of sets of segments (or pages) which possess many of the characteristics associated with a locality.

An *Activity Set of size i* exists at time t if every element in the first i positions of the LRU stack vector has been re-referenced more than once since that set was formed at the top of the first i positions of the LRU stack vector. A *Bounded Locality Interval* (BLI) was then defined as the two tuple (A_i, τ_i), where A_i is the activity set and τ_i is its *lifetime* at the head of the LRU stack vector. This definition allows for a hierarchy of BLI's to exist over a given time period as illustrated in Fig. 6, which shows an example reference string and the corresponding BLI structure. The notion of the *level* of a bounded locality interval in the hierarchy can also be introduced and is defined as the distance of the BLI down in the hierarchy. The *level one* BLI's are those at the top of the hierarchical structure, and they have special significance in that they subdivide the reference string into the longest possible subintervals of distinctive referencing behavior.

For the data reference strings of ALGOL 60 programs, Madison and Batson observed that, if one chooses to define the long-lived stable phases in the program's execution in term of level-one BLI's, then transitions between these states usually involve a considerable amount of uncorrelated, unordered activity. There is little correlation between the locality set size before and after a transition. Note that the empirical results of Madison and Batson [Madison (1976), Batson (1976b)] are limited to the description of data segments, and more specifically, to array segments declared in the source language Algol 60 programs; i.e., there is a one-to-one correspondence between array names in the source programs and segment identifiers in the data segment strings. Although similar model would be applicable to instruction reference strings, as pointed out by Spirn and Denning [Spirn (1972)], one may expect very different reference patterns for these two types of information.

Whereas the above concept of BLI is extremely convenient for the study of the phase/transition behavior in the reference string, there are several problems with this concept;
(i) The BLI definition classifies some reference patterns as locality intervals that do not completely satisfy our intuitive concept of an interval of localized reference behavior. One such example is a BLI for which all of the members of its activity set are referenced at the beginning of the interval and then one or more members are not referenced

at all for the rest of the lifetime of the activity set.

(ii) The definition of BLI is very strict because if a program reference
a new segment, the BLI is terminated. But intuitively, we might conside
a program to be in a single phase even if it occasionally references a
new data (e.g., a source program that contains conditional branches and
procedure calls within the computational loops).

(iii) If we correlate the BLI's structure of a program with its syntacti
structure, the existence of a hierarchy of BLI is a necessary but not
sufficient condition for the existence of nested loops in the source
program. The existence of a multilevel BLI structure can be due to othe
reasons, and therefore, BLI at some level of the hierarchy may be mean-
ingless and give false indication of localities.

Beside the above deficiencies, the concept of BLI is ill-suited to
the design of rules that would manage a memory hierarchy while dynamically estimating the characteristics of the current program. The algorithm used to find the BLI's in a reference string is more complex and
therefore there must be a delay between the formation of a BLI and the
first time when it can be acknowledged.

6. PROGRAM LOCALITY MODEL BASED ON PROGRAM STRUCTURE

We think that the difficulties of modeling program behavior may
result from the following reason. In the previous models, programs are
used only as *black boxes* to generate a reference string, i.e. the original structure of source program was ignored. However, the center of
concern should really be the program itself and not the reference strin
Details of the process by which reference string is generated are clear
contained in the source program and data. There is almost nothing impo
tant in a reference string which is not reflected in the source program
Thus, our approach will be to study and analyse programs by correlating
their dynamic behavior during execution with their syntactic structure.

SCHEMATIC CHART OF PROGRAM

Usually, the flowchart is used to describe the flow of the execution of the program. Unfortunately, certain control structures in programming languages, such as iteration, have to direct translation to th
conventional flowchart language and must be built from simpler control

structures. With the advent of structured programming, top-down programming, and GOTO-free programming, a method is needed to model computation in simpler ordered structures. Recently, Nassi and Shneiderman [Nassi (1973)] have proposed a flowchart language whose control structures are closer to that of structured programming language.

Iteration or looping structures have long been recognized as a central feature of program behavior. Our intuition leads us to speculate that these looping structures in a program might correspond to the intervals of localized references, and that it may be possible to recognize such localized referenced intervals by analysis of the program's looping structures in the program's syntactic structure. To represent explicitly the program's looping structures, we will introduce a flowchart language, called *schematic chart*, which uses the following symbols to represent the program's logic structure.

The *process symbol* (Fig. 7a) is used to represent sequential statements (e.g., assignment, read, write, etc.).

The *decision symbol* (Fig. 7b) is used to represent the IF-THEN-ELSE statement found in PL/I, ALGOL, and similar languages.

The *repetitive contour symbol* (or simply *countour*)(Fig. 7c) is used to represent a group of statements which can be executed more than one time. Usually, the repetitive contour symbols are created by the iterative statements such as DO, WHILE, REPEAT statements, but in programming language having GOTO statement, they may be created by the branch backward GOTO statement.

Fig. 8 shows an example of a program with its schematic chart.

DEFINITIONS AND ASSUMPTION

To simplify the analysis, we will make the following assumption.

(A) There is only one entry statement in the repetitive contour symbol.

Note that this assumption is satisfied for structured programming or GOTO-less languages.

In each repetitive contour symbol, there may exist two types of decision symbols. One type, called *exit-decision symbol*, is used to exit from the contour, and another type, called *selective-decision symbol*, is used to describe the choice between two alternatives. In Fig. 8b, the decision symbol Test 1, which is used to exit from the contour C, is an exit-decision symbol, and the decision symbol Test 2, which is used to choose between S_2 and S_3, is a selective-decision symbol.

A decision symbol is said to be a *decision point* of a statement S if the execution of statement S depends on the test of that decision symbol. The decision symbol Test 2 in Fig. 8b is a decision point of S_2 and S_3, but it is not a decision point of S_4.

A statement S_2 is said to be *reachable* from a statement S_1 if there is a path from S_1 to S_2. A *reachability degree of S_2 from S_1* is defined to be equal to the maximum number of decision point on each path from S_1 to S_2 plus 1. In Fig. 8b, the statement S_4 is reachable from Test 1 with reachability degree equal to 2, and the statement S_2 is also reachable from Test 1 but with reachability degree equal to 3 since Test 1 is the decision point of S_2.

Let S be a statement in a repetitive contour symbol C. We define the *reachability degree of S*, in relation to C, to be equal to the maximum number of selective decision symbols, which are the decision points of S, on each path from the entry statement of the contour C to the statement S plus one.

The reachability degree of a contour C_2 in relation to a contour $C_1 (C_2 \subset C_1)$ is defined to be equal to the reachability degree of the entry statement of C_2 from the entry statement of C_1.

The *stability degree* of a contour is defined to be equal to the number of selective-decision symbols in that contour plus one. Fig. 9 shows an example of a stable contour and an unstable contour. In the contour C_1 of Fig. 9a, there is no selective-decision symbol (Test is an exit-decision symbol), then it is a stable contour with stability degree equal to 1. In Fig. 9b, the contour C_2 contains one selective-decision symbol (Test 2), then it is an unstable contour of stability degree 2.

Property. - With the assumption (A), the repetitive contour symbol of a program form hierarchies of contours.

From the above definitions, each repetitive contour symbol is characterized by:
(i) its stability degree. A stable contour never changes its members during its existence in the dynamic behavior (i.e., reference string) of a program;
(ii) its reachability degree in the hieararchy of contours, which characterizes the existence of the contour in the program's dynamic behavior.

RELATIONSHIP OF THE NOTION OF CONTOUR AND THE NOTION OF LOCALITY

The notion of locality is derived from the dynamic behavior in the program's reference string. In this section, we will correlate the

notion of contour defined in the previous section to this dynamic behavior of the program.

A contour C is said to be *active* at time t if it contains the
statement being executed at time t. If a contour C is active, all contours containing C are also active.

Let C be a contour. Each simple path from the entry statement to
the exit statement of C is called an *iteration* of the contour C. If
the stability degree of a contour C is greater than 2, C has many iterations. The stable contour C_1 of Fig. 9a has only one iteration {Test,
S_2, S_3}, and the unstable contour C_2 of Fig. 9b has two interations
{Test 1, S_2, Test 2, S_3, S_5} and {Test 1, S_2, Test 2, S_4, S_5}.

Let the string in Fig. 10b be the reference string generated by
the contour C in Fig. 10a during the program's execution. The times
t_0, t_1, t_2, t_3 in the figure correspond to the ends of the successive
iterations of reference to members of the active contour C, and we call
such times as *cycle points*. There are two distinctive periods in the
interval $[t_0, t_f]$. The first part $[t_0, t_3]$ is the *body* of the active
contour C. It consists of one or more complete iterations. The second
part $[t_3, t_f]$ is an incomplete iteration. The number of iterations in
the body of an active contour is called *rank*.

A *locality contour* is defined as a two tuple (C, τ), where C is an
active contour with rank > 1 and τ is the period at which C is active.

Locality contours, as defined here, have the following characteristics:
(i) they correspond strongly to the most intuitive notion of what constitutes a *locality*. All members of an active contour have a high re-
referenced probability;
(ii) they can be used to divide reference strings into *phases, transitions within phase* (corresponding to the phenomenon that the locality
set changes slowly its members.), and *transitions between phases*;
(iii) the definition of the locality contour is independent of parameters, such as window size, and is independent of any characteristics of
the computer systems used to generate the reference string. It depends
only on the characteristics of the program at the source language level;
(iv) the definition of the locality contours allows a *hierarchy of locality contours* to exist over a given time period.

The locality contour is a novel approach to correlate the program's
dynamic behavior in the reference string with the syntactic structure
of the source language level program. Another interesting possibility
is that the structure of program's repetitive contours in the source
program can be detected by the compilers. Then there is possibility

that compilers can implant instructions (e.g., at the entry and exit of
each repetitive contour) that advise dynamically the memory management
(such as working set algorithm) when certain pages or segments have been
referenced for the last time in the current phase. We are currently
investigating some of the applications of the locality contour concept
to control the parameter of the memory management, and the validation
of this model in the actual reference strings.

7. CONCLUSION

We have first discussed several reference string models for program
behavior, ranging from non-locality models, locality models to phase/
transition models. Then we have proposed a new model for program behavior, which uses the information of source programs. The previous
program behavior models and program locality concept are based only on
the information in the reference string generated by the program during
its execution. Our approach is to utilize the information in the source
programs as well as the one in the program's reference string. This
approach seems to be very useful not only for modeling of program behavior, but also it suggests a new locality concept and must be useful
in the choice of parameters of memory management strategies. In our
current research project, we are implementing this new approach in the
actual compiler.

REFERENCES

Aho A.V., Denning P.J. (1971). Principles of optimal page replacement.
J. ACM, Vol 18, No 1, January 1981, pp 80-93.

Arvind, Kain R.Y., Sadeh E. (1973). On reference string generation
process. Proc. 4th ACM Symposium on Operating Systems Principles.
October 1973, pp 80-87.

Baskett F., Rafii A. (1976). The A_0 inversion model of program paging
behavior. Stanford University, Computer Science Dept., Report STAN-CS-
76-579, November 1976.

Batson A.P. (1976a). Program behavior at the symbolic level. Computer, Vol 9, No 11, November 1976, pp 21-26.

Batson A.P., Madison A.W. (1976b). Measurements of major locality phases in symbolic reference strings. Proc. Int'l Symposium on Computer Performance Modeling, Measurement, and Evaluation. ACM SIGMETRICS and IFIP WG 7.3 March 1976, pp 75-84.

Belady L.A. (1966). A study of replacement algorithms for virtual storage computers. IBM Syst. J., Vol 5, No 2, 1966, pp 78-101.

Courtois P.J., Vantilborgh H. (1976). A decomposable model of program paging behavior. Acta Informatica, Vol 6, No 3, 1976, pp 251-276.

Courtois P.J. (1977). Decomposability. Academic Press. 1977.

Denning P.J. (1968). The working set model for program behavior. Comm. ACM, Vol 11, No 5, May 1968, pp 323-333.

Denning P.J. (1972). On modeling program behavior. AFIPS Conf. Proc. 40. 1972 JSCC, pp 937-944.

Ferrari D. (1974). Improving program locality by strategy oriented restructuring. Proc. IFIP Conf., 1974, pp 266-270.

Franklin M.A., Gupta R.K. (1974). Computation of page fault probability from program transition diagram. Comm. ACM, Vol 17, No 4, April 1974, pp 186-191.

Graham G.S. (1976). A study of program and memory policy behavior. Ph.D. Thesis, Dept. Computer Sciences, Purdue Univ., December 1976.

Gupta R.K. (1974). Program reference behavior and dynamic memory management. Ph.D. Thesis, Washington University, 1974.

Hatfield D., Gerald J. (1971). Program restructuring for virtual memory. IBM Syst. J., Vol 10, No 3, 1971, pp 168-192.

Hofri M., Tzelnic P. (1979). On the working set size for the markov chain model of program behavior. Performance of computer systems, edited by M. Arato et al., North-Holland, 1979, pp 393-405.

Kahn K.C., Denning P.J. (1975). A study of program locality and life-time functions. Proc. 5th ACM Symposium on Operating Systems Principles, November 1975, pp 207-216.

Kobayashi M. (1980). Instruction reference behavior and locality of reference in paging.   Ph.D. Thesis, Univ. of California, Berkeley, 1980.

Madison A.W., Batson A.P. (1975, 1976).   Characteristics of program
localities.   Proc. 5th ACM Symbosium on Operating System Principles,
November 1975, pp 64-73.   See also Comm. ACM. Vol 19, No 5, May 1976,
pp 285-294.

Masuda T., Shoita H., Noguchi K., Ohki T. (1974).   Optimization of
program organization by cluster analysis.   Proc. IFIP Conf., 1974, pp
261-265.

Mattson R.L., Gescei J., Slutz D.R., Traiger I.L. (1970).   Evaluation
techniques for storage hierarchies.   IBM Syst. J., Vol 9, No 2, 1970,
pp 78-117.

Shedler G.S., Tung C. (1972).   Locality in page reference strings.
SIAM J. Computing, Vol 1, No 3, September 1972, pp 218-241.

Spirn J.R., Denning P.J. (1972).   Experiments with program locality.
AFIPS Conf. Proc. 41.   1972 FJCC, pp 611-621.

Spirn J.R. (1976).   Distance string models for program behavior.
Computer, Vol 9, No 11, November 1976, pp 14-20.

Spirn J.R. (1977).   Program behavior: Models and Measurement.   Elsevier/
North-Holland Publishing Co., 1977.

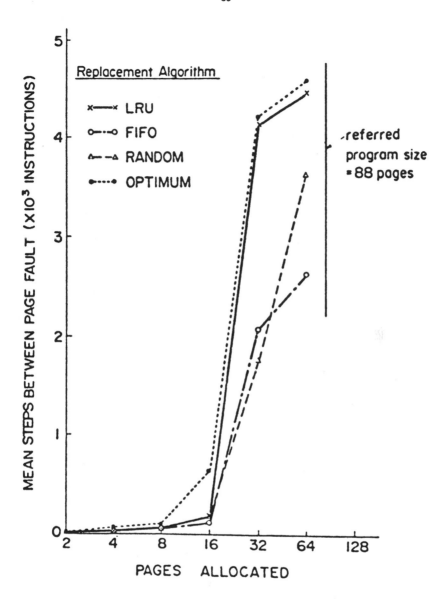

Fig. 1   Lifetime functions of fixed memory policies

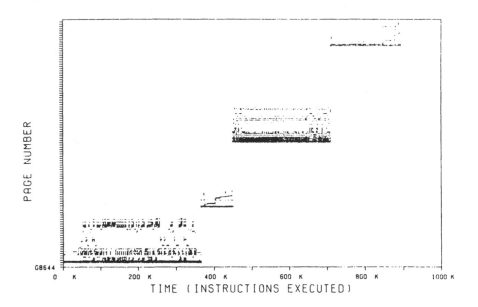

Fig. 2a Address reference pattern of a FORTRAN compiler: all phases

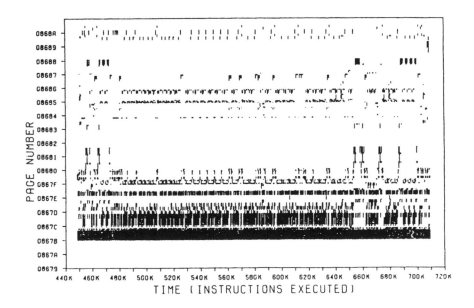

Fig. 2b Address reference pattern of a FORTRAN compiler: third phase

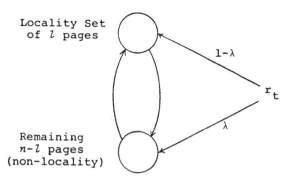

Locality Set
of l pages

Remaining
$n-l$ pages
(non-locality)

$1-\lambda$

λ

r_t

Fig. 3 Very simple locality model [Spirn(1977)]

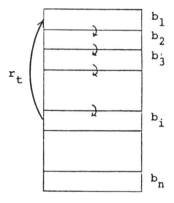

r_t

b_1
b_2
b_3'

b_i

b_n

Fig. 4   LRU stack model [Spirn(1976)]

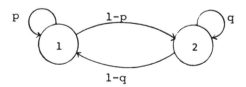

p $1-p$ q

1   2

$1-q$

Fig. 5   Two-state Markov chain [Spirn(1976)]

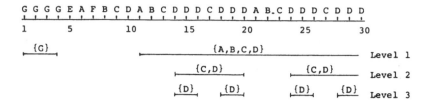

Fig. 6   Hierarchy of Bounded Locality Intervals
for an example symbolic reference string

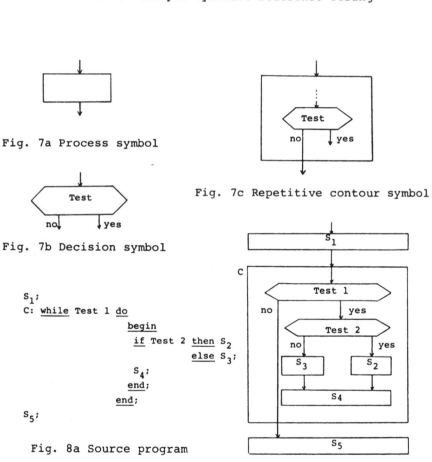

Fig. 7a Process symbol

Fig. 7b Decision symbol

Fig. 7c Repetitive contour symbol

```
S₁;
C: while Test 1 do
            begin
                if Test 2 then S₂
                          else S₃;
            S₄;
            end;
          end;
S₅;
```

Fig. 8a Source program

Fig. 8b Schematic chart

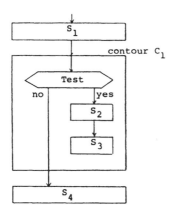

Fig. 9a A stable contour

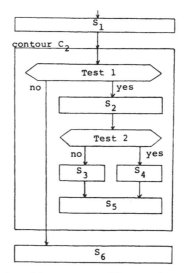

Fig. 9b An unstable contour

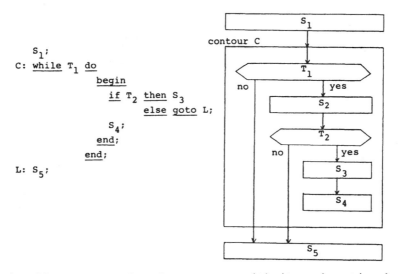

```
       S_1;
    C: while T_1 do
               begin
                 if T_2 then S_3
                         else goto L;
                 S_4;
               end;
           end;
    L: S_5;
```

Fig. 10a An example of a program with its schematic chart

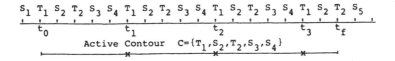

Fig. 10b Cycle points and active contour

CPU SCHEDULING FOR EFFECTIVE MULTIPROGRAMMING

Hisao Kameda

Department of Computer Science
The University of Electro-Communications
Chofu, Tokyo, Japan

ABSTRACT

Several analytically solvable queueing models of multiprogramming with different jobs and various scheduling disciplines are investigated. It is shown that the analysis of these models supports the optimality of the already proposed CPU scheduling discipline which assigns higher processing priority to a more I/O bound job. Furthermore, the effects of some endogenous scheduling disciplines such as preemptive-resume last-come-first-served are compared with that of this discipline using some queueing models.

1. INTRODUCTION

In any multiprogrammed computer system, jobs may suffer from congestion at the central processing unit (CPU) of the system. Thus we have the problem of providing an appropriate scheduling

A close version of this paper appeared in Trans. IECEJ, Vol.E64, No.3 (March 1981), pp.120-125.

discipline to handle this congestion. Jobs in the system do not usually have the same characteristics: Some jobs have short CPU time bursts (I/O bound) while others require long CPU processing between two consecutive I/O operations (compute bound). A scheduling discipline (here we call it H-schedule) has already been proposed which gives higher preemptive priority at the CPU to a more I/O bound job than to a more compute bound job [Ryder (1970)]. This discipline was recognized through some empirical works as giving better throughput of multiprogrammed computer systems than any other disciplines already devised.

However, there seem to have been few comprehensive theoretical works on the effectiveness of this discipline. This may be partly because it is difficult to solve analytically general queueing models of multiprogramming which allow different classes of jobs and various scheduling disciplines, although we have quite a general queueing model developed by Baskett et al. (1975) if the scheduling disciplines are limited. Moreover, some author states that the H-schedule may produce less throughput, in his study of some restricted priority queueing models.

In this paper, we investigate several restricted queueing models with various scheduling disciplines and see the effectiveness of the H-schedule. Furthermore, we compare the effect of the H-schedule with that of some endogeneous scheduling disciplines such as preemptive-resume last-come-first-served (LCFSPR) and processor sharing (PS-a limiting case of round-robin discipline).

2. MODELS OF MULTIPROGRAMMING

The models that we want to use in evaluating the effect of CPU scheduling should be so simple that relevant characteristics of the model may be obtained in some analytic fashion. Those models which are solvable only numerically may give us little insight into the real effect of CPU scheduling. Baskett el al. (1975) developed a method of solving analytically a very broad category of queueing models with different classes of customers. By means of their theory (called BCMP theory), we have, for example, the following model of multiprogramming that can be solved analytically: The model has one CPU server and several I/O servers. At any I/O servers, the service time distribution is the same for any jobs and is exponential, and the service discipline is first-come-first-served. At the CPU server, each program may have a distinct service time distribution, but the CPU scheduling discipline is either processor sharing or preemptive-resume last-come-first-served (or any one of last-batch-processor-sharing (LBPS) disciplines with the fixed number of servers [Noetzel (1979)]. The model has a product form solution for each of its state probabilities. Each job, say j, may have the different probability, P_{ji}, of selecting an I/O device, i, at the end of each CPU burst (i.e., $P_{ji} \neq P_{ki}$, for $j \neq k$). If we want to have a more general model than the above, we may have quite cumbersome procedures for obtaining analytic solutions under the current status of knowledge. For example, such models as have preemptive priority scheduling disciplines at their CPU do not have any product form solutions, and we can not use the BCMP theory.

Now we must turn to less general queueing models to evaluate the effect of CPU scheduling. We may impose several different restrictions on models: As for I/O servers- A. The number of I/O servers is one; B. The number of I/O servers may be greater than one. The service time distribution of each I/O server is identical and the probability of each job's selecting any I/O server is also identical (i.e., $P_{ji} = P_{jk}$ for $i \neq k$); C. The service time distribution of each I/O server is identical, the number of I/O servers is greater than or equal to the number of jobs in the system, and each job selects any vacant I/O server when it requires (machine repairman model). As for the number of jobs in the system — I. N = 2; II. N is arbitrary. The following table shows the authors who solved each restricted case. In most cases, it is assumed that service time distributions are exponential for each job although the mean service time may be different for each job.

In the following section, we investigate the solutions obtained by these authors and derive some results out of them, if necessary, for the purpose of evaluating the effect of CPU scheduling. We consider that, in real situations, the service time distribution at I/O servers for each job may be regarded as similar while those at CPU server may vary much from job to job. Thus, we assume that the service time distribution at each server is identical. Under this assumption, the model of Lazowska and Sevcik's (A-I) can be included in that of Spirn's (B-I) as a special case. Also the model of Spirn's (C-I) is included in that of Kameda's. Thus, in the

Table 1. The authors of the reports on queueing models with
different jobs and various scheduling disciplines.

	A No. of I/O = 1.	B No. of I/O > 1.	C Machine repairman.
I No. of jobs = 2.	Lazowska & Sevcik(1974)	Spirn (1976)	Spirn (1976)
II No. of jobs is arbitrary.	Mitrani* (1972)	———	Kameda (1979) Price** (1972)

* CPU has only a preemptive priority discipline. The priority at
CPU and that at I/O are identical for each job.
** All jobs are statistically identical. The service time
distribution at CPU may be general.

following section, we investigate those models such as Mitrani's,
Spirn's, Price's, and Kameda's to discuss the effect of CPU
scheduling.

The term throughput is sometimes defined to be the number of
jobs processed by the system during the unit time interval. It is
not appropriate to use this definition directly in evaluating the
effect of scheduling of different jobs, because, under this
definition, we can increase the throughput of the system by simply
giving higher processing priority to jobs with short total
processing time. Let us replace 'the number of jobs processed by
the system' in the definition by 'the total job processing time'.
Let us illustrate this here. The total processing time, t_j, of job
j during the time interval t must be t under uniprogramming
environments if the job has no overlap operation in itself. Let
t_{ji} be the time length job j spends at server i during
$t(\Sigma_i t_{ij}=t_j)$. Under multiprogramming environments, the system may

have congestion at several servers and $t_j \leq t$. Let us call $t_j/t = e_j$ the processing rate of job j at that interval. The total amount of processing during the unit time interval is to be:

$$\Sigma_j t_j/t = \Sigma_j e_j.$$

And this is to be defined as throughput U in our discussion. Furthermore,

$$U = \Sigma_j e_j = \Sigma_j (\Sigma_i t_{ij}/t) = \Sigma_i (\Sigma_j t_{ij}/t) = \Sigma_i U_i.$$

where U_i denotes the utilization factor of server i. Thus we consider that the throughput of the system is the sum of the utilization factors of the servers in the system.

3. THE EFFECT OF CPU SCHEDULING

In this section, we investigate the effect of CPU scheduling using several analytically solvable queueing models of multiprogramming. We assume the following throughout this section unless otherwise stated. These models consist of a 'CPU' server and one or several 'I/O' servers. Jobs are indexed by the integers 1, 2, ..., N, and N denotes the number of jobs in the system. The mean service time length of job j at the CPU server and those at the I/O servers are u_j^{-1}, and v^{-1}, respectively, for j = 1, 2, ..., N. Let $r_j = v/u_j$.

THE CASE OF MITRANI'S MODEL

Mitrani (1972) considered a cyclic queueing system consisting of two servers, CPU and I/O. The system serves a constant number, N ($N \geq 1$) of customers or jobs, each of which is given a distinct priority. Jobs in the system and their priorities are both indexed by the integers 1, 2, ..., N. Let a smaller integer mean higher preemptive priority at both CPU and I/O servers. That is, job j means the job which has priority j, j = 1, 2, ..., N, and job 1 has the highest priority at both CPU and I/O, etc.

The period of time between two consecutive joinings of the CPU queue by the same job will be called a 'cycle'. Denote the steady-state average cycle for job j by c_j. In this model, it is assumed that the average I/O service time of job j is given by v_j^{-1}. Then c_n for job n is given by,

$$c_n = c_{n-1} + \{u_n[1 - \sum_{j=1}^{n-1} (u_j c_j)^{-1}]\}^{-1} + \{v_n[1 - \sum_{j=1}^{n-1} (v_j c_j)^{-1}]\}^{-1},$$

$$c_1 = u_1^{-1} + v_1^{-1}.$$

Let us derive from this the total utilization, U, of CPU and I/O servers for the case where $v_1 = v_2 = \ldots = v_N = v$ and N = 3, for example. Then, we have,

$$U = 1 + r_1(1+r_2)(1+r_1)^{-1}(1+r_1+r_1 r_2)^{-1}$$

$$+ r_1^2(1+r_2)(1+r_3)(1+r_1+r_1 r_2)^{-1}[(1+r_1)+(1+r_2)r_1 + r_1^2(1+r_2)(1+r_3)]^{-1}.$$

Note that if r_1 is close to zero, i.e., if top priority is given to extremely I/O bound jobs, the throughput U is close to the infimum, 1. Mitrani (1972) has similar arguments on the CPU utilization, and states that the commonly accepted practice of giving the highest priorities to jobs which are most I/O bound is not necessarily the most efficient. Notice, however, that, in this situation, top priority is given to extremely I/O bound jobs not only at the CPU server, but also at the I/O server. We can understand this situation intuitively as follows. Job 1 almost occupies the capacity of the I/O server, since it is extremely I/O bound and is given the highest preemptive priority at both CPU and I/O servers. Thus all other jobs can receive almost no processing, since they usually require a certain amount (on the average, v^{-1}) of I/O service between two consecutive services of CPU. Thus we cannot say that the above statement by Mitrani still holds true even if different scheduling disciplines are employed at the I/O server.

Mitrani also showed how to solve the model where non-preemptive priorities are given at the I/O server. The solution is much more complicated even when N = 3, and we do not work out the details here. However, the situation is similar to the above. That is, if there are two extremely I/O bound jobs in the system and they are given the highest priorities at both CPU and I/O, the capacity of the I/O server will be almost completely used up by the two jobs and no other jobs can receive processing. Note that, if the priority assignment at the I/O server is different, the results may also be different. In any case, we can consider that Mitrani's model has little concern with the prevalence of the H-schedule.

THE CASE OF SPIRN'S MODEL

Consider a central server model consisting of a 'CPU' server and m 'I/O' servers. The model has only two jobs, 1 and 2. A job leaving CPU chooses one of the m I/O units at random. Assumptions concerning service time distributions are the same as appear at the beginning of this section. Let R_1 and R_2 denote the utilization factors of CPU for jobs 1 and 2, respectively. Let us define T as follows: $T = C_1 R_1 + C_2 R_2$, where C_1 and C_2 are given constants.

Consider a class of scheduling disciplines, called (p,q) schedules, which includes FCFS, LCFSPR, PS, preemptive priority, etc. [It is defined as follows. Suppose jobs 1 and 2 are both in a queue; they will be processed in parallel by the server. If job 1 entered the queue first, then job 1 will receive a fraction p of server capacity, and job 2 a fraction of 1-p. Likewise, if job 2 entered the queue first, then job 2 will receive a fraction q and job 1 a fraction 1-q. Examples are: p=q=0 LCFSPR; p=q=1 FCFS; p=q=1/2 PS; p=1, q=0 job 1 has preemptive priority over job 2.] Spirn (1976) states the following property: The CPU schedule that maximizes T among the class of disciplines is to give higher preemptive priority to either job 1 or job 2; The same holds true for I/O schedule. Notice that we need to consider only the case where the I/O schedule is FCFS, since only two jobs are in the system and no preemption is allowed at I/O servers, usually. Thus, since $U = (1+1/r_1)R_1 + (1+1/r_2)R_2$, we see, from the above property, that the throughput U is maximum when either job 1 or job 2 has preemptive priority over the other.

To see this in more detail, let U_{ij} denote the value of the throughput U when job i has preemptive priority over job j. We can obtain U_{ij} as follows:

$$U_{ij} = t \cdot \frac{(1+r_i)(1+r_i+r_j+tr_i r_j)+(1+r_j)(1+tr_i)}{(2+tr_i)+t(1+r_i)(r_i+r_j+tr_i r_j)} ,$$

for $(i,j) = (1,2)$ and $(2,1)$ where $t = 2m/(m+1)$.
We assume $r_1 \leq r_2$ without losing any generality. Then the H-schedule in this model is to give job 1 preemptive priority over job 2. From the above equation, we can derive,

$$(U_{12}-U_{21})/U_{21}$$

$$= (r_2-r_1)(r_1+r_2+tr_1 r_2) \{[2-(t-2)^2]+t(r_1+r_2)+t^2 r_1 r_2\}$$

$$\cdot [(1+r_2)(1+r_1+r_2+tr_1 r_2)+(1+r_1)(1+tr_2)]^{-1}$$

$$\cdot [(2+tr_1)+t(1+r_1)(r_1+r_2+tr_1 r_2)]^{-1}.$$

From this we see that $U_{12} \geq U_{21}$ since $r_2 \geq r_1$. Thus, from the above property, we see that the H-schedule optimizes the throughput. Furthermore, we can easily see that $(U_{12}-U_{21})/U_{21}$ has its supremum, 2, when r_1 is zero and r_2 is infinite. In that case, U_{12} becomes 2, which is the most desirable throughput since it means that the processing of two jobs is almost completely overlapped, while U_{21} becomes 1, which is the least desirable throughput since it is like the throughput of uniprogramming. The latter is the same as the case where the FCFS discipline is employed at the CPU server, as we can see intuitively that, once job 2 occupies the CPU, job 1 should wait for the completion of job 2 in vain under this scheduling discipline.

MACHINE REPAIRMAN MODELS

The following two subsections treat two different extensions of the machine repairman model. The model considered here is a closed queueing network model which has two service stations and a finite number, N, of jobs. The one service station consists of only one server ('CPU' server) where jobs may suffer from queueing delays.

The other service station has multiple servers ('I/O' servers) the number of which is greater than or equal to the number of jobs, N, where no job suffers from queueing delays. This can be a good model of multiprogrammed computer systems, when the congestion at I/O servers can be neglected. Boyse and Warn (1975) suggest that this is a reasonably good model of a real multiprogrammed computer system.

THE CASE OF PRICE'S MODEL

Price (1972) considered a machine repairman model where each job is statistically identical (i.e., $u_j = u$ for all j) and the service time distribution at CPU server is general. He has shown that the shortest remaining processing time first (SRPT) discipline maximizes the CPU utilization in this model. Since all the jobs in the model are statistically identical, the I/O utilization is proportionate to the CPU utilization. Thus, SRPT maximizes also the total throughput of the system. If the service time of the CPU server for each job is known at each entry of the job into the CPU server, the H-schedule in this model is the SRPT discipline even though each job is statistically identical and has the same mean service time at the CPU server. Thus we see that also in this model the H-schedule optimizes the throughput of the system.

However it is impossible to know the length of CPU service time of each job when the job enters the CPU server unless the same sequence of operation of the job has already been executed and necessary information has already been collected. Furthermore, we cannot generally assume that all the jobs are statistically identical. So we need to investigate other cases further.

THE CASE OF KAMEDA'S MODEL

The model investigated in Kameda (1979) is an extention of the machine repairman model, where each job j has a distinct mean CPU service time u_j^{-1}. Other assumptions on this model are the same as appeared at the beginning of this section, although the results of

Kameda (1979) may apply to the cases a bit broader than the case of these assumptions. We assume that each job has the same mean I/O service time v^{-1}. Consider a class of scheduling disciplines that includes FCFS, preemptive and nonpreemptive priority, LCFSPR, LCFS, PS, generalized PS, etc. to be employed at the CPU. [This class is characterized as follows: Regard each group of states of the model in all of which the same set of jobs stay at CPU, as one aggregated state (say S) of the model. Let $P(j/S)$ denote the conditional probability that CPU is processing job j in state S. Here we consider only such a class of disciplines that the CPU departure rate of each job j is $u_j P(j/S)$ while the model is in an arbitrary state S. Thus we do not consider such disciplines as require the exact knowledge on the service time length in advance, e.g., SRPT, which is practically unrealizable.] The following three properties have been obtained.

I. The utilization factor, R, of the CPU is constant with respect to CPU schedules:

$$(1-R)^{-1} = \sum_{d_1=0}^{1} \sum_{d_2=0}^{1} \cdots \sum_{d_N=0}^{1} [(\sum_{j=1}^{N} d_j)! \prod_{j=1}^{N} r_j^{d_j}],$$

where $r_j = vu_j^{-1}$ for $j = 1, 2, \ldots, N$.

Let C_j be a constant associated with job j and let $C = \Sigma_j C_j R_j$ where R_j is the utilization factor of the CPU for job j ($\Sigma_j R_j = R$).

II. C is maximum if and only if each job has higher preemptive priority at the CPU than any other job that has a lower weight factor than it has.

Since job j uses the fraction of $r_j^{-1} R_j$ of I/O, then we have $U = \sum_{j=1}^{N} (1+1/r_j) R_j$. And, from II, we have the following property.

III. The throughput, U, is maximized if each job has higher preemptive priority than any other jobs having r_j's larger than its own (more compute bound jobs).

The H-schedule in this model is such a scheduling discipline as gives higher preemptive priority to the job with less r_j. Thus the H-schedule optimizes the throughput also in this model. We have seen, throughout the investigation on these models, no evidence against the optimality of the H-schedule while we have seen that the H-schedule optimizes the throughput of the system in any relevant models discussed here.

4. SOME IMPLEMENTATION PROBLEMS

The H-schedule requires some means of predicting the CPU service time length of each job, for example, based upon the measured history of the sequence of the CPU bursts of each job. However, we cannot always predict it exactly and sometimes we may have such chances that a program which has transferred to the phase of being extremely CPU bound is predicted to be still I/O bound, and vice versa. In such occasions, the H-schedule may cause serious degradation of multiprogramming performance.

On the contrary, there are several scheduling disciplines in which the decision may be based solely or partially on other considerations relating to the existing state of the system, e.g., the type of job last serviced or the waiting time of the jobs present. Such disciplines do not require any forecasting on the length of CPU service time, etc. Let us call these discipline 'endogenous'. Among such endogenous scheduling disciplines are FCFS, PS, RR, LCFSPR, etc.

In this section, we investigate whether such endogenous disciplines as PS and LCFSPR give us the throughput close to the optimal throughput given by the H-schedule. We consider the case of the machine repairman model with different customers, which is solvable for PS, LCFSPR and preemptive-priority (the H-schedule). Assume job 1, 2, ..., N are given preemptive priority in decreasing order (i.e., job 1 has the highest preemptive priority, etc.). Let $R^{(i)}$ denote the sum of the utilization factors of the CPU for jobs 1, 2, ..., i. Then from Kameda (1979),

$$(1-R^{(i)})^{-1} = \sum_{d_1=0}^{1} \sum_{d_2=0}^{1} \cdots \sum_{d_i=0}^{1} (\sum_{n=1}^{i} d_n)! \prod_{n=1}^{i} r_i^{d_n}.$$

The utilization factor of CPU for job i is as follows.

$$R_i = R^{(i)} - R^{(i-1)}.$$

In the case where PS or LCFSPR is employed at CPU, we can obtain R_i using the BCMP theory.

Let U_{PR}, U_{PS}, U_{FF}, and U_{LCFSPR} denote the values of the throughput when the scheduling displines at the CPU are preemptive priority, PS, FCFS, and LCFSPR, respectively. Naturally $U_{PS}=U_{LCFSPR}$. First, we consider the case where N=2 (two jobs). Let us assume $r_1 \le r_2$. Then we have from Kameda (1979),

$$U_{PR} = 1 + \frac{(1+r_2)(1+2r_1)}{(1+r_1)(1+r_1+r_2+2r_1r_2)} ,$$

$$U_{PS} = \frac{2(1+r_1)(1+r_2)}{1+r_1+r_2+2r_1r_2} , \text{ and}$$

$$U_{FF} = [(1+r_1)^2(1+2r_2)+(1+r_2)^2(1+2r_1)]/E,$$

where $E = (1+r_1+r_2)(1+r_1+r_2+2r_1r_2)$.

During the investigation in Section 3, we know that $U_{PR} \ge U_{PS}$, U_{FF}. And we have by simple calculations,

$$U_{PS}-U_{FF} = (r_1-r_2)^2 E^{-1} \ge 0, \text{ and}$$

$$\frac{U_{PS}-U_{FF}}{U_{PS}} = \frac{(r_1-r_2)^2}{2(1+r_1+r_2)(1+r_1)(1+r_2)} \le \frac{1}{2} .$$

The equality in the last relation holds where r_1 is zero and r_2 is infinite. Also we have,

$$\frac{U_{PR}-U_{PS}}{U_{PS}} = \frac{(r_2-r_1)r_1}{(1+r_1)(1+2r_1+2r_2+2r_1r_2)} \le \frac{1}{8} .$$

The equality in the above holds where $r_1 = 1$ and r_2 is infinite. Thus $U_{PR} \ge U_{PS} \ge \frac{8}{9}U_{PR}$ while $2U_{FF} \ge U_{PS} \ge U_{FF}$. We can see that U_{PS} is generally closer to U_{PR} than to U_{FF}.

Next, we consider the case where N = 3. By calculating, we have the following,

$(U_{PR}-U_{PS})/U_{PS}$

$= \{(r_3-r_2)(1+2r_1)(r_1+r_2+4r_1r_2)+2r_1[(1+r_3)(r_2-r_1)+r_2(r_3-r_1)]F\}$

$\times (1+r_1)^{-1}F^{-1}(3+3r_1+3r_2+3r_3+4r_1r_2+4r_2r_3+4r_3r_1+6r_1r_2r_3)^{-1}$

where $F = 1+r_1+r_2+2r_1r_2$.

Then,

$(U_{PR}-U_{PS})/U_{PS} \leq 0.20786\ldots$.

The equality holds where $r_1 = 0.61305\ldots$, $r_2 = 3.2053\ldots$ and r_3 is infinite. Thus we see that $U_{PR} \geq U_{PS} \geq U_{PR} \times 0.82791\ldots$, while intuitively we have

$3U_{FF} \geq U_{PS} \geq U_{FF}$.

Throughout these examples, we see that such endogeneous disciplines as PS and LCFSPR may be substantially good alternatives to the H-schedule. As for the cases where N > 3 or where more general service time distributions are employed, it might be cumbersome to work out calculations. However, we can see intuitively that both the H-schedule and PS (or LCFSPR) can give the maximum throughput near N if r_j is near zero for j = 1, 2, ..., N-1, and r_N is infinitely large, where FCFS gives the minimum throughput near 1.

Notice that Anderson (1973) proposed a method of approximating preemptive priority dispatching in a multiprogramming model by processor sharing. His proposal comes out of a viewpoint entirely different from this study, that is, merely providing an approximation method of models that are difficult to solve analytically. Furthermore, he checks his method only through several numerical examples. However, the implication of his research is along the line of the study in this section.

5. CONCLUDING REMARKS

In this paper, we investigated several models of multiprogramming which are analytically solvable, and observed that the CPU scheduling discipline (called H-schdule in this paper) which gives higher preemptive priority to a more I/O bound job maximizes the throughput in the framework of these models of multiprogrammed computer systems. We found no evidence so far against the optimality of the H-schedule although some author stated that this discipline sometimes produces low throughput.

The implementation of the H-schedule requires some means of predicting program behavior. Errors in prediction may cause the degradation of the throughput of the system. Thus we considered some endogenous CPU scheduling disciplines such as processor sharing (PS) and preemptive-resume last-come-first-served (LCFSPR). We investigated how close the throughput these endogeneous disciplines produce is to that of the H-schedule, using some machine repairman models.

Most of these models assume exponential service time distributions for each job. The work yet to be done is to relax this restriction, but in that case we might feel much more difficulties in deriving analytical results than before. Also, experimental validation of the discussion of Section 4 will be wanted.

REFERENCES

Anderson, H.A., Jr. (1973). Approximating Pre-emptive Priority Dispatching in a Multiprogramming Model. IBM J. Res. Develop, Vol.17, No.6, November 1973, pp. 533-539.

Baskett, F., Chandy, K.M., Muntz, R.R., and Palacios, F.G. (1975). Open, Closed, and Mixed Networks of Queues with Different Classes of Customers. J. ACM, Vol.22, No.2, April 1975, pp. 248-260.

Boyse, J.H., and Warn, D.R. (1975). A Straightforward Model for Computer Performance Prediction. ACM Computing Surveys, Vol.7, no.2, April 1975, pp. 73-93.

Kameda, H. (1979). A Finite-Source Queue with Different Customers. Technical Report 79-01, Dept. of Computer Science, The University of Electro-Communications, October 1979. To appear in J. ACM, Vol.29, No.2, April 1982.

Lazowska, E.D., and Sevcik, K.C. (1974). Scheduling in Systems with Two Scarce Resources. Proc. ACM Nat'l Conf. San Diego (Calif.), November 1974, pp. 66-73.

Mitrani, I. (1972). A Queueing Model of Priority Multiprogramming. Technical Report 41, Computing Laboratory, University of Newcastle Upon Tyne, December 1972.

Noetzel, A.S. (1979). A Generalized Queueing Discipline for Product Form Network Solutions. J. ACM, Vol.26, No.4, October 1979, pp.779-793.

Price, T.G. (1972). An Analysis of Central Processor Scheduling in Multiprogrammed Computer Systems. Technical Report No. 57, Digital Systems Laboratory, Stanford University, October 1972.

Ryder, K.D. (1970). A Heuristic Approach to Task Dispatching. IBM Systems Journal, Vol.9, No.3, July 1970, pp.189-198.

Spirn, J.R. (1976). Multi-queue Scheduling of Two Tasks. Acta Informatica, Vol.7, Fasc.2, 1976, pp.217-226.

DYNAMIC TUNING OF OPERATING SYSTEMS

Chiaki Ishikawa
Ken Sakamura
Mamoru Maekawa

Department of Information Science
Faculty of Science
University of Tokyo

Abstract

This paper discusses the effect and the feasibility of dynamical tuning of operating systems. There are many factors which can be modified dynamically in order to handle jobs with different characteristics and they interact with each other in various ways. Repeated tuning procedure that takes the correlation among these factors into consideration is reported to achieve the improved cost performance of existing computer systems. Many examples including an adaptive multiprogramming scheduler are given.

This paper also refers to the influence of the adaptive operating systems over future software architecture and a means of personalization of VLSI architecture.

1. INTRODUCTION

The advent of microelectronics has decreased the cost of computer hardware. The number of computer used in industry, business and government is increasing ever more due to this cost-down. People using these computers for their work demand application-oriented capability from computer systems. Software has played a major role in supplying application-oriented capabilities by supplying good user-interface, application-oriented languages, etc.

But as the use of computer systems becomes sophisticated, application software alone cannot meet the users demand. Certain change in more fundamental parts other than the application software must be made to satisfy the wide spectrum of users request. What are those parts that should be modified? For many application users, operating systems and instruction set processor (ISP for short) define the computer architecture upon which their application programs are built. Hence operating systems and ISP should be modified according to application requirements.

An operating system (OS for short) maps the user job requests to given hardware resources and performs services such as scheduling and interfacing with devices. A well organized OS should map user job requests without much overhead to the hardware resources of computers and achieve a good performance. An OS should be flexible so that it can be adapted to handle jobs that have widely different and time-varying characteristics.

Adaptation of OS and ISP will become more important in the future. Tuning is presented and discussed as an important concept to deal with such adaptation. Tuning means the following in this paper: tailoring the operating system, language support system, user interface and other parts of the computer systems to suit the needs of the user and thus making it easy for the user to perform his own computing task.

In this paper we pay attention mostly to the tuning of OS. We show that the concept of tuning can give a framework for the construction of operating systems and give examples that show tuning procedures can achieve improved performance in many cases.

The rest of this paper is organized as follows. The second chapter presents the concept of tuning in detail. OS from the viewpoint of tuning is defined. The third chapter describes real examples of tuning procedures. The fourth chapter discusses considerations. The fifth chapter is the conclusion of this paper.

2. TUNING

In this chapter we define OS and tuning.

What is an OS?

We can think of several structural layers of computer systems. They are hardware device, instruction set processor (ISP for short), language, OS, user program and user interface layers(Figure-1).

USER COMMUNITY

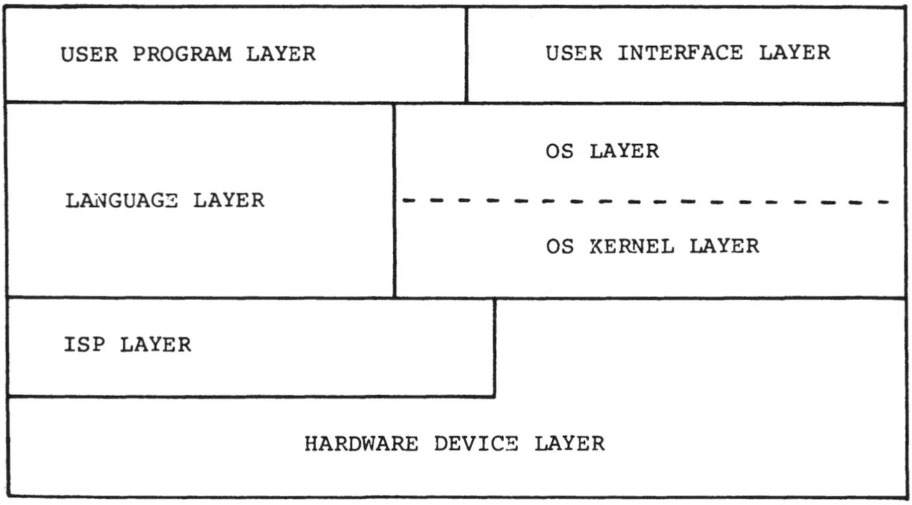

USER PROGRAM LAYER	USER INTERFACE LAYER

LANGUAGE LAYER

OS LAYER

OS KERNEL LAYER

ISP LAYER

HARDWARE DEVICE LAYER

FIGURE-1. LAYERS OF COMPUTER SYSTEM

The OS layer maps the logical flow of information inside user jobs to the physical data flow over the real resources in a computer system. So let us define an OS to be a collection of program modules which transforms the user job requests to logical devices into requests to physical devices in this hierarchy of layers.

"Job" refers to the user program processed by the computer systems. The jobs can be classified in terms of their requests to the system resources. Let us regard the system as a network of resources. These resources include CPU, main memory, secondary storage device, I/O channels, disk and drum etc. Each job has its own amount of requests to these resources and the routing frequency which indicates how often the job moves from one resource to another after getting service from the former. We call this doublet of requests to devices and the routing frequency the "job pattern". A good example of a modeling of computer systems utilizing this job pattern is the queuing network modeling (Figure-2).

Using the definition of OS and jobs above, we define tuning as the process of changing operating systems configuration to handle jobs with particular job pattern so as to achieve predefined objectives. System configuration, here, refers to the entities such as the policies ,algorithms, data structures, etc. used in the OS which we can modify during the system operation. Tuning is thus used to remove bottlenecks which appear in the resource network when the system configuration does not match the job pattern. As the job pattern varies in time and from one computer installation to another, tuning mechanism should be able to adapt OS to such changes.

There are several categories of tuning in the framework of OS and the job outlined above. The first category is the change of the policy to pick up the jobs to be processed so that the best job mix for a given resource network is obtained for a predefined objective. Job mix determines the total amount of service and the number of visits to devices.

The second category is the change of scheduling policy to achieve the predefined objective once the job mix is established. Once the resource network connection and the job mix are given, the scheduler

TERMINALS

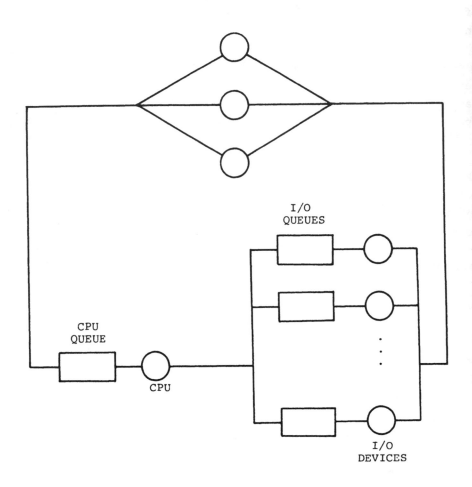

FIGURE-2. Queueing Network Model

should try to improve the performance without destroying the load balance over devices which has been achieved by the choice of a suitable job mix. Scheduling here has a very broad meaning. Scheduling of CPU is, of course, included. Furthermore it includes the scheduling of

other devices such as secondary storage devices. Careful allocation
of files over devices so that devices are uniformly utilized is
included in this category.

The third category is the increase of processing speed at each
device. The device connection is fixed, but the processing speed at
each device can be increased either by removing the overhead or by
speeding up of device function (via microprogramming, for example).

This third category can be further divided into two parts, namely
the tuning of the user programs and the tuning of OS (including the
computer architecture itself in a wider sense). OS exists as the
interface between the programs and the system resources, and the overhead, i.e. the amount of requests to devices which are not essential
to the user job, can be decreased by changing the algorithm used in
the OS or system parameters such as buffer size.

Tuning in Practice

Let us follow how a user program should be executed in a computer
system to see how these tuning concepts should be used in combination.
First, a performance objective function has to be supplied as the target of optimization.

At the job mix selection, we have to consider the execution speed
at each server in the resource network. For each job, we have to
estimate the job pattern on an individual basis.

After evaluating the job profile at each device, the job mix
which brings in the best performance of the system is sought. Given a
resource network and the given a workload from the user community, we
can, at least in principle, pick up the jobs so that the optimal value
of the objective function of the system can be obtained.

Then, given the objective function, the resource network and the
job mix to be processed, we can, again in principle, choose the best
scheduling policy to achieve the optimal performance. This best policy
maps the logical flow of the information intrinsic to the user job
onto the flow of information in the physical device network in such a

way to optimize the objective function.

In this way, a given user job is executed when the system picks it up and allocates necessary resources to it. If a satisfactory value of the objective function is not attained at the first trial, the OS is modified and the tuning step is repeated, until a satisfactory result is obtained or other termination conditions are met.

There are many implementation details that are left to the implementors in OS design. It is a huge burden on implementor to decide which implementation method to use to realize flexible parts of OS because there are so many trade-off decisions. Tuning approach which tries to optimize the objective function should be used to implement the flexible parts of OS as it can give a clear guideline in choosing which implementation methods to use and eases implementor's task.

OS construction was an art in the past. Describing the fixed and flexible parts of OS separately and tuning the flexible parts according to the actual user workload characteristics seem to be the only reasonable way to construct an OS in an 'engineering' fashion.

3. TUNING METHODS.

In this section we discuss tunable parts of OS by giving examples. The examples treated and the categories they belong to are; I/O buffer size (the third category of tuning), schedulers and file allocation methods (the second category of tuning), and instruction tuning, an APL machine and OS enhancement through firmware (the third category of tuning using firmware). Example of I/O buffer size is treated first because it is straightforward and should be easily understood.

Example: I/O Buffer Size

The third category of tuning is to increase the execution speed of devices by removing overhead of OS and user jobs. The number of supervisor calls (SVCs, for short) which indicates the amount of overhead of OS can be reduced in various ways. Take I/O data transfer block size for example. The larger the block size is, the less transfer SVCs are required to transmit the same amount of data. When the number of I/O SVCs is reduced, the time required for search, seek and the setup time of I/O channels and CPU time for the SVCs are reduced, too. Table-1 taken from [SHAR80] shows the relation between block size, CPU time and channel time to transfer the same amount of data. We have to be careful, though, not to make the buffer size too large. For too large block size may require transfer of unnecessary data or keep some part of block unused. Characteristics of each application determines the best size of block.

We can perform tuning of user programs as well as tuning of OS. Tuning of user programs is the modification of particular implementation of application programs to reduce overhead. Examples of such user program tuning are found in program restructuring to reduce the number of page faults [SNYD78] and to increase concurrency of CPU and I/O processing [MAEK74,76].

Table-1.   RELATION BETWEEN BUFFER SIZE AND   OVERHEAD

BLOCK	SIZE	200	1,000	2,000	4,000	6,000	(bytes)
CPU	TIME	73.6	21.6	14.3	10.6	9.3	(seconds)
CHANNEL	TIME	95.2	46.9	38.4	36.5	33.3	(seconds)

(to transfer the same amount of data)

The second tuning category is the change of scheduling to achieve the optimal performance objective once the job mix is selected. Schedulers with tuning mechanisms that respond to the change of workload are described next.

Example: Scheduler - 1

Geck reported an experimental scheduler that changes the degree of multiprogramming to control the overall load on the system[GECK79]. The scheduler tries to balance the load over I/O devices, CPU and memory system by changing the amount of overlayable area in the memory when the jobs impose time-varying load on these resources.   The performance objective function is the throughput. A certain performance index to decide whether CPU, I/O and memory system is heavily or lightly utilized was constructed, and the system was controlled according to the decisions made upon this index.   Experimental runs showed the improvement of the performance by 9-14%. In this way choosing a job mix which is suitable for the given resource network has an important effect on the system performance.

Example: Scheduler - 2

Figure-3 is taken from an experimental simulation of the scheduler which changes the degree of multiprogramming by monitoring paging activity to change the size of memory allocated to each process [ISHI80].   The system which is a batch system with I/O spooling is modeled using closed queueing network. When a process at CPU produces a page fault, it moves to a paging device station. The job paging model is a semi-Markovian model which has two states, one corresponding to the low paging activity period, the other corresponding to the page burst period. The interpage-fault time at each state is assumed to be exponentially distributed. CPU utilization was chosen as the objective function. For the model, the CPU utilization can be calculated using queueing network theory (appendix). According to the calculation, the memory size given to each process affects the objective function. To keep CPU utilization at a high level, we have to keep the degree of multiprogramming high and at the same time have to prevent thrashing. An optimal level is calculated by using the formula in the appendix. The scheduler tries to keep the degree of multiprogramming at the optimal level given by the queueing network theory by blocking and releasing the processes entering the CPU queue. The CPU utilization of the system controlled by the scheduler discussed above (an adaptive scheduler) and that of a FCFS scheduler with a fixed degree of multiprogramming is given in figure-3. The scheduler would try to prevent thrashing, and if thrashing occurs, it will recover more rapidly. This is an example of dynamic tuning which prevents a serious system performance degradation when the job pattern changes much in a short time. In this case the job mix was chosen mainly in terms of the paging activity. The modeled computer system itself is a little old-fashioned. We are planning to apply our tuning methodology to a powerful modern personal computer system built on VLSI chips.

Example: Scheduler - 3

The decision by the scheduler of CPU to switch the processes affects the system performance substantially. It is known that process preemption is favorable when the service time distribution is hyperexponential. Maekawa reported a scheduler and the analysis of its performance[MAEK74,76]. The scheduler does not use time slicing method for process switching. It preempts the job only when I/O completion occurs. Time slicing usually brings in some overhead. The proposed scheduler has less overhead for process switching than time slicing scheduler, but was shown to perform almost as well. So if the service time of CPU is hyperexponentially distributed, the fact which is

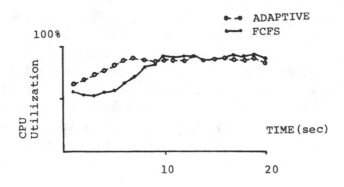

FIGURE-3. SCHEDULER EXAMPLE

determined by the characteristics of application, such a scheduler becomes advantageous. We can further refine the scheduler so that it measures the distribution of service time on individual basis so that it preempts certain jobs and never preempts other jobs. Such a scheme needs a good measurement facility.

Example: File Allocation Methods

File allocation decision is, in a wide sense, a scheduling problem of OS. It is very important to decide where the files should reside. The good decision must be such that the load is balanced and secondary storage devices are used uniformly. OS overhead, such as seek, search and channel setup time, can be reduced significantly by load balancing, i.e. by moving the information stored in the devices so that accesses are uniformly distributed over devices. These access frequencies, of course, change according to the job pattern and the allocation policy.

Hughes and Moe reported that the information replacement over different drums brought in 12% improvement of CPU utilization[HUGH73]. The system was modeled by a queueing network and

some files were moved from the most utilized drum to others. The
improvement was very close to the value predicted by the model.

When file device uses a moving-arm head, we may decrease the
seek distance by rearranging files on the same device or decrease the
contention of different requests to the same device by placing files
over different devices[GURI78]. How the rearrangement should be done
is determined by accessing pattern, which reflects the characteristics
of user workload.

The third category of tuning treated in the previous chapter is
the speed-up of device either by removing the overhead of OS or by
changing the device function, i.e. by the introduction of
application-oriented function. Examples of using firmware to support
application-oriented functions are given in the following.

Example: OS enhancement through firmware

Firmwarization of OS is an important step toward the construction
of dynamically tunable systems, and more research is desired in this
direction. The OS kernel routine which should be moved into firmware
first is the most frequently used one or the most time consuming one.

Figure-4 indicates the relation among the relative execution time
of OS kernel, number of kernel routines implemented in firmware and
WCS (Writable Control Storage) capacity of a simulated minicomputer
OS. By measuring the execution time and the number of calls of each
routine, the choice as to which routine is moved to the firmware was
made one by one in order to decrease the execution time of the simulated OS. The data is a rough estimate based upon the estimated execution time and the number of calls to each OS routine and is meant
to be the probe for the detailed monitoring planned.

Firmware can be used to enhance the ISP architecture and the
language system as well as OS.

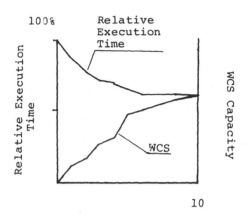

FIGURE-4. OS EXAMPLE

Example: Instruction tuning

The idea of instruction tuning is based upon the following observation. Each program uses the instruction repertoire of a given computer in a particular way. Some instructions are used more frequently
than others. By making new instructions out of often used patterns of
instruction sequence, the program would run faster because of less
instruction fetching and of better utilization of CPU resources such
as registers. Figure-5 is taken from [SAKA79]. New instruction was
implemented in microprogram. As more instruction are implemented in
the firmware, the relative speed is increased much. Different workload requires different new instructions to be implemented. The code
generation part of the compiler has to be modified. The profile of a
program is measured in one run and the system can take advantage of
instruction tuning after the program is recompiled using the new
instructions.

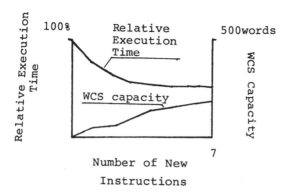

FIGURE-5. INSTRUCTION TUNING EXAMPLE

Example:An APL Machine

In an experiment, an APL interpreter was enhanced by using firmware[MAEK79]. The APL interpreter was originally written in machine language and in APL itself. Figure-6 indicates the relation between execution time of an APL interpreter and WCS capacity to hold the microprogrammed interpreter routines. As can be seen, the interpreter was speeded up by the use of microprograms. This is an example of vertical migration of functions. Which functions to migrate into firmware can be determined by tuning mechanism by considering the user workload characteristics. The use of firmware will become more popular in the future because of advancement of VLSI technology. Tuning mechanism can give clear guideline where to use firmware effectively.

These examples indicate how OS should map the intrinsic logical flow of information in the user job to the physical hardware device network by considering particular workload characteristics.

Table-2 sums up briefly the tuning mentioned in this chapter and other tuning methods.

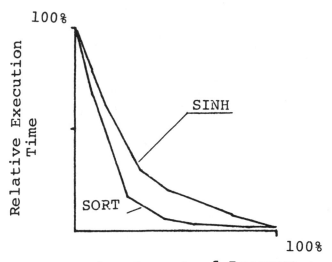

FIGURE-6. APL INTERPRETER EXAMPLE

Table-2.

The decision for job mix and scheduling

Regulation of the system load

---so that CPU, I/O system and memory system is used in
a balanced way.

Regulation of the degree of multiprogramming

---so that Each job can receive enough memory in order
to keep page fault rate at a low level.

Scheduling of CPU

---use a best policy to suit the service time distribution.

File reallocation over devices to remove bottleneck device,
and decrease seek distance and arm contentions.

Increasing the execution speed of user jobs and OS modules at devices

The change of buffer size to decrease I/O SVCs.

The use of virtual I/O instead of real I/O to decrease the
I/O SVCs and interrupts.

The decision of program library memory residency
to speed up the linking process.

Program restructuring:

---to reduce page fault rate.

---to increase the concurrency of CPU computation and
I/O processing.

Instruction tuning for programs.

Microprogram support system for high-level
language constructs.

Moving OS kernel to firmware.

4. CONSIDERATIONS.

Objective Function

The decisions on what objective function is to be optimized, how to optimize it and how to measure the performance are the most difficult parts of the design of the tuning mechanism. One should pay more attention to the orthogonal extensions of computer systems such as ease of debugging and maintainability in the future.

Although examples with only one objective function were discussed, there may be occasions when multiple objectives are desired. Even one user would like to achieve different goals from time to time. We believe the answer to this is the use of dynamic microprogramming and virtual machines. Virtual machine approach to support various operating system environments where different objective goals exist may be justified if we can decrease the overhead of the kernel substantially [LYCK78]. Extensive use of microprograms, we think, substantially solves the problem.

An example of the change of performance objective from one installation to another is seen in "personal computer". Powerful mini- and micro- computers based on VLSI chip would realize the concept of true "personalization" of computer systems to individual needs. OS of such personal computer system can benefit from having a built-in tuning mechanism for personalization.

Evolutionary Development of Operating Systems

Tuning process should begin as early as possible in the design process of OS. From the view point of tuning, the evolutionary development of computer operating systems is modeled as follows.
Step 1.---The user service requirements are specified. Predicted user workload is given.
Step 2.---The first version of OS is designed according to the information given in step 1.

Step 3.---The OS designed is put into use under actual workload. The actual workload may be different from the predicted one given in step 1. Also the workload shows fluctuation over time. So various scheduling decisions of OS should be modified according to such fluctuations in order to achieve the optimal performance. Actual workload data is stored in database for tuning.

Step 4.---New version of OS is created using the tuning database that stores user workload information.

Step 3, step 4 are repeated until a satisfactory result is obtained.

In the above model of OS development, tuning concept manifests itself in step 2, step 4 and step 3. Tuning in step 2 and step 4 is the modification of the structure of OS. Tuning in step 3 is the modification of scheduling decisions.

We must incorporate the monitoring facility and much flexibility necessary for tuning into the OSs as early as at the step 2. Tuning mechanism should not be built into the system as an afterthought.

Model of Tunable OS

The model of tunable operating system should be built to apply our tuning approach to OS. This model has fixed parts and tunable, i.e., changeable parts. Logical specification of operating system function given by user must be satisfied by design. Hence such specifications define fixed parts of OS. Other fixed parts are determined by the limitation of physical resources such as the bandwidth of data paths. Each implementation environment has such physical limitation. Flexible parts of OS are the algorithms that are used to implement the specified functions and the data structures used in the algorithms.

We should be able to write down specification of OSs so that fixed parts and flexible parts are clearly distinguished. Description language that enables the OS designers to describe the two parts separately has to be devised.

Automated Tuning Mechanism

Tuning mechanism should be automated. Idealy the computer system itself should take care of its tuning process without much human intervention. A computer systems with automatic tuning mechanism may seem to change their outer appearance according to the given require- ments of users. The feasibility to build such computer systems is under current investigation.

Interference of Tuning

Adaptation of different layers in a computer system affects the adaptation of other layers. We have to take this interaction into account when we perform the adaptation of computer systems in prac- tice. For example, the ISP tuning may cause the program to show dif- ferent paging behavior. Here the OS has to be modified to take full advantage of the ISP tuning.

Loose Feedback Control

The adaptation mechanism has feedback control of the system based upon the measured information. This feedback should be loose to sta- bilize the system operation. Badel's scheduler has certain hysteresis in the choice of the level of multiprogramming to keep the control stable[BADE75].

5. CONCLUSION

This paper addresses the problem of the construction of OS architecture with adaptation mechanism by considering the feasibility and the effect of tuning of various parameters of operating systems. There are numerous factors which can be modified during the execution of OS and they interact with each other in various ways. A repeated tuning process that takes the interactions among these factors, namely job mix, scheduling and the execution speed at devices into consideration can bring in an improved performance. Dynamic characteristics of the user workload must be paid due attention in the tuning process.

Tuning also has an important connection with the true personalization (adaptation) of personal computers based upon VLSI chips. Future personal computers will be built with specific application in mind such as file processing, editing or numeric computation. These applications would be supported by a tunable OS and personalized instruction set of microprogrammable VLSI CPU.

Tuning not only works to improve the performance of existing systems but also supplies data that affects the design of future systems. Data collected for tuning supplies valuable information on how users exploit system resources and it is important to use this data in the design of computer systems to produce the best computer architecture that satisfies the needs of users.

Modeling and analysis of computer systems has to be refined before we will be able to build dynamically tunable systems with much confidence. We believe that tuning concept will become an important framework to build computer systems that satisfy user request with ease.

APPENDIX

In a system in the figure given below, the probability
that the system is at state $\vec{n}$ is given by (A-1).

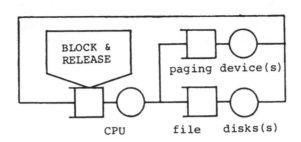

$$P(\vec{n}) = 1/g(N,M) B_{cpu}(n_M) W_{cpu}^{n_M} \prod_{i=1}^{p} (W_i \tau_p)^{n_i} \prod_{j=p+1}^{p+f} (W_j \tau_f)^{n_j} \quad (A-1)$$

The meaning of symbols are as follows.

$\vec{n} = (n_1, \ldots, n_p, n_{p+1}, \ldots, n_{p+f}, n_M)$

$n_1, \ldots, n_p$: number of jobs at paging devices.

$n_{p+1}, \ldots, n_{p+f}$: number of jobs at file disks.

n_M : number of jobs at CPU.

N : the total number of jobs.

M : the total number of servers.

$$g(N,m) = \sum_{k=0}^{N} g(n-k, m-1) B_m(k) W_m^k$$

$$B_M(k) = B_{cpu}(k) = \prod_{i=1}^{k} 1/C_{cpu}(i)$$

$C_{cpu}(i)$: the processing speed of the cpu stations when there are i jobs.

$B_j(k) = (W_j \tau_f)^k$ $p+1 \leq j \leq p+f$

$B_i(k) = (W_i \, _p)^k$ $1 \leq i \leq p$

W_j : the routing probability of the j-th disk.

τ_f : the mean service time of the file disk.

$W_i = W_{cpu}/L \cdot f_i$

W_{cpu} : the mean inter-I/O time.

$L = L(m)$: the life time function. "m" is the amount of memory given to a process.

f_i : the routing probability of the i-th paging device.

τ_p : the mean service time of the paging device.

Using the above formula, we can calculate the CPU utilization numerically for a given set of parameter values. The CPU utilization ρ_{cpu} is given by

$$\rho_{cpu} = 1-\Sigma \; p(\vec{n}) \tag{A-2}$$
$$(\text{for all } \vec{n} \text{ such that } n_M=0)$$

REFERENCES

[BADE75] Badel M. et al(1975). Adaptive Optimization of a Time Sharing System's Performance. Proc. IEEE, 63, No. 6(1975), pp. 958-965.

[GECK79] Geck A. (1979) Performance Improvement by Feedback Control of Operating Systems. Proc. 4th Int'l Symp. on Modelling and Performance Evaluation of Computer Systems, Vienna, Austria, Feb. 1979, pp. 459-471.

[GURI78] Gurin N. N., et al (1978).   A Heuristic Approach to File Allocation Problem. Proc. 2nd Int'l Symp. on Operating Systems Theory and Practice, Rocquencourt, France, Oct. 1978, pp. 199-206.

[HUGH73] Hughes J., and Moe G. (1973) A structured Approach to Computer Performance Analysis, Proc. AFIPS Conf., Vol. 42, pp. 109-120.

[ISHI80] Ishikawa C., Sakamura K., and Maekawa M. (1980). Operating Systems with Adaptation Mechanism. (in Japanese) Architecture Workgroup of Japan Information Processing Society, June 1980.

[LYCK78] Lycklama H., and Bayer D. L. The MERT Operating System.   The Bell System Technical Journal, Vol. 57, No. 6, July-August 1978, pp. 2049- 2086.

[MAEK74] Maekawa M., and Boyd D. L. (1974). A Model of Concurrent Tasks within Jobs of a Multiprocessing System, Proc. 8th Princeton Conference on Information Science and Systems, pp. 97-101.

[MAEK76] Maekawa M., and Boyd D. L.(1976). Two Models of Task Overlap within Jobs of Multiprocessing Systems. Proc. 1976 Int'l Conference on Parallel Processing, pp. 83-91.

[MAEK79] Maekawa M., and Morimoto Y. (1979). Performance Adjustment of an APL Interpreter. Microprocessors and their Applications, EUROMICRO 1979, pp. 65-75.

[SAKA79] Sakamura K., and et al. (1979). Automatic Tuning of Computer Architectures. Proc. AFIPS Conf., Vol. 48, pp. 499-512.

[SHAR80] Shardt R. M. (1980). An MVS Tuning Approach. IBM Syst. Journal, Vol. 19, NO. 1, pp. 102-119.

[SNYD78] Snyder R. (1978). On a priori Program Restructuring for Virtual Systems. Proc. 2nd Int'l Symp. on Operating Systems Theory and Practice, Rocquencourt, France, Oct. 1978, pp. 207-224.

ON PSEUDO WORKLOAD FOR PERFORMANCE MEASUREMENT OF INTERACTIVE SYSTEMS

Masatoshi Miyazaki*
Shigeru Matsuzawa*
Seiziro Obata*
Shoichi Noguchi**

* Tohoku University Computer Center
** Tohoku University Research Institute of
Electrical Communication

ABSTRACT

A workload problem in performance evaluation of interactive systems is discussed. A simple method to create a pseudo workload usually called a synthetic job is proposed. A pseudo workload can be generated by using two functions. One of these functions is to execute deferred jobs in a time-sharing environment, and another one is to place a program being executed into waiting status during a required time.

A detail process to generate the pseudo workload using the functions such as deferred processing and the waiting function is shown. Appropriateness of the pseudo workload is discussed. Finally, several examples of performance measurement under the pseudo workload operation are given.

1. INTRODUCTION

Performance evaluation of computer systems, especially for large-scale computers, may be one of the most important subjects in computer science. In fact, as computer systems become large in scale, a cost-performance tends to be more concerned interest for both computer manufacturers and users. In the discussion of cost-performance, performance evaluation and prediction are inevitable.

Criteria of performance may be a serious problem. The well-known criteria may be a total throughput, a turnaround time and a response time [Goodman(1972), Kobayashi(1978)]. The total throughput and turnaround time are meaningful in batch processing systems; the response time is used in interactive systems such as time-sharing system(TSS). The total throughput is represented by number of jobs executed in a unit time. The turnaround time means the time duration which each job spends in the system. The response time is an interval from final submission of request(usually carriage return) to the system until the first output comes out to the terminal. A utilization of resources such as a CPU, an I/O channel and a main memory might affect these criteria mentioned above. The CPU utilization is the most popular measure. If the CPU utilization of the problem state, which represents a time that a CPU executes a user program, is kept in high level, the total throughput must increase, and the turnaround time may become short. The response time may not be discussed by only the CPU utilization, but it is true that the CPU utilization fairly affects the response time.

In performance evaluation, there are several methods. The typical techniques are an analysis of job accounting records collected under actual operating conditions [Schwetman(1969)], a measurement with a hardware or software monitor [Ruud(1972), Schwartz(1973)], use of an analytic model [Boyse(1975)] and a simulation [Noe(1972)]. The analytic model and simulation may be useful for a performance prediction. On the other hand, the analysis of job accounting and the measurement may be a powerful method to evaluate performance of real systems which are already under operation.

Performance evaluation of real systems is of concern to computer users. The users might have several questions such as "Is the cost-performance of this system reasonable?", "Are there bottle necks in some where?", "Can we expect an improvement of performance when the system parameters or resources are changed?", et cetra. In order to give answers to these questins, an analysis of job accounting or a performance measurement should be performed.

The job accounting records collected from a usual service system is not enough to evaluate the system in detail. A workload to the service system will change every day, and hence reproducibility of the same workload cannot be assured. Therefore, benchmarks or synthetic jobs are preferable for performance evaluation of real systems. These jobs are usually used for batch processing systems. It may be difficult to prepare such workload for the interactive systems, especially for TSS.

In this paper a simulated workload for TSS, which we call a pseudo workload, is discussed.

2. WORKLOAD PROBLEM IN TSS

As mentioned above, in performance evaluation of a real TSS, it is most crucial problem to prepare a proper workload. There are several methods to generate a workload. The most feasible way is to use a real workload which is caused by the terminals under actual operating conditions. This method is desirable if many terminals can be made concurrently active for the measurement. But usually it may be nearly impossible to make a great number of terminals active.

The second method is to use a terminal simulator which generates the simulated terminals using another CCP(communication control processor) and CPU(if necessary). The CPU creates a workload which is series of commands obtained from actual accounting records and gives them to the evaluating system through communication lines. This method may be comparatively reasonable in the point of view that the whole system including a CCP and communication lines can be evaluated if the suitable series of commands could be collected. On the other hand, it is fairly difficult to carry out the evaluation with this method because extra CCP and CPU may be required and a reconfigulation of the system is inevitable for the measurement.

The third way is to generate a pseudo workload in the system to be evaluated. Some software tools are necessary to perform this method, which tools and their applications are discussed in this paper. Performance evaluation using this method is easily done since the other resources such as a CCP, a CPU and terminals are not required. But there are some limitations caused by using only software tools. For example, a traffic problem in the CCP and communication lines can not be evaluated. Moreover, we may obtain only approximate data because the workload is just simulated one. In spite of the fact that this method has several limitations, it should be emphasized that the simulated workload can be easily created without extra resources, terminal operators and expenditure. For this reason, we have proceeded to study performance evaluation of a interactive system by the use of a simulated workload. We call a simulated workload in TSS a pseudo workload.

3. MECHANISM FOR PSEUDO WORKLOAD

In order to create a pseudo workload, two functions or tools are required. The one is that, in a time-sharing environment, a system can automatically execute jobs or commands which are already submitted to the system. We call this type of processing "a deferred processing". The other function is that a program being executed can be placed into a waiting status during a time requested. We call it "waiting function".

DEFERRED PROCESSING

ACOS-NEAC System 900 which we are concerned with has a deferred processing mechanism. Fig.1 illustlates the deferred processing conceptually. In this figure, a deferred file contains workload programs and their parameters. The deferred file

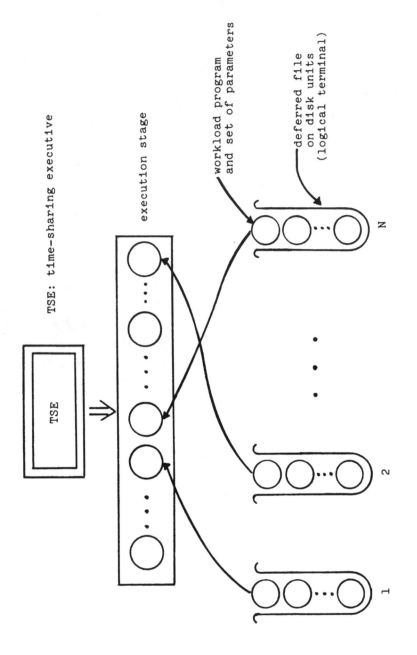

TSE: time-sharing executive

execution stage

workload program
and set of parameters

deferred file
on disk units
(logical terminal)

TSE

Fig.1 Deferred processing

corresponds to a logical terminal. Number of the deferred files(N in Fig.1) means number of active terminals under concurrent operations. A circle in the deferred files means a workload program and its parameters. These programs are submitted into the deferred files previously.

TSE(time-sharing executive) is a submonitor of ACOS-6 which is the operating system of System 900. TSE creates the time-sharing environment in System 900. When the operation of time-sharing starts, TSE derives the workload programs from each deferred file as much as N, and puts them on an execution stage and executes them. An execution stage means a main memory and swapping area. The workload programs in the same deferred file are picked up one by one.

The workload program stated above is a synthetic program. These synthetic programs should be nearly series of actual commands. If the synthetic programs can be made as same as the actual command programs, the deferred processing could created a simulated time-sharing workload. The synthetic program to simulate the commands will be discussed in section 4.

WAITING FUNCTION

A workload program being executed in the real service environment will request terminal I/Os in certain intervals. When the terminal I/O is requested, the workload program will be swapped out if there are other programs in the swapping area waiting to be executed. The terminal I/O time may include a time of transmission of characters and a think time of a terminal operator. The CPU time consumed during the command execution and disk I/O operation may be easy to realize in the synthetic program. But it is difficult to generate a terminal I/O time in a simulated workload environment.

In order to realize the terminal I/O time, we use the waiting function. This function brings a program that invoked the function to the waiting status during the time required, in which status the program is not executed. The program in this status is eligible to be swapped out. So that, the terminal I/O time may be approximated by the waiting time.

The waiting function in ACOS-6 is used by calling a subroutine called WAIT from FORTRAN program with parameter S, where S is a time (sec) to be waiting.

4. PSEUDO WORKLOAD

COMMAND PARAMETERS

Inherrent parameters to characterize a actual command program may be as follows.

    (1)* CPU time(used for actual execution of command program)

    (2)* number of I/Os for disk unit

    (3)* number of terminal I/Os

(4)* terminal I/O time (including think time)

(5) characters transmitted

(6) memory size

For our purpose of performance evaluation with a pseudo workload, in a first step, we select only four parameters (1)-(4) shown with asterisk, which we call workload parameters, because these parameters seem to be enough to compose quite simple workload program. The workload program we deal with consists of only three types of operation such as a CPU time consumption, a disk I/O and a terminal I/O.

The statistical data of these parameters except terminal I/O time can be obtained from accounting records of ACOS-6. The terminal I/O time cannot be measured in ACOS-6. So that, this parameter must be estimated by using other parameters. In ACOS-6's accounting information, there are another parameters such as a elapsed time, a CPU time used for swapping and a processing time in a memory. The elapsed time means the difference of start and end time of a command program. The processing time means that a program is in a main memory, and it mainly contains a CPU time used for a program execution and a disk I/O time including a waiting time for a disk operation. Then, an approximate terminal I/O time can be estimated by subtracting the CPU time, the swapping time and the disk I/O time from the elapsed time.

This terminal I/O time may include the time that a program is being swapped out according to consumption of quantum of a CPU time. But this swapped out time may be much small compared with the terminal I/O time if number of active terminals is not so large.

Fig.2 shows a process of generating workload parameters and executing the workload programs. The service system under usual operation gives the job accounting records. The distributions of parameters such as a CPU time, number of disk I/Os, number of terminal I/Os and a mean time for each terminal I/O which is given by deviding the terminal I/O time by number of terminal I/Os are obtained from the accounting records.

The parameters for the pseudo workload are created from these distributions by using random numbers. The set of these four parameters is submitted to each workload program. We assume that these four parameters are mutually independent.

WORKLOAD PROGRAM

A flow of the workload program written by FORTRAN is shown in Fig.3. At first step, the program reads the following prameters;

CT: CPU time (msec)

ND: number of disk I/Os

NT: number of terminal I/Os

TT: mean time of terminal I/O (sec)

CT': CT/(ND+NT)

RD: [ND/NT+0.5] if ND>NT, else 1

RT: [NT/ND+0.5] if NT>ND, else 1

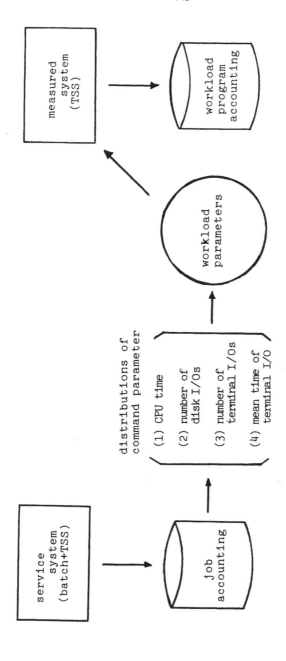

Fig.2 Process of generating pseudo workload

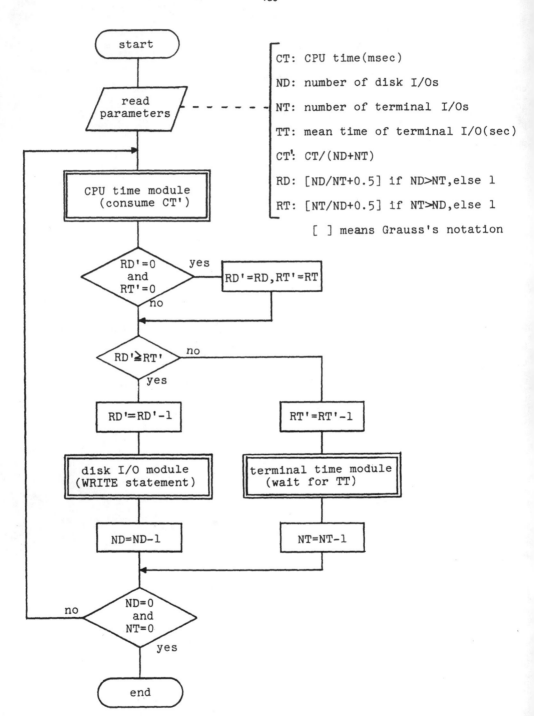

CT: CPU time(msec)

ND: number of disk I/Os

NT: number of terminal I/Os

TT: mean time of terminal I/O(sec)

CT': CT/(ND+NT)

RD: [ND/NT+0.5] if ND>NT,else 1

RT: [NT/ND+0.5] if NT>ND,else 1

[ ] means Grauss's notation

Fig.3   Flowchart of workload program

[] means Gauss's notation

The first four parameters are used for the pseudo workload. The parameters of last three are used to control the loops. CT' sliced by ND and NT is a CPU time to be consumed in each CPU cycle. RD and RT, which are a ratio of ND and NT, are used to scatter the disk I/Os and terminal I/Os into the time sequence of the workload program. But, in order to decrease a overhead in the workload program, they are previously calculated and submitted.

The workload program consists of three modules. The CPU time module just only consumes a processor time as much as CT'. The disk I/O module executes a WRITE statement which transmits a basic record to a disk unit. The terminal time module calls the subroutine which places the program being executed to the waiting status during the time TT. A memory size of the workload program is about 56 KB.

The workload program has an overhead such as an analysis of the workload parameters (5 msec), an operation of file opening (14 msec), an execution of a WRITE statement (3 msec for each statement) and call of WAIT (2 msec for each call). When the workload parameters are given, an overhead time is simulated previously in the program which constracts the set of workload parameters. If the overhead time is greater than a CPU time in the workload parameters, then the difference of the CPU time and the overhead is taken as a new CPU time parameter, otherwise the CPU time is not adopted. When a CPU time is smaller than 5 msec and number of disk I/Os and terminal I/Os are both zero, the special workload program which consumes a CPU time just only 1 through 5 msec.

5. EXAMPLES OF MEASUREMENT

MEASURED SYSTEM

A measured system is ACOS-NEAC System 900 at Tohoku University Computer Center. The system is a multiprocessor system with two EPUs (execution processing unit). A EPU corresponds to a CPU. A capacity of a main memory is 4MB . A secondary storage consists of disk units, and a total capacity is 4,000MB. In our measurement, only four units(200MB per each) were used. Two FNPs(front-end network processor) are used to control communication lines.

An opereating system of ACOS System 900 is called ACOS-6. ACOS-6 is designed to support multi-dimensional processing, that is, a local batch processing, a remote batch processing, a time-sharing service and a conversational remote batch processing. A virtual memory is not provided in our system.

The time-sharing service is realized by TSE that is a submonitor of ACOS-6's monitor as mentioned before. A memory is normally assigned to programs in a manner analogous to IBM's OS/MVT with dynamic program relocation. A total user's area of main memory is limited up to about 750KB.

VALIDATION OF PSEUDO WORKLOAD

It is important to confirm an appropriateness of a pseudo workload before a performance measurement with a pseudo workload is commenced. The worklord program issues the three kinds of accounting informations such as a CPU time, number of disk I/Os and a terminal I/O time(waiting time). The distributions of each parameter are given from different sources, that is, user's job(command) accounting records of an actural service system, the worklord parameters submitted to the worklord programs and workload program's accounting records of the measured system. So that, we are to compare the distributions for each parameter.

Fig.4 is a graph displaying the CPU time distributions. A dotted line(A), broken line(B) and solid line(C) represent the distributions of a user's accounting, a workload parameter and a workload accounting respectively. There is a little difference between A and B. It is considered that this difference may be caused by the adjustment of the overhead of a worklord program stated in section 4. On the other hand, B and C are considerably similar. The distributions of a disk I/O count and terminal I/O time are shown in Fig.5 and Fig.6 respectively. A little difference between A and B of the distributions of the disk I/O count may also be due to the overhead adjustment. For the distribution of the terminal I/O time, A and B are comparatively same. In either case, C is nearly equal to B. Consequently it can be concluded that the pseudo workload proposed in our study may reflect an actual wokload.

EXAMPLES OF PERFORMANCE

Appropriateness of the pseudo workload we proposed was proved by investigating the distributions of several parameters. Then, we will show some examples of performance measure that were measured with the pseudo workload.

Fig.7 shows a CPU utilization for number of logical terminals. The CPU utilization means a ratio of a CPU time used for only the workload programs, and it is calculated as that a total capacity of two EPUs is 2 (1 for each). A logical terminal means a deferred file and it corresponeds to a active user's terminal in an actual service system. The CPU utilization increases lineally according to increase of logical terminals while number of logical terminals is less than about 40. When number of logical terminals exceeds 50, it seems that the CPU utilization cannot increase move over 0.7, so that a response time must be affected.

Number of workload programs executed in a unit time for number of logical terminals is shown in Fig.8. As same as the CPU utilization in Fig.7, number of executed programs may be saturated at 50 logical terminals. This phenomenon can be considered to be caused by saturation of the CPU utilization.

Finally, a discussion of a response time will be given. As mentioned in section 1, a response time may be most important measure in performance evaluation of interactive systems. A definition of a response time is well-knowen as an elapsed time between end of text and beginning of first output.

We use another measure of a response time because it is difficult to obtain an

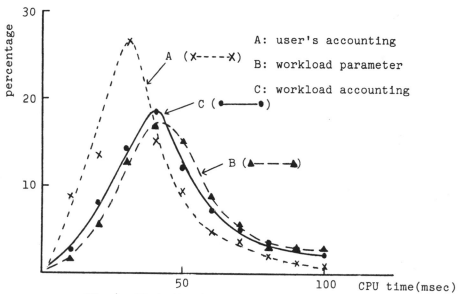

Fig.4 Distributions of CPU time

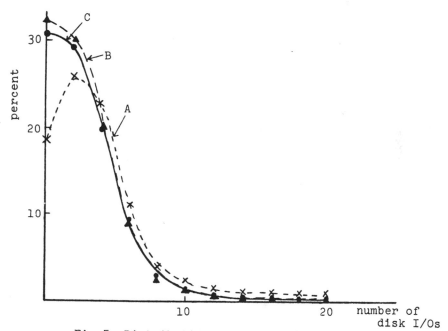

Fig.5 Distributions of disk I/O

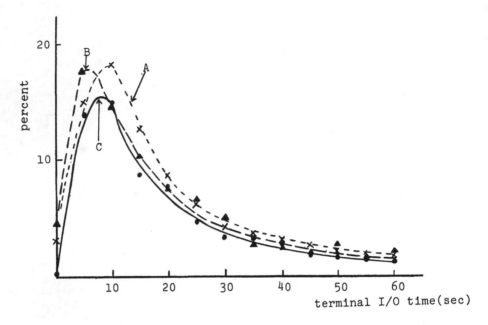

Fig.6 Distributions of terminal I/O time

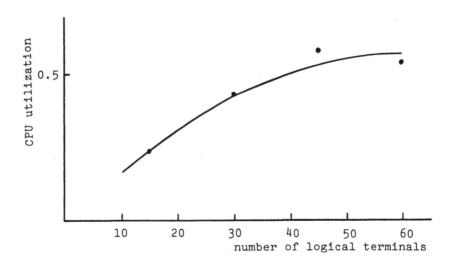

Fig.7 CPU utilization

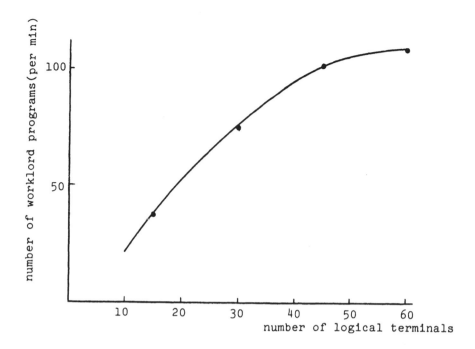

Fig.8 Number of executed workload programs

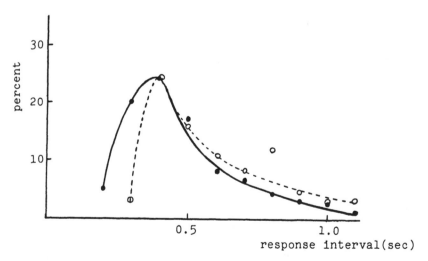

Fig.9 Comparison of response intervals

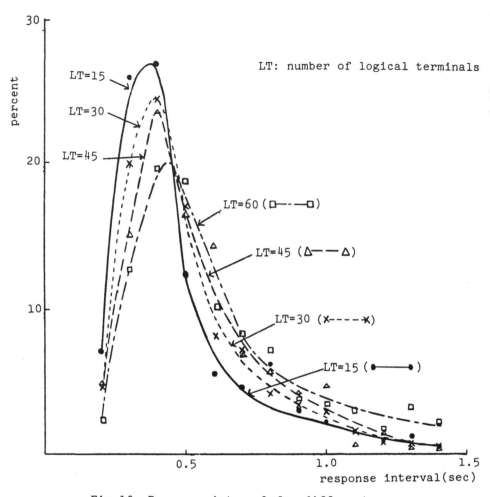

Fig.10   Response interval for different
number of logical terminals

exact response time in our system. Other terminology should be used to avoid an occurence of confusion. We call the new measure a response interval. A special purpose program is executed during the measuement to observe the response interval. The program is designed to repeat a simple loop. In the loop, the waiting function is called with a parameter one second and the real times of that the waiting started and the next dispatch of the CPU commenced after the termination of the waiting are obtained. The elapsed time between the end time of waiting and the first time of dispatch is defined as the response interval. The end time of waiting can be given by adding one second to the start time of the waiting.

Fig.9 shows a comparison of response intervals between the actual service system and the measured system. Number of active (logical) terminals is about 30. The dotted line shows the distribution of the response interval in the actual system, and the solid line shows that in the measured system. These two response intervals may be considered nearly similar.

The distributions of each response interval for different number of logical terminals are depicted in Fig.10. As number of logical terminals increases, a curve of the distribution moves to the right and the maximum value of percent goes down. This result represents a typical performance characteristic of a interactive system.

6. CONCLUSIONS

This paper has described a pseudo workload for evaluating performance of interactive systems. We have confirmed that a pseudo workload for interactive systems could be easily created using the two functions which are the deferred processing in a time-sharing environment and the waiting mechanism to place an executing program into a waiting status during a reqired time.

The pseudo workload consists of the workload programs. Each workload program executes simple FORTRAN statements so as to consume a CPU time, to issue an I/O operation and to call the waiting function. Appropriateness of the pseudo workload has been discussed by comparing the distributions of each parameter of a real workload in the real service system and the pseudo workload. Several results of performance measurement with the pseudo workload have been displayed. The method to creat the pseudo workload can be applicable to any system which has the two functions stated above.

The study represented in this paper is just only first step. There are some problems to be discussed furthermore. A memory size of the workload program must be taken into consideration. A dependency between parameters that are a CPU time, a disk I/O count and a terminal I/O time may not be negligible. More detail measurement must be performed using a software monitor in order to obtain more precise performance measures. The study will be performed to cope with these problems.

REFERENCES

Boyse J.M., et al. (1975). A Straightforward Model for Computer Performance Prediction. Computing Surveys, Vol 7, No 2. 1975, pp 73-93.

Goodman A.F. (1972). Measurement of computer system - An Introduction. Proc. of FJCC, 1972. pp 669-680.

Kobayashi H. (1978). Modeling and Analysis: an Introduction to System Performance Evaluation Methodology. Addison-Wesley Publishing Company, 1978.

Noe J.D., et al. (1972). Validation of a trace-driven CDC 6400 simulation. Proc. of SJCC, 1972. pp 749-757.

Ruud R.J. (1972). The CPX-A A systems approach to performance measurement. Proc. of FJCC, 1972. pp 949-957.

Schwartz J.M., et al. (1973). Use of the SPASM software monitor to evaluate the performance of the Burroughs B6700. Proc. of NCC, 1973. pp 93-100.

Schwetman H.D., et al. (1969). An operational analysis of a remote console system. Proc. of SJCC, 1969. pp 257-264.

Part III.

Operating System Evolution

Operating systems are expected to have long life spans.
They evolve during their life spans because operating system
programs are, after all, representations of real life
procedures and artifacts. They are subjected to changes,
enhancements and modifications, continually performed by
developers and maintainers. This program evolution is one
of the most challenging aspects of software engineering and
must be coped with a powerful method. The first paper by L.
A. Belady describes an ongoing project which is the application of data abstraction for redesigning an existing
operating system component. It developed, among others,
tools to facilitate the work with existing systems and to
design new systems. The second paper by M. Maekawa proposes
an operating system structuring concept "resource module" to
help design an easily modifiable operating system. The
concept is a formalization of the view that an operating
system is a collection of resources, as has been recognized
by industrial programmers, and is similar to data abstraction.

Modifiability of Large Software Systems
L. A. Belady
IBM Research
June 1980

ABSTRACT: The problem of software modifiability is two-fold: that of modifying existing systems and of designing new systems which are easier to modify.

An ongoing project is described which is the application of data abstraction for redesigning an existing operating system component. The results of this project are tools to facilitate the work with existing systems (a graphic program notation called GREENPRINT and an automatic clustering program to regroup modules and control blocks of an operating system) and to design new systems (a new language called XPLI to enforce data abstraction, and the associated External Structure expressing intermodule connectivity, for the computer aided design of large systems out of components).

1 Introduction

Modifiability of procedures and artifacts is an increasing problem in modern civilizations. On one hand, social progress brings about an increase in freedom of choice and action. This would mean that, as individuals or members of communities, we are free to change that part of the world over which we have legitimate control. Yet, as we all know, it has become increasingly difficult to exercise this right, for many of the changes have unpredictable or predictably unpleasant side-effects.

Changes are often results of choices made of alternatives. The availability of alternatives is of course made possible by the recent massive increase in productivity, due to social cooperation in modern societies. But this is unfortunately coupled with a growing interdependence of all participants - producers and consumers. It is this interdependence which makes choices risky and the often unavoidable changes painfully expensive. Let us look at a few examples.

The woman scientist with a heavy publication record gets married, and if she chooses to change her family name to that of her husband's, she may lose, at least for a while, the continuity of her professional reputation. (We don't even mention problems of mailing address, driver's license, bank accounts, etc., which almost all marrying women must face). This problem is that of "information *investment*" in the minds of fellow scientists.

Or take the architect of the beautiful medieval cities, for example the ones which surround the Mediterranean. The streets are too narrow for automobile traffic - whom can we blame for not having foreseen the 20th century? Modification of the streets would be difficult because we want to *preserve,* not destroy and replace them just to accommodate a new function for which the original setting was not designed.

The last example is the current changeover to the metric system in the U.S. In this case the consequences are predictable but, as most of us know quite well, the *cost* of replacing the many tools and instruments of one of the most advanced industries in the world is horrendous, not to mention the *inertia* in people's mind, which acts against the development of a new "feel" for quessing, comparable to the one within the old system.

Investment, preservation, cost - these are some of the issues which must be considered whenever we contemplate modification. The main question is then how to reduce the impact on the different issues of a change. Clearly, the smaller the domain and the shorter the expected time of the impact the better we are off. *Locality,* in space and time, of the impact of modification seems to be the central concept. The narrower the field and the shorter lived the scientific results, the less unpleasant is the   name change; the more primitive the society the easier the changeover to new standards.

We are also interested, as mentioned earlier, in the predictability of the effects of change: we would like to easily *locate* the consequences of planned modifications. It is intuitive to accept that modifiability increases with the ease of indentifying and locating its consequences, and increases with locality, with its "impact size".

It seems that large software too displays the mentioned characteristics of modifiability. After all, programs are representations of real life procedures and artifacts: banking, maufacturing, flight dynamics, airplanes. And since they are models, i.e. abstractions of reality, they are better bounded than parts of the complex real world and thus easier to study. They too must be constantly modified, as was shown almost a decade ago in *Evolution Dynamics* (1), (2) the study of ever changing large programs.

These studies distinguish between two entirely different dynamics of computer programs. The first and traditional subject is that of *execution* which takes place when a computer, guided by a program, processes data by changing the state of variables stored in the memory. This dynamics is the domain of computational complexity and of the many efforts collectively called performance modeling and evaluation.

The other, and the perhaps more challenging, dynamics is that of *program evolution* which takes place when the program is not running on the machine at all - in fact it itself is subjected to changes, enhancements and modifications continually performed by developers and maintainers. There is not enough space here to give much detail on program evolution dynamics and only one of its major observations is reviewed herewith.

Large operating systems, such as OS-360/370, whose evolution was first studied, are built of modules - components small enough to understand and worked upon by one programmer, relatively independently of, and with little need to communicate with, others. OS-360/370 consists of several thousands of these modules.

During the first ten years of its history the system had about twenty releases. The amount of modification - change and enhancement in each release - was more or less the same over the entire period. At release changeover, some modules remained identical, some others were new versions of old modules, while a third category consisted of brand new modules. It was interesting to observe that for the entire observation period the fraction of modified modules was monotonically and faster than linearly increasing, and towards the end of this twenty-release period actually approaching the saturation point at which all modules must be modified to make the next release (Figure 1).

This observation was interpreted as clear indication that repeated modification of software systems is increasingly difficult - each modification creates an extra bit of obstacle to the next one. The reasons for this is that the original structure which was deduced from and well matched to the original requirements is gradually deteriorating as more recent requirements induce changes which do not fit the old structure. Since one must live with an ever changing environment, one must explore methods which at least reduce this deterioration of structure during unavoidable program evolution.

Another way of looking at modifiability is to observe what kind of work is being done by programmers. Following many surveys (3), (4), it is safe to say that significantly more than half of the world's programmer population works with existing programs, and only the minority is involved in developing programs from scratch. It appears that "modify we must", and our paper is founded on this premise. For the time being we do not question the wisdom of modifying rather than replacing the old program in response to new requirements, nor do we consider to develop techniques for deciding whether modification or replacement is more economical.

2. *The Modification Process*

First, we want to examine what classes of modifications are usually performed on software. The obvious number one category is that of repair, i.e. the elimination of faults found during development and subsequent operation on the field. The important issue here is that while hardware repair is *not* modification but replacement of parts or subassemblies to get the product back to its original designed state, software repair is always changing *away* from the original state because it is found faulty.

This leads us to the important observation that the so-called maintenance activity is actually *redesign,* corresponding roughly to engineering changes in hardware. If we assume that in product development even low level detail decisions must have been deduced from requirements, then we must also expect that changes at the same level, but now under the name of maintenance, may cause the possible perturbation of higher level choices, or even of the initial requirements.

But in reality maintenance ignores the redesign aspects of its task and actually much less skilled people than software designers are employed for performing modifications. The maintainers' knowledge of the original design is marginal. In addition to this, documentation of design is not only too sketchy, but usually rapidly loses its validity, thanks to long series of earlier modifications. Moreover, maintainers focus on individual building blocks, the modules, of the system, instead of studying the interaction of the components before effecting a change. The top-down approach, if practiced at all in the first place, is replaced by low level patching, whose consequences, uncontrolled and unpredictable, propagate into the system, and thus affect clarity of the entire structure.

But repair is not the whole story. Driven by expanding market requirements for new function and, in the case of operating systems, by the introduction of new, advanced, pieces of hardware, enhancement becomes the other large category of continuing changes. And if performance is critical and the desire to save machine resources is great, system tuning becomes another source of modification because, in practice, modifications introduced by tuning rarely observe clarity of structure or understandability of program text.

But what is usually modified in software? After all, software is a fiction, simply information to guide a machine's operation. At the same time it appears to humans in form of documents - either printed text or projection on a CRT. In fact, several levels of documents must be prepared for developing and maintaining software if it is large enough and employs many people organized into specialist groups: architects, designers, testers, etc. In fact, one way of viewing the process or life cycle is as a sequence of documents, that of requirements, specifications, programs, etc., and transformations from one document into the next. It happens that only the last of these transformations - program text into machine code - is fully automatic and done by a compiler. The other transformations - design out of specifications, or programs out of design - are manual.

We can then make two important observations. The first is related to the labor intensiveness of the process. This leads to high cost which is further amplified by low reliability of human beings in contrast to reliability of machines. Moreover, iteration in the process is also often necessary to iron out errors introduced by fuzzy and noisy communication between development and maintenance groups, who work under schedule and cost pressure. In this environment only machine processed documents (compiled text) are modified and promptly updated, namely the ones which comprise the end-product to be delivered, while the associated higher level design documents are left unchanged, reflecting the state in which the software was, and not is. It would cost extra money to keep these documents aligned with code. Of course, this neglect makes the next generation of modifications again a bit more difficult and forces the crew to work with the only trustworthy document, namely the one which runs on the machine: the low level code itself.

3. Research in operating system modifiability

Up to about three years ago the problems of software modifiability did not seem to be appreciated much by the software engineering community. This was indicated by the fact that no exploration - research or other - was conducted at all on maintainability or modifiability. Rather, most efforts were directed at the design of software from scratch. Our software engineering group in Yorktown thus found it first necessary to invent *how* one should do research in software modifiability.

It was felt that modifiability would most directly impact the world of maintenance - excluding major enhancements. We learned from the company's maintenance organization that the major cost contributor was labor, and most of this was spent on familiarization, i.e. learning the system to be maintained. Relatively less time was spent on the actual definition and implementation of the modification. From this and other observations made earlier in this paper we reached the following conclusions:

- There would be little chance for success if we just speculated and theorized about maintenance. Hence we decided to make hands dirty by working on an *existing software* system, in order to build a more modifiable version of it.

- We should have a double objective:
  - Improved methods and tools for modifying *existing systems* - with good or bad structure
  - Methods and tools to construct new software which is *easier* and safer to *modify*
- We should not invent and introduce new tools; rather select and, in the process of exploration, test and *refine the already proposed* and promising *ideas* which help achieve the above objectives.

Let us elaborate a little bit on the last point. For a decade or so the concept of *abstraction* has been in the focus of programming methodology. Recently this concept has gone well beyond, and become broader than, the traditional procedural abstraction implemented by a subroutine. Abstraction has been manifested for example in information hiding (5), or abstract data types (6). Common to them is the following rationale:

the task of working with complex systems is significantly simpler if one explicitly separates the relevant from the irrelevant while modifying or maintaining the system.

This fits well the many formal or intuitive models of complexity, in which it is regarded synonymous to uncertainty or variety (variety, since repetitive occurrence of the same thing does not add to complexity). Following this idea, simplification in working with software can be achieved by decreasing the uncertainty, either by reducing the information (i.e. the number of items to examine) necessary to correctly perform the modification, or by prescribing, as a recipe, with certainty, the steps to be taken (or objects to consider) when modification is performed.

Let us illuminate this by examples. It seems intuitively obvious that modification of a module is simpler if we know that

a) it does not impact the interface, i.e. the calling pattern and associated parameter definitions are left unchanged and

b)there is no way but through call invokation that the module is ever accessed from other parts of the system.

In the same vein, if one finds on a single page or at least on adjacent pages in the documentation all data structures which are potentially accessed by a single module, the verification of the impact of a changing module is much simpler than performing a frantic search through the entire program documentation for direct or indirect references issued by the module.

Let us now put the pieces together. Our reading into the then current technical literature and discussions with members of the software engineering community led us to the adoption of *data abstraction,* a concept which integrates information hiding, structural simplification and advanced language ideas into a tool. This tool we thought could have the potential to enforce a particular design in which locating and localizing changes are easier to perform.

Relatively soon we opted for VTAM as a research vehicle. It is an OS370 component of reasonable complexity, a good balance between a perhaps impossibly large operating system (too large for a small research team) and a small "toy" example which would not help us to validate the experiment. The result was a firm plan of experimentally redesigning parts of VTAM *specifically* for modifiability, using data abstration (6).

Soon we learned also that our project would have two major phases: the first to work with the existing, official, version of VTAM to extract its functional content, and the second to redesign it anew. We found later that these two phases already predetermined the final output of the effort: on one hand we would develop tools and techniques of "scoping", i.e studying, existing systems, and on the other construct facilities to aid the design of new, more modifiable, systems.

Based on our discussions and cooperation with several development and maintenance organizations, we have become convinced that current conditions in both domains - work with the old and constructing the new - demand a great deal of substantial improvement. In the following we will describe the tools developed so far for working with existing systems, then turn our attention to problems of constructing modifiable software.

3.1 Work with existing systems

The first obstacle which we encountered was the great difficulty to understand and accurately redocument the actual functional content of VTAM. But this difficulty created just the right milieu: we were in fact playing the role of maintainers who were given a piece of software to work with - debug or update. As already mentioned, if you *really* want to know what the program does during evolution, you cannot trust manually produced documents, which are not automatically coupled to the compilable program text.

We found the reading and understanding of the PL/I* written VTAM
*Actually it is based on a dialect of PL/I used internally by IBM to write system programs.

code quite slow, in spite of the ample comments supplied in the program text. We therefore started experimenting with different, mostly graphical, program representations, as a possible enhancement of the text proper. After long considerations we rejected the number one contender, the Nassi-Scneiderman (NS) diagram, mostly because of the complications of displaying it on a, say, IBM-3270 terminal. We remind the reader that NS-charts are nested representations of program segments which then appear to shrink indefinitely if surrounded by repeatedly nested constructs. Obviously, a simple alphnumeric terminal, or a line printer, cannot easily cope with this, and the increased complexity of image construction would severely limit widespread applicability.

We were therefore literally forced to invent another program notation which we later designated *GREENPRINT* (in contrast to engineering "blueprints", programmers use CRT terminals with green phosphorous images). At present GREENPRINTs are generated as follows: a program, developed by us, takes the (PL/I) text as its input and then produces as output an enhanced listing. In the process the program text and the order of statements are left unperturbed, while along the left margin the program tree, i.e. the control flow, is displayed, as indicated in Figure 2. Procedures, loops and decisions are distinguished by the different vertical column types. Detailed information on GREENPRINT can be obtained from (7).

In addition to our own positive experience with GREENPRINT - aided program "scoping", an increasing number of co-workers has become interested in using this inexpensive and machine generated scheme. Current work is in the direction of making GREENPRINT interactive, the idea being to permit editing the graph and thus using it as a design tool for from scratch efforts.

The second major obstacle to working with VTAM was the small size of our research team: the already mentioned difficulty of rapidly learning this operating system component, and the sheer size of it (in excess of 100K lines of code) made a complete redesign prohibitive and we had to satisfy ourselves with redesigning only selected subcomponents of VTAM. But the subcomponents, the ones identified by the original design documents, appeared quite intertwined at the code level. Again, due to size, it seemed impractical to search manually for reasonably self-contained chunks, namely those having relatively sparse communication or little shared information with the rest of VTAM. To do this automatically, we had to find a new tool again.

At this point we must describe the notion and interconnected control blocks and modules which span the basic structure of most operating systems. Control blocks hold the state information - of the machine and its resources, of the jobs, tasks, users, messages and other data stored for processing - while modules are the "actors" - programs which induce state transitions. After having gathered information out of some control blocks, a small set of modules typically updates one or more control blocks. The operating system functions as an aggregate of these individual actions, hence a module has access to many control blocks, while a control block is accessible by several modules and thus becomes a shared object serving as the main communication link between modules.

In the original design the set of modules and the set of control blocks are neatly laid out: modules grouped by function, control blocks by meaning. But during subsequent maintenance and enhancement, clarity of interfaces suffers by ad hoc extensions of the crisply defined control blocks, and extensions become necessary to accommodate new and originally unforeseen functions. The long chain of these modifications results in the already mentioned and observed increase in change penetration into the system, as the number of modules accessing a control block, and the number of control blocks accessed by a module, increase during program evolution.

Figure 3 displays this interconnectedness by a two-dimensional matrix. A matrix provides for the most general, indeed most generous, pattern with which elements of two sets can be connected: m modules and n control blocks may have up to (mxn) two-way connections. Clearly only a sparse sub-set of this is desirable for a neatly structured system, if we expect not only the reasonably independent development of individual components, but also predictable maintenance during which the number of potentially impacted elements is not too large.

In order to carve out well isolated sub-components, we first machine-stored the connectivity matrix of VTAM. After that we were fortunate enough to find within our building an already and immediately usable heuristic program which, although originally developed for the placement of circuit elements on chips, was directly applicable to our problem of identifying *relatively independent clusters of modules and control blocks*. The detail of this work was reported in (8). This is how our short term action of looking for a tool of this type to master the complexity of VTAM, led to the supply of a generally useful tool for others for work with evolving software and for control of its complexity. (Incidentally, we also made some attempts to formalize complexity on the basis of the connectivity matrix as given in (8)).

3.2 Design for Modifiability

As mentioned earlier, we selected data abstraction as our approach to software modifiability. Data abstraction can be applied immediately as a design principle: structure programs (modules) and data (control blocks) such that the access code is packaged with the data rather than interspersed with the actual logic of the programs. Paraphrased, data should interface programs in behaviorial, operational terms rather than in terms of implementation. This would result in the much desired hiding of the detail of the chosen data structure implementation.

A simple analogy is a team of several office workers sharing a file cabinet of several drawers. The particular arrangement of the files in the cabinet is a matter of implementation; what is really wanted is to store certain documents such that they be easy to retrieve later. This means just two fundamental operations: store and retrieve. Yet, in order to perform them, each person in the office must know the rituals of how to get access to any required file. If someone, perhaps in order to optimize, perturbs the order in which the drawers, and the files within, are organized, the others must also be retrained - their knowledge "modified" - if efficient office operation is to be retained. The other alternative is chaos.

A possible solution is to hire another agent who then personally stores and retrieves the requested files. He can optimize the process by using any desired implementation or reshuffling of the files, without the need to reveal this to the actual users who will be quite happy as long as the files become stored and retrieved rapidly and as requested. This is actually the case of isolating the implementation (physical storage) from the usage of the documents.

Similarly, while writing or reading a program, we usually try to concentrate on the program's real function - perhaps some algorithmic procedure or mimicking a phycial process - and do not like to be distracted by occasionally having to read unimportant yet complex data-access code. It would be like reading a book intensely, but getting occasionally interrupted with the description of the type setting processes which were used in the production of the book.

If several programs share the same data, then it is even more important that data be associated with its own access code, otherwise each program using these data must contain the access code individually. Thus, if the implementation of the data structure changes, this must be reflected in each program - a certainly error prone process.

Experience with large software indicates that new design and programming principles are rarely followed readily and rapidly, due to inertia in the programmers' mind, and to the usual schedule and cost pressures which force the choice of methods offering the shortest time to put the program together, and not of schemes making modification easier in the future. Indeed, optimizing development and optimizing the entire life-cycle (development *plus* the long period of maintenance and enhancement) are far from being coincidental. This is why we thought that short of a tool which *enforces* the use of data abstraction, we would probably not improve modifiability too much.

Accordingly, we decided to develop a language which encourages, in fact enforces, the use of data abstraction. The language was made a strongly typed one, and one which permits the user to define abstract data types in addition to the usual built-in types such as integers, characters, Boolean, etc., along with operations associated with each type (as the four arithmetic operations defined on integers). This we did by designing a language *called XPL/I,* an extended PL/I (see footnote earlier). The design was guided by the existing language CLU developed at MIT. In order to avoid the burden of writing a new compiler, we wrote a preprocessor which now accepts XPL/I programs and generates PL/I code for the run-off-the-mill compiler, which in turn produces executable machine code.

Two kinds of *modules* can be written in XPL/I: *procedure* (a la PL/I) and *capsule* which is an abstract data type. Figure 4 displays an example for procedure and capsule in the syntax of the language.

Having a new language, we were ready to write new, more modifiable operating systems - or were we? The new language indeed helped us only to construct individual modules, and the compiler helped to establish the internal consistency of a single module, but left open the even more important issues of how the modules are interconnected, and of machine aided checking of intermodule consistency. So we put forward an effort to develop a tool for *machine aided design* based on data abstraction.

On closer examination it became clear that the structure of an operating system, redesigned with having data abstraction in mind, could become significantly different than a traditional composition by modules and control blocks. Indeed, the experimental redesign of VTAM resulted in a single set of quite similar objects: procedures and capsules, which are implemented in terms of each other.

In order to explain this better, let us examine Figure 5 which is a VTAM function after redesign. Arranged from "northwest to southeast" are the modules: procedures and capsules. Lines between them indicate the direction of "uses" relations. For example the capsule "RPH" (module A) uses for its implementation "DVT", "QUEUE", "MEL" and some primitive types. We call the interconnected set on Figure 5 the *external structure* (ES) of the software design.

There are several important attributes of ES which we would like to emphasize. First, a line represents the set of operations used by the module originating this line, and is performed on the module forming the end point of the line. The operations in the set must be consistent with the "type rules", and can thus be checked by the compiler, which is now extended into the world of intermodule communication. This world is the "programming in the large", in contrast to the implementation of individual modules - the "programming in the small".

Visualize a community of software designers - or maintainers - who share and view at their individual display terminals the machine stored single copy of the evolving design, the interconnected objects and recall at will the detail specification of the operations defined on capsules. In the future the semantics of individual modules will also be added such that the participants understand rapidly *what* the programmed function is and *how* it is implemented. When a function must be extended, the designers may become easily familiar with the already implemented components, some of which could be included in the extension; *reuse of parts* is thus encouraged. Once, for example, a generic queue is built, it can be used as a template at other places in the system, or even in other systems, by properly "wiring it" into the external structure. Preservation of consistency will of course be checked by the extended compiler.

Or consider maintenance. Each module has two faces: its "left profile" is the specification, i.e., its functional capabilities, while the "right profile" is the implementation. If one modifies the specifications of say module A, the lines to the left (and up) clearly identify the domain of impact within the set of higher lever modules - the modules which rely on module A's definition. Changing module B's implementation, on the other hand, can be followed along the lines leading to its "building blocks". Figure 5 illustrates the "limited domain" impact sets and clearly contrasts the new structure's simplicity against the generality of the two-dimensional matrix with its rich connectivity.

We consider the exernal structure a machine aided design tool which is particularly well suited to the construction of large software systems, for which a human organization is employed, in contrast to the informal development and modification process by small teams. In our own experience in redesigning VTAM, consequences of changes, even during the design process, are easier to follow, exploring alternatives is more rapid, and the compiler's typechecking superior to manual testing in catching bugs early. Our current efforts are now in the direction of enriching the external structure to contain formal specifications of capsules wherever possible.

4 Conclusions and Future Work

Tools are useful for both the maintenance of existing systems and the design of new modifiable software. The experimental approach taken by our research team turned out to be productive since certain problems of design and maintenance can be understood and appreciated only by experiencing them. Also, the actual use of the newly developed tools led to their further refinement and consequent increase in usability and credibility for successful technology transfer.

The project's current emphasis is two-fold. First, modifiability must be evaluated by comparing the new version to the old. This we plan to do by employing two groups of programmers performing the same set of modifications, one group on the new and the other on the old version. Difficulty of the modification, the time it takes, and the performance of the resulting programs, will all be used in the quantitative comparison. Second, we will extend both the language and the external structure, the former to facilitate concurrent processing and the latter to accommodate all formal and informal specification for the entire duration of a software's life cycle.

5 Acknowledgments

The project mentioned here is headed by Hamed Ellozy. He and the other members: Jerry Archibald, Carlo Evangelisti, Burt Leavenworth, and Leigh Power, as well as many visitors from the United States and other Universities, have been doing the creative work which lead to the presented results.

6 References

(1)   Belady, L. A. and M. M. Lehman: "Programming Systems Dynamics IBM Research Report, RC-3546, September 1971.

(2)   Belady, L. A. and Lehman, M. M.: *IBM Systems Journal,* Vol. 15, No. 3, 1976, pp. 225-252.

(3)   Proceedings of the Symposium on "The High Cost of Software", Monterey, CA, Sept. 1973.

(4)   Boehm, B. W.: "Software Engineering", IEEE-TC, Vol. C-25, No. 12, Dec. 1976.

(5)   Parnas, D.L.: "On the Criteria to be Used in Decomposing Systems into Modules", CACM Vol. 15, No. 12, Dec. 1972.

(6)   Liskov, B. and S. Zilles: "Programming with Abstract Data Types", SIGPLAN Notices, Vol. 9, No. 4, and Proceedings of Conference on Very High Level Languagues, April 1974.

(7)   Belady, J. Cavanagh and C. J. Evangelisti: "GREENPRINT - A Graphical Representation for Structured Programs", IBM Research Report, RC-7763, July 1979.

(8)   Belady, L. A. and C. J. Evangelisti: "System Partitioning and Its Measure", IBM Research Report, RC-7560, March 1979.

Complexity

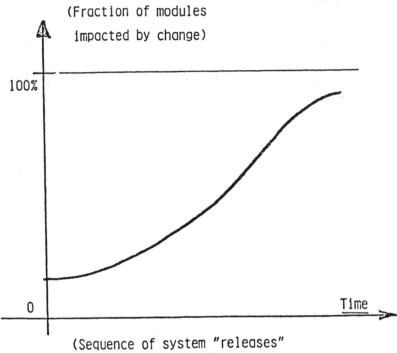

(Fraction of modules
impacted by change)

100%

0

Time

(Sequence of system "releases"
in roughly equal increments)

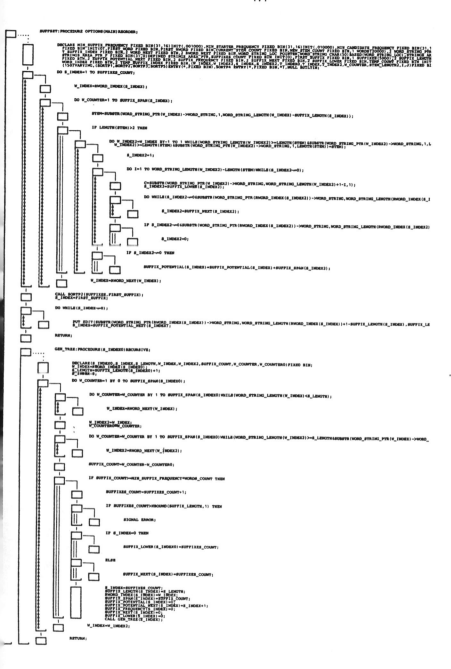

```
SUFFSET:PROCEDURE OPTIONS(MAIN)REORDER;

   DECLARE MIN_SUFFIX_FREQUENCY FIXED BIN(31,16)INIT(.001000),MIN_STARTER_FREQUENCY FIXED BIN(31,16)INIT(.010000),MIN_CANDIDATE_FREQUENCY FIXED BIN(31,1
   6)FIXED BIN INIT(10),FIRST_WORD FIXED BIN,FIRST_SWORD FIXED BIN,CURRENT_STEM_COUNT FIXED BIN,WORDS_COUNT FIXED BIN,1 WORDS(20000),2 WORD_STRING_PTR
   T_SUFFIX_INDEX FIXED BIN,2 WORD_NEXT FIXED BIN,2 WORD_NEXT FIXED BIN,WORD_STRING_LOC_POINTER,WORD_STRING_CHAR(50)BASED(WORD_PTR(6C_LOC)),STRINGR_PTR
   STRINGS_AREA PTR,2 FIXED BIN(31)DEFINED_STRINGS_AREA_PTR,SUFFIXES_COUNT FIXED BIN INIT(0),FIRST_SUFFIX FIXED BIN,1 SUFFIXES(5000),2 SUFFIX_LENGTH
   FIXED BIN,2 SUFFIX_POTENTIAL_NEXT FIXED BIN,2 SUFFIX_FREQUENCY FIXED BIN,2 SUFFIX_NEXT FIXED BIN,2 SUFFIX_LOWER FIXED BIN,TEMP_COUNT FIXED BIN INIT
   WORD_INDEX FIXED BIN,2 TEMP_SUFFIX_INDEX FIXED BIN,(W_INDEX,W_INDEX2,S_INDEX,S_INDEX2,T_INDEX,T_INDEX0,T_INDEX,T_INDEX2,W_COUNTER,STEM_LENGTH2,I,J)FIXED BI
   (150)VARYING,(SORTP1,SORTP2,SORTP5)ENTRY(*,FIXED BIN),SORTP4 ENTRY(*,FIXED BIN,*T,NULL BUILTIN;

   DO S_INDEX=1 TO SUFFIXES_COUNT;

      W_INDEX=RWORD_INDEX(S_INDEX);

      DO W_COUNTER=1 TO SUFFIX_SPAN(S_INDEX);

         STEM=SUBSTR(WORD_STRING_PTR(W_INDEX)->WORD_STRING,1,WORD_STRING_LENGTH(W_INDEX)-SUFFIX_LENGTH(S_INDEX));

         IF LENGTH(STEM)>2 THEN

            DO W_INDEX2=W_INDEX BY-1 TO 1 WHILE(WORD_STRING_LENGTH(W_INDEX2)>=LENGTH(STEM)&SUBSTR(WORD_STRING_PTR(W_INDEX2)->WORD_STRING,1,L
            W_INDEX2)>=LENGTH(STEM)&SUBSTR(WORD_STRING_PTR(W_INDEX2)->WORD_STRING,1,LENGTH(STEM))=STEM);
               S_INDEX2=1;

               DO I=1 TO WORD_STRING_LENGTH(W_INDEX2)-LENGTH(STEM)WHILE(S_INDEX2~=0);
                  C=SUBSTR(WORD_STRING_PTR(W_INDEX2)->WORD_STRING,WORD_STRING_LENGTH(W_INDEX2)+1-I,1);
                  S_INDEX2=SUFFIX_LOWER(S_INDEX2);
                  DO WHILE(S_INDEX2~=0&SUBSTR(WORD_STRING_PTR(RWORD_INDEX(S_INDEX2))->WORD_STRING,WORD_STRING_LENGTH(RWORD_INDEX(S_I
                     S_INDEX2=SUFFIX_NEXT(S_INDEX2);
                  IF S_INDEX2~=0&SUBSTR(WORD_STRING_PTR(RWORD_INDEX(S_INDEX2))->WORD_STRING,WORD_STRING_LENGTH(RWORD_INDEX(S_INDEX2)
                     S_INDEX2=0;

               IF S_INDEX2~=0 THEN

                  SUFFIX_POTENTIAL(S_INDEX)=SUFFIX_POTENTIAL(S_INDEX)+SUFFIX_SPAN(S_INDEX2))

         W_INDEX=RWORD_NEXT(W_INDEX);

   CALL SORTP2(SUFFIXES,FIRST_SUFFIX);
   S_INDEX=FIRST_SUFFIX;

   DO WHILE(S_INDEX~=0);

      PUT EDIT(SUBSTR(WORD_STRING_PTR(RWORD_INDEX(S_INDEX))->WORD_STRING,WORD_STRING_LENGTH(RWORD_INDEX(S_INDEX))+1-SUFFIX_LENGTH(S_INDEX),SUFFIX_LE
      S_INDEX=SUFFIX_POTENTIAL_NEXT(S_INDEX);

   RETURN;

GEN_TREE:PROCEDURE(S_INDEX0)RECURSIVE;

   DECLARE(S_INDEX0,S_INDEX,S_LENGTH,W_INDEX,W_INDEX2,SUFFIX_COUNT,W_COUNTER,W_COUNTER0)FIXED BIN;
   S_LENGTH=SUFFIX_LENGTH(S_INDEX0)+1;
   W_INDEX=RWORD_INDEX(S_INDEX0);
   S_INDEX=0;
   DO W_COUNTER=1 BY 0 TO SUFFIX_SPAN(S_INDEX0);

      DO W_COUNTER=W_COUNTER BY 1 TO SUFFIX_SPAN(S_INDEX0)WHILE(WORD_STRING_LENGTH(W_INDEX)<S_LENGTH);

         W_INDEX=RWORD_NEXT(W_INDEX);

      W_INDEX2=W_INDEX;
      W_COUNTER0=W_COUNTER;
      DO W_COUNTER=W_COUNTER BY 1 TO SUFFIX_SPAN(S_INDEX0)WHILE(WORD_STRING_LENGTH(W_INDEX2)>=S_LENGTH&SUBSTR(WORD_STRING_PTR(W_INDEX)->WORD_

         W_INDEX2=RWORD_NEXT(W_INDEX2);

      SUFFIX_COUNT=W_COUNTER-W_COUNTER0;

      IF SUFFIX_COUNT>=MIN_SUFFIX_FREQUENCY*WORDS_COUNT THEN

         SUFFIXES_COUNT=SUFFIXES_COUNT+1;

         IF SUFFIXES_COUNT>HBOUND(SUFFIX_LENGTH,1) THEN

            SIGNAL ERROR;

         IF S_INDEX=0 THEN

            SUFFIX_LOWER(S_INDEX0)=SUFFIXES_COUNT;

         ELSE

            SUFFIX_NEXT(S_INDEX)=SUFFIXES_COUNT;

         S_INDEX=SUFFIXES_COUNT;
         SUFFIX_LENGTH(S_INDEX)=S_LENGTH;
         RWORD_INDEX(S_INDEX)=W_INDEX;
         SUFFIX_SPAN(S_INDEX)=SUFFIX_COUNT;
         SUFFIX_POTENTIAL(S_INDEX)=0;
         SUFFIX_POTENTIAL_NEXT(S_INDEX)=S_INDEX+1;
         SUFFIX_FREQUENCY(S_INDEX)=0;
         SUFFIX_NEXT(S_INDEX)=0;
         SUFFIX_LOWER(S_INDEX)=0;
         CALL GEN_TREE(S_INDEX);

      W_INDEX=W_INDEX2;

   RETURN;
```

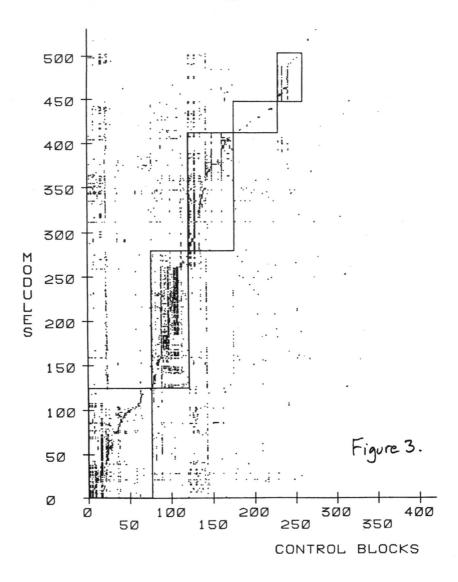

Figure 3.

```
PROC  MSG_QUEUE_BUILD(BUFFER<<MESSAGE>>, MOD QUEUE<<MESSAGE>>)

    USES ( BUFFER<<MESSAGE>> {OBTAIN, GETVAL} ,
           QUEUE<<MESSAGE>> {OBTAIN, ADD},
           MESSAGE { },
           LOCK { })


TYPE QUEUE<<T:TYPE>>

    DEFINES
         ( •
           OBTAIN(QUEUE<<T>>, MOD LOCK) -> BOOL ,
           ADD(MOD QUEUE<<T>>, T, LOCK),
           • )

    USES ( •
           BOOL,
           LOCK,
           • )


TYPE BUFFER<<T:TYPE>>

    DEFINES
         ( •
           OBTAIN(BUFFER<<T>>, MOD LOCK) -> BOOL,
           GETVAL(BUFFER<<T>>, LOCK) -> T,
           • )

    USES ( •
           BOOL,
           LOCK,
           • )


TYPE MESSAGE

    •
    •
```

174

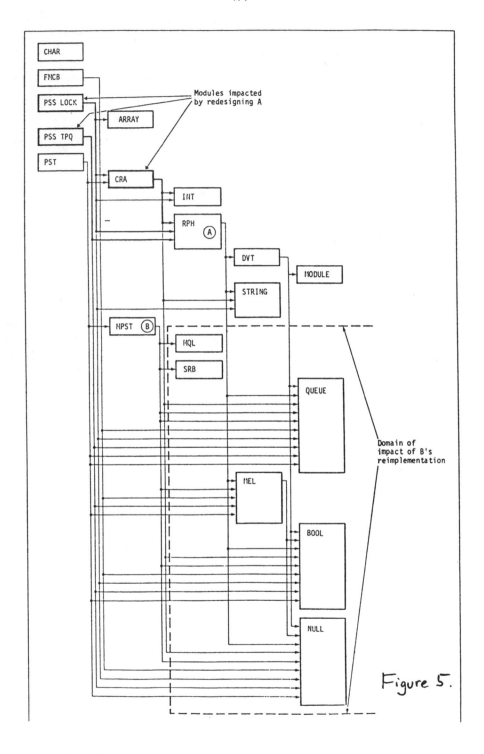

Figure 5.

OPERATING SYSTEM CONCEPTUAL MODEL FOR EASE OF EXTENSION

Mamoru Maekawa

Department of Information Science,
Faculty of Science,
University of Tokyo
7-3-1 Hongo, Bunkyo-ku Tokyo, 113 Japan

ABSTRACT

An operating system structuring concept and method is proposed. The method recognizes "resource" as the most important structuring concept and unit of the operating systems. A resource module can be of two kinds; a reusable resource module or a consumable resource module, and it contains a set of functions through which the resource is accessed. The consumable resources are primarily used for process synchronization whereas the reusable resources are used to carry information which is accessed and manipulated by functions. The proposed structuring method helps to build operating systems which are robust for changes of many kinds and whose properties are readily estimated.

KEYWORDS

Operating systems, Resources, Family of Operating Systems, Maintenance, Data Abstraction, Computer-Aided Design

1. INTRODUCTION

MOTIVES

This paper is motivated by the following complaints about operating systems.

(a) We want to add a simple capability to an operating system, but to do so would mean rewriting most of the current code.

(b) We want to simplify an operating system by removing the unneeded capabilities, but to do so would require to rewrite major sections of the code.

(c) Some programmers left an operating system project at the middle of development and the successors would only find that it is easier to redesign the unfinished programs all over again from scratch.

(d) So many similar operating systems are developed for different machines and applications, but they are difficult to be transported from one machine to another or from one application to another.

(e) The SYSGEN is intended to allow us to tailor a system to its user's needs, but it is not flexible enough.

(f) The performance of an operating system can not be predicted beforehand precise enough to make any performance commitments to its potential customers.

These complaints are very common but they are one of the most difficult problems in software development [Ross (75)] and their successful solutions have not been found yet. The fact that a large portion (two thirds to three quarters) of the total software development efforts is spent for maintenance underlines the importance of the above problems because the maintenance is mostly additions, deletions and modifications of capabilities caused by the changes of hardware and applications. In addition, the recent advance and the wide spread use of microprocessors make the above problems more important because a large number of different but similar systems for various applications must be developed. These systems should be built in a more efficient way, otherwise an enormous amount of labour will be required to develop them.

GOALS

Our goal is to find a solution for the above problems. More specifically, we want to have;

(a) an operating system model which can serve as a basis to build a variety of operating systems,

(b) a design methodology which can create a variety of operating systems with ease,

(c) a way of expressing user requirements,

(d) a way of expressing hardware constraints, and

(e) a method of evaluating the system properties beforehand.

2. APPROACH

PREVIOUS APPROACHES

Although the above complaints have been well recognized, the proposals of solutions are limited, chiefly because it is difficult to formulate the problems themselves. The family of operating systems by Parnas is one of the limited number of proposals [Parnas (76)]. It is based on the concept of hierarchy of "uses," and is an extension of the Price and Parnas's work [Price (73)]. It was extended in a somewhat different direction by Habermann and Cooprider [Habermann (76)]. The Habermann's approach is based on the concept of "incremental machine design," similar to the Dijkstra's approach in the "T.H.E." system [Dijkstra (68)].

OUR APPROACH

Our approach is based on the following two concepts:

(a) Resources as modules.

(b) A three-level model of families of operating systems.

The first concept is to recognize a resource as the basic unit of modularization. It will be elaborated and expanded in later sections. The second concept is best illustrated in Fig. 1. The conceptual model is a pure "conceptual" and "structural" model of the general operating system. Key words are "conceptual" and "structural." The "conceptual" means that no physical considerations are included in this model. This is contrasted to the "incremental machine design," in which the physical considerations are spread among the layers, the lower layer being more physical while the higher layer being more logical. The "structural" means that the conceptual model represents the interconnection structure of components or "modules" composing a general operating system. The conceptual model is highly modularized so that

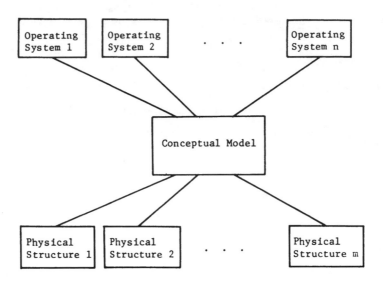

Figure 1. Operating system conceptual model

many families of operating systems can be built on different machines for different applications. The basic process of building an operating system is shown in Fig. 2. The requirements are specified in three areas.

(a) Function

This specifies what functions should be performed.

(b) Performance

This specifies the performance of the system.

(c) Others

This specifies other system properties such as reliability and security.

The constraints are mainly the hardware limitations. They include the main memory size and its access time, the secondary memory size and its access time, the input/output device configuration and their characteristics, the interactive terminal configuration and their characteristics, and the number of CPU's and their processing speed. We discuss, in the next section, the conceptual model which plays the central role of our methodology.

3. CONCEPTUAL MODEL

GENERAL MODEL VERSUS SPECIALIZED MODEL

The conceptual model is intended to be a general operating system model, from which a variety of operating systems can be built. It is a structural model, and its success or failure is most critically affected by how proper a set of structuring or modularization criteria are chosen. There are two basic approaches to select structuring criteria.

(a) General approach

Follow the general guidelines such as hierarchical decomposition, stepwise refinement, encapsulation, layers of virtual machines, information hiding and data abstraction, and then apply them to an individual operating system and its subsystems.

(b) Specialized approach

Identify the specific operating system objects and concepts, around which modules are formultated.

Most of the past approaches are "general approaches." They are certainly useful but may not be revolutional. The specialized approaches are more tailored to operating systems and thus can be much more significant. Our approach is a specialized approach. The understanding of the target systems is far more important than the general methodology and the characteristics

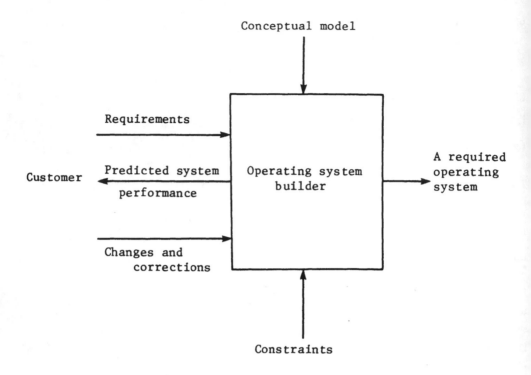

Figure 2.   Operating system buildidng process

of the target systems should be reflected on the methodology.

OPERATING SYSTEM OBJECTS

The following four objects are identified as the most important objects of operating systems.

(a) Resources: Resources perform or help perform operations requested by processes.

(b) Processes: A process is an active entity which issues requests to resources to accomplish its goal. Processes are also resources.

(c) Messages: Messages and signals are passed between processes to communicate and synchronize. Messages are also resources.

(d) Access control and scheduling: The access control and scheduling governs the access and use of resources by processes.

The basic perception of an operating system is that a series of actions are executed by functions of resources whose sequence is specified by a process description. Each access or use of resource is always trapped and validated before its execution by the access control and scheduling.

We call messages "consumable resources" and the rest of resources "reusable resources," following Holt [Holt (72)]. Other objects and concepts will be introduced when they become necessary.

The operating system structure based on the above objects is more modular and makes easier to estimate and evaluate the operating system properties, as will be demonstrated later. We introduce the representation of each object next.

4. RESOURCE MODULE

RESOURCE MODULE

A resource is represented by

(i) static information such as the type and the structure of resource, the total number of units, access time, and the name of the producer in case of a consumable resource,

(ii)   dynamic information such as the number of currently available units,

(iii)   its inherent access characteristics such as read only, sequential access only, etc., and

(iv)   access functions which are invoked by a process to access or use the resource.

A resource forms a module and its general structure is shown in Fig. 3. The *resource* states the resource's inherent access characteristics. The *resource type* specifies whether it is "reusable," "consumable" or "virtual." The reusable resource becomes available for use when it is released whereas a consumable resource ceases to exist when it is acquired. Files and common variables are reusable resources whereas messages and signals are consumable resources.

The *resource structure* defines the structure of the resource and their initial values if necessary. The resource structure is defined in terms of other resource modules as well as the basic data structures defined below.

A. Directly accessible basic data structures

The following data structures are directly accessible; namely, they can be accessed directly without using any functions. However, they can, of course, be declared as the data structures accessible only through access functions.

(a) Integer

An integer data is defined with its value range.

integer v[lower bound, upper bound] *initial* 50.

(b) Character string

A character string data is defined with its maximum length.

string v[length] *initial* "system."

(c) Boolean

A Boolean data is defined as follows.

Boolean v *initial* false.

(d) Binary

A binary data is defined with maximum length.

binary v[length] *initial* 1010.

(e) Pointer

A pointer is an off-set from some base address. It is defined with its range. The lower

```
resource name: resource module;
               resource information;
       name: resource;
               resource type "reusable", "consumable" ro "virtual";
               virtualization virtualization method;
               resource structure definition of resource structure
                               and initial values;
               access type "random" access, "block random" access
                           or "unit device";
               usage type "exclusive" or "sharable";
               scheduling discipline specification of scheduling
                                    discipline;
               access time mean, minimum, maximum, distribution func-
                           tion of access time;
               access mode "direct" or "function";
       name: resource
               definition of the next resource
                               .
                               .
                               .

           function definition;
               function name (parameter list);
                   parameter definition definition of parameters;
                   usage "exclusive", "copy sharable" or "original
                         sharable";
                   execution time mean, minimum, maximum, distribu-
                                  tion function of the execution
                                  time;
                   execution resource;
                       reusable resource names of necessary reusable
                                       resources;
                       local variable definition of local variables;
                   input port;
                       consumable resource names of resources and
                                       their functions required;
                       reusable resource names of resources and their
                                       functions required;
                   output port;
                       consumable resource names of resources and
                                       their functions required;
                       reusable resource names of resources and their
                                       functions required;
                   body
                       function body which can access and use only
                       the resources declared in execution resource,
                       input port, and output port through their
                       declared functions except the directly accessi-
                       ble resources;
               function name (parameter list);
                       definition of the next function
                               .
                               .
                               .
```

Figure 3. Resource module definition

bound can be negative.

pointer v[lower bound, upper bound].

(f) Block

A block is an unstructured area. It is defined with its size.

Block v[100].

(g) Record

A record consists of several fields of different types.

record r
  integer i[0,1000];
  string s[10];
end.

(h) Array

An array consists of elements of the same type.

array v[1:100] *of*
  record
    integer i[0,100];
    string s[10];
  end.

An array element can be directly accessed by the notation v[i] when the array is in the main memory.

(i) Stack

A stack is a first-in-last-out list.

stack v[maximum size] *of*
  record
    integer i[0,100];
    string s[10];
  end.

B. Basic data structures accessible only through access functions

(a) Queue

A queue is a first-in-first-out list.

queue v[maximum size] *of*
  record
    integer i[0,100];
    string s[10];
  end.

(b) Set

A set is a collection of non-ordered records. A necessary record is content-addressed; namely, a set of functions are provided to access records, given a condition of (attribute, value) pair.

set v[maximum size] *of*
  record
    integer i[0,100];
    string s[10];
  end.

(c) File

A file is an array of records possibly with a label. A file can reside either on secondary memory or on main memory. However, the access must be made through one of its access functions. This is the major difference between array and file. An end indicator "end" is always associated with a file and remains false until the end is reached.

file v[maximum size]
  with label record
      string name[20];
      string date[8];
       end
  of record
    integer i[0,100];
    string s[10];
  end.

(d) Tree

A tree is a hierarchical structure of records. Like a file, a tree can reside either on secondary memory or on main memory, and a tree node must be accessed through one of its access functions. The tree leaves can have different structures from the other node.

tree v[maximum depth]
  with root pointer r[A] *of*
 node array [1:3] *of*
   record
     string key[10];
     pointer next[A3]
   end
 leave array [1:10] *of string* [50].

The *access type* specifies whether this resource is random access, block random access or a unit (sequential access). This restricts the type of access functions attachable to this resource. The *usage type* specifies whether access to this resource must be exclusive or sharable. Most of reusable resources are exclusive. The *access time* specifies the mean, minimum and maximum of access time. The distribution function of access time can be specified if it is available. This access time information is used to estimate the system performance. The *access mode* specifies whether this resource is directly accessible or can be accessed only through access functions.

The *function definition* consists of six major parts. The *usage* defines the type of use of this function. It can be "exclusive," "copy sharable" or "original sharable." The "exclusive" allows only one process to use this function whereas "copy sharable" allows each process to use a copy of this function and "original sharable" allows any number of processes to use the original of this function. This function usage is subject to the usage type of the resource. The copy sharable and the original sharable functions are allowed only for the sharable resource.

The *execution resources* specifies the necessary resources to execute this function. The *input port* and the *output port* specify the input channel and the output channel of the function. They are used in a function body to input and output information. The *function body* is a specification of the function's actions. A function is basically of three types; input function, manipulate function, and output function. Their usage and operation principles are discussed next.

FUNCTION USAGE

A function is used either to obtain information from a resource module, to store information into a resource module or to manipulate information in a resource module. In any case, a function must access data structures inside or outside its resource module. The following rules are applied to the access to data structures by a function.

(a) Internal data structures

Directly accessible data structures (access mode = "direct") can be accessed directly; any other data structures must be accessed through their access functions.

(b) External data structures

Any external data structures can be accessed only through their access functions.

(c) Process's working data structures

Each process is allowed to possess data structures as its temporary information storage. These data structures are all directly accessible.

Any input or output function assumes at least one of the source and the destination to be a directly accessible data structure. If both the source and the destination are accessible only through functions, they must be connected via a directly accessible data structure.

RESOURCE MODULE SKELETONS AND RESOURCE SKELETONS

Many resource modules are often of the same structure except some minor differences. It is much more convenient to specify these modules based on a standard resource module skeleton or class. Since it is difficult to predetermine which variables are to be parameterized and which variables are to be prespecified, we allow any variable values to be changed by use of the design system. A resource module skeleton is defined in the same way as shown in Fig. 3 except the first line to be

resource module skeleton name: *resource module skeleton* (# 1, # 2, . . . , # n)

instead of

resource name: *resource module*

where parameter # 1, # 2, . . . , # n are replaced as texts with actual arguments when a resource module is defined. The variables can be parameterized as described above, prespecified or left unspecified (denoted by *). The prespecified values remain so unless respecified at the resource module definition time whereas the *'ed values must be explicitly specified. The design system, to be described later, explicitly asks the designer to fill the *'ed values whereas the prespecified values are changed only when requested by the designer.

A resource skeleton can be similarly defined to denote a class of resources. The definition and use are similar to those of the resource module skeletons.

HIERARCHICAL STRUCTURING OF AN OPERATING SYSTEM

The method, "conquer by divide," is the only way to understand a large software system. Whatever the design process is, either top-down, bottom-up or any other, the designed system should be described in a hierarchical manner. Therefore, the description of a resource module must provide a way of describing a hierarchical structure. A resource module may have the following relations with other resource modules, as shown in Fig. 4.

(a) Port relation. Information can be received or sent to another resource through a port. Two resource modules are in the same hierarchical level. Neither includes the other.

(b) Inclusion relation. A resource module is included in a higher level resource module. This inclusion relation is strictly hierarchical. That is, a resource module can be included in a single resource module only.

(c) Virtualization relation. A resource module can be virtualized or multiplexed into multiple resource modules. The virtualized resource modules are considered to be the higher level modules.

The port relations are defined by the *input port* and *output port* declarations. The inclusion relation is declared by the *resource structure*, which lists the names of the included resource modules. The entire resource module including its functions is always included. This rule allows only a strictly hierarchical relation among resource modules. The virtualization relation is declared by "virtual," which stated that this resource is a virtual resource created on the resource declared in the *resource structure*. The *virtualization* specifies which multiplexing method is used. The multiplexing mechanisms are included in the access control and scheduling.

DYNAMIC CREATION AND DELETION OF RESOURCES

In an operating system, it is often necessary and convenient to dynamically create and delete resources. If dynamic creation or deletion is necessary, then such special functions must be provided to a concerned resource module. Most of the characteristics of the resource are defined in the resource definition whereas some characteristics can be dynamically specified as parameters of the create function. The create and delete functions are, like any other functions, under the control of the access control and scheduling, and their executions must be validated.

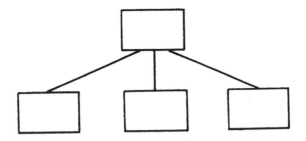

(a)   Inclusion relation

(b)   Port relation

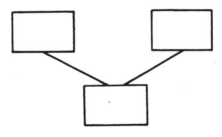

(c)   Virtualization relation

Figure 4.   Resource module relations

EXAMPLES

As an example of a resource module definition, two files are defined in Fig. 5.

5. CONSUMABLE RESOURCE

The consumable resource at the conceptual level must be independent of physical implementation, yet be precise enough so that elaborate process coordination is describable.
Implementation-oriented descriptions such as the description by a ring buffer with P and V
primitives should be rejected. The best method is "tagged messages" [Maekawa (80)]. Combining with the eventcount and sequencer method proposed by Reed and Kanodia [Reed
(79)], we adopt the following method.

We define an eventcount and a sequencer to be a non-decreasing integer number, on
which the following primitives are allowed.

ticket(s):increment the sequencer s by 1 and returns its value; the sequencer is mutually
excluded and two uses of ticket(s) primitives must return different values.

await(e,t):wait until the value of eventcount e reaches t; this primitive need not be mutually
exclusive.

advance(e):increment the absolute value of eventcount e by 1 and activate any process waiting for e to reach the new value; this primitive need not be mutually exclusive
either.

replace(B,s,M,t):obtain a unit of consumable resource B whose sequence number is s and
replace it with a message at location M with sequence number t; if there is no unit
of resource B with sequence number s, the process waits until the required unit
becomes available. Note that this replace operation can be considered as a combination of an advance and an await with a data transfer capability.

grab(B,s,M,t):grab a unit of consumable resource B whose sequence number is s, and then
set its sequence number to t and return its address into M. This operation sets the
grabbed unit to be empty and not available for a "replace" operation.

mark(t):mark the unit with sequence number t as available. The grab and mark primitives
are useful to avoid additional data transfers between two directly accessible resources.

```
file system: resource module;
             resource information;
  name file: resource skelton ( );
                resource type reusable;
                resource structure
                    file [1000] of string name [10] with end indicator
                          end;
                access type random;
                usage type exclusive;
                access time (10 ms, 1 ms, 50 ms);
                access mode function;
master file: name file ( );
working file: name file ( );
             function definition;
                function copy (F1, F2);
                parameter definition file F1, F2;
                usage copy sharable;
                execution resource;
                   local variable block W[10];
                body;
                   while F1.end=false
                   begin
                      get (F1,W);
                      put (F2,W);
                   end
             function definition;
                definition of get and put;
```

Figure 5. A resource module definition example

await($e_1, t_1; e_2, t_2;,.,.; e_n, t_n$):wait until each e_i reaches t_i.

replace($B_1, s_1, M_1, t_1; B_2, s_2, M_2, t_2; ...; B_n, s_n, M_n, t_n$):wait until all the messages with number s_i are available and replace them with the messages with number t_i.

delete(B, t):delete any messages whose absolute values of the event number part are less than t. This primitive is useful to delete any possibly left-out messages.

The use of the above primitives is shown in the following two examples.

(a) Message transfer (producer-consumer)

An input process places a message which is picked up by a consumer process. There are multiple producers and consumers.

(b) I/O synchronization

A computation process waits for the completion of an input/output operation. We assume that an input/output device may fail to send an interrupt signal of notifying the completion of an input/output operation in spite of the successful input/output completion. We assume that the input/output device is perfect but this failure. In order to avoid the computation process's permanent wait, we start a timer at the input/output operation initiation so that it acts on behalf of the input/output device if it fails. The timer interval is set long enough for any input/output operation to complete within it.

The solutions for the above two examples are shown in Figs. 6 and 7.

6. PROCESS

A process is a sequence of actions performed by functions of resources and it is most conveniently described by a decision table or by a graph, as shown in Fig. 8. Each line specifies an action to be performed, time constraint and next action. An action is specified by a resource module and its function to be invoked. The time constraint specifies the maximum time allowed to perform this function. The severeness specifies the degree of severeness of the time constraint. This information is used in scheduling processes. Each process possesses a set of state variables and a set of working data structures, all of which are directly accessible. The state variables are primarily used to determine the next action to be performed whereas the working data structures are used as temporary storage to transfer information from one action to another. We assume that the definition of a process is

```
comment sequencer S,T (initially 0);
        consumable resource B of N units
        whose event counts are initialized
        to -1,-2,...,-N
```

Producer	Consumer

```
loop                             loop
   produce a message and place      t:=ticket(T);
      it into M;                    replace(B,t,M,-(t+N));
   s:=ticket(S);                    consume the message at M;
   replace(B,-s,M,s);           end of loop
end of loop
```

Figure 6. Message transfer in a multiple producer
            multiple consumer problem

```
comment sequencer S;
        consumable resource B of N units
        whose event counts are initialized
        to -1,-2,...,-N;
```

Computation process	I/O device	Timer

```
loop
    s:=ticket(S);
    activate the I/O device          .                              .
    and the timer with               .                              .
    their access functions           .                              .
    with s as a parameter;
                  .      place the completion
                  .      information into M;
                  .      replace(B,-s,M,s);

    replace(B,s,M,-(s+N));
      delete(B,s)                            place the completion
end of loop                                  information into M;
                                             replace(B,-s,M,s);
```

Figure 7. I/O synchronization

Action	Module	Function	Time constraint	Severeness	Capability	Next action
1	Input line	Get	Module's own time limit	Suspend	Input line Get	2
2	Program library	Command analysis	Module's own time limit	Suspend	Program library Command analysis	3
. . .	. . .	. . .	. . .	. . .	. . .	. . .
20	Exception	Abort	None			End

(a) Process by a decision table

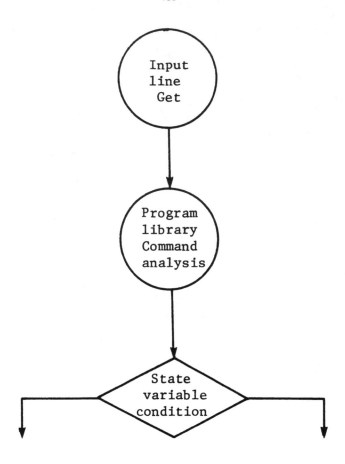

(b) Process by a graph

Figure 8. Process description

simple and short. This is usually the case for a majority of operating systems.

7. ACCESS CONTROL AND SCHEDULING

The access control and scheduling (ACS) is a set of mechanisms and a set of rules to govern the entire operating system and, as such, is a core of the system. Each and every access to a resource through one of its function must always be reported to the access control and scheduling, unless so specified, for it to be validated and to be scheduled properly. The access control and scheduling insures the following three properties of the system.

(a) Security,

(b) Deadlock free.

(c) Proper scheduling.

Because the control of them is separated from the rest (the majority part) of the system, a new or a different access control and scheduling method can be relatively easily tried. We discuss some of the issues involved in the access control and scheduling.

SECURITY

The security of an operating system can be assured by validating each and every access attempt. There are basically two approaches to do access checking; capability based or access right based. Since the capability-based method is faster, we adopt this approach. As shown in Fig. 8, a process is specified with its capability at each action. The process's capability can be passed, increased and decreased from action to action. The capabilities can be dynamically passed between processes for resource sharing. A set of special primitives are provided for this purpose. An invocation of a function usually increases its capability because the function's local resources become available. The definition of capabilities for each action can be done almost automatically because the necessary resources can be determined from the definition of the function. Although a hierarchical arrangement of capabilities may be more convenient, we adopt a one-level arrangement as suggested in Fig. 7 because it is more flexible.

QUEUE FORMULATION FOR SCHEDULING

A queue must be formulated for each resource when competition arises. Although a queue is necessary for each resource, we formulate queues in the access control and scheduling area because each process can join to only one queue. This simplifies the queue structure and handling. The scheduling discipline can be stated by the *scheduling discipline* of a resource module definition. Some of the available choices are FCFS (first-come-first-served), SSTF (shortest service time first), PS (priority scheme), and EDTF (earliest due-time first). A consistent selection of the scheduling discipline is important. This is ultimately the responsibility of the designer. However, the simulation capability of the design system would be a great help to choose a proper scheduling discipline. The above scheduling disciplines are modularized so that the designer can choose an appropriate one with ease.

DYNAMIC CREATION AND DELETION OF RESOURCES AND PROCESSES

Dynamic creation and deletion of resources and processes is allowed as stated before. When an object is created or deleted, it must be explicitly reported to the access control and scheduling by a special function, *create* object or *delete* object. In this way the access control and scheduling knows the entire resource modules and processes. Any process or resource module not known to the access control and scheduling cannot access or be accessed. It is assumed that any resource and process is given a unique identification number.

VIRTUALIZATION

Virtualization or multiplexing is one of the most fundamental functions that the operating systems provide. Because of its importance, we provide several standard virtualization mechanisms from which the designer choose one. They are

(a) round robin,

(b) round robin with input/output completion interrupts,

(c) base register,

(d) segmentation, and

(e) paging.

The first two choices are specified in the process definition whereas the last three are specified in the resource module definition.

NUCLEUS OR PROCESS

The access control and scheduling can be run as a nucleus; namely, independent of any processes, or as a master process. It is conceptually easier to run as a nucleus. However, there ar some cases that it must run as a process because operations may involve wait conditions. Virtualization, in particular, may cause waits. Such a part must be run as a process.

PROGRAM STRUCTURE

The non-process part of the access control and scheduling is also structured based on the resource modules although the access to them may never cause wait states and does not need the clearance of the access control. The program is hierarchically structured for better understanding. The process part of the access control and scheduling works in the same way as a regular process except that this process is given a somewhat larger capability. The process part is thus also based on the resource modules.

6. COMPARISONS WITH OTHER STRUCTURING METHODS

It may be noticed that our resource module is somewhat similar to an abstract data and that our process model is similar to a transaction model like SREM [Alford (77)]. In fact, they share some common properties.

The evaluation of structuring methods is a difficult task because there is no agreed set of evaluation criteria, not to mention that any criterion is at best qualitative if not subjective. The Ross's seven principles and four goals [Ross (75)] are one of the useful sets of evaluation criteria. For our purpose, however, our initial motives stated in section 1 would serve as a more effective set of criteria. They can be summarized as the changes of the four major characteristics of the system as follows.

a) Changes of hardware configuration
Addition or deletion of an equipment, increase or decrease of the main memory and even a shift to a new machine.

b) Changes of job characteristics
Increase of workload, changes of workload characteristics, addition of a new application such as real-time processing.

(c) Addition or deletion of system capabilities

Addition of a new file processing capability, addition of a new logging capability, and so forth.

(d) Changes of system properties

Changes of severeness of response times, changes of performance objectives, changes of reliability requirements, and so forth.

Since these changes are in many directions, the evaluation of modularization methods must be multidimensional. Some method is robust for changes in one dimension but weak for changes in another dimension while other methods have strength and weakness in different dimensions. Since it is too huge a job to compare our method with all the other conceivable structuring methods, we here compare our method only with the currently most common method, which is outlined below.

COMMON METHOD

The currently common method is to decompose or synthesize a system with functional modules. Some common functions of operating systems are as follows.

(a) Input function: obtain a set of data from a card reader, a terminal, or a magnetic tape unit.

(b) Command analysis: analyze a command.

(c) Allocate function: allocate necessary resources to a job.

(d) Initiate function: initiate the execution of a required program.

(e) Read/write function: read/write data from/onto a secondary memory such as magnetic disk.

(f) Terminate function: terminate the execution of a program.

(g) Release function: release the allocated resource from the job.

(h) Output function: output the result.

(i) Sequencing function: control and monitor the above sequence for a program.

(j) Logging function: record the activities in the system.

The above modularization is quite common and easy for both operating system designers and users to understand. However, the method is not robust for the changes stated before.

As for the hardware configuration and characteristic change, in our structure, each hardware resource is usually confined in one resource module and thus changes of hardware are more easily confined in smaller areas. In the functional modularization, the change tends to spread over many modules because many modules utilize the information of the hardware configuration and characteristics.

The job characteristic is represented, in our method, as a process and its time constraints can be more easily stated. Simulation and performance prediction are easier because job flow patterns and their queuing networks are readily formulated because the process representation is immediatedly seen as a queuing network. In the function modularization, the queuing model formulation is not straightforward because servers and queues are not immediately recognized.

An addition of a new function would be also easier in our structure because its data are more likely to be concentrated in some module. This is the principle that the Parnas's method and the data abstraction methods are claimed to be more robust for changes. It is considered that data are more unstable than functions. If a system is modularized based on functions, necessary data tends to be spread over many modules.

The system properties such as performance, reliability and security are, in our structure, confined in the access control and scheduling, thus they are more easily evaluated and controlled. In the functional modularization, the system properties are spread over many modules and difficult to be evaluated.

9. DESIGN SYSTEM

Our conceptual model can become a model of a general operating system, from which families of operating systems are built, as shown in Fig. 1. We briefly discuss other components of this design system.

PHYSICAL MODEL

We recognize any physical resource to be an information carrying device. Any physical resource is characterized by

(a) structure,

(b) access restriction,

(c) access primitives, and

(d) access time.

The main memory, for instance, has a homogeneous structure with random access. Its access primitives are "load" and "store" with access time less than a microsecond. A card reader has a queue structure with sequential access. Its access primitives are "read" and "check status" with access time, for instance, 50 ms and 5 μs, respectively. As such, a physical resource can be represented by the same notation proposed for a conceptual resource. Instead of directly listing physical commands as access primitives, we define a little more logical and systematic primitives. The basic primitives are:

(a) read (p, d, e); read a basic information unit at location p into d with eventcount's value into e.

(b) write (p, d, e); write the basic information item at d into location p with eventcount value into e.

(c) wait (e); wait until the eventcount reach to e.

(d) initialize; place the physical resource at the initial position.

There are two important issues concerning the physical resource representation.

(a) Simultaneous executions of a physical resource and a process.

(b) Notification of the end of operation.

An operation of a physical resource may take a considerably longer time than a unit operation of a process, and thus they are allowed to be performed simultaneously. we do not consider this simultaneous operation by a physical resource to be a process. This much simplifies the allocation of CPU at the initiation time of an operation of a physical resource. If a physical resource operation is considered as a process, the CPU must be allocated to this operation with priority; otherwise the operation will not start. This problem occurs because the physical resource lacks the capability of doing process synchronization. This lack of capability also causes the second problem of notifying the end of an operation.

We assume that the notification of the end of an operation is made by interrupt. An interrupt is a CPU time stealing and is given a priority over ordinary processes. An interrupt condition and its action is specified by *trigger on* condition statement. On the completion of an operation, the eventcount is *advanced*, which will wake up the waiting process.

REQUIREMENTS AND CONSTRAINTS

Our ultimate objective of the design system is to produce an operating system by specifying a list of required system properties. This is an interactive design process as indicated in Fig. 2. The resource module definition is designed so that the designer can choose a necessary module or can build a necessary one by combining modules rather than programming it. This goal will of course not be reached immediately, but after an integration of resource modules and knowledges, some of the design will be automatically done by the design system.

10. CONCLUSIONS

The operating system is probably one of the worst piece of software for which a concrete system model does not exist. Any system can be understood and placed under our control only when we have developed a reasonable model for it. Operating system building has been done based on a set of know-hows collected by the past experience. The most important advancement we have to achieve in the system area is to develop reasonable models for information processing systems. We have to approach it from both general and specific stands. A general model covers a wider range of systems but is weak to express a specific system whereas a specialized model covers a narrower range of systems but has stronger power to express a specific system. A general model can have impact on a wider range of systems but the improvement for each system is moderate whereas a specialized model can have impact only on a narrow range of systems but the improvement for each system can be revolutional. If we want to have revolutionary effects, we must develop specialized models. Our approach is such a specialized approach.

There can be many forms of models for systems. However, except for some special cases, the only promising approach is to model the structure of a system. Our approach is also a structural approach. In modeling a system as a structure, the most important thing is which view or views are taken to see the system. We have taken the view that a system consists of resources. This view is convenient to evaluate many system properties, and the system based on this view tends to be more robust for changes of many kinds. Since the maintenance occupies a large portion of software development cost, this improvement in system changes is significant. It turns out that our idea of "resource" is similar to the concept of abstract data. The readers may also notice that the view of operating system as a collection of resources has been recognized among industrial programmers. Our approach can be said to be a formulation of this vague idea among industrial programmers which happens to match the recent research direction in software systems. The concept expressed in this paper should thus be acceptable to practitioners without much difficulty.

REFERENCES

Alford M. W. (1977). A requirements engineering methodology for real-time processing requirement. *IEEE Trans. Software Eng.* Vol. SE-3, No. 1, Jan. 1977, pp. 60-69.

Dijkstra E. W. (1968). The structure of the "T.H.E."-multiprogramming system. *Comm. ACM* Vol. 11, No. 5, May 1968.

Habermann A. N., Flon L., and Cooprider L. (1976). Modularization and hierarchy in a family of operating systems. *Comm. ACM* Vol. 19, No. 5, May 1976, pp. 266-272.

Holt R. C. (1972). Some deadlock properties of computer systems. *Computing Surveys* Vol. 4, No. 3, Sept. 1972.

Maekawa M. (1980). A classification of process coordination schemes. Dept. of Information Science, University of Tokyo, Japan.

Parnas D. L., Handzel G., and Wurges H. (1976). Design and specification of the minimal subset of an operating system family. *IEEE Trans. Software Engineering.* Vol. SE-2, No. 4, Dec. 1976, pp. 301-307.

Price W. R. and Parnas D. L. (1973). The design of the virtual memory aspects of a virtual machine. *Proc. ACM SIGARCH – SIGOPS Workshop on Virtual Computer Systems.* March 1973.

Reed D. P. and Kanodia R. K. (1979). Synchronization with eventcounts and sequencers. *Comm. ACM* Vol. 22, No. 2, 1979, pp. 115-123.

Ross D. T., Goodenough I. B., and Irvine C. A. (1975). Software engineering: process, principles, and goals. *Computer.* May 1975.

Part IV.

User Interfaces

One of the goals of the operating system is to minimize the
human efforts needed to program and operate the system. To
this end, the interface between operating system and its
users of various kinds (application programmers, users at
terminals, operators, casual non-DP users, and so forth)
must be made easier and less complicated for efficient,
error-free communication. With this in mind, the first
paper by T. Takeshita has attempted to review the main
aspects of the OS interface, classifying them into several
categories, tracing back the evolution of their characteristics, and then projecting its future. The author predicts
that low-cost, colour/graphics displays with both interactive
dialogues and procedural command languages, supported by a
powerful full-screen editor and a library management facility
will become prevalent in the future. While this first paper
discusses the OS interface from the overall viewpoint, the
second paper by I. Arita discusses a rather specific case.
It proposes "Intelligent Console (INC)," which is a microcomputer inserted between a computer and its operator's
console. It offers an effective means for users to add new
non-standard operating system functions without modifying
the operating system. Its usefulness is successfully
demonstrated by the actual implementation of non-trivial
operating system functions such as an inter-job communication facility and a remote entry system.

PERSPECTIVE OF OS INTERFACE TO USERS

Toru Takeshita

Development No.1, Software Development Center,

IBM Japan, Ltd.

1-14, Nisshin-cho, Kawasaki-ku,

Kawasaki 210, Japan

ABSTRACT

An attempt has been made to classify various aspects of the OS interface, to review evolutionary changes in each aspect, and to project the future.

The advancement of the OS, the changes in its environment, and the future of the OS with particular emphasis on end-user orientation are briefly covered.

The author predicts that low-cost, colour/graphics displays with both interactive dialogues and procedural command languages, supported by a powerful full-screen editor and a library management facility will become prevalent in the future.

1. Preface

An operating system of a large computer system is a huge software package, reaching to several million lines of code, with accumulated techniques, inventions, knowledge and experiences. Its users are steadily increasing and vary vastly. Its interface to the users is extensive and of multiple purposes. Discussion of its total aspects is not possible without the entire knowledge of design objectives, functions and usage of the operating system and without the good analysis of its users in term of their needs and satisfaction.

Two major goals of the operating system are 1) maximizing the effective use of computer resources for increased system performance and 2) minimizing the human effort needed to program and operate the system. The second objective is really to ease the communication between man and machine. That is for a human to tell the machine what to do and to learn what is being done by the machine. As dramatic improvements of computer power and of price/performance have been achieved, two conflicting phenomena, 1) the use of computers by less trained people and 2) the complexity and sophistication of computer hardware, software and applications have been increasing. The higher the machine capability, the more applications are run on a system, and the more set-up, IPL, responses to system messages, and other operator jobs are required.

In order to facilitate application development and operation, the interface between the computer system (operating system) and the user (application programs, application developers at the terminals, operators and casual non-DP users) must be made easier and less complicated for efficient, error-free communication. Indeed, the interface to the user is becoming a critical aspect of the operating system.

With this in mind, the author has attempted to review the main aspects of the OS interface, to classify them into several categories, to trace back the evolution of their characteristics, and then to project its future with emphasis on end user orientation and finally to summarize problems and requirements.

2. Evolution of OS Interface to Users

When the predecessors to today's OS' made their debut in the late 1950's,
they were a simple collection of I/O routines called "IOCS", or a FORTRAN
monitor sequentially handling compilation and execution of FORTRAN programs. Now in a complex case, multiple job streams including network
interdependency and multiple on-line tasks with different priorities
are randomly received from peripheral devices connected to the channels
and from terminals located at remote locations; all to be processed by
multiple CPUs. Unlike the past when applications in one area, commer-
cial or scientific, were sequentially run on a single system, many jobs
in the two areas are mixed and run concurrently -- batch and real-time
-- on a single system.

The users of the OS interface at first were trained programmers and
operators in the central location of a large enterprises. Now, the OS
interface is exploited by non-DP professionals.

As computer thechnology has evolved, applications and users have expanded, and the physical devices used for the interface have changed
and been diversified. Before the introduction of CRT's, typewriter-
like devices were popularly used by operators. Now, the use of a colour
display as console is not unusual. The console was initially used for
operation of just a single stand-alone system. But, today, it may be
used as master operator console for tightly-coupled or loosely-coupled
multi-CPU system, or for a distributed system consisting of many CPUs
located at nodes of a large network. They may be located remotely from
the CPUs with alternate consoles in different locations. The use of a
single console for multiple CPUs helps to achieve a 'single systm image
as well as the logical isolation of operator functions.

3. Users of Interface and Information Communicated

Let me discuss "who are the users of the OS interface" and "what information is communicated" and "what changes have happened" in the following areas:

    - System Programmers and Operators to OS (cf. fig.1)
    - OS to System Programmers and Operators (cf. fig.2)
    - Application Programmers to OS (cf. fig.3)
    - OS to Application Programmers (cf. fig.4)

---

1. SYSTEM GENERATION (CONFIGURATION, FUNCTIONAL AND PERFORMANCE OPTIONS)

STATIC SYS. GEN ⟶ DYNAMIC RECONFIGURATION - - - - - - - ⌐

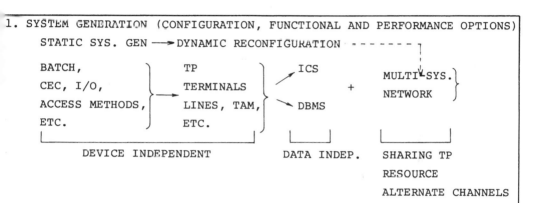

BATCH,   TP   ICS   MULTI SYS.
CEC, I/O,   TERMINALS   +   NETWORK
ACCESS METHODS,   LINES, TAM,   DBMS
ETC.   ETC.

      DEVICE INDEPENDENT   DATA INDEP.   SHARING TP
                                                RESOURCE
                                                ALTERNATE CHANNELS

2. START, CHECKPOINT, RECOVERY/RESTART

KEY, SWITCHES, ⟶ BOOTSTRAP ⟶ IPL ⟶ AUTO IPL
ETC. SET MANUALLY

COLD START ⟶ WARM START ⟶ HOT START

3. JOB SET-UP

NAMES OF JOBS,   DEFFINITION
PROGRAMS, FILES, ⟶ OF OTHER
DEVICES, ETC.   RESOURCES,
                     PRIORITIES,
                     SECURITIES, ETC.

. SINGLE JOB STREAM ⟶ MULTI-JOB STREAM
. SEQUENTIAL JOB-SCHEDULING ⟶ PRIORITY JOB SCHEDULING ⟶
  DEPENDENT JOB SCHEDULING
. MANUAL SET-UP USING JCL ⟶ AUTOMATIC PREPARATION OF JOB STREAM
  ⟶ AUTOMATIC HANDLING OF DEPENDENT JOBS

4. MONITORING SYSTEM STATUS AND ADJUSTING ACTIONS

. OPERATOR RESPONSES TO MESSAGES ⟶ AUTOMATIC (PROGRAMMED)
  RESPONSES

```
. SINGLE CONSOLE → MULTI-CONSOLE → REMOTE
  CONSOLE → CENTRAL CONSOLE FOR DISTRIBUTED CPU's

. MANUAL SHUT OFF → AUTOMATIC SHUT OFF

5. MAINTENANCE  ⎫
     INDIVIDUAL  ⎬ → SMP (SYSTEM MODIFICATION PROGRAM)
     PATCHING   ⎭
```

FIGURE 1   System programmers and operators to OS

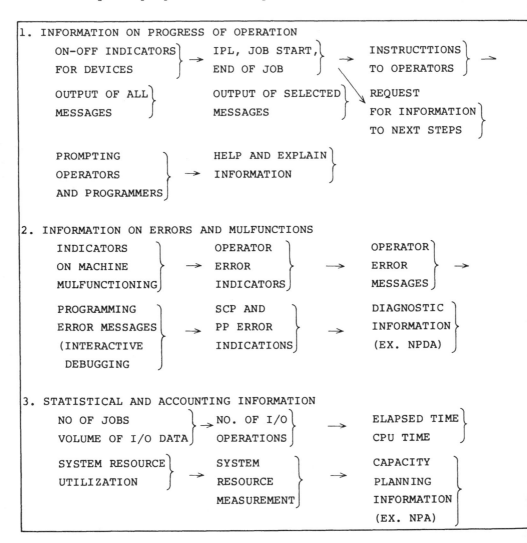

1. INFORMATION ON PROGRESS OF OPERATION

    ON-OFF INDICATORS⎫→ IPL, JOB START,⎫ → INSTRUCTTIONS⎫→
    FOR DEVICES   ⎭ END OF JOB   ⎭   TO OPERATORS ⎭

    OUTPUT OF ALL⎫ OUTPUT OF SELECTED⎫ REQUEST
    MESSAGES   ⎭   MESSAGES   ⎭ FOR INFORMATION⎫
                                        TO NEXT STEPS ⎭

    PROMPTING   ⎫ HELP AND EXPLAIN⎫
    OPERATORS   ⎬→ INFORMATION   ⎭
    AND PROGRAMMERS   ⎭

2. INFORMATION ON ERRORS AND MULFUNCTIONS

    INDICATORS   ⎫ OPERATOR   ⎫   OPERATOR⎫
    ON MACHINE   ⎬→ ERROR   ⎬→ ERROR   ⎬→
    MULFUNCTIONING   ⎭ INDICATORS ⎭   MESSAGES⎭

    PROGRAMMING   ⎫ SCP AND   ⎫   DIAGNOSTIC ⎫
    ERROR MESSAGES   ⎬→ PP ERROR   ⎬→ INFORMATION⎬
    (INTERACTIVE   ⎪ INDICATIONS⎭   (EX. NPDA) ⎭
     DEBUGGING   ⎭

3. STATISTICAL AND ACCOUNTING INFORMATION

    NO OF JOBS   ⎫→NO. OF I/O⎫ → ELAPSED TIME⎫
    VOLUME OF I/O DATA   ⎭ OPERATIONS⎭   CPU TIME   ⎭

    SYSTEM RESOURCE⎫ SYSTEM   ⎫   CAPACITY   ⎫
    UTILIZATION   ⎭→ RESOURCE   ⎬→ PLANNING   ⎬
                      MEASUREMENT ⎭   INFORMATION⎪
                                      (EX. NPA) ⎭

FIGURE 2   OS to system programmers and operators

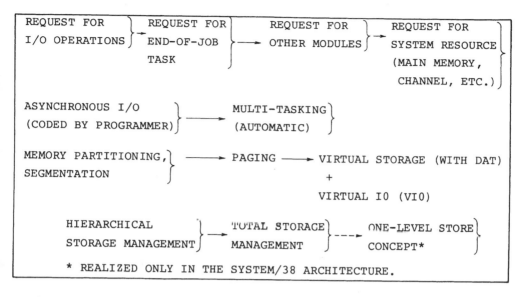

FIGURE 3   Application programmers to OS

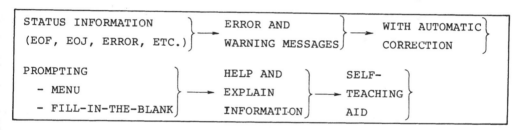

FIGURE 4   OS to application programmers

examples are shown in separate charts (cf. figs. 5, 6, 7 and 8) atta-
ed to this paper, the purposes of the interface and information commu-
cated through it have become complex and diversified, implementing
rious new concepts and facilities of the operating system. Accurately
pressing definitive and control information and feeding it into the
stem requires much training, experience and thoroughness.

4. Representations and Formats

The languages are representations and formats of informartion passed
through the interface and are very important. They deserve much discussion and evaluation as computer scientists, developers, and users try
to find better ways to interact with the OS.

The media for communicating system environmental information, such
as addresses of I/O devices, the location of the first instruction, the
end-of-job actions, were initially switches, or keys on the console or
wiring of control panels for card readers and line printers. With the
introduction of the operating system (for the second generation systems)
control cards substituted these for flexibility (e.g. to give device in-
dependence to application programs) and ease of control. Then, with
the development of IBM OS/360, a formalized way of representing control
information, called "job control language (JCL)" was developed. It is
still in dominant use today.

It is a parametric language with one or more identifiers to indicate
a type of control card and one or more items of specifying information
in the format of "variable=numeric or character string (as value)". Since
it has many keywords and rules for writing and machine entry, and, in
addition, many cards must be prepared with absolute accuracy; JCL has
been often criticized by programmers and operators in spite of its obvious advantages and various types of information it contains. These
are exemplified in the charts, "System Programmers and Operators to OS"
(fig. 1) and "Application Programmers to OS" (fig. 3), which should be
appreciated by users.

The symbols used for this kind of communication are similar to those
used for application programming. At first, just numerical digits or
alphabetic characters were used for control purposes. Then, alphanumer
character strings, and, in Japan, katakana strings were to be used in
the JCL. Now, some people even prefer the use of kanji in Japan. I
believe the use of colour and graphical representations will become pop
lar from now on. Also, some limited use of voice recognition may be
realized in the future.

To make all the capabilities of OS functions available to users on
a terminal, the JCL was converted to a command language for use on a
time sharing system (interactive sub-system). Its example is TSO commands initially for IBM MVT (OS-360) and now for IMB MVS (OS/370). It
is rather complex and has a thick grammar book to be mastered, because
it accommodates all the functions of MVS specifiable by the operator.
In the meantime, TSS's (such as MAC at MIT, and TSS/360 and CP/360 both

by IBM) primarily for personal computing were developed by many people. One of most efficient, well-recognized interactive computing system is IBM VM/CMS under IBM VM/370, a virtual machine system which was originally developed at IBM Cambridge Scientific Center. Its command language is much simpler and easier to use partly because it is intended to serve the non-DP professional from the beginning.

The use of VM/CMS commands has become even simpler and more convenient with the introduction of EXEC procedures, which allows specifying and storing a set of commands which are repeatedly used. At execution time, the terminal user can select from the library the entire sequence of commands just by specifying its EXEC name; and, if required, can insert new parameters and/or modify existing ones. With these command procedure capabilities, it has been reported that the use of an interactive subsystem has increased very significantly. W. J. Doherty of IBM T. J. Watson Research Center reported in 1977 that there were twice as many EXEC;s as all other source programs in conventional programming languages combined at the center. Also, in 1977, the Stanford Line Accelerator Center (SLAC) installation observed an average of 25 commands executed per command typed at a terminal when using the WYLBUR interface. The EXEC 2 language which has been developed by IBM seems to be a very good one.

When a terminal user keys in TSS commands, HLL statements, texts and data, he makes mistakes and must correct them. Later, he must make changes (add, delete, update) to what has already been entered into the system. A software aid for this is called "Editor".

The editing function incorporated into early TSS systems was a "line editor "which allows the terminal user to change previously entered information line by line with the specification of "line number and character positions". Then, a "context editor" was developed, which relieves the users from the burden of counting lines and characters, and which automatically finds the position of the substring of characters specified.

On display terminals, a full screen editor is presently considered to be a most efficient tool, substantially reducitng the editing workload of the user. X-Edit which was also developed at IBM T. J. Watson Research Center seems to be a powerful tool. Other examples are TSO/SPF, CMS/SPF, and APL Full Screen Editors.

By the way, technique to define screen formats have evolved from macro (SCL-like) definition to interactive definition with prompting and fill-in-the blank technique. (cf. fig. 12)

The commands and command procedures are difficult for untrained people because they have to learn the keywords and syntax, not to mention the system functions and control information items to be specified. Much of this is not directly related to the problems they want to solve.

The languages used as OS interface have evolved as explained above. The modes of communication have also changed. At first, operators and programmers had mostly one way or delayed two-way communication--batched card feed-in and some printed feedback at the end of job. Then, with a console typewriter, the operator began to receive from the system some messages, to which he can take action. With the use of an interactive system, the operator can now confirm what he is putting into the system is syntactically valid and whether the requirements and conditions given by him are acceptable to the system. More recently, the system has grown "intelligent" enough to urge the user by "prompting" him for what to do next and to help him by explaining the meanings of words, syntaxes, procedures, etc.

With various dialogue procedures utilizing display screen, it is possible to develop an application development system which allows the user to specify data base definitions, to do interactive coding with incorporation of existing commonly used blocks of code, to create data bases and job streams, and to execute the object programs. (cf. fig. 12)

The application programmers want to have friendly interfaces with the operating system, since the execution of his program depends heavily on the services and control of the OS supervisor. Soon after computer programmers came into existence, they learned to develop and share common subroutines for I/O operations, utility functions, etc. These functions were combined into the IOCS (input-output control system) which was called by the user via IOCS macros. Then, with development of IBM's OS/360, the user program used SVC call macro statements to request services provided by the operating system. However, now, with heavier maintenance workload, even assembler programmers avoid the use of low-level types of interface. They prefer to use higher-level macros (of subsystems such as VSAM and VTAM). In order to use DBMS packages, the programmer uses an even higher level type of interface -- e.g. simple DL/I calls in case of IMS/VS. Successful attempts have already been made to bring the interface much higher -- much closer to the user. Namely, in case of generator-type software, just a set of parameters, rules, entries into tables and the like are interface information from application developers. (cf. fig. 13)

By the way, APL has taken different approaches for a programmer to communicate with someone outside his workspace. He utilizes "shared variables: and "auxiliary processors" to talk with other APL workspaces (concurrently running) as well as Operting System Subsystems.

6. An Ideal OS Interface (with emphasis on end users)

The ideal interface (cf. fig.14 and 15) to such an operating system should be something like the following:

The physical media will be a low-cost, compact and portable display terminal with the capability of supporting multiple partitions, and windows. It will be equiped with colour and graphic features. Its international version will have multi-language support. A full-screen text editor, will be a must, but more pictures and graphs will be utilized for easier representation of information than strings of characters.

For novice users, menus and "fill-in-the blank" formats will be used to specify what he wishes to do. It will have "Help" and "Explain" function depending on the need, and, in addition, provide examples for easier and faster understanding.

Particularly for end users, it will provide "user friendly", self-teaching dialogues. And, to eliminate the need for specifying many items, default features, both system-defined and user-defined, will be extensively used. Also, depending on the level of a user, the amount and level of information to be shown on the screen will be changed.

For the professional experienced programmer, it will give the conventional procedural languages, command procedures and editing capabilities.

Error detection, automatic correction and retry, and diagnostic aids will be incorporated. Greater convenience for testing will be provided.

It is desirable that the same, common formats be used for all subsystems, although the contents, languages and types of information may be different depending on types of users, types of applications, and phases of development. Customization approaches will be implemented for tailoring to specific needs.

Increasingly important are human factors which are essential to make the OS interface an easy-to-use, efficient one to far more users, if not everyone.

If we can tell what kind of an operating system and what interface we want, then we may be able to specify functional requirements to its designers.

First, the OS interface should be standardized across subsystems, with proper integration with key software components to allow the programmer, operator and end user to have convenient access to any modules, functions, data files on any of computer facilities. These are all to achieve a single system image. Just as a hand-calculator of any make can be used by anyone, the computer system should be made accessible by anyone with no knowledge of its internal mechanism.

On the other hand, flexibility which varies depending on types of users should be provided. A user can choose either a procedural language or non-procedural language. These should be a number of standard options which are treated as default so that the user need not specify many options. Unless the user is highly experienced and sophisticated, as much complexity and difficulty as possible should be hidden under the cover.

To attract users, especially untrained people, the system should support their own languages, colour and graphics. User friendliness is a very important attribute of the interface.

5. A Future Operating System (with emphasis on end users)

More and more emphasis is currently placed on the direct use of computer-resources by the end users. A question most frequently asked is what will be a future operating system, which is much more oriented to the end users. Assuming that end users have little training in DP and occasionally use the computer, the operating system should be able to meet the following needs.

Firstly, to show the end user what functions, ready-made packages, tools and aids, and data are available and to guide him in the selection and usage of the proper tools are essential functions.

Once the user has decided to use a particular set of tools, the system should prompt the user to provide the definitions of the application following a particular syntax or a set of rules and to enter the data to be processed in proper formats. If the user is in trouble, the system sould offer help by displaying on the terminal textual and pictorial explanations.

If the user wishes to develop new modules or functions to be commonly shared by multiple users or in some of his programs, the system should also show how to develop them, prompt, and help in the actual development and testing of these tasks.

It should provide the data base into which new modules, functions and packages are stored. Also, required is the system directory which tells what data, modules, functions, and packages are stored, who has developd them, who has used or are using them, which data are used by what programs and by which persons, etc. This directory should be a central repository of definitions of data resources used in the enterprise and may be by its nature used for change management.

Also, accounting information is required. The system should save use of resources for possible charge back, performance tailoring and vendor servicing.

Lastly, security management will become even more important in such an "open" and powerful system.

7. Problem Areas and Requirements

The problem areas which I see in the design and use of the OS interface
are the diversity and proliferation of languages and formats now in use
and to be developed; trade-off of 'ease of use' vs processing speed and
cost to achieve these in term of CPU and memory cost and software development efforts; sharability of common data and programs; their integ-
rity, security and maintenability.

Also, important is the definition of "ease of use". Unless desired
"ease of use" is clearly described, the developer cannot design the
system acceptable to the end users.

It is hoped that these problems will be solved as computer technology, human factors studies and most importantly users' experience and
feedback will enable further advancement.

I look forward to the day when the new OS interface described above
become a reality and ordinary people can use the computer system more
easily and effectively.

8. Acknowledgement

The author wishes to thank Mr. T. Sugawara of LSSC, IBM Japan for his technical review of all the charts and some useful comments, Mr. J. D. Waugh of IBM World Trade Americans/Far East Corp. for his review of the draft and valuable suggestions, and Mr. A. Suzuki of Product Line Management, IBM Japan who provided a few charts attached to this paper.

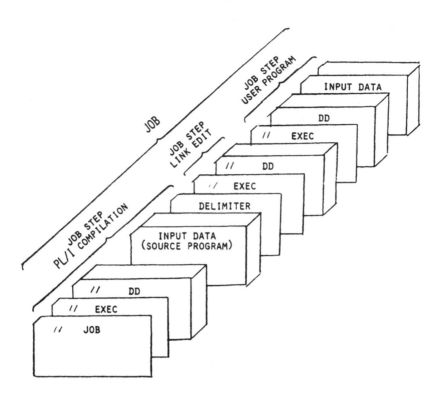

Fig. 5   JCL required for a job with several steps

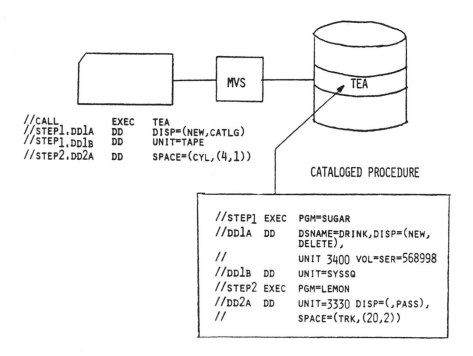

```
//CALL       EXEC   TEA
//STEP1.DD1A DD     DISP=(NEW,CATLG)
//STEP1.DD1B DD     UNIT=TAPE
//STEP2.DD2A DD     SPACE=(CYL,(4,1))
```

CATALOGED PROCEDURE

```
//STEP1 EXEC  PGM=SUGAR
//DD1A  DD    DSNAME=DRINK,DISP=(NEW,
              DELETE),
//            UNIT 3400 VOL=SER=568998
//DD1B  DD    UNIT=SYSSQ
//STEP2 EXEC  PGM=LEMON
//DD2A  DD    UNIT=3330 DISP=(,PASS),
//            SPACE=(TRK,(20,2))
```

Fig. 6   Cataloged procedure

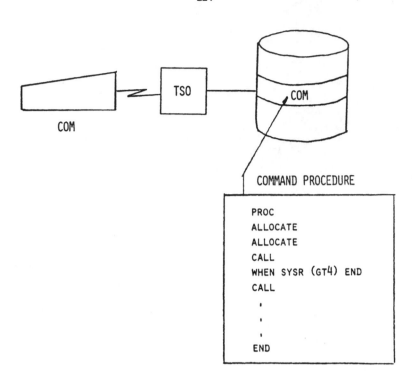

Fig. 7   TSO command procedure

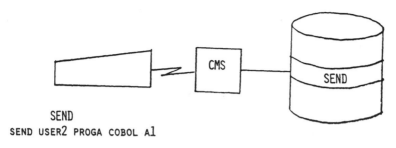

SEND

SEND USER2 PROGA COBOL A1

EXEC PROCEDURE

```
CP SPOOL 00D TO &1
PUNCH &2 &3 &4
CP MSG &1 FILE IS &2 &3 &4
CP SPOOL 00D OFF
& EXIT
```

```
CP SPOOL 00D TO USER2
PUNCH PROGA COBOL A1
CP MSG USER2 FILE IS PROGA COBOL A1
CP SPOOL 00D OFF
```

Fig. 8   CMS EXEC procedure

```
                    ELIAS-I PRIMARY MENU
                                              ELI¥KO

   オコナイタイ コウモク ヲ エランデ クダサイ。
   ----------------------------------------------------------------
   1. SYSTEM              ELIAS-I データ・ベース ノ テイギ
      ADMINISTRATION      ト ファイル ノ テイギ ヲ オコナイ マス。ˎ

   2. APPLICATION         ELIAS-I プログラム ト
      PROGRAMMING         マップ ヲ サクセイ シマス。

   3. JOB PREPARATION     ICCF ヲ ツウジテ バッチ ニ オクル
                          ジョブ ヲ ジュンビ シマス。

   4. SYSTEM SETUP        ELIAS-I システム ノ ショウリャク ジ
                          ノ アタイ ヲ テイギ シマス。
   ----------------------------------------------------------------
   ==>

     EXPLAIN  RETURN  ICCF  INITIAL
```

Fig. 9   ELIAS-1 procedure (prompter)

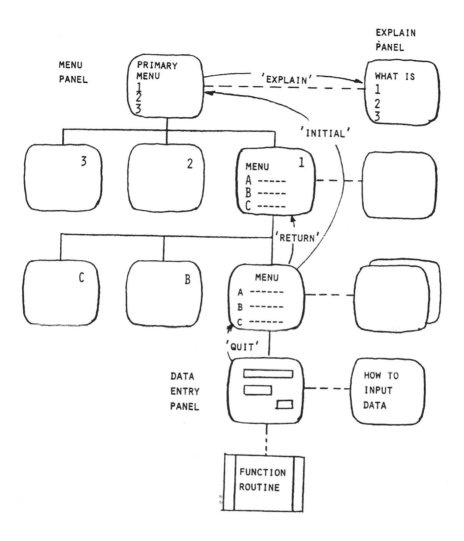

Fig. 10   Hierarchy of menu panel

APPLICATION
SCREEN

X   FILE BROWSE

        NUMBER   NAME   AMOUNT

        XXXXX   XXXXXXXXXXXXXXXXXXX   XXXXXXX
        XXXXX   XXXXXXXXXXXXXXXXXXX   XXXXXXX
        XXXXX   XXXXXXXXXXXXXXXXXXX   XXXXXXX
        XXXXX   XXXXXXXXXXXXXXXXXXX   XXXXXXX

        PRESS PF1 OR TYPE F TO PAGE FORWARD

        PRESS PF2 OR TYPE B TO PAGE BACKWARD

SCREEN
DEFINITION
FACILITY

W/ SDF/CICS
INTERACTIVE DEFINITION

1.3 --- FIELD DEFINITION ---- MAPSETC SDFHAMC 3270-1

==> TEST_

LINES 1 12 ----- C(#) V(¬) G(%) S(/) ----- COLS 1 40

¬,1
                         #FILE BROWSE

#NUMBER   #NAME   #AMOUNT

¬,6   ¬,20   ¬,8
¬,6   ¬,20   ¬,8
¬,6   ¬,20   ¬,8
¬,6   ¬,20   ¬,8

#PRESS PF1 OR TYPE F TO PAGE FORWARD

#PRESS PF2 OR TYPE B TO PAGE BACKWARD

W/O SDF/CICS
MACRO DEFINITION

```
MAPSETC DFHMSD TYPE=&SYSPARM, MODE=INOUT, CTRL=(FREEKB,FRSET),  *
        LANG=ASM, TIOAPFX=YES
SDFHAMC DFHMDI SIZE=(12,40)
DIR     DFHMDF POS=(1,1),LENGTH=1,ATTRB=IC
        DFHMDF POS=(1,3),LENGTH=1
        DFHMDF POST=(1,15),LENGTH=11,INITIAL='FILE BROWSE'
        DFHMDF POS=(3,1),LENGTH=6,INITIAL='NUMBER'
        DFHMDF POS=(3,17),LENGTH=4,INITIAL='NAME'
        DFHMDF POS=(3,32),LENGTH=6,INITIAL='AMOUNT'
NUMBER1 DFHMDF POS=(4,1),LENGTH=6
NAME1   DFHMDF POS=(4,9),LENGTH=20
AMOUNT1 DFHMDF POS=(4,30),LENGTH=8
NUMBER2 DFHMDF POS=(5,1),LENGTH=20
NAME2   DFHMDF POS=(5,9),LENGTH=20
AMOUNT2 DFHMDF POS=(5,3),LENGTH=8
NUMBER3 DFHMDF POS=(6,1),LENGTH=6
NAME3   DFHMDF POS=(6,9),LFNGTH=20
AMOUNT3 DFHMDF POS=(6,30),LENGTH=8
NUMB.R4 DFHMDF POS=(7,1),LENGTH=6
NAME4   DFHMDF POS=(7,9),LENGTH=20
AMOUNT4 DFHMDF POS=(7,30),LENGTH=8
MSG1    DFHMDF POS=(11,1),LENGTH=39,                            *
        INITIAL='PRESS PF1 OR TYPE F TO PAGE FORWARD'
MSG2    DFHMDF POS=(12,1),LENGTH=39                             *
        INITIAL='PRESS PF2 OR TYPE B TO PAGE BACKWARD'
        DFHMSD TYPE=FINAL
        END
```

Fig. 11 Example of software support for screen formating

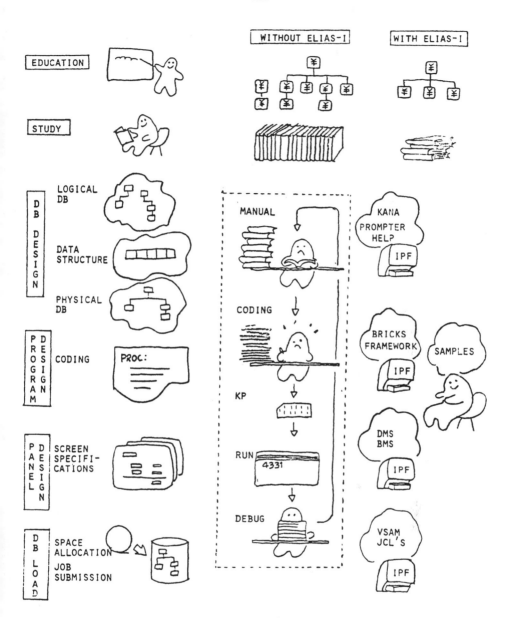

Fig. 12   DB/DC implementation using ELIAS-1

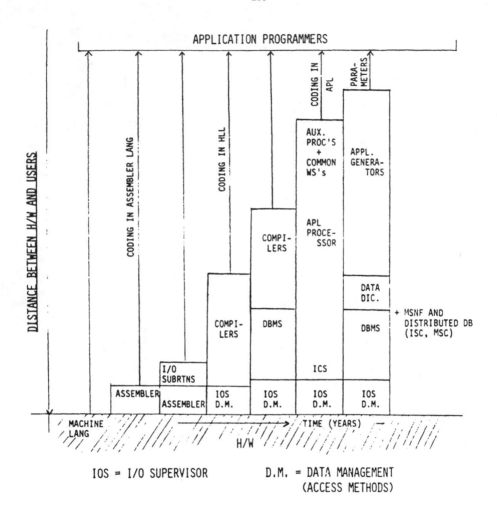

DISTANCE BETWEEN H/W AND USERS

APPLICATION PROGRAMMERS

IOS = I/O SUPERVISOR   D.M. = DATA MANAGEMENT
                                    (ACCESS METHODS)

Fig. 13   Advancement of programmer's interface to computer system

231

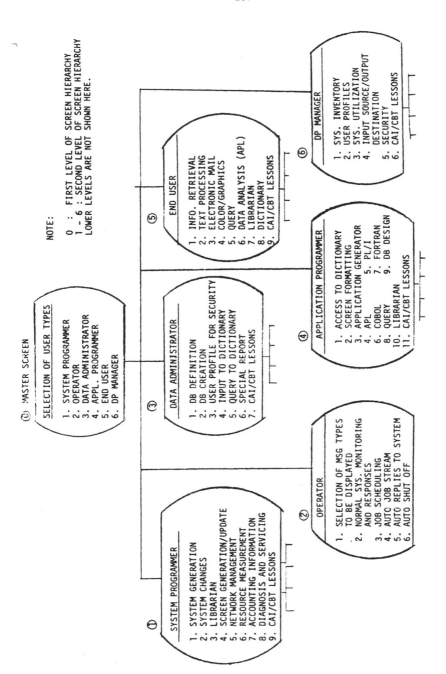

Fig. 14   Screens for ideal OS interface to users

232

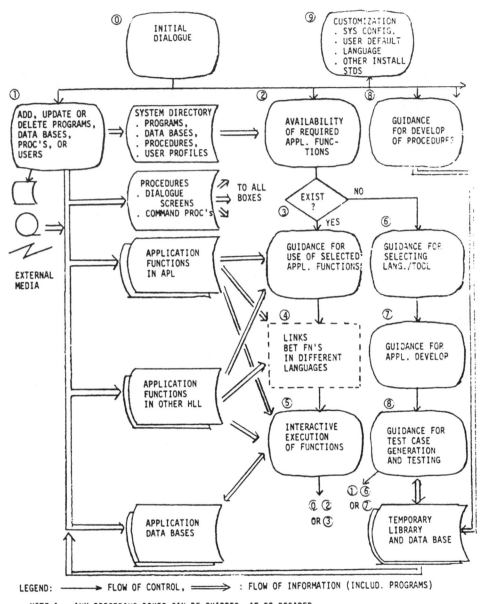

LEGEND: ———→ FLOW OF CONTROL, ===⇒ : FLOW OF INFORMATION (INCLUD. PROGRAMS)

NOTE 1. ANY PROCEDING BOXES CAN BE SKIPPED, IF SO DESIRED
NOTE 2. COMMAND LANGUAGE IN STEAD OF MENU AND FILL-IN-THE-BLANK CAN BE CHOSEN BY EXPERIENCED PROGRAMMERS

Fig. 15   Ideal OS interface to application programmers and end users

INTELLIGENT CONSOLE

A UNIVERSAL USER INTERFACE OF A COMPUTER SYSTEM

Itsujiro Arita

Faculty of Engineering,
Kyushu University
Fukuoka, Japan

ABSTRACT

The intelligent console (INC) is a microcomputer inserted between a computer and its opetator console. Although INC is simple, it offers a very flexible user interface of a computer system. Usually, a user interface of a computer system is pre-specified by its operating system. So, if we want somewhat non-standard usage of a computer system, such as remote access to a batch opetating system, we must provide new hardware and software. It is very difficult for a user to implement such a system, because it requires the users to improve or modify the operating system. Using INC, we can easily add a new function to the computer system, without modification of its operating system.

In this paper, we discuss the concept of INC and some of its applications. Although INC is a supplementary method to extend an operating system, it is very useful when we want a new function on a ready-made opetating system. This seems to suggest a method to construct user extensible operating systems.

1. INTRODUCTION

The functions of a computer system are determined by its operating system. If we want a new function or facility, we must extend or modify the operating system. Some operating systems for large computers are extensible by appending a new control module as a sub-monitor. But, most of operating systems for medium or small computers do not have such a means, so we must modify the operating system directly.

To make or to modify the control module of an operating system is very difficult, or almost impossible for computer users because of the following reasons:

(1) A recent operating system is so large and complicated that users can hardly understand all over it.

(2) Users cannot get precise information (internal specifications) of the operating system.

(3) Most of control modules must be written in an assembly language, but usually users are unskillful at programming in assembly languages.

(4) Debugging or testing of a control modules is very troublesom. Users have not effective tools for debugging control modules.

(5) Maintenance becomes difficult by adding or exchanging control modules.

This situation is the same for the computer manufacturers. When we require somewhat non-standard usage of the computer system, such as the connection of non-standard I/O devices, the remote access to a batch operating system or the interconnection to other computers, our requests are always rejected by computer manufacturers for the reasons of difficulty in software, but in hardware. Indeed, the modification or the reconstruction of operating systems is vert troublesome and undesirable.

A solution of these problems is to construct a operating system on which we can implement a control module as a user job. In such a system, since we can write a control module in high-level programming languages, coding, debugging, and maintenance or improving of the system become very easy for us. A user job must be able to communicate with any control module and the other user jobs in such a system. But, usually an operating system enables user jobs to communicate with only specified control modules.

The user interfaces of operating systems provide, at least, job control languages, system macros and operator commands. The job contro languages and the system macros are provided for programmers, and the operator commands for operators. Usually, user cannot use the operator

commands in his program. But if the system permit him to use the
operator commands in his program, the user job can communicate with the
control modules or other jobs using suitable operator commands. This
indicates that the user program can act as a control program.

In this paper, we discuss a method to extend a user interface of
a computer system, using attached simple hardware, without the modification or the reconstruction of the operating system. Each application
shown here is realized in many operating systems. Since it is impossible for any operating system to cover all needs of various users, the
user extensible feature of the operating system is meaningful,
especially for small operating systems.

2. CONCEPT OF INTELLIGENT CONSOLE

The intellignent console (INC), which is a microcomputer inserted
between a host computer and its operator console, acts as an extended
monitor. Fig.1 shows the hardware configuration of the system, where
CCI is the console interface of the host computer, and SCI, DCI, and
ECI are the system control interface, the device control interface and
the environment control interface respectively.

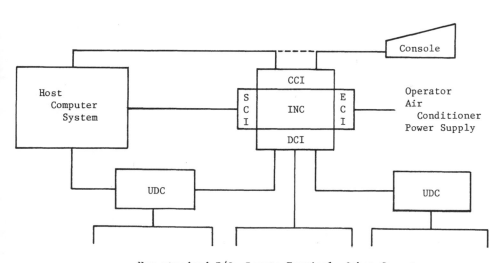

Non-standard I/O, Remote Terminal, Other Computer

Fig.1 Configuration of INC

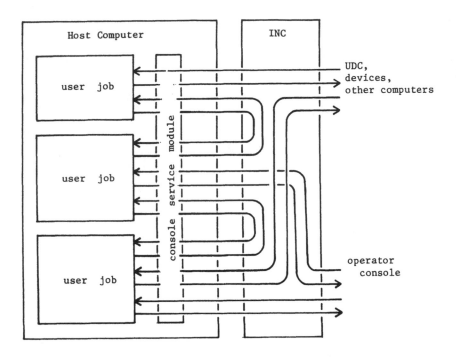

Fig.2 Message paths on INC

SCI, ECI, and DCI are provided if the application needs them. SCI is the interface to the operation panels of CPU and other devices, and is used to read displayed information or to control switches. ECI is the interface to devices or facilities other than computer systems such as air conditioners, power supply or the buzzer for operator call. DCI is for non-standard I/O devices such as cassette MT's, flopy disks, telephone lines and other computers.

The universal device controller (UDC) is also a microcomputer and used for an interface controller when the device interfaces are so complex or so fast as to be controlled by INC. UDC2 in Fig.1 is an example of high-speed data transfer. On the UDC2, only control messages are sent to INC and data are sent to the host computer through another high-speed interface.

Operating systems have console management or conversation service as its elementary function module. This module enables operator to communicate with control modules or user jobs using operator console. The messages from a program are displayed on the console and the messages from an operator are typed in as opetator command for control

modules or operator messages for user jobs. All of these messages pass
through INC. So, by inserting into messages a special code that does
not appear in any system messages, user job can communicate with the
extended monitor in INC. Finding such a special code in a message,
INC regards it as not a console message but the message to extended
monitor in INC. Messages from the extended monitor have the same
format as operator messages do, and are sent to the host computer as if
they were sent from the console. Thus, using the extended monitor,
user programs become capable of such as controling each interface of
INC, issuing operator commands receiving system messages, or communicating with the other user programs. Fig.2 shows realizable communication paths by INC.

There are many applications of INC. The following are examples
of such applications.
(1) System control
    Automatic or remote start-up and shutdown of systems, self run-
    ning with no operators, automatic recovery of system crashes.
(2) Environment control
    Watch and control of air conditioners, operator calls.
(3) Monitoring
    Monitor and control of executing job streams, dynamic dispatching
    of control modules, dynamic allocation of system resources.
(4) Implementation of control modules as a user job.
(5) Control of non-standard I/O devices.
(6) Remote job entry system, interactive system.
(7) Computer complex, computer network.

Although INC is a very simple and flexible user interface of an
operating system, it has following weak points due to using a console
interface and consisting of a microcomputer.
(1) All of the messages must consist of charactors, so binary data
    must be coded in hexadecimal.
(2) The transfer rate of the console interface is usually low, so
    high-speed data transfer by INC is impossible.
(3) The length of data transfered per I/O operation is short, so the
    number of I/O operations increases when large amounts of data are
    transfered.
(4) The capacity of INC is not so large as we can implement many
    functions on INC.
(5) The greatest care is necessary in the security of the system,
    because all operator commands can be accessed in user programs.

In spite of these defects INC is useful for users to readily implement a function, which is not available in a ready-made operating system.

3. SYSTEM CONFIGURATION AND COMMUNICATION PROTOCOL

SYSTEM CONFIGURATION

Fig.3 shows a computer complex and remote accessing system using INC. F-45S is a medium scale computer FACOM 230-45S, used for the purpose of education in the Department of Communication Engineering and Computer Science of Kyushu University, and M-200 is a large scale computer FACOM M-200 in the Computer Center of Kyushu University, for the general use of researchers.

INC1 and INC2 are M6800 microcomputer systems and are connected as a sub-console of each computer. UDC1 is also a M6800 microcomputer and UDC2 is a NEAC-6300 model 50 data terminal. They are distant from F-45S and are used as the device controller of I/O devices. UDC1 can be used as a stand-alone microcomputer system. It has various peripheral devices such as a charactor display with a keyboard, IBM 735 selectric typewriter, a digital cassette MT, an audio cassette MT, an acoustic coupler, a serial printer, a P-ROM writer, and so on. The data transfer rates are 48 Kbps between INC1 and INC2, and 1200 bps between INC1 and UDC's. INC's have some other I/O interface, namely modem interfaces for terminals and parallel ports for special devices.

The aims of this system are as follows:

(1) Remote accessing to F-45S

The operating system of F-45S has the facilities of remote accessing and interactive usage. But we cannot use this feature at all time for lack of primary memory, because they are made so generally that they require large memory space, but our system is not a virtual memory system. So, we want readily to implement such functions on the batch operating system.

(2) Control of non-standard I/O devices on F-45S

To connect non-standard I/O devices to a computer, it is required to convert the I/O interface of the host computer ot the interface of connecting device. It is easily accomplished using a microcomputer. But, if many devices are connected to the same device controller, namely the same I/O channel of the host computer, the operating system regard them one device. Then, while a job is using one of the devices, the other jobs can not use them even if they are free. So we want to allow many jobs to access at a time to different devices connected to the same device controller.

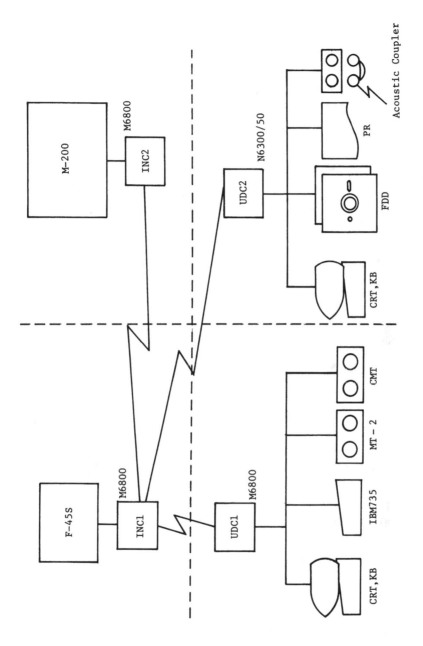

Fig. 3 System Configuration

(3) Usage of files on M-200 from F-45S

Since F-45S has only a small amount of files we want to use a large file system of M-200. We wish to use the files of F-45S as a staging file of the files on M-200.

(4) Remote entry system of M-200

M-200 is a large scale computer. We want to send jobs that are beyond the capacity of F-45S.

BASIC COMMUNICATION PROTOCOL

Most of operating systems have system macros to enable operators to communicate with a user program. In our system, they are WTO(Write To Operator) and WTOR (Write to Operator with Reply). WTO sends a message with sender's job caode to the operator, and WTOR receive a message from the operator after sending a message. A message from a job to INC is sent using WTO if the job need not any answer, and sent using WTOR if the job want to get some answer from INC.

There are various types of messages on INC. They are system messages from control modules, operator messages from jobs to operators, messages from jobs to the extended monitor in INC, reply messages or operator commands from operators, answer messages from extended monitor to the jobs, and operator commands issued by the extended monitor.

Fig.4 shows the format of these messages. ID0 appended by console service, contains the identification code of WTO or WTOR and sender's job code. ID1 is a special string which does not appear in any system messages and usual operator messages from jobs. It shows this message must be processed in INC. FC1 is the function code to INC, and UNO, DNO, FC2 are parameters of FC1. If FC1 is 0, for example, then this message is sent to UDC indicated by UNO, and the operation specified by FC2 is executed on the device shown in DNO. ID2 contains a destination job code, and the console service send this message to the specified job in ID2.

Fig.5 shows the basic communication protocol between a host computer and INC using WTO and WTOR. Since we use WTO and WTOR as basic communication means, the initiative of communication is always on the host computer. Namely, INC cannot send any messages until the program in the host computer issue a WTOR, except the commands for a control module.

Hight-level protocols such as job to job in the same host computer job to extended monitor in INC, job to device handler in UDC, and job to job in different computers, are determined on a case-by-case basis for each application.

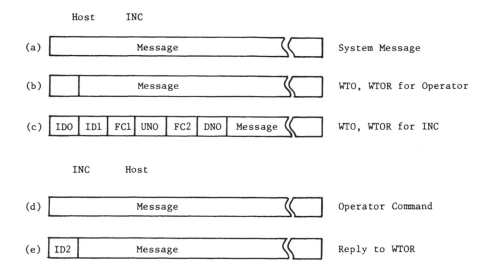

Fig. 4 Message Format

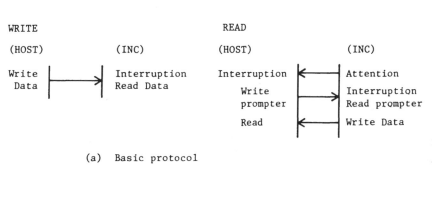

(a) Basic protocol

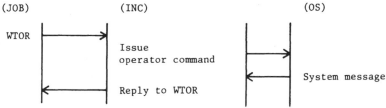

(b) Issuing operator command from job

Fig. 5 Host-INC protocol

STRUCTURE OF SOFTWARE

The application software on our system consist of some programs related to each other. They are library subroutines built in user jobs in the host computer, application programs in INC, application programs in UDC and control jobs in the host computer. Fig.6 shows the relationship among these programs.

Our system is flexible enough to construct application software in various structure. For example, we consider a "proxy system" that watches system messages and issues suitable operator commands if necessary. This system can be constucted of programs in INC. But we can also make this system into two parts, the one in host acting as proxy of operator, and the other in INC only exchanging messages. In the former case, we must implement all of the system using the assembly language of a microcomputer. While in the later, we can use a high level programming language to implement most of the system. Thus we can select the structure of the system according to the requirement of the applications.

4. APPLICATION OF INC

Although INC is a very simple system, there are many interesting applications for INC. In this chaper, some applications are shown briefly. Some of them were implemented on our system. We does not discuss the details of the implementation, because the concrete implementaion is different for each system, but not so difficult.

INTER-JOB COMMUNICATION SYSTEM

The control module or service module of an operating system must be able to communicate with the other control modules or unspecified user jobs. Then, inter-job communication feature is essential to construct control module or service modules as a user job. Conventional operating systems does not permit a job to communicate with the other jobs, because jobs are logically independent each other in such systems. We can easily realize this function on the convertional operationg system using INC.

The desired functions to make control modules as jobs, are the following three.
(1) To receive a message from an unspecified job.
(2) To receive a message from a specified job.
(3) To send a message to a specified job.

Our system consists of IJAM (Inter-Job Access Method) and IJCCP

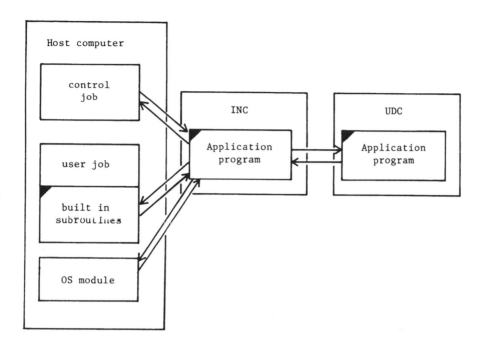

Fig. 6 Structure of application software

Inter-Job Communication Control Program). IJAM contains three sub-
outines, namely RCIVA, RCIV, and SEND corresponding to the functions
entioned above.   They are coded in assembly language and built-in jobs
n the host computer. The calling sequences are as follows:

> CALL   RCIVA(SJID, RVMSG)
>
> CALL   RCIV(WJID, RVMSG)
>
> CALL   SEND(DJID, SDMSG)

here, SJID is a return parameter and yield sender's job code, while
JID and DJID are the job codes of the partners to communicate with.
hese subroutines make the header for INC that contains the information
ɔ IJCCP, and issue WTOR to post the occurrence of a request of IJCCP.

IJCCP, a control program in INC, has next functions.

ynchronization:

For this purpose, IJCCP has RT (Rendezvous table), entries of
hich are the requests to IJCCP. They contain a macro code, a sender's
ɔb code, a partners job code and an arrival time. At each arrival of

the request, IJCCP searches this table and enters it if the partner is not there.

Message transfer:

When the partner is in RT, IJCCP receives the message from its sender and sends it to the receiver. The matched request is removed from RT.

Timer:

IJCCP renovates RT at a constant time interval. The old requests other than RCIVA are removed from RT, and IJCCP posts the time out signal to the corresponding jobs.

We can conctruct a control job or a service job using RCIVA, RCIV, and SEND. The control job waits for the request by RCIVA and post the completion of the serives by SEND. User jobs calls the control job by SEND and wait for the completion by RCIV.

Fig.7 shows the communication protocol between the control job and the user jobs. For this application, INC needs no other interfaces than CCI.

TERMINAL I/O CONTROL SYSTEM

TIOCS (Terminal I/O Control System) enables a user job to use non-standard I/O devices connected to UDC, as if they aere supported by their operating system. TIOCS consists of BDAS (Basic Device Access Subprogram), TIOJC (Terminal I/O Job Control), and TIOCP (Terminal I/O Control Program). BDAS contains subroutines coded in an assembly language. They are built-in jobs in their host computer. They correspond to the entry points of access macros. TIOJC on INC manages the jobs that are using TIOCS. TIOCP consists of DM (Device Management), AM (Access Management), and IOP(I/O Program).

The relationship among these programs is shown Fig.8. BDAS contains the following subroutines.

TOPEN (TN, FNAME, BSIZ, DIRC, CC)
TCLOSE(TN)
READ   (TN, BADR, LNG, CC)
TWRITE(TN, BADR, LNG, CC)
TCONT (TN, CONT, CC)

where, TN, a terminal number consists of a UDC number and a device number. FNAME is a file name for a file device and BSIZ, DIRC are the buffer size and the direction of data transfer respectively. BADR is a buffer address and LNG is the length of data actually transfered. Specified actions for each device such as rewinding MT or line feed for printer, are proceeded by TCONT. These subroutines perform data transfer or device control, communicating with AM in UDC.

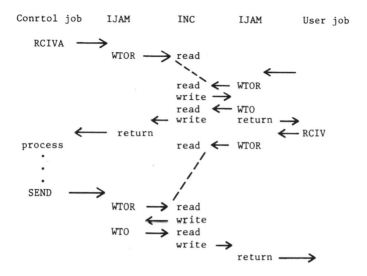

Fig. 7   Inter-job communication protocol

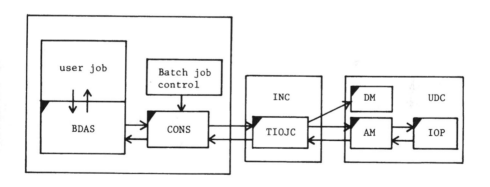

Fig. 8   Configuration of TIOCS

TIOJC has JT (Job Table), the table of jobs that use TIOCS. When TOPEN is called, TIOJC enters the job code in this table. At each arrival of a job end message from the batch job control, TIOJC removes the ending job code from JT if there is, and posts DM the completion of the job to release the occupied devices. DM assigns devices to jobs exclusively by DCT (Device Control Table). The job code is put into DCT by TOPEN and deleted from it by TCLOSE. AM is the executive routines for each macro, and IOP is the device handlers for the I/O devices under UDC.

REMOTE ENTRY SYSTEM FOR F-45S

We can construct RJES (Remote Job Entry System) as an application of TIOCS. RJES consists of RINCON (Remote Input Control), ROUTCON (Remote Output Control), RJC (Remote Job Control), and RBCP (Remote Batch Control Program).

RINCON, an operator job in F-45S is waked up by a "execute job" command from RJC. Using TIOCS, RINCON reads input data from the device specified by RJC, and makes a stack file. Sending parameters such as the name of the stack file, input jobs, and output files, RINCON requests RJC to issue the "job stack" command.

RJC manages remote jobs using RJT (Remote Job Table). Each entry of RJT contains a remote job code, a job status, and an output file name.

ROUTCON, also an operator job in F-45S, is waked up by RJC. Getting the output file name of a remote job and the output device number from RJC, RINCON sends the output file to the sepcified device using TIOCS.

RBCP is a command interpreter on UDC. It accepts remote batch commands from the UDC console and requires RJC to proceed these commands. The remote batch commands are the following three:

INPUT   DNO: Input from device DNO

OUTPUT JID, DNO: Output the results of job JID to device DNO.

STATUS JID: Display the status of job JID to console.

REMOTE FILE ACCESS SYSTEM

Extending the inter-job communication system over multiple hosts, we can construct RFAS (Remote File Access System). Fig.9 shows the configuration of RFAS.

FACP (File Access Control Program), a control job in M-200, is waked up by START command issued from INC2 and proceeds file operations to the data sets on M-200. BFAS (Basic File Access Subprogram) built-in each user job, communicates with FACP and accesses the data sets on

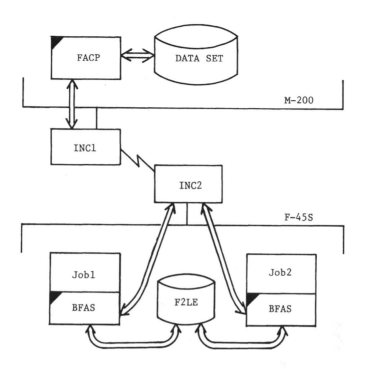

Fig.9 Remote file access system

M-200. RFAS has two modes, namely a redord access mode and a transfer mode. In the record access mode, jobs in F-45S can access to the data sets on M-200 as if they were files on F-45S. On the other hand, in the transfer mode, the jobs in F-45S transfer files from F-45S to M-200 or vice versa, and each access is proceeded on F-45S.

The following subroutines are provided in BFAS for record accesses.

RALLOC(DD, DS, UNIT, DSP1, DSP2, SP1, SP2, REC, CC)

ROPEN(DD, TYP, CC)

RREAD(DD, BUF, BLK, CC)

RWRITE(DD, BUF, BLK, CC)

RCLOSE(DD)

RFREE(DD)

Where, DD: DD name,

DS: Data set name,

UNIT: 'PUB'/'WORK',

DSP1: 'NEW'/"OLD'/...,

```
DSP2: 'CATALOG'/'DELETE"/...,
SP1, SP2: Initial space, increment in track,
REC, BLK: Record size, block size,
TYP: 'INPUT'/'OUTPUT'/'UPDATE',
BUF: Buffer address, and
CC: Completion code.
```

The subroutines for the transfer mode are the following:
RLOAD(AC, DD, CC)
RSTORE(AC, DD, CC)
Where, AC and DD are the access names for the files on F-45S and M-200 respectively.

APPLICATION FOR OPERATION OR USER SERVICE IN COMPUTER CENTER

Self operating system:

Attaching some hardware, a "proxy system" becomes a self operating system. For this purpose, we must prepare the following interfaces on INC.
SCI(System Control Interface)
    CPU: Switches; power on/off, reset, IPL
        Lamp signal; ready, machine check
    DISK: Switches; power on/off, unload
        Lamp signal; ready, lock
ECI(Environment Control Interface)
    Digital watch: Date, time
    Air conditioner: Power on/off switch
    Thermometer: Temperature alarm signal
    Buzzer: Buzzer on/off switch

Remote console:

In a time sharing environment, we can vary any terminals to an operator console using INC. Initiating a special job which communicates with its operating system through INC, a TSS terminal changes into an operator console. It is very dangerous that a terminal user uses this function. But, for the operator or the manager of the computer center, it must be favorable to know the status of the computer system, or to control it in everywhere from the TSS terminal. For this purpose, INC requires only CCI.

Announcing system:

It is favorable for the users of the computer center to know the circumstance of job processing. Especially, on batch or open batch

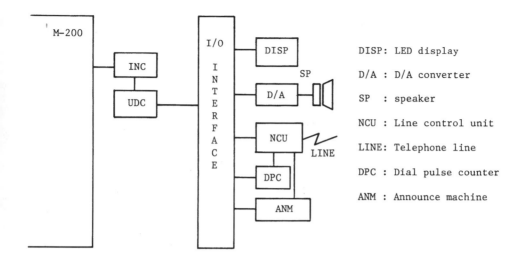

Fig. 10   Announcing system in computer center

opetation, users always maind turnarround time or the completion of
their jobs.   It is the same in the time sharing environment, when users
submit   their jobs to background batch operating system.   The system
shown Fig.10 is an announcing and inquiry system for a computer center.
     The function of this system are the following:
     (1) Display and announcement of ended jobs
     The batch job control sends an ending message to the operator
console.   Being checked by INC, this message is sent to UDC to be
displayed or announced.   UDC converts the job code to a sequence of
phonemes that are previously provided, and sends it to a D/A converter.
     (2) Notice of job completion by telephone
     The users, who want to know the completion of their jobs, provides
another job step in their job.   In this job step, the completion sign
of his job and his telephone number are sent to INC using WTO.   Receiving this message from INC, UDC controls NCU to call the user, and sent
the message "Your job is over now." by an announcing machin.
     (3) Inquiry from telephone
     Users can ask for turnarround times, the status of their job and
other information concerned with the computer center, through this
system.   To know the sorts of inquiry, a dial pulse counter is provided.
The user indicates his request by dialing the number assigned to his

request. If the request is related to the computer system, UDC issues
a suitable operator command through INC, and gets the answer from the
computer. The answer for the user is selected out of the messages in
the announcing machine.

5. CONCLUSION

The concept of INC and some of its applications are described.
INC is very simple but it offers very flexible user interfaces, both
on software and hardware. Of cource, this is an easy and supplementary
method to extend an operating system. But, this is the realization of
an extensible operating system at user job level. Indeed, the application systems shown here, can be implemented mostly as user jobs, with
no extra information other than the user manuals.

INC suggests a desirable function of a user extensible operating
system. If an operating system has a communication means like INC,
the systems discussed here are also realizable as user jobs.

More essentially, the elementary operation for synchronization and
communication between processes, must be implemented on message level.
Then a job can easily communicate with any control modules and the
other jobs.

REFERENCES

Brinch Hansen P. (1970). The Nucleus of a Multiprogramming System.
Comm. ACM, Vol. 13, No. 4, April 1970.

Arita I. et al. (1972) The Development of an Alarm System of the
Computer. KOHO, Kyushu University Computer Center, Vol. 5, No. 3, 1972.

Carrol H. (1974). OS Data Processing with Review of OS/VS. Wiley, 1974.

Arita I. (1979). Intelligent Console and its few Applications. Techn.
Reports of Kyushu University, Vol. 52, No. 3, June 1979.

Part V.

Distributed Operating Systems

Due to the recent development of hardware technology, distributed systems suitable for high-speed parallel processing appear now more economically and technically viable. The following topics, however, require more research for further development of such systems; (1) distributed synchronization mechanisms, (2) reliability mechanisms and (3) system configurations with a large number of processors. The first paper by M. Tsukamoto is concerned with the topics (1) and (2). A general and flexible concurrency control facility called Guarding Processes is proposed, which is designed to specify communication and synchronization mechanisms as well as to detect control faults. The second paper by Y. Takahashi discusses the topic (3). The binary tree structure is selected since its average path length is shortest among those of all organizations in which the number of connections is equal to or less than the number of processors. The binary tree system CORAL and its operating system CORALOS are discussed. In addition, the implementation of the system and an example of application are given.

Structuring Distributed Programs with Control Fault Detection[*]

Michiharu TSUKAMOTO

Electrotechnical Laboratory
1-1-4 Umezono, Sakura-mura, Niihari-gun
Ibaraki 305, JAPAN

ABSTRACT

This paper introduces a language concept, guarding processes, as a method of structuring concurrent programs in distributed computing systems without a common memory. In the concept a program consists of modules each of which defines objects and servers with multi-processes The concept is based on two types of path expression. One type is used to achieve synchronization, mutual exclusion, and autonomous resource access in the module. The other type is used to specify interactions and to detect impermissible sequences of communication between modules. The paper gives some examples of this new concept and demonstrates its potential.

INDEX TERMS: communication, concurrent programming, control fault detection, distributed computation, distributed programming, error detection, master and slave, module, mutual-checking, object, path expression, reliable software.

---

*) This paper is a revised version of the paper presented at the 14th IBM Computer Science Symposium; Working Conference on Operating Systems Engineering held in Amagi, Japan, 1980.

1. INTRODUCTION

Recent advances in hardware technology have made it economically feasible to construct distributed computing systems (DCS) where nodes are connected by local networks. DCS is attractive for real-time application, distributed office automation, and for a distributed database. The reasons are reduced contention, high speed of access, its potential for better reliability and high availability, and its natural extensibility to accomodate changing needs [Liskov (1979)]. However there are some technical difficulties in developing the potential of DCS [Liskov (1981)]. The reasons are as follows:

- Many distributed functions must be coordinated.
- Systems must be highly reliable and available.
- Systems must fit their purpose.

Significant milestones have recently been reached in overcoming the first problem. Hoare [Hoare (1978)] has introduced a set of language primitives called communicating sequential processes (CSP). Brinch Hansen [Brinch Hansen (1978)] has also proposed a concept named distributed processes (DP), a developed version of monitor. Many approaches to the second and the third problems have been proposed and implemented. But they have been ad hoc, and none have been greatly significant [Kim (1979)].

In this paper, we will introduce a new programming concept, guarding processes, for writing high quality distributed programs in a structured manner. The concept allows the software components to detect control faults, that is, to detect impermissible sequences of communications.

The idea was used in developing PPSC, a prototype DCS composed of four nodes [Nagata (1979)], and in constructing a distributed robot system [Tsukamoto (1981)].

2. REAL-TIME DISTRIBUTED PROGRAMMING

DCS has great potential for distributed office automation, a distributed database, and especially for distributed real-time

applications. There are important reasons why DCS is attractive for
real-time application [Jensen (1978)]:

- In real-time systems the exchange of information between the
  computer and the environment should be performed at fixed intervals
  or in time. The requirements are satisfied by increasing the
  number of available computers (nodes).
- DCS is potentially more reliable than a centralized system, as DCS
  is more redundant and is able to prevent propagation of errors.
- Since individual nodes are simpler than centralized systems, user
  application systems are easily developed and maintained for each
  node.

Handling the real-time DCS in a more formal and unified manner is
necessary to develop such potential. From that point of view,
scheduling, resource allocation, and DCS planning are studied [Matelan
(1976)]. On the other hand, more practical approaches are also
necessary.

One of the approaches is to develop a programming language for
real-time DCS. It is desirable to construct a program using a
universal programming language so that the user need not be conscious
of many nodes or their distribution. Programming for DCS is called as
distributed programming and the programming language for such purpose
is called as a distributed programming language. Some distributed
programming languages have been proposed [Hoare (1978), Brinch Hansen
(1978), Feldman (1979), Liskov (1979), Mao (1980)]. However, some of
them seem to be inadequate for real-time applications.

What features should be included in the distributed programming for
real-time applications?

- A modular unit called a *module* is needed that can be used to model
  the task and can be used as the smallest unit. This means that the
  module is indivisible and encapsulates internal information from
  its environmnets. Inside information cannot be directly obtained
  or modified from the outside.
- Modules make interactions with each other via communications. The
  transfer of information between nodes introduces variable delays.
  However, each node must do its mission in time and must therefore,
  be autonomous.

- Some modules or their components may be ready-made, and others are developed and improved through the life time of the DCS. They should be integrated with the total system with consistency.

3. STRUCTURE OF MODULE

Introducing a virtual node in distributed programming is necessary. Concurrent programming was successfully formalized by introducing a process as a virtual processor, and this is the same approach. We call the virtual node a module. It means that a module has some processes as its activities and they share data, and that modules communicate with each other via messages.

3.1 MODULE

A module consists of objects, servers, and an initializer. The object contains data and operations to be accessed in the module. The server is a description of a sequential program and its instances are refered to as processes. The initializer sets up objects and initiates processes. Thus the form of the module is:

```
MODULE <module id>
  <const declarations>
  <type declarations>
  <object definitions>
  <server definitions>
  <initializer>
```

where the initializer has the form:

```
DO <statement list> END
```

The process is initiated by the initializer or a process which may belong to any module, and performs its work according to the program of the server. During the computation, the population of processes will vary. A module exists until its initializer and all of its processes terminate.

In the module processes share objects and communicate with each other via the objects. On the other hand, the process and its initiating process communicate via messages. The names of servers and their interfaces called ports are visible across the modules. One module can reside in only one node, and a node can be occupied by one or more modules.

In general, the cost of inter-module communication is higher than that of intra-module communication. This characteristic is naturally reflected in language constructs. A module may resides in any node unless it is concerned with the specialities of the node such as special hardware. The problem of placing modules at appropriate nodes is not dealt with in this paper. The reason why we separate a module into objects and servers is discussed in the following sections.

3.2 OBJECT

If shared variables and resources are accessed at any place in a module, the accesses are so tangled that understanding the program is difficult and the program is prone to error. Moreover, treating the program formally is difficult as well as being able to confine and recover the errors. Thus we introduce objects in which to confine the shared variables and resources as follows:

```
OBJECT <object id>
   <const    declarations>
   <type     declarations>
   <var      definitions>
   <counter  definitions>
   <path     expression>
   <proc     definitions>
   <initializer>
```

The objects include variables and exist as far as the module exists. They are accessed and modified directly by processes only through the procedures of the object in the module. Device handlers are also programmed as procedures of the objects. Mutual exclusion, concurrent execution, and synchronization among processes are controlled by counters and paths [Andler (1979)]. This is described in the next section. Nothing except the procedure which appears in the path expression is visible from the outside. The initializer sets up the object when the module is loaded.

3.3 SERVER

A server defines the scenario of computations or accesses to the
objects of the same module. The form is:

```
SERVER <server id> (<in vars> # <out vars>)
   <const   declarations>
   <type    declarations>
   <var     definitions>
   <port    definitions>
   <proc    definitions>
   DO <statement list> END
```

When the server that is visible from the outside of the module is to
be defined, '*SERVER' is used instead of 'SERVER'. In that case, its
ports are also visible from the outside.

In this form, <statement list> is a body of the server, and it is
executed by processes, namely instances of the server.

Any process can make an instance of the server by a WITH statement:

```
WITH <module id>.<server id> (<exprs> # <vars>)
     : <statement list> END
```

When the process reaches this statement, it sends the values of
<exprs> to the server <server id> of the module <module id> and waits
until it succeeds in initiation. On the other hand, the received
server creates a process including ports as an instance of the server,
and initiates the process to execute its body.   When the initiating
(initiator) process and the initiated (service) process reach the end
of the WITH statement and the body of server respectively, the values
of <out vars> are replied to the initiator process and are bound to
<vars> and the initiator continues its processing. Then the service
process disappears.   The initiator and the service process
communicate through the ports according to each <statement list>.

We should keep in mind that the process is instantiated including its
ports and that the ports correspond to the process, not to the server.
In other word, ports are shared by the initiator process and the
service process, and not by other processes (Fig. 1).

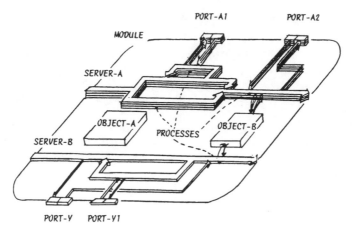

Fig. 1   Architectural Overview of Module

4.   COMMUNICATION AND SYNCHRONIZATION

A module consists of objects, servers, and an initializer.   But its
activities are processes.   In order to do missions by many processes
they must communicate and be synchronized with each other.   When the
communication and synchronization method is designed for real-time
applications, we have to pay attentions to the followings:

- Processes must work autonomously as far as possible, unlike
  monitor, DP, and CSP.
- Run time costs must be cheap.
- Programming must be easy.

This section describes communication and synchronization via shared
objects in a module and communication via ports between modules.

4.1   INTRA-MODULE COMMUNICATION AND SYNCHRONIZATION

In order to specify intra-module synchronization, we use path
expressions [Campbell (1974)].   The path expression defines the
allowable sequence of operations on the corresponding object in terms
of a regular expression.   The operators in the path expression are
selection(|), sequencing(;), and repetition(*).   In the pure path
expression the executions of all operations are mutually exclusive and
it lacks programmability [Lauer (1975)].

As all operations are mutually excluded, large programs with shared variables are difficult to define as operations for real-time applications. Such a case often occurs when the programs are coded in conventional languages. Lack of programmability is also fatal because real-time programs need fine controllability.

Such difficulties are overcome by introducing a parallel operator(,), a concurrent operator(#) and predicates [Andler (1979)]. Predicate path expressions allow the use of predicates associated with the name of the procedures. The name of the procedures may be followed by predicates enclosed with square brackets ([,]). For example:

PATH (a;(b[p]|(c;d)*)

means that 'a' must be followed by execution of 'b' if predicate 'p' is true, or by repetition of 'c' and 'd'. If 'b' is able to be executed concurrently by many processes, the above expression is defined as follows:

PATH (a;(b[p]#|(c;d)*))

Suppose that the number of pending procedure requests, active procedure invocations, and completed procedure invocations are denoted by #f, f, and f# respectively for a given procedure f. Using this notation, a counter is defined by the following linear expression:

COUNTER c= Σ $a_i*\#p_i$+ Σ b_i*p_i+ Σ $c_i*p_i\#$+d

where a_i, b_i, c_i, and d are integer constants.

The predicate is an expression of the relationship of the counters connected by the boolean operators 'not', 'and', and 'or'. The predicate path expression is easy to implement and manipulate formaly. An external interrupt can also be specified by these counters as described in section 6.

.2 INTER-MODULE COMMUNICATION

It is necessary to invent inter-module communication primitives that do not tangle the communication links or the programs. At first, in order to avoid tangled links, it may be necessary to restrict the structure of the links.

We will adopt communication primitives of Ada [Ichbiah (1979)] as a candidate, namely, entry call, accept statement, and select statement for multiple requests. Nevertheless, in Ada one process (called a task) must handle the requests from a number of processes. Therefore, the servicing process should be programmed to search the requests frequently in order to achieve fast responses. Thus the program becomes unnecessarily complicated. So we extend the Ada scheme from one service process to many. In addition, we restrict each process to serve only one calling process. Hence, there is a one to one correspondence between service processes and calling processes. The calling process has to make an instance of the server defined in another module with the WITH statement before it starts communications. Instantiation may be carried out with the parameters stated above.

After instantiation, the calling process can send requests to and receive answers from the service process by calling the port as follows:

    <module id>.<server id>.<port id> (<vars> # <exprs>)

On the other hand, the called process receives the requests by ACCEPT statements.

    ACCEPT
        <port1> : <statement list> {THEN <statement list>} ELSE
        ....
        <portN> : <statement list> {THEN <statement list>} END

The service process waits until one of the ports receives the request. The received requests are reconstructed and bound to formal parameters. Then the corresponding <statement list> is executed. When the process finds THEN or ELSE in the list, the values of variables specified in the port are sent back to the caller via the port. The ACCEPT statements can be nested when they are used between THEN and ELSE in the list.

In this scheme the service process devotes its service to its initiator. The program of the service process describes its relationship with the initiator.

Regarding the data type of messages, communicating modules may reside in different nodes, and therefore, messages cannot be addresses or pointers. Instead of an address or a pointer, tokens, namely symbols corresponding to the address, may be transmitted. When messages are of a complex type, for example, arrays or records, it is necessary for the sending nodes to decompose the messages and for the receiving nodes to reconstruct them.

5. DETECTION OF CONTROL FAULTS

A large system is usually designed and implemented by many people, and may be improved and extended during its life time. In these situations modules are liable to be misused, e.g. they may encounter invalid parameters and impermissible interractive sequences. Illegal parameters may be detected by checking the inconsistency of their types by a compiler. Nevetheless, impermissible interactive sequences which may be induced not only by defects of a program but also by unexpected failures, are hard to detect. Erroneous states may cause an impermissible sequence of control in the long run. Such errors are called *control faults* [Kane (1975)].

In our scheme it is possible to detect impermissible sequences as follows: A service process is instantiated by the initiator using a WITH statement, and requests received via ports are restricted from its initiator by the definition of section 3.3. Therefore, when the service process receives the request from any processes other than the initiator, the situation is erroneous. Furthermore, if the request received from the initiator is not included in the port list of the ACCEPT statement which are issued in the locus of the service process, the situation is also erroneous.

In Fig. 2, a process MASTER of a module M1 makes an instance of a server SLAVE of a module M2, and it sends requests P, Q, and R to the service process in a sequence. On the other hand, the service process can accept requests in a sequence of P, Q, S or P, R, S. Thus the service process finds that the request R is impermissible by the ACCEPT statement of S.

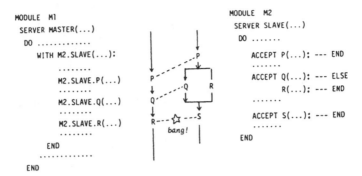

Fig. 2   Concept of Control Fault Detection

The more frequently processes communicate, the more they can detect
impermissible sequences. This scheme can also be applied to
conventional sequential programs. We term this scheme *guarding
processes*, because the scheme detects the misuse of objects and guards
against such misuse.

6. EXAMPLES

To give a concrete image of how the concepts are used in programming,
we present here some examples of the construction of a remote terminal
control module. In addition, a concurrent version of the sieve of
Eratosthenes and a file transfer protocol are presented.

A. BOUNDED BUFFER

The first is a producer/consumer problem with a finite buffer [Andler
(1979)]. The messages are produced by 'put' and consumed by 'get'.
If the initial number of available slots is 'n', the object 'buffer'
is defined as follows:

```
OBJECT   buffer;
  VAR      buf: ARRAY [0..n] OF message;
           inx,outx: INTEGER;
  COUNTER msgs = put#-#get;
           slots = n-put+get#;
  PATH     (put[slots>0]*,get[msgs>0]*);
  PROC     put(msg:message);
    DO       buf(inx):=msg; inx:=(inx+1) MOD n END;
  PROC     get(# msg:message);
    DO       msg:=buf(outx); outx:=(outx+1) MOD n END;
  DO       inx:=0; outx:=0 END
```

The predicates specify that 'put' and 'get' are delayed until any slot
and any message are available respectively.

B. INPUT AND OUTPUT WITH INTERRUPT

This example shows that input and output operations with interrupt are
programmed in the form of objects and the operations are synchronized
by path expressions.

```
OBJECT    keyboard;
 COUNTER  intreq = interrupt#-acknowledge#;
 PATH     (acknowledge[intreq>0]|inchar)*;
 PROC     Interrupt; INTERRUPT(n);
 PROC     acknowledge; DO clear_interrupt END;
 PROC     inchar (#ch:CHAR); DO ch:=input_from_device END;
 DO       END;

OBJECT    display;
 COUNTER  intreq = interrupt#-acknowledge#;
 PATH     (outchar|acknowledge[intreq>0])*;
 PROC     interrupt; INTERRUPT(n);
 PROC     acknowledge; DO clear_interrupt END;
 PROC     outchar (ch:CHAR); DO output_to_device END;
 DO       END;
```

'INTERRUPT' is defined in the kernel and the kernel inclements
counters '#interrupt', 'interrupt', and 'interrupt#' when the
interrupt is occured through the vector specified in the argument.

C. INPUT AND OUTPUT PROCESS

The objects consist of data and codes, but not of activities.   The
following examples define the scenarios for activities to manipulate
objects.   The server 'keyboard_server' reads characters from the
keyboard and puts them into the input buffer while the server
'display_server' gets characters from the output buffer and prints
them on the display through the above objects.

```
SERVER keyboard_server;
 VAR   ch:CHAR;
 DO    WHILE TRUE: keyboard.inchar(#ch);
                   keyboard.acknowledge;
                   inbuffer.put(ch) END END;

SERVER display_server;
 VAR   ch:CHAR;
 DO    WHILE TRUE: outbuffer.get(#ch);
                   display.outchar(ch);
                   display.acknowledge END END;
```

This scheme is adequate for real-time applications, because each process is devoted to reading or printing and it is not blocked in buffering.

D. SERVER

This example is a server for communicating with external modules. It can accept 'get' or 'put' until 'end'.

```
SERVER server;
  VAR    continue:BOOLEAN;
  PORT   get(#ch:CHAR);
         put(ch:CHAR);
         end;
  DO     continue:=TRUE;
         WHILE continue:
           ACCEPT get(#ch):  inbuffer.get(#ch) ELSE
                  put(ch):   outbuffer.put(ch) ELSE
                  end:       continue:=FALSE END END
```

E. TERMINAL MODULE

By collecting the above examples into a module, it becomes an aimed module. 'Server' and its ports are visible from the outside. The initializer initiates 'keyboard_server' and 'display_server' to be devoted to their missions.

```
MODULE   terminal;
  OBJECT inbuffer;         ... {the same as example A}
  OBJECT outbuffer;        ... {the same as example A}
  OBJECT keyboard;         ... {the same as example B}
  OBJECT display;          ... {the same as example B}
  SERVER keyboard_server;  ... {the same as example C}
  SERVER display_server;   ... {the same as example C}
 *SERVER server;           ... {the same as example D}
  DO     WITH terminal_server: WITH display_server: END END END
```

F. THE SIEVE OF ERATOSTHENES

This example is more complicated than above examples, and shows the following points:

- A lot of instances are generated from the same server and how they disappear.
- Communication between service processes are structured by ACCEPT statements.

The example is a concurrent version of the sieve of Eratosthenes [Hoare (1978)] to print all primes less than the number given from the terminal. When an instance of 'sieve' is generated with a prime 'p', it prints the number and checks whether the numbers received from its initiator are multiples of 'p' until it accepts 'end'. If the number is not a multiple and the process does not initiate its service process, it initiates another service process with the number. Whenever the number is not a multiple and the process has already initiated the service process, it sends the number to the service process. On the other hand, the initializer generates the numbers in ascending order and sends them to its service process. When the number reaches the limit, the initializer sends 'end'. And then the service processes disappear in the reverse order.

```
MODULE prime;
  VAR     limit,i:INTEGER;
  SERVER  sieve(p:INTEGER);
  VAR     continue:BOOLEAN;
  PORT    next(n:integer);
          end;
  DO      continue:=TRUE;
          WITH terminal.server.putnumber(p): END;
          WHILE continue:
           ACCEPT next(n:INTEGER): THEN
                      IF (n MOD p)<>0:
                         WITH sieve(n):
                          WHILE counter.continue:
                           ACCEPT next(n:INTEGER): THEN
                                      IF (n MOD p)<>0:
                                         sieve.next(n) END ELSE
                                  end: continue:=FALSE;
                                         sieve.end END END END END ELSE
                      end: continue:=FALSE END END END;
  DO      WITH terminal.server:
          terminal.server.putstring("Key in the limit of primes");
          terminal.server.getnumber(# limit);
          terminal.server.putnumber(1);
          WITH sieve(2):
           i:=2;
           WHILE i<=limit: sieve.next(i);
                           i:=i+1 END;
          sieve.end END END
```

3. FILE TRANSFER PROTOCOL

The last example is a file transfer protocol (FTP) of the computer network T-NET. It shows how our scheme is used for structuring communication and detecting its impermissible sequences.

The permissible commands sequence of FTP is defined in Fig. 3 and

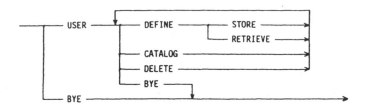

Fig. 3 Permissible Sequence of Commands

explained in natural language by Kawai [Kawai (1981)]. The following
skeleton program is coded according to it. For simplicity we do not
define modules, objects, and servers as data types, therefore modules
and servers are programmed for each node, i.e. 'src' and 'dst'. The
ftp consists of a 'server' and many 'requester' corresponding to each
node. When the user wants to transfer files across the nodes, the
user initiates the 'requester' and sends request commands to it.   The
requester accepts the commands from the user according to the locus of
control. So, user's commands are checked by the requester whether
each request is included in each alternative of ACCEPT statement. If
the command is honored, the command is transfered to 'server' of the
destination module. On the other hand, the 'server' also accepts the
request from the 'requester' and checks it similarly.

```
MODULE   src_ftp;
 OBJECT control_link; ... ;
 SERVER dst_requester;
  DO     control_link.open;
         WITH dst_ftp:
          dst_ftp.server.open(# ack:code); ... ;
          ACCEPT
           user(userid,password:TEXT # ack:code):
            dst_ftp.server.define(filetype # ack): ... THEN
            ACCEPT
             define(filetype:ftype # ack:code):
              dst_ftp.server.define(filetype # ack); ... THEN
              ACCEPT
                store(srcfid,dstfid:fid # ack:code):
                 dstftp.server.store(srcfid,dstfid # ack); ... ELSE
                retrieve(srcfid,dstfid:fid # ack:code):
                 dstftp.server.retrieve(srcfid,dstfid # ack); ... END
                                                       ... ELSE
             catalog(# ack:code,cat:TEXT):
               dst_ftp.server.catalog(#ack,cat); ... ELSE
             delete(filename:fid # ack:code):
               dst_ftp.server.delete(filename # ack); ... ELSE
             bye: dst-ftp.server.bye(# ack:code); ... END ELSE
           bye: dst_ftp.server.bye(#ack:code); ... END;
          dst_ftp.server.close(# ack:code); ... END;
       control_link.close END;
```

```
SERVER server;
  DO    control_link.open;
          ACCEPT open(# ack:code): ... END;
          ACCEPT
            user(userid,password:TEXT # ack:code): ... THEN
              ACCEPT
                define(filetype:ftype # ack:code): ... THEN
                  ACCEPT
                    store(srcfid, dstfid:fid # ack:code): ... ELSE
                    retrieve(srcfid, dstfid:fid # ack:code): ... END ELSE
                  catalog(# ack:code,cat:TEXT): ... ELSE
                  delete(filename:fid # ack:code): ... ELSE
                  bye: ... END ELSE
              bye: ... END;
          ACCEPT close(# ack:code): ... END;
          control_link.close END
```

7. CONCLUSION

We have proposed Gaurding Processes as a general and flexible
distributed programming concept. We have implemented the concept by
introducing modules which consist of servers and objects with path
expressions by introducing the initiator-server model, and by
proposing the rule that the initiator process and the service process
correspond on a one-to-one basis and the service process serves only
the initiator process. This simple rule allows us to obtain a
powerful mechanism by which complex problems are specified easily and
in a structured manner. Furthermore it allows us to detect control
faults between processes.

The scheme uses the path expression in two ways. In one way, it uses
the expression to specify the synchronization and the mutual exclusion
of processes with respect to the object. This is the so-called *object
oriented* interpretation of the path expression. In the other way, it
uses the expression to detect impermissible sequences of requests.
This is *subject oriented* interpretation of the path expression.

The first version of Guarding Processes has been implemented for the
PPSC computing system [Nagata (1979)], and has been used to realize a
multiple robots system. In this case, a delay-statement is included
in the ACCEPT statement as Ada. In this paper we have avoided
discussion of the problem of error recovery, but it is discussed by
Tsukamoto [Tsukamoto (1981)].

ACKNOWLEDGEMENTS

This research has been encouraged by Dr. K. Sato, the manager of Automatic Control Division of ETL, Dr. T. Nagata, former chief of Information and Control Section of ETL, and Dr. M. Kakikura, the chief of Information and Control Section of ETL. The author is grateful to the members of the PPSC project who have provided the PPSC system to apply the ideas.

REFERENCES

Andler, S. (1979). Predicate Path Expression: A High-Level Synchronization Mechanism. CMU-CS-79-134, Depart. of Comput. Science Carnegie-Mellon Univ.

Brinch Hansen, P. (1978). Distributed Processes: A Concurrent Programming Concept. Comm. ACM, Vol 21, No. 11, pp 934-941.

Campbell, R.H. and Habermann, A.N. (1974). The specification of Process Synchronization by Path Expressions. LNCS, Vol 16, pp 89-102.

Feldman, J.A. (1979). High Level Programming for Distributed Computing. Comm. ACM, Vol 22, No 6, pp 353-368.

Hoare C.A.R. (1978). Communicating Sequential Processes. Comm. ACM, Vol 21, No 8, pp 666-677.

Ichbiah J.D. et al. (1979). Preliminary ADA Reference Manual. ACM SIGPLAN Notices, Vol 14, No 6, Part A.

Jensen, E.D. (1978). The Honeywell Experimental Distributed Processor -- An overview. IEEE Computer, Vol 11, No 1, pp 28-39.

Kane J.R., and Yau S.S. (1975). Concurrent Software Fault Detection. Trans. on Software Engineering, Vol SE-1, No 1, pp 87-99.

Kawai, H. (1981). High-Level Protocols in Heterogeneous Computer Networks. Res. of ETL, No 817, Electrotechnical Lab.

Kim K.H. (1979). Error Detection, Reconfiguration and Recovery in Distributed Processing Systems. Proc. IEEE Distributed Computing Systems, Huntsville, pp 271-295.

Lauer, P.E. and Campbell, R.H. (1975). Formal Semantics for a Class of High-Level Primitives for Coordinating Concurrent Processes. Acta Informatica, Vol 5, pp 297-332.

Liskov, V. (1979). Primitives for Distributed Computing. Proc. 7th Symp. on OS Principles, pp 33-42.

Liskov, V. (1981). Reports on the Workshop on Fundamental Issues in Distributed Computing. ACM SIGOPS, Vol 15, No 3, pp 9-38.

Mao T.W., and Yeh R.T. (1980). Communication Port: A Language Concept for Concurrent Programming. IEEE Trans. on Software Engineering, Vol SE-6, No 2, pp 194-204.

Matelan, M.N. (1976) A Model for Real Time Control System Production. ACM SIGDA, Vol 6, No 2, pp 14-61.

Nagata T. et al. (1979). An Outline of Poly Prosessor System for Control (PPSC). Bull. of ETL, Vol 43, No 4, pp 208-212.

Tsukamoto M. (1981). Language Structures and Management Method in a Distributed Real-Time Environment. Proc. 3rd IFAC Workshop on DCCS, Beijing.

A DISTRIBUTED OPERATING SYSTEM FOR
A BINARY TREE MULTIPROCESSOR

Yoshizo Takahashi

Department of Information Science
Faculty of Engineering
Tokushima University
Minami Jyosanjima-cho, Tokushima 770
Japan

ABSTRACT

In a massively parallel processing system consisting of hundreds
or thousands of processors, the shared data system is unfeasible and
the distributed data system seems more promising.   Among other architectures the binary tree structure is considered most excellent.   Some
characteristics of the binary tree multiprocessor, which is named CORAL
are discussed.   An operating system for CORAL is designed and named
CORALOS.   CORALOS is a distributed operating system which has an intensively hierarchical structure.   The elementary functions of the operating system are distributed to the groups of OS modules, each one of whi
consists of a master module and as many slave modules as the processors
Although the slave modules operate independent of each other, they have
to respond to the requests delivered from their master module and also
report to it when any unusual conditions ocurr.   Among the groups of
OS modules, the packet handler takes a key role interprocessor communic
tions.   Distribution and broadcasting of data are supported by a maste
packet handler and slave packet handlers.   The job program is decompos
and distributed to the processors and is executed as job processes.   As
an example of the operation of the system, parallel solution of partial
differential equation in one dimensional heat conduction problem is illustrated.

1. INTRODUCTION

A binary tree multiprocessor, which we name CORAL, has an architecture well adapted to the massively parallel processing systems in which hundreds or thousands of processors are interconnected. This paper first reviews the architecture of CORAL [Takahashi(1980)], then presents the results of the preliminary design of a distributed operating system for CORAL. The operating system is tentatively called CORALOS.

In Chapter 2, the architecture of binary tree multiprocessor is introduced and its characteristics are described in comparison with those of other possible distributed data systems. In Chapter 3, the design objectives of CORALOS are discussed. Chapter 4 describes the hierarchical structure of CORALOS. In Chapter 5, methods of the interprocessor communications in CORALOS are discussed. Chapter 6 defines functions and structures of the OS modules. In Chapter 7 the behavior of job processes is described. Chapter 8 gives the concluding remarks.

2. BINARY TREE MULTIPROCESSOR:CORAL

After having studied various architectures of distributed data parallel processing systems, the author has concluded that the binary tree architecture is one of the most promising systems for implementation of a massively parallel processing system [Takahashi(1980)]. To date the binary tree architecture has been adopted in several computer systems in different ways[Lipovski(1970),Davis(1978),Harris(1979)]. The binary tree multiprocessor CORAL is shown in Fig.1

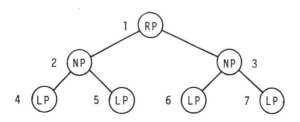

Fig.1 Binary Tree Multiprocessor CORAL of Level 2

The characteristics of the binary tree architecture, including data distribution time, data broadcasting time, average path length, and over all speed-up ratio, are shown in Table 1 with those of other architectures. In Fig.2 and in Fig.3 are shown the speed-up ratios and the average path lengths obtained from the formulae in Table 1. The advantage of the binary tree architecture is clearly observable from these diagrams.

Table 1. Characteristics of Various Architectures

Architecture	Distribution Time	Broadcasting Time	Average Path Length	Speed-Up Ratio
Star	d	nd	2	$\dfrac{n_0+1}{n_0+n}n$
Chain	$(2n-1)\dfrac{d}{n}$	nd	$\dfrac{n+1}{3}$	$\dfrac{n_0+1}{n_0+2n}n$
Loop	d	$nd/2$	$\dfrac{n+1}{4}$	$\dfrac{n_0+1}{n_0+n}n$
Lattice	$2(1+\dfrac{1}{k})m$	$(k+m)d$	$\dfrac{k+m}{3}$	$\dfrac{n_0+1}{n_0+2n}n$
Binary Tree	d	$2[\log_2(n+2)-1]d$	$\dfrac{(L-2)2^{2L+2}+(L+4)2^{L+1}}{(2^{L+1}-1)(2^L-1)}$	$\dfrac{n_0+1}{n_0+n}n$

where d: time to pass a data to next processor
      n: number of processors
      k: number of rows of lattice
      m: number of columns of lattice
      L: number of levels of balanced tree
     n_0: ratio of distribution time to processing time per data

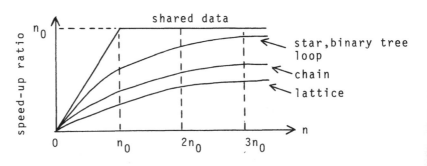

Fig.2 Speed-Up Ratios

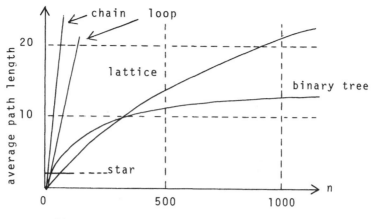

Fig.3 Average Path Lengths

Referring Fig.1 we now define several terms. The processor at the root of the tree is called a <u>root processor</u> and is denoted by RP. The processor at each node is called a <u>node processor</u> and is denoted by NP. The one at each leaf is called a <u>leaf processor</u> denoted by LP.

The processors have their own addresses which are integers. The address of RP is 1 and those of other processors are as indicated in Fig.1. There is a relation that the address of the left son of a processor of address i is 2i and that of the right son is 2i+1.

A node processor is connected to its parent and to the left and right sons through paths called top, left, and right paths respectively. We also define the direction of the interprocessor communications by T, L and R corresponding to the top, left and right paths. We also define S direction which represents the path to its own processor. They are indicated in Fig.4.

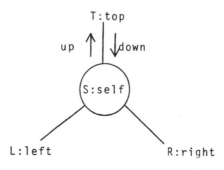

Fig.4 Paths and Directions

The features of the CORAL are as follow.

(1) The structure is recursive so that it is feasible to construct a massively parallel processing system.

(2) The structure of the element processor is simple, as it has only three ports for interprocessor connections.

(3) It is a distributed data system instead of a shared data system and does not require a shared storage.

(4) The data distribution time is small.

(5) The data broadcasting time is small.

(6) The average path length, that is the average distance between any two processors, is short especially when the number of processors is large.

(7) Hiearchical structure is imbedded, so that the grouping of process-ors is easily implemented.

(8) The processing power of the element processor is rather small.

(9) The size of the storage of the element processor is small.

(10) The cost of the element processor is low.

The parallel processing of a job in CORAL is performed with a pro-cessor called a <u>job control processor</u> and a group of processors called the <u>working processors</u>. The job control processor distributes program and data to the working processors. These programs are identical in code while the data are different from processor to processor. The working processors execute this program with the given data. They ex-change intermediate results among themselves during the execution. Whe the execution is completed, they send back the calculated results to th job control processor.

In order to prove the feasibility of the binary tree architecture in the parallel processing system, a prototype of CORAL shown in Fig.5 is being developed at Tokushima University. It is a two levels binary tree multiprocessor with SORD M223 Mark II microcomputer as RP and six sigle-board microcomputers as NP and LP.

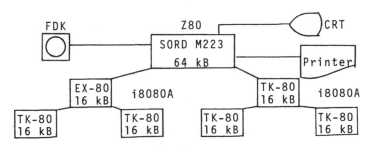

Fig.5 CORAL Prototype

3. A DISTRIBUTED OPERATING SYSTEM: CORALOS

The preliminary design of an operating system for CORAL is finished and is being implemented on CORAL prototype. The operating system is tentatively called CORALOS. The design objectives of CORALOS are:
(1) The function of the operating system is divided into many modules which fit the small storage and small cpu power of the element processor.
(2) Communication overheads between OS modules may be as small as possible.
(3) Taking advantage of the binary tree architecture.
(4) Covering some drawbacks of CORAL architecture if any.

The functions implemented in CORALOS are as follow.
Interprocessor communication
Process management
Job management
Resource management
I/O management
File management
Access control
Data distribution and collection
Mutual exclusion
Command processing
Error recovery

These macro functions of the operating systems are decomposed into elementary functions which are implemented in each one of the OS modules. These OS modules are distributed to the processors and operate concurrently. While the concurrent operation of OS modules increases the throughput, the increased interprocessor communications tend to decrease t. There may be an optimum number of OS modules to achieve high thruughput.

In the course of the designing CORALOS, the author is greatly influenced from the existing distributed operating systems as StarOS [Jones 1978)], Medusa [Outerhout(1980)], and NETWORK (Brich Hansen(1978)]. He is grateful to the authors of these operating systems.

4. STRUCTURE OF CORALOS

CORALOS is a set of OS modules which are distributed to the elemen processors of CORAL. The job is also divided into many job processes which are executed by different working processors. The job processes have an identical object code which processes individual data. Each job process is executed in different processor. In some processors a job process and OS modules are executed, while in other processor only OS modules are executed. The former processors are called the working processors denoted by WP, and the latter ones are called the control proce-sors denoted by CP. The control processor which distributes program and data is called the job control processor. Although there may be more than one control processors, it is always possible to unite them to be one master control processor. The root processor may best be used as the master control processor. In other cases, RP and the NPs around RP are used as control processors.

The OS modules are divided into several groups. The members of a group are executed in different processors. Each one of the groups executes roughly one macro fuction of the operaitng system. In one group of the OS modules, there is one master module and as many slave modules as the processors. The master module operates in CP and the slave modules operate in WPs. The slave modules operate independent of each other and communicate with the job process and with other slave modules of different groups. The slave module also communicates with slave modules of the same group that operate in the processors directly connected to the current one. The master module can always send commands to the slave modules and controls their operation. The slave modules report to their master whenever an abnormal condition is encoun tered. Thus the slave module has a firm loyalty to the master as well as a limited freedom. Fig.6 illustrates the relation between the mast and the slave modules.

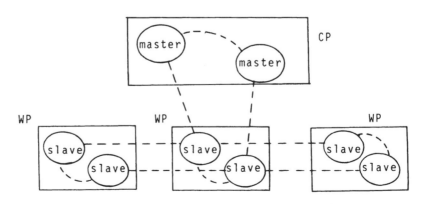

Fig.6 Master and Slave OS Modules

The OS module groups of CORALOS and their functions are as follow.

(a) Kernel

The kernel group handles interrupts and schedules processes.

(b) Packet Handler

The messages are transmitted between processors in packets.   The
packet handler group supports the routing of the packets.

(c) Job Scheduler

The job scheduler group distributes job processes and parameters
to the working processors.

(d) SYSIN

The SYSIN group handles input from the system input device connected to the input control processor and sends the input data to the
processor which requested.

(e) SYSOUT

The SYSOUT group handles output to the system output device which
is connected to the output control processor.

(f) File System

The file system group handles requests to access files on DASD
which is connected to the file control processor.

(g) Command Processor

The command processor group reads commands from the system console
connected to the system control processor and sends informations to
other OS modules.   It also writes system messages on the system console.

5.INTERPROCESSOR COMMUNICATIONS

5. INTERPROCESSOR COMMUNICATIONS

In a processor there exists at most one job process and several OS
modules.   The communications among these processes are carried
out by exchanging the messages.   When the processes residing in different processors communicate, the messages are divided and enclosed in
packets which are transmitted between the processors.   The processor
which exists on the path of the communication routes the packets to
others.

A packet is composed of a preamble and a text.   The informations
contained in the preamble are as follow.

```
Text size
Destination address
Broadcasting address
Number of packets constructing the message
Packet sequence number
Category
Other informations
```

The text size may not exceed 256 bytes. The destination address
is the processor address, mentioned in Chapter 2, of the processor to
which the packet is delivered. The broadcasting address indicates a
group of processors to all of which the packet is delivered. There
are following broadcasting addresses.

(1)   Processors belonging to a branch
(2)   Processors of addresses from N1 to N2
(3)   Processors belonging to a branch and of address from N1
       to N2.
(4)   Processors on the path between two processors

These broadcasting addresses are illustrated in Fig.7

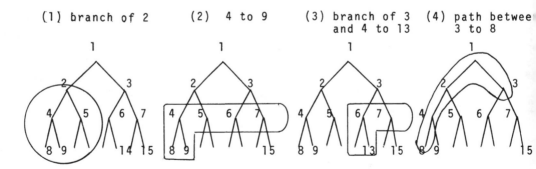

Fig.7 Broadcasting Addresses

The category indicates the kind of informations contained in the
message. By looking at the category one can find the appropriate process to which the message is to be delivered. The categories and the
processes to be delivered are listed in Table 2.

Table 2. Category of Messages

Category	Process to Receive
data	job process
job packet	job scheduler
print data	SYSOUT
read data	SYSIN
write data	command processor
get data	file system
put data	file system
read request	SYSIN
get request	file system

5.2 ROUTING OF PACKETS

When a slave packet handler of a processor receives a packet, it reads the preamble and finds the directions of retransmission according to the following algorithm.

```
begin
    a:=destination_address; s:=own_address;
    left:=s*2; right:=left+1;
    T:=false; L:=false; R:=false; S:=false;
    if a=s then S:=true;
    repeat
        case a of
            left : L:=true;
            right: R:=true
            else : if a < s
                        then T:=true
                        else a:=a div 2;
        end
    until T or L or R or S=true
end.
```

6. DESCRIPTION OF OS MODULE GROUP

6.1 KERNEL

Kernel is a group of OS modules that consist of a master kernel and several slave kernels. The slave kernel handles interrupts that arise within the processor by which it is executed. It also schedules processes being executed in the processor. Whenever an error is detected the slave kernel reports to the master kernel which resides in CP. The source of interrupts differs from processor to processor. For instance the leaf processors have only one connection port and only few processor have I/O devices. The master kernel sends commands to the slave kernel when some processes are to be scheduled or to be stoped.

6.2 JOB SCHEDULER

The job scheduler consists of a master job scheduler and slave job schedulers. The master job scheduler, which is executed in the job control processor, prepares the job packets which contain a job program, and distributes them to the slave job schedulers in the working processors. As each slave job scheduler receives a job packet, it loads the program into the program area and asks the kernel to activate it as a job process. When the job process terminates, the slave job scheduler is notified and reports to the master job scheduler.

6.3 PACKET HANDLER

The packet handler also consists of a master and many slave module The master packet handler prepares informations concerning the configuration of the system and notifies to individual slave packet handler when the configuration is changed. The slave packet handler in each processor performs routing of the packet depending on the informations supplied by the master packet handler.

The packets transmitted between the processors are temporarily stored in the packet buffer. The packet buffer is a pool of buffers each storing one packet. The state of each buffer, which is either free, not_free, full, or empty, is indicated with buffer status word. Buffer pool is a resource which is distributed throughout the processor and managed by the slave packet handlers. When a slave packet handler becomes unable to manage it in such an occasion that no more free buffe is available, it asks to the master packet handler if it can force to

release any buffers.   In this communication a special buffer reserved
in each of the packet handlers is used instead of the buffer pool. Fig.8
illustrates a state in which the buffer pool of a processor P2 becomes
fully occupied and blocks the packet transmission in other directions.
In response to the report from the slave packet handler of P2, the master
packet handler sends order to release all buffers containing the packets
to R direction.   Thus the deadlock is avoided.

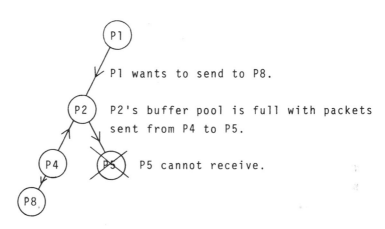

Fig.8 A State of Deadlock

When a slave packet handler is activated, it searches for buffers
which are either full or empty.   When an empty buffer is found the buffer
status word is changed to free.   When a full buffer is found, the preamble of the packet is analyzed to obtain the direction of transmission.
If the direction is S, that is toward its own processor, it further analyzes the category and finds the process to receive the packet which is
waken up.   The category of the message is so determined that the different processes never wait for the same message.

6.4 SYSIN

SYSIN modules consists of a master SYSIN, which resides in th input
control processor, and many slave SYSIN which reside in working processors.   The function of the master SYSIN is to read data from the system
input device and to send them to the processors which requested them.
The slave SYSIN, which has requested to the master, receives the packet
and after assembling the message forwards it to the process which has

requested input.   As the amount of input data is usually large, the
master SYSIN takes care of not sending too many packets successively so
that the routing processors may be blocked with full buffers.   This is
achieved by deliberate cooperation of the master and the slave SYSIN
modules.

6.5 SYSOUT

There are a master and many slave SYSOUT modules.   The master
SYSOUT module resides in the output control processor and the slave SYS_
OUT modules reside in the working processors.   When a process wants to
print data, it activates the slave SYSOUT module which requests the mas
ter module to reserve the system output device.   When granted it sends
data in packet to the master which print them.   The slave SYSOUT sends
request for disconnection to the master SYSOUT after sending the last
packet so that the latter can release the system output device.

6.6 FILE SYSTEM

The master file system resides in the file control proce-sor.   It
receives access requests from the slave file systems residing in other
processors.   When a job process wants to access a file, it activates
slave file system in the same processor.   The slave file system then
requests to master file system and waits until the requested record of
the file arrives.

6.7 COMMAND PROCESSOR

The command processor receives and analyzes the system coomands
inputted from the system console.   The master command processor reside
in the system control processor and the slave command processor in othe
processors.   When the master command processor reads a system command,
it recognizes the command name and finds which OS modules should be not
fied.   It then sends the entire system command to the master module
of the related OS module group.   It is the task of this master module

that analyzes the command and sends orders to its slave modules.   When a process wants to output a message on the system console it activates the slave command processor.

7. JOB PROCESS

As mentioned previously, a job is decomposed into many job processes of identical code.   They are distributed to different processors and activated as the job processes.   To illustrate the behavior of the job process, the parallel solution of a partial differential equation in one-dimensional heat conduction problem with CORALOS is described.

The one-dimensional heat conduction problem is described in the following partial differential equation.

$$\frac{\partial u}{\partial t}(x,t) = c^2 \frac{\partial^2 u}{\partial x^2}(x,t) \qquad (0 \le x \le L) \qquad (1)$$

$$
\begin{aligned}
&u(x,0) = f(x) \\
&u(0,t) = f(0), \quad u(L,t) = f(L)
\end{aligned}
\qquad (2)
$$

By expansion and denoting

$$r = \frac{kc^2}{h^2}, \quad \text{where } h = \frac{L}{M}, \qquad (3)$$

$$u_m^n = u(mh, nk) \qquad (4)$$

the following difference equations are obtained.

$$u_m^{n+1} = r[u_{m-1}^n + (\frac{1}{r} - 2)u_m^n + u_{m+1}^n] \qquad (m=1,\dots,M) \qquad (5)$$

The data flow graph of eq.(5) is as shown in Fig.9.

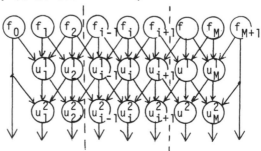

Fig.9 Data Flow Graph

When p working processors are available, each processor computes M/p equations of eq.(5). As the processors computing the adjoining regions have to exchange the boundary variables at every iteration, the strategy of allocating these regions to the processors located as near as possible is required. One such strategy is shown in Fig.10.

Regions

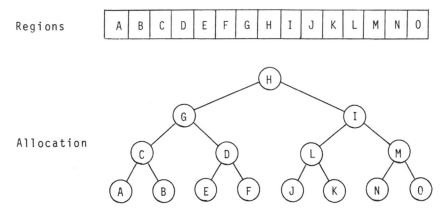

Allocation

Fig.10 Optimum Allocation Strategy

Each slave job process is supplied with the following parameters by the master job process.

leftmost mesh-point no.:	ml
rightmost mesh-point no.:	mr
address of processor allocated to its left region:	Pl
address of processor allocated to its right region:	Pr
number of iterations:	N

One possible program code of slave job process will be as follows.

```
for n:=1 to N do begin
    receive(Pl,u[ml-1]^[n-1]); receive(Pr,u[mr+1]^[n-1]);
    send(Pl,u[ml]^[n-1]); send(Pr,u[mr]^[n-1]);
    for m:=ml to mr do
        u[m]^n:=r*[u[m-1]^[n-1] + (1/r -2)*u[m]^[n-1] + u[m+1]^[n-1]]
end.
```

$$u_m^n := r*[u_{m-1}^{n-1} + (\frac{1}{r} -2)*u_m^{n-1} + u_{m+1}^{n-1}]$$

This program does not work however. All slave job processes wait to receive data forever. The sequence of data exchange must be carefully considered in order to avoid the deadlock. To release programmers from this task, the packet handler is assigned to perform the data exchange without causing a deadlock. The job process needs only to call a procedure exchange which is as follows.

$$exchange(((sendaddress_1,data_1),(sendaddress_2,data_2),...$$
$$(sendaddress_M,data_M)),((receive\ address_1,area_1),$$
$$(receiveaddress_2,area_2),...,(receiveaddress_N,$$
$$area_N)))$$

The operation of the packet handler will be:

> wait until all data are transmitted and all areas are
>   received;
> wake-up job_process.

Thus the job process is waken up when all data exchanges are completed. The slave packet handlers so communicate each other that no deadlock takes place.

8. CONCLUSIONS

Outlines of CORAL system and its operating system CORALOS are described. As CORAL is a loosely coupled multiprocessor, the performance of the operating system may affect the overall performance seriously. The hierarchical structure of the binary tree makes it easy to implement a distributing operating system like CORALOS. Performance of the CORALOS will be measured on the CORAL prototype as soon as it is implemented.

REFERENCES

Brinch Hansen,P.(1978). NETWORK: A Multiprocessor Program. IEEE Trans. on Software Engineering, Vol.SE-4,No.3,May 1978,pp.194-199.

Davis,L.A.(1978). The Architecture and System Method of DDM1: A Recursively Structured Data Driven Machine. Proc. of 5th Annual Symposium on Computer Architecture,1978,pp.210-215.

Harris,J.A.,Smith,D.R.(1979). Simulation Experiments of a Tree Organized Multicomputer. Proc. 6th Annual Symposium on Computer Architecture,1979 pp.83-89.

Jones,A.K.,et al.(1978). Programming Issues Raised by a Multiprocessor. Proc. IEEE,Vol.66,No.2,Feb. 1978,pp.229-237.

Lipovski,D.H.(1970). The Architecture of a Large Assiciative Processor, Proc. SJCC,1970,pp.385-396.

Outerhout,J.K. et al.(1980). Medusa: An Experiment in Distributed Operating System Structure, Comm. ACM, Vol.23,No.2,Feb. 1980,pp.92-105.

Takahashi,Y.,Wakabayashi,N.,Nobutomo,Y.(1980). A Binary Tree Multiprocessor: CORAL, Technical Repaort of IECE of Japan,EC-79-60, Jan.1980, pp.1-8.

Part VI.

Network Operating Systems

A computer network is an efficient way of distributing
computing power by sharing common resources and a way of
improving reliability, availability and serviceability
(RAS) of computing systems. The design of the computer
network entails the construction and validation of standard
protocols through which component systems are connected to
the network. Four papers are included in this part. The
first paper by K. Ikeda, Y. Ebihara, M. Ishizaka, T. Fujima,
T. Nakamura and K. Nakayama gives an introduction to an
large-scale computer network called "GAMMA-NET" which is
being developed at the University of Tsukuba. The paper
presents an overview of the system and discusses the structure of the ring bus system and the network protocols. The
second paper by T. Saito, T. Kato and H. Inose is concerned
with the validation of a node connected to a given computer
network. The protocol implemented in a node is assumed to
be defined in terms of state transition matrices and is
tested based on an automaton model. The authors give a
detailed exposition of the validation procedure. The third
paper by J. Livesey and E. G. Manning proposes a language,
Task Graph Language, for the centralized representation of
distributed control in the Mininet distributed operating
system. This context-free language allows a programmer to
specify the inter-process communication between a suite of
distributed processes in the form of a task graph and to
have the constraints of the task graph enforced at run-time
by cooperating token lists, one at each task. The language
is more powerful than ordinary capability checking because
it allows the specification of sequencing. The forth paper
by M. G. Gouda, E. G. Manning and Y. T. Yu considers the
general problem of communication progress between two
machines. This analysis is useful in characterizing communication progress properties such as boundedness, and freedom
of deadlocks and unspecified receptions.

GAMMA-NET:

COMPUTER NETWORK COUPLED BY 100 MBPS OPTICAL FIBER RING BUS

-SYSTEM PLANNING AND RING BUS SUBSYSTEM DESCRIPTION-

Katsuo IKEDA(*)   Yoshihiko EBIHARA(*)
Michihiro ISHIZAKA(**)   Takao FUJIMA(**)
Tomoo NAKAMURA(*)   Kazuhiko NAKAYAMA(*)

   * University of Tsukuba
     Ibaraki, Japan
  ** Mitsubishi Electric Co.
     Kamakura, Japan

ABSTRACT

Planning and design considerations are presented for a full scale high performance heterogeneous computer network coupled by a 100 MBPS optical fiber ring bus. The design goals of this system are efficient resource sharing and improved RAS. All common resources, such as processors, peripheral devices, terminals and file devices, are directly connected to the ring bus, instead of directly to a processor. This network includes two or more large computers of different types, a guide subsystem to manage common resources and to control their usage, peripheral and terminal control subsystems, and a gateway processor.

1. INTRODUCTION

Much of the progress of computers has been in processing speed and storage capacity. However, as computers become more and more important in society, the quality of processing and the reliability, availability and serviceability (RAS) of computer systems are becoming critical, along with speed and capacity.

Computer utilization by inter-university computer networks is expanding in both volume and distance. A plan to build a nation-wide science information processing system has been proposed. These trends have common aims: To distribute large computing power and to share common resources among a great number of people throughout a large area.

Augmenting the processing power and the storage capacity of a single computing system alone is not an efficient way of coping with the variety of requests. A distributive processing system, however, might meet these requirements efficiently.

Distributive processing improves response time, communication cost, and Ras. It is effective even when the distance between two processors is short. Groshe's law on cost/performance does not apply to very large computers; it is economical to build a computer complex, connecting two or more computer systems, to augment processing power. Distributive processing is superior to a single computer system in RAS, computing power growth potential, and the capability to add new functions. The purpose of this paper is to make a case for the feasibility of constructing a distributive processing system using new LSI technology and optical fiber communication technology. One such full scale distributive processing system is now being developed at the Science Information Processing Center of the University of Tsukuba (SIPC).

LSI technology reduces the size and cost of logical processing units and memory units, and permits the system designer to employ compact function elements. Optical fiber technology provides high speed, low noise figures, and low cost transmission lines.

In view of these circumstances, there is a need for a standard method to build a distributive processing system and standard protocols to connect computing systems.

There are several papers describing standard protocols along with the development of computer network systems; examples include the ARPA networks (Frand 1972) and CYCLADES (Pouzin 1974) over telephone switching or leased lines and the ALOHA network (Abramson 1970) through a communication satellite. Other network protocols have been

or are being developed by computer manufactures and by the Nippon
Telegraph and Telephone Public Corporation (NTT) (IBM, NEC, Inoue 1976
and Toda 1979). All of these examples involve rather slow speed
communication among computers and terminals long distances apart.

This report describes the planning and design of the GAMMA-NET
(General purpose And Multi-Media Annular NETwork) system now
implemented at the SIPC. The system is tightly ocupled by a high-speed
optical fiber ring bus in order to satisfy a large variety of requests
for computing facilities. Section 2 gives a more detailed description
of the motivation for a distributive information processing system,
and explains the demands for computing facilities in the SIPC. Section
3 outlines the configuration of the system. Section 4 describes the
service functions of the network system. Section 5 explains the
structure of the ring bus subsystem and of the network protocol as
well as the plan for the performance measurement of the system.
Section 6 discusses the issues of heterogeneous networks.

2. TICIPS BECOMES A DISTRIBUTIVE SYSTEM

TICIPS (Tsukuba Integrated Campus Information Processing and
Sharing system) has been in service in the SIPC for a large variety of
processing of scientific, educational and administrative data, and has
served also for research and development of the science information
processing system. This has been done by a single large computing
system. We have often experienced bottlenecks in this system because
of local imbalances in processing power, and demands for computing are
becoming more and more complex and diverse.

In order to handle a large variety of requests by a single
large-scale computer, it is necessary to raise its processing capacity
greatly, and this is neither economical nor an effective way to
improve RAS.

Thus, we have decided to build a heterogeneous computer network
to improve the performance of the system. Our design goals are as
follows:

1) Improvement of response time for interactive processing and
   on-line information retrieval.
2) Sharing of hardware, software, and data.
3) Large volume and long time processing capacity.
4) Special processing capability, such as image processing and kanji
   (Japanese writing) processing, with the potential to add, change
   and expand system functions easily.
5) Automated system management and operation.

The implications of sharing hardware and software resources are as
follows:

1) Better utilization of various peripheral devices, remote
   terminals, and file space.
2) Easier conversion between protocols used in our network and
   external network protocols by sharing a gateway processor.
3) Improved RAS.
4) Larger variety of functional capabilities available to the user.
5) Easier system upgrading.

It is helpful to system users if they do not need knowledge about
their individual host processors. This requires the following:

1) Guiding facility for managing resources in the network.
2) Compatibility between different types of computers.

3. SYSTEM CONFIGURATION

Our system includes several functional subsystems (called nodes) connected by an optical fiber ring bus. The design philosophy of the ring bus subsystem is as follows:

1) Connect common resources directly to the bus, and minimize the number of local devices at individual host processors as much as possible.
2) Introduce a guide node to manage system resources and to guide users in system utilization.
3) Improve communication efficiency, by adopting simple protocols.
4) Establish standard protocols to link computer systems and unify protocol conversion between internal and external networks.

Functional subsystems connected to the ring bus subsystem are:

host processors which offer processing power,

a file subsystem,

a resource managing and guiding subsystem,

I/O subsystems which connect and control common I/O devices and on-line terminals,

a gateway processor which connects this system to external computer networks and converts protocols, and

a ring bus supervisor.

Fig. 1 shows the system configuration.

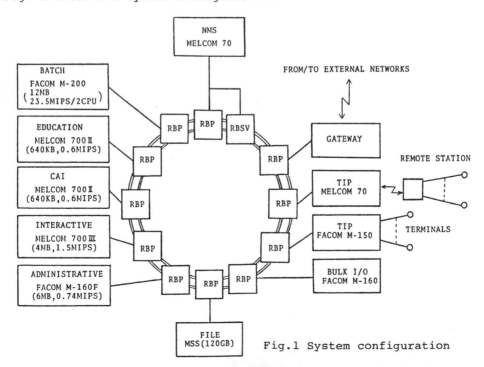

Fig.1 System configuration

3.1 HIGH-SPEED OPTICAL FIBER RING BUS

Each node is connected by a high-speed bus whose transmission
capacity is greater than the maximum direct memory access speed, so
that the transmission line does not become a bottleneck in the network
system.
Transmission lines form a loop in order to reduce the line cost
(Zafilopulo 1974), (Yasuboshi 1978). The ring bus system employs dual
100 MBPS optical fiber lines; these lines are identical, and there is
no separate control line (Dual bus). Transmission channels of each bus
are divided into nine subchannels or frame channels as shown in Fig.2,
one of which is used for transmission control and the rest for data
links (950 KB/S). Channels may be bundled, by combining up to five
subchannels to expand bandwidth, according to the transmission
capacity of the communication host processors (Multi-channel access;
Max 4.8 MB/S). Though one node can send or receive only one message at
a time, an express message can interrupt ongoing communication
(Priority transmission). When part of a line or a node fails, the
defective part is cut off by bypassing the defective node or by
turning back the bus, and the rest of the system can continue
operations.
A node is connected to the ring bus through a ring bus processor
(RBP) in which communication protocols of data link level are
implemented by firmware.

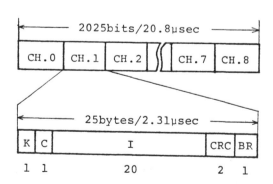

K :	channel access key
C :	command field
I :	information field
CRC :	cyclic redundancy check
BR :	busy/response

Fig. 2 Frame structure

The ring bus system (RBS) is structured by RBP's and a ring bus supervisor (RBSV). RBP's are linked by dual optical fibers via optical repeater (REP) into the ring computer network. Functional subsystems are connected directly to the RBP without a front-end-processor, for the purpose of decreasing data transmission delay. Major portions of the RBP are duplicated in order to guarantee reliable, high performance system operation, and these operate simultaneously under normal conditions. The detailed design of the ring bus subsystem is described in Section 5. Table 1 compares the performance of several ring bus systems.

3.2 HOST PROCESSORS

Our system includes several large computing systems; each is installed as a general purpose system, but is specifically tuned to interactive processing (MELCOM 700III-2CPU, 4 MB, 1.5 MIPS), to interactive programming as a method of instruction (MELCOM 700II, 0.64MB, 0.6MIPS), or to batch processing (FACOM M200-2CPU, 12 MB, 23 MIPS; M160F, 6 MB, 0.74 MIPS), for efficient operation and good response. Host processors are not identical, since a variety of processing capabilities is expected.

Under current policy, system service to the public is closed from time to time in order to insure secrecy of administrative processing. However, if a distributive processing system is realized, this public service will remain available, while confidential jobs are processed by a system which is temporarily cut off from the network.

	UNIV. OF TSUKUBA	OHIO STATE UNIV. (')	PIPS (TOSHIBA) (")
COMMUNICATION LINE	OPTICAL FIBER CABLE 100 MBPS x 2 (32 MBPS - 1980)	UNKNOWN	OPTICAL FIBER CABLE 100 MBPS x 2 (10 MBPS - 1976)
NUMBER OF STATIONS	MAX. 32	UNKNOWN	16 (MAX. 127)
STATION DISTANCE	MAX. 1KM	UNKNOWN	MAX. 300M
TYPE OF NODES	LARGE/MEDIUM-SCALE COMPUTERS	MIDI/MINI/MICRO-COMPUTERS	SPECIAL-PURPOSE INTELLIGENT I/O DEVICES
PURPOSE	CREATION OF MULTI-PURPOSE, MULTIFUNCTIONAL LARGE-SCALE SYSTEM	EFFECTIVE USE OF MIDI/MINI/MICRO-COMPUTERS	INSTALLATION OF VARIOUS SPECIAL-PURPOSE I/O FUNCTIONS INTO NETWORK SYSTEM
PRACTICAL/EXPERIMENTAL	PRACTICAL	EXPERIMENTAL	PRACTICAL

' Liu 1977
" Okuda 1978

TABLE 1 Comparison of ring bus systems

3.3 RESOURCE MANAGING AND GUIDING SUBSYSTEM

Our network aims to be an ultra high-performance computing
system. Thus, an executive subsystem is introduced which selects the
virtual processing host that executes the required processing. This
subsystem guides users, interprets network commands given by users,
reconnects remote terminals, and gives network commands to host
processors.

If we imagine that the processing of this network is executed by
a virtual system, this resource managing subsystem acts as a resource
dispatcher. The root directory of files in this network is also
included in this node. But a "direct link" can be used to process
files in a particular host directly, instead of passing through the
root directory.

When a node is activated or terminates its operation, it notifies
this guide node of its status, and it also transmits its operating
status periodically to the guide node. The guide node also examines
operating status of nodes in the network periodically. Thus, by
maintaining a resource management table, the node performs resource
management and user guidance.

This guide node lies on one of the higher level application
protocols in the hierarchy of the ring bus protocols, instead of being
palced at the nucleus of the system. Thus, the whole system does not
crash when this node fails. This node is one of the important features
of this network.

3.4 FILE SUBSYSTEM

Each functional subsystem holds only the minimum amount of file
space necessary for its operation. The files of network users are, in
general, placed in the space prepared in file subsystems. A mass
storage systen (MSS) whose storage capacity is 102 GB will be included
in a file subsystem. Files can be referred to and from any node using
file access protocols.

3.5 PERIPHERAL AND TERMINAL CONTROL SUBSYSTEM

Efficient sharing and utilization of remote terminals, remote job
entry devices and many other peripheral devices is important. In the
past, each such device has been connected directly to a single host

processor. In our network all of these devices are connected to the
ring bus through a Termical interface Processor (TIP). Telephone lines
are also connected to the ring bus in the same manner. Thus, every
device can be connected to any host, for better utilization of
hardware resources.

3.6 GATEWAY SUBSYSTEM TO CONNECT EXTERNAL COMPUTER NETWORKS

Several inter-university computer networks employing N1 protocols
are being developed in Japan and NTT is developing a data
communication network (DDX). The trend is toward the establishment of
large area information processing networks in tne near future. We wish
to participate in large area resource sharing, connecting our network
system to these external networks.

Our system employs simple, uniform communication protocols.
External protocols need only to be converted to internal ones by a
gateway subsystem, and need not be converted according to the
conventions of each individual system. This scheme would not be
affected by changes to a subsystem. In addition, terminals connected
to the ring bus can be connected directly to external hosts through
this gateway subsystem.

4. NETWORK SERVICE FUNCTIONS

Service functions of this network are as follows:
1) Interactive processing / remote job entry / batch processing / special processing and special input output functions of individual subsystems.
2) Inter-computer communication.
3) Inter-computer file access / file transfer functions.
4) Guide service for resource utilization / load leveling functions.
5) Data collection and management functions for network operation statistics.
6) Supervisory functions for the network.

In order to support these applications, high level protocols are established in the network subsystem. These are:
1) File access protocol.
2) Interprocess communication protocol.

And several application protocols are established utilizing these high level protocols. These include:
1) TSS protocol.
2) RJE protocol.
3) Resource managing protocol.

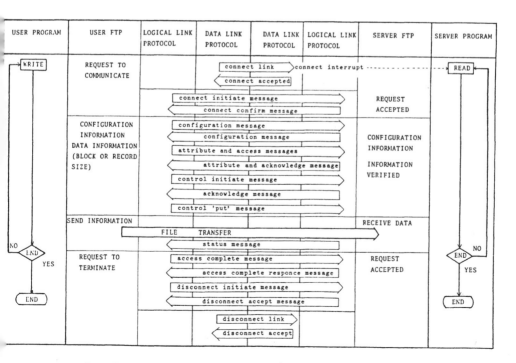

Fig. 3 General sequence of file access procedure

4.1 FILE ACCESS PROTOCOL

File access protocols (FAP) are prepared for transferring,
accessing and controlling virtual files in any node of the ring bus
subsystem. When a remote file is accessed, a logical link is
established first between the file access server in the remote host
processor and the user process, and then the remote 'file is opened by
using the file access protocols. Fig. 3 shows the general sequence of
remote file access. The basic functions of the file access protocols
are as follows:

1) Read / write / position records of sequential files.

Function	Message type and direction (User) (Server)
Establish a logical link	Connect link Request(CR) $\longrightarrow$ Confirm link Connection(CC) $\longleftarrow$
Exchange configuration messages	CONFiguration message(CONF) $\longrightarrow$ CONFiguration message(CONF) $\longleftarrow$
Send or receive file atribute and access messages	ATRiBute message(ATRB) $\longrightarrow$ ACCeSs message(ACCS) $\longrightarrow$ ATRiBute message(ATRB) $\longleftarrow$ ACKnowledge message(ACK) $\longleftarrow$
Send or receive file control messages	CONTrol message(CONT) $\longrightarrow$ ACKnowledge message(ACK) $\longleftarrow$
Send or receive file data messages	CONTrol message(CONT) $\longrightarrow$ DATA(Record) 1 (DATA) $\longleftarrow$ DATA(Record) n (DATA) $\longleftarrow$ STATus message(STAT) $\longleftarrow$
Transfer completion messages	transfer COMPletion message(COMP) $\longrightarrow$ transfer COMPletion message(COMP) $\longleftarrow$
Disconnect a logical link	Disconnect link Request(DR) $\longrightarrow$ Disconnect link Confirmation(DC) $\longleftarrow$

Fig. 4 FAP control sequences

2) Read / write / position file records at random by key or record address.

3) Error recovery.

4) Delete or rename files.

5) List or search file directories.

These functions are performed by using nine types of FAP messages as shown in Fig. 4.

The file organizations that the first version of FAP supports are as follows:

1) Sequential file organization.

2) Realtive file organization.

3) Indexed file organization.

4.2 INTERPROCESS COMMUNICATION PROTOCOL

Interprocess communication protocols (ICP) are prepared for communication between processors of remote nodes (Walden 1972). These protocols standardize the logical link as an access method interface for interprocess communication. These are performed by eight types of ICP commands which include:

1) Establish a logical link and confirm the connection.

2) Accept or reject connect requests.

3) Send or receive messages.

4) Send interrupt messages.

5) Terminate and release a logical link.

6) Synchronize command executions.

Standard library routines to utilize the inter process communication facilities will be prepared for higher level language programming.

4.3 TSS PROTOCOL

TSS protocols are virtual termical protocols (VTP) prepared for acquiring TSS servies offered by any host computer from any TSS terminal on the ring bus subsystem. TSS protocols utilize FAP protocols to specify data transfer, access and control of terminal input / output as if a terminal were a sequential file. These protocols define a standard code set, control characters and terminal control sequences between a host computer and a virtual terminal (a standard terminal on the ring bus subsystem) on a logical link pair (full duplex mode) established by a request from a terminal.

When a remote terminal is turned on, it is first connected to the guide node. The user on the terminal logs on to this node, and then he is allowed to utilize the system resources. Through the resource guidance of this node, an appropriate host is selected, and the terminal is connected to the selected host; then, the wanted TSS service begins, as shown in Fig. 5. The user is also able to log on directly to a designated host that he designates, without this resource guidance, if the guide node is down.

4.4 RJE PROTOCOL

RJE protocol is prepared by applying the file access protocols for remote batch processing. They determine standard procedures for job entry, for remote output control, for job execution control, and for other service functions from a remote terminal.

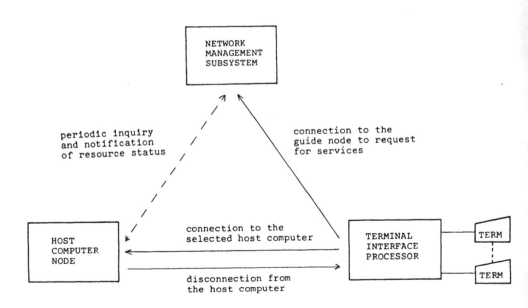

Fig. 5 TSS service connection procedure

5. IMPLEMENTATION OF THE RING BUS SUBSYSTEM

The logical structure of the ring bus subsystem is constructed in a hierarchical manner (Wecker 1978) as shown in Fig. 6.

When a terminal or a process wants to receive services using higher level protocols, it is first necessary to establish a logical link. A logical link is dynamically established by a demand from a terminal or a process. This link is supported by a lower level data link. There are two alternatives, a multiplexed mode link and a burst mode link; selection depends on the amount of data (see Fig. 7). This option makes the performance of the ring bus subsystem more efficient.

This ring bus subsystem will begin basic operations at the beginning of October 1980, at the speed of 32 MBPS, and enhanced mode operation with dual 100 MBPS lines from April 1981.

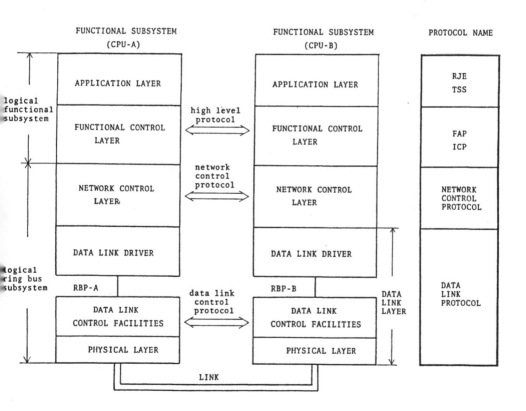

Fig. 6 Layered structure of RBS

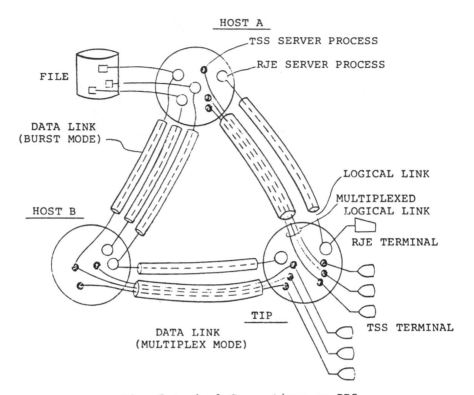

Fig. 7 Logical Connections on RBS

5.1 NETWORK CONTROL LAYER

This layer provides a logical data path (logical link) between dialogue processes under the interprocess communication protocols. The main functions of this layer are as follows:
Establish or terminate a logical link.
Send or receive messages.
Control flow on each logical link.

5.2 DATA LINK CONTROL LAYER

The main functions of this layer are achieved by the RBP. The software of this layer is a simple 'driver' which transmits the request from the network control layer to the RBP. The main functions of this layer are as follows:
Establishment or termination of data links between RBP pairs when so requested by the network control layer.

Data flow control by a synchronous (or rendezvous) transfer mechanism.

Completely ensured message transfer, with error detection and recovery.

5.3 RING BUS PROCESSOR

A RBP communicates with a channel connected to a time division multiplexed bus through a bus interface adaptor (BIA) and a transmission control unit (TCU).

To improve communication performance, several transmission mechanisms are implemented in the RBP by microprograms.

An attached service processor (ASP) is also included in the RBP to improve reliability. The communication functions of the RBP is always monitored, and RBP status is reported to the ring bus supervisor (RBSV) for system diagnosis. This monitoring is separate from the high speed transmission.

5.4 RING BUS SUPERVISOR

The RBSV contains a bus control unit (BCU) which maintains bus synchronization and a bus service processor (BSP) which supervises system operations. The BSP always monitors the communication functions and their quality, and the recovery operation is automatic when failure occurs somewhere in the RBP.

5.5 DATA LINK CONTROL PROCEDURE OF THE RBP

The RBP performs data link control depending upon commands from the data link driver.

5.5.1 ESTABLISHMENT PHASE (see Fig. 8(a))

When a CONNECT LINK command with a destination address B is given from CPU-A by a start-input-output command (SIO), RBP-A, which keeps an available link control table position (LCTi), assigns a link number (LNi) and then transmits a bus command LCM with link control command CL to the receiver (RBP-B). This command gets an available LCT

position and assigns a link number j (LNj) at the RBP-B. Then RBP-B
sends an attention interrupt (attention IT) to CPU-B. If the data link
driver on CPU-B returns a CONNECT ACCEPT command to RBP-B, a data link
(LNi, LNj) is established on the RBS.

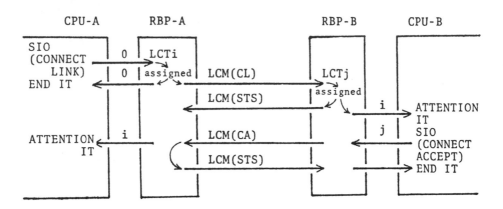

Fig. 8(a)   Link establishment sequence

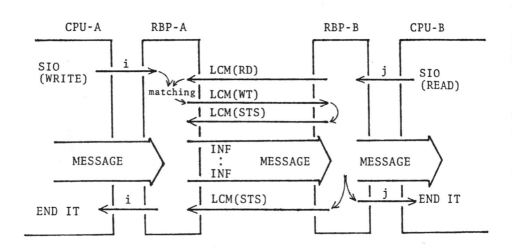

Fig. 8(b)   Data transfer sequence

bus command:	LCM INF FIN	
link control command:	CL...connect link	STS...status
CA...connect accept	RD...read	WT....write

Fig. 8 Data link control sequence

5.5.2 DATA TRANSFER PHASE

Two data transmission types are available in this phase: normal synchronous type and forced synchronous type.

(1) Normal synchronous type (NS-type)

NS-type transmission is a fundamental communication function, in which a 'matching' action is taken at the sending LCTi position. (see Fig. 8(b))

If CPU-B issues a READ command through the previously established data link, RBP-B captures an available channel and sends a bus command LCM(RD) followed by the destination address A and by the link number (LNi, LNj) to RBP-A. This read request is stored in the LCTi.

The matching is accomplished at the table position (LCTi) after a WRITE command is issued from CPU-A. After RBP-A receives a response status LCM(STS) from RBP-B for the first bus command LCM(WT), it begins to send a portion of a message with a bus command INF from a source buffer on CPU-A to a sink buffer on CPU-B.

When RBP-A sends the final part of the message with a bus command FIN, RBP-B releases the channel assigned to the data link (LNi, LNj).

(2) Forced synchronous type (FS-type)

By using FS-type operation an RBP is able to start sending without waiting for a read request bus command LCM(RD). The data link driver issues an FWRITE command forcing the receipt of a message.

5.5.3 TERMINATION PHASE

By issuing a DISCONNECT LINK command to terminate a link to an RBP from the driver, two RBP's release the link control table positions LCTi and LCTj as soon as each receives a DISCONNECT ACCEPT command from the other.

5.6 MEASUREMENT OF SYSTEM PERFORMANCE

Measurement of system performance is essential for performance analysis and assessment of this system. Modules for performance measurement, both hardware and software, are designed and implemented from the design stage of this system. The following are the major items of performance measurement:

A) Hardware factors:

1) Distribution of destinations for each node.

2) Distribution of processing times, by node.

3) Distribution of message lengths, by node.

B) Software factors:

1) Number of times transmission or reception of messages has begun, by subchannel.

2) Total length of messages, by subchannel.

3) Average rendezvous time for each subchannel.

4) Total amount of transmission time, by subchannel.

5) Average channel busy ratio for each subchannel.

6. DISCUSSION

In order to attain design goals for distributive processing, it is necessary to resolve the problem of compatibility between different types of computers. And it is desirable for regular users of this network system to be able to use computers without being clearly conscious of machine types. Further, the network system should operate in optimum loading condition according to the system status. A few points in question are discussed below.

FILE SHARING   There are few problems of sharing sequential files. For index sequential files, the relation between key and data depends on computer type. Random access to file records, such as read, write, and position by key or record address, may be supported by establishing standard file access protocols for the ring bus subsystem.

PORTABILITY OF PROGRAMS   Portability of programs which are written in high level programming languages and whose program logics are independent of internal expressions is satisfied by this system, with the exception of character code. Portability problems occurring frequently may be identified as follows:
  1) Problems relating to the size of a machine word or a set of words, such as precision of arithmetic operations, internal character arrangement, or number of bits in a character.
  2) Problems relating to internal expressions such as character code or the expressions of numeric data or logical data.
  3) Problems relating to special functions of a particular system. Problems of type 1 and 2 can be resolved to a vertain extent by transforming data form automatically.
      Currently, it is very difficult to attain compatibility of machine executable or relocatable binary programs. This problem may be resolved when machines are built that can directly execute programs written in high level languages.

COMPATIBILITY OF DATA   While data in the form of external expressions are accepted by any system, data in the form of internal expressions can not be directly processed by different machines. Thus, the problem lies in the conversion of data from external form to internal form.

COMPATIBILITY OF PERIPHERAL DEVICES AND TERMINALS   Control sequences of input / output devices are different from system to system; the standardization of protocols in the ring bus subsystem is intended to resolve this problem.

7. CONCLUSION

Our motivation for implementing a computer network tightly coupled by a high speed optical fiber ring bus is discussed above in detail, and the planning and design considerations of such a network system at the SIPC are presented. This system is a full scale, practical system that tightly connects several large computer systems of different types. We do not know of another such system. The development of this system might well lead to better organization and design of interfaces between hardware and/or software modules. This would be a major accomplishment of this project.

This project is being jointly carried by the Science Information Processing Center of the University of Tsukuba and by Mitsubishi Electric Company; it is not possible to list every participant here. The authors would like to express their appreciation to Mr. Akira Sakaguchi and to Mr. Tomoaki Tsuruoka for their discussion, and to all the other participants. Finally, this paper has been greatly improved by the insightful comments of Professor Yasuhiko Ikebe and Professor James W. Higgins of the University of Tsukuba.

REFERENCES

Frank, H., R. E. Kahn and L. Kleinrock (1972). Computer Communication Network Design - Experience with Theory and Practice, AFIPS Conference Proc. 40, 255-270, SJCC, 1972.

Pouzin, L. (1974). CIGALE, The Packet Switching Machine of the CYCLADES Computer Network, IFIP Congress, 155-159, 1974.

Abramson, N. (1970). The ALOHA system - Another Alternative for Computer Communications, AFIPS Conference Proc. 37, 281-285, FJCC, 1970.

Liu, M. T. and C. C. Reames (1977). Message Communication Protocol and Operating System Design for the Distributed Loop Computer Network (DLCN), Proc. of 4th Annual Symp. on Computer Architecture, 193-200, 1977.

Okuda, N., T. Kunikyo and T. Kaji (1978). Ring Century Bus - An Experimental High Speed Channel for Computer Communications, Proc. of ICCC, 161-166, 1978.

IBM. System Network Architecture General Information, IBM Manual, GA 27-3102-0.

NEC. Outline of DINA (Distributed Information-processing Network Architecture, Manuals, Nippon Electric Co., Ltd.

Inoue, Y. T. Nakamura, K. Yamaguchi and H. Koretomo (1976). FACOM Network Architecture (FNA), in Japanese, FUJITSU journal 27, 1976.

Toda and Nakata (1979). Basic Architecture of Data Communication Network (DCNA), in Japanese, IPSJ 20, 153-158, 1979.

Zafiropulo, P. (1974). Performance Evaluation of Reliability Improvement Techniques for Single-Loop Communications System, IEEE Trans. on Comm. COM-22, 742-751, June 1974.

Yasuboshi, R. et al. (1978). An In-House Network Configuration for Distributed Intelligence, Proc. of 4th ICCC, 155-160, Sept. 1978.

Wecker, S. (1978). Computer Network Architectures, COMPUTER 58-78, 1978.

Walden D. (1972). A System for Network, Comm. of the ACM 15, 221-230, April 1972.

PRODUCT VALIDATION FOR STANDARDIZED NETWORK PROTOCOL

Tadao Saito, Toshihiko Kato, and Hiroshi Inose

Faculty of Engineering
University of Tokyo
Bunkyo-ku, Tokyo 113, Japan

ABSTRACT

To connect a new node to an established computer network, it is needed to confirm that the new node is constructed conforming to the network protocol. This paper describes a method to validate the protocol of the product based on an automaton model. The node to be tested is connected to protocol tester which applies a test sequence and observes the response from the node. Considering the fact that protocols are specified in terms of the responses to inputs from higher level as well as external inputs, to validate the protocol for input from higher level, an additional higher level program called validation task may be needed. This paper describes two method for validation of HDLC-BA* protocol. The first method uses the validation task and the second method does not use the validation task. Detail of test sequence and the completeness of the validation are described in this paper.

1. INTRODUCTION

To construct and maintain a largescale computer network, the establishment of network protocol and to exact conformity to the established protocol is essential. If a node which does not conform to the protocol is connected to the network, various difficulties may happen in the network.

Therefore, if a new node is to be connected to an established computer network, the new node is to be tested if the node is implemented conforming to the established network protocol. In the implementation process of a node, tests to verify correctness should be performed in various phases. The programs used to implement the protocol must be intensively tested from the view point of program debugging. In the last phase of the test the node is to be tested by connecting the node to the network or the network simulator and by applying various signals to the node in the real network or a network simulator which can simulate the network environment in a controlled manner. If the network simulator is designed to generate a test sequence which can validate all the specification in the network, the node can be completely validated.

The present paper proposes a method to validate the protocol implemented in a node. The validation in this sense may be called a "product validation of the protocol" [Kawaoka (1978)].

Recently various standardization activities are made to establish internationally or nationally standardized network architecture. If the protocol of the standard architecture can be validated by a product validation procedure, the usefulness of the standard will be great. For this purpose, the description of the standard itself should be formalized to support the product validation.

The product validation described in this paper is based on an automata model. The model is established assuming that the protocol is defined in terms of state transition matrix. The formulation of the validation model, the environment of the validation and an example to apply the model to HDLC-BA protocol are described in this paper.

---

* High Level Data Link Control Procedure – Ballanced Asynchronous.
This procedure is defined by IS 3309, 4335, 6159, 6256, JIS 6363, 6364, 6365, and CCITT X.25.

2. PRODUCT VALIDATION PROCEDURE OF A PROTOCOL

The protocol validation of this paper is assumed to be performed by connecting the node to be tested to a protocol tester through a communication channel. Protocol tester will apply various test sequences to the tested node and will receive the response from the tested node.

The protocol implemented in the node can be modeled as a finite state automaton. The automaton is called the protocol machine. Thus the validation procedure can be reduced an identification problem of an automaton.

The automaton is defined by a set of states and transitions between states. The transitions are caused by the input to the automaton. Figure 1 shows three classes of inputs to the protocol machine.

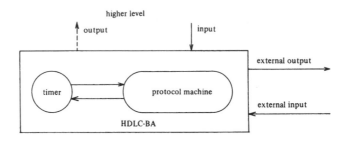

Fig. 1 Protocol machine and its inputs/outputs

The input from the protocol tester is the external input. In addition to this, input from the higher level protocol is applied to the automaton. The input form higher level is not directly controlled by external input. The input is also applied from timers which is to be implemented as a part of HDLC control program. The input from timer is controlled indirectly by the external input but they can be controlled by external input without additional programming effort for the validation.

To control the input from higher level directly by the external input, some programs which controls the HDLC level from higher level must be implemented which is not needed in usual operating environment. This is called higher level test aid or validation task. To generate input from higher level to control the HDLC level control information should be imbedded in the incoming HDLC frame applied from the protocol tester. The higher level test aid generates higher level input in response to the control information.

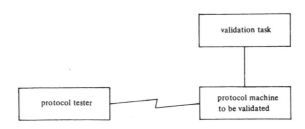

Fig. 2 Validation scheme using input from higher level

In this paper a validation scheme using the higher level test aid is described first. Although nearly complete validation is possible using this scheme, to eliminate the necessity of additional programming, a validation scheme which does not use the higher level test aid is also described. The completeness of the validation schemes is evaluated at the conclusion.

3. GENERATION OF TEST SEQUENCE INCLUDING HIGHER LEVEL INPUT

In the scheme using higher level input, the protocol machine can be modeled as a completely specified strongly connected finite state automata. The validation of the protocol machine can be reduced to an identification problem of a finite state automaton.

Outline of the test sequence generation can be summarized as follows [Hennie (1964)].

The protocol machine is specified as a finite automaton M.

$$M = (S, I, O, \delta, \omega) \tag{1}$$

S: set of states, I: set of inputs,

O: set of outputs,

δ: $S \times I \to S$ state transition function

ω: $S \times I \to O$ output function

$|S| = n$, $|I| = m$. The distinguish sequence of the automaton M is denoted by $\tilde{x}_D$. By sequence $\tilde{x}_D$, the state is transferred from s_i to s_i (l) and an output sequence $\tilde{z}_i$ is generated in this transition. The sequence $\tilde{z}_i$ is called the "characteristic sequence" for state s_i. The transition sequence which transfers the state from s_i to s_j is denoted by $\tilde{x}(s_i, s_j)$.

The automaton is assumed to be in state s_1 at the beginning of the validation. At first, n states are identified using the input/output response (2). In the following notations first row specifies the input sequence $(\tilde{x})$ and the second row specifies the output sequence $(\tilde{z})$ which is generated in response to the input sequence. In the output sequence, only the response to the distinguish sequence has meaning.

$$
\begin{aligned}
\tilde{x} &: \tilde{x}_D \ \tilde{x}(s_1 \ ^{(l)}, s_2) \ \tilde{x}_D \cdots \cdots \cdots \tilde{x}(s_{n-1} \ ^{(l)}, s_n) \ \tilde{x}_D \\
\tilde{z} &: \tilde{z}_1 \text{\textemdash\textemdash\textemdash\textemdash} \tilde{z}_2 \cdots \cdots \cdots \cdots \text{\textemdash\textemdash\textemdash} \tilde{z}_n
\end{aligned}
\tag{2}
$$

Then the state is transferred back to s_1, and the transition is confirmed.

$$
\begin{aligned}
\tilde{x} &: \tilde{x}(s_n \ ^{(l)}, s_1) \ \tilde{x}_D \ \tilde{x}(s_1 \ ^{(l)}, s_n) \ \tilde{x}_D \ \tilde{x}(s_n \ ^{(l)}, s_1) \\
\tilde{z} &: \text{\textemdash\textemdash\textemdash} \tilde{z}_1 \text{\textemdash\textemdash\textemdash} \tilde{z}_n \text{\textemdash\textemdash\textemdash}
\end{aligned}
\tag{3}
$$

Then all the possible state transition from state s_1 and output for every possible transition is tested.

$$
\begin{aligned}
\tilde{x} &: x_1 \ \tilde{x}_D \ \tilde{x}(s_1 \ ^{(1)} \ ^{(l)}, s_n) \ \tilde{x}_D \ \tilde{x}(s_n \ ^{(l)}, s_1) \ x_2 \ \tilde{x}_D \\
\tilde{z} &: z_1 \ (1) \ \tilde{z}_1 \ (1) \ (1) \text{\textemdash\textemdash} \tilde{z}_n \text{\textemdash} z_1 \ (2) \ \tilde{z}_1 \ (1) \ (2) \\
&\quad x(s_1 \ ^{(1)(l)} (2), s_n) \ x_D \ x(s_n \ ^{(l)}, s_1) \cdots x_m \ \tilde{x}_D \\
&\quad \text{\textemdash\textemdash\textemdash\textemdash} \tilde{z}_n \text{\textemdash} \cdots z_1 \ (m) \ \tilde{z}_1 \ ^{(1)} (m)
\end{aligned}
\tag{4}
$$

Then the state is transferred to s_2. Because the state transition $s_1 \ ^{(l)} \to s_2$ for $\tilde{x}(s_1 \ ^{(l)}, s_2)$ is validated in the formula (2),

$$
\begin{aligned}
\tilde{x} &: \tilde{x}(s_1 \ ^{(1)} \ ^{(l)} (m), s_1) \ \tilde{x}_D \ \tilde{x}(s_1 \ ^{(l)}, s_2) \\
\tilde{z} &: \text{\textemdash\textemdash\textemdash\textemdash} \tilde{z}_1 \text{\textemdash\textemdash\textemdash}
\end{aligned}
\tag{5}
$$

The state transition from s_2 and output for every input x_i are validated in an identical manner as Eq. (4). States $s_3, \ldots, s_n$ are also validated in a similar way.

The state transition and the output of a finite state automaton can uniquely be identified by this test sequence when total number of state of the automata is known. Therefore under the limitation that an implemented protocol has less states than given number, any error in the protocol can be detected.

4. STATE TRANSITION TABLE OF HDLC-BA PROTOCOL

As an example of the protocol validation, HDLC-BA protocol for a packet switching system is selected. An example of the HDLC-BA protocol is found in the specification of the packet switching network by NTT. The specification is given in terms of a state transition table [NTT(1978)] .

The state of HDLC-BA protocol machine is specified by the control state and a variable corresponding to the sequence number of HDLC frames. The control state is the state defined in the following state transition table and this state is not influenced by each value of the sequence number. Therefore the performance about the control state and the sequence number can be validated separately. In this paper only the validation of performance about the control state is considered [Kato (1979)] .

The state transition table used to specify the HDLC-BA protocol contains two classes of state. When a certain kind of input command frame is applied, the receiving station is expected to return a corresponding response in its earliest convenience. In this case, the state of the station is transferred to one of transient states, in which the station is to transmit the response, at which time the state of the station is again transferred to another state. The transient state can be observed by the response signal. The other class of states is stable states which can be validated only by giving some sensing frames.

In our protocol validation system, since the transient state can be automatically tested by observing the output which is given at the end of the transient state, only the stable states are included as states to be validated.

The stable state of HDLC-BA protocol machine and the input for HDLC-BA protocol machine are listed in tables 1 and 2 respectively The state transition table for the product validation is shown in table 3. An entry of the transition table includes the next state, the output, and the timer control. The symbol "o" in the transition table means that the next state is identical to the present state and the entry with the slash "/" means that the input is neglected inthe state. The entry which has a plurality of next states and outputs is indicated by symbol "or". This means that one of these transition happens depending upon implementation.

5. PRODUCT VALIDATION USING THE INPUT FROM THE HIGHER LEVEL

As the distinguishing sequence of the HDLC-BA protocol machine specified in table 3, the input sequence

$$B \ C, \ I < \ > P, \ DATA, \ REJF, \ DMF, \ I = P$$

can be used. The transient of state from the initial state by this sequence is shown in Fig.3. In Fig.4 a part of the test sequence to identify the states of HDLC-BA protocol machine is shown. Complete sequence is shown in Appendix A. In Fig.5 examples of the test sequence validating the state transition and output in each state for each input is shown. The upper sequence is an input sequence and the lower sequence is the response sequence corresponding to the input sequence. In the case that the response to the given input have several possibilities. In these cases, all the possible output sequences are shown in the figure. The non-deterministic entry of the state transition table can be excluded from the transition sequence.

The generation of time out input and N_2 times repeated times out input is to be devised for each state first for the external input and the input from higher level and then for the timer input. The timer input is not used in the distinguishing sequence nor in the transition sequence.

In states N and AA the timer cannot be started hence the timer input cannot be applied. In state CA time out input can be applied only once. Hence N_2 times repeated time out input cannot be applied.

In states AC, B41, through, B55, CA, CB, and CC, the timer input can be applied as an external input or an input from the higher level.

In states B01, through, B55 respectively. Therefore in these states, the N_2 times repeated time out input cannot be applied.

The test sequence composed this way consists of 12411 inputs signals, 8166 of them are external input frames.

state	discon-nected	wait for DM	wait for UA response	not polling							
				DCE ready				DCE busy			
				DTE ready		DTE busy		DTE ready		DTE busy	
				normal sequence	REJ-exception	normal sequence	REJ-exception	normal sequence	REJ-exception	normal sequence	REJ-exception
code	N	AA	AC	B01	B02	B04	B05	B11	B12	B14	B15

polling								RNR command to be sent	DISC command to be sent	wait for UA response	FRMR exception
DCE ready				DCE busy							
DTE ready		DTE busy		DTE ready		DTE busy					
normal sequence	REJ-exception	normal sequence	REJ-exception	normal sequence	REJ-exception	normal sequence	REJ-exception				
B41	B42	B44	B45	B51	B52	B54	B55	CA	CB	CC	DA

Table 1. States of HDLC-BA protocol machine

input	code	input	code
set up data link	STAT	RRF ($N(R) \geq J$)	RRF
wait for DM	WAIT	RRF ($N(R) < J$)	RRF+
reset	REST	$\overline{RRF}$	RR
data link shut down	END	RNRF	RNRF
forced data link shut down	FEND	$\overline{RNRF}$	RNR
busy	BH	REJF	REJF
busy clear	BC	$\overline{REJF}$	REJ
time out	TOUT	UAF	UAF
N_2 times repeated time outs	N_2T	DMF	DMF
data transmission requested	DATA	$\overline{DMF}$	DM
$\overline{IP}$ ($N(S) = R$)	I =	FRMRF	FRMRF
$\overline{IP}$ ($N(S) \neq R$)	I <>	$\overline{FRMRF}$	FRMR
IP ($N(S) = R$)	I = P	ERROR F = 1	ERRF
IP ($N(S) \neq R$)	I <> P	ERROR P/F = 0	ERR
		ERROR P = 1	ERRP

Table 2. Input for HDLC-BA protocol machine

STATE\INPUT	N	AA	AC	B01	B02	B04	B05	B11	B12	B14	B15	B41	B42	B44	B45	B51	B52	B54	B55	CA	CB	CC	DA
STAT	AC/ SABM P TS																						
WAIT	AA																						
REST																							AC/ SABM P TS
END				CB/ RNRP TS	CB/ RNRP TS	CB/ RNRP TS	CB/ RNRP TS	CB/ RNRP TS	CB/ RNRP TS	CB/ RNRP TS	CB/ RNRP TS	CA	CA	CA	CA	CA	CA	CA	CA				
FEND		N		CC/ DISC P TS	CC/ DISC P TS	CC/ DISC P TS	CC/ DISC P TS	CC/ DISC P TS	CC/ DISC P TS	CC/ DISC P TS	CC/ DISC P TS	CB	CB	CB	CB	CB	CB	CB	CB				CC/ DISC P TS
BH				B44/ RNRP TS	B45/ RNRP TS			B54/ RNRP TS	B55/ RNRP TS			B44/ RNR	B45/ RNR			B54/ RNR	B55/ RNR						
BC					B41/ RRP TS	B42/ RRP TS				B51/ RRP TS	B52/ RRP TS			B41/ RR	B42/ RR			B51/ RR	B52/ RR				
TOUT			o/ SABM P TS	B41/ RRP TS	B42/ RRP TS	B44/ RNRP TS	B45/ RNRP TS	B51/ RRP TS	B52/ RRP TS	B54/ RNRP TS	B55/ RNRP TS	o/ RRP TS	o/ RRP TS	o/ RNRP TS	o/ RNRP TS	o/ RRP TS	o/ RRP TS	o/ RNRP TS	o/ RNRP TS	CB/ RNRP TS	o/ RNRP TS	o/ DISC P TS	o/ FRMR TS
N₂T			N	N	N	N	N	N	N	N	N	N	N	N	N	N	N	N	N		N	N	
DATA				o/ I TS or B41/ IP TS	o/ I TS or B42/ IP TS	o/ I TS or B44/ IP TS	o/ I TS or B45/ IP TS					o/ I TS	o/ I TS	o/ I TS	o/ I TS								
I =				o/ (RR) (TP) or B41/ RRP TS	B01 (RR) (TP) or B41/ RRP TS	o/ (RNR) (TP) or B44/ RRP TS	B04 (RR) (TP) or B44/ RNRP TS	o/ (RR) (TP) or B51/ RRP TS	B11 (RR) (TP) or B51/ RRP TS	o/ (RR) (TP) or B54/ RRP TS	B14 (RNR) (TP) or B54/ RNRP TS	o/ (RR)	B41/ (RR)	o/ (RNR)	B44/ (RNR)	o/ (RR)	B51/ (RR)	o/ (RNR)	B54/ (RNR)				
I < >				B02/ REJ (TP) or B42/ REJP TS	o/ TP	B05/ (RNR) (TP) or B45/ RNRP TS	(RNR) (TP) or B45/ RNRP TS	B12/ REJ (TP) or B52/ REJP TS	o/ TP	B15/ (RNR) (TP) or B55/ RNRP TS	o/ (RNR) (TP) or B55/ RNRP TS	B42/ REJ	o/	B45/ (RNR)	o/ (RNR)	B52/ REJ	o/	B55/ (RNR)	o/ (RNR)				
I = P	o/ DMF			o/ RRF	B01 RRF	o/ RNRF	B04 RNRF	o/ RRF	B11 RRF	o/ RNRF	B14 RNRF	o/ RRF	B41 RRF	o/ RNRF	B44 RNRF	o/ RRF	B51 RRF	o/ RNRF	B54 RNRF				o/ FRMR F TS
I < > P	o/ DMF			B02/ REJF	o/ RRF	B05/ RNRF	o/ RNRF	B12/ REJF	o/ RRF	B15/ RNRF	o/ RNRF	B42/ REJF	o/ RRF	B45/ RNRF	o/ RNRF	B52/ REJF	o/ RRF	B55/ RNRF	o/ RNRF				o/ FRMR F TS

Table 3. State transition table for HDLC-BA protocol machine (1/2)

STATE / INPUT	N	AA	AC	B01	B02	B04	B05	B11	B12	B14	B15	B41	B42	B44	B45	B51	B52	B54	B55	CA	CB	CC	DA
RRF												B01/ (TP)	B02/ (TP)	B04/ (TP)	B05/ (TP)	B01/ (TP)	B02/ (TP)	B04/ (TP)	B05/ (TP)	CB/ RNRP TS	CC/ DISC P TS		o/ TP
RRF+												B01/ I TS or o/ IP TS	B02/ I TS or o/ IP TS	B04/ I TS or o/ IP TS	B05/ I TS or o/ IP TS	B01/ I TS or B41/ IP TS	B02/ I TS or B42/ IP TS	B04/ I TS or B44/ IP TS	B05/ I TS or B45/ IP TS	CB/ RNRP TS	CC/ DISC P TS		o/ TP
RR			o/ (TP)	o/ (TP)	o/ (TP)	o/ (TP)	o/ (TP)	B01/ (TP)	B02/ (TP)	B04/ (TP)	B05/ (TP)	o/	o/	o/	o/	B41/	B42/	B44/	B45/	o/	o/		
RNRF												B11/ (TP)	B12/ (TP)	B14/ (TP)	B15/ (TP)	B11/ (TP)	B12/ (TP)	B14/ (TP)	B15/ (TP)	CB/ RNRP TS	CC/ DISC P TS		o/ TP
RNR			B11/ (TP)	B12/ (TP)	B14/ (TP)	B15/ (TP)	o/ (TP)	o/ (TP)	o/ (TP)	o/ (TP)	B51/	B52	B54/	B55/	o/	o/	o/	o/	o/	o/			o/ TP
REJF												B01/ I TS or o/ IP TS	B02/ I TS or o/ IP TS	B04/ I TS or o/ IP TS	B05/ I TS or o/ IP TS	B01/ I TS or B41/ IP TS	B02/ I TS or B42/ IP TS	B04/ I TS or B44/ IP TS	B05/ I TS or B45/ IP TS	CB/ RNRP TS	CC/ DISC P TS		o/ TP
REJ				o/ I TS or B41/ IP TS	o/ I TS or B42/ IP TS	o/ I TS or B44/ IP TS	o/ I TS or B45/ IP TS	B01/ I TS or B41/ IP TS	B02/ I TS or B42/ IP TS	B04/ I TS or B44/ IP TS	B05/ I TS or B45/ IP TS	o/ I TS	o/ I TS	o/ I TS	o/ I TS	B41/ I TS	B42/ I TS	B44/ I TS	B45/ I TS.				
UAF			B01/ TP																			N/ TP	
DMF			N/ TP									AC/ SABM P TS	AC/ SABM P TS	AC/ SABM P TS	AC/ SABM P TS	AC/ SABM P TS	AC/ SABM P TS	AC/ SABM P TS	AC/ SABM P TS	N/ TP	N/ TP	N/ TP	AC/ SABM P TS
DM		AC/ SABM P TS		AC/ SABM P TS	AC/ SABM P TS	AC/ SABM P TS	AC/ SABM P TS	AC/ SABM P TS	AC/ SABM P TS	AC/ SABM P TS	AC/ SABM P TS	AC/ SABM P TS	AC/ SABM P TS	AC/ SABM P TS	AC/ SABM P TS	AC/ SABM P TS	AC/ SABM P TS	AC/ SABM P TS	AC/ SABM P TS			N/ TP	AC/ SABM P TS
FRMRF			DA/ TP									DA/ TP	DA/ TP	DA/ TP	DA/ TP	DA/ TP	DA/ TP	DA/ TP	DA/ TP	DA/ TP	DA/ TP	DA/ TP	
FRMR			DA	DA	DA	DA	DA	DA	DA	DA	DA	DA	DA	DA	DA	DA	DA	DA	DA	DA	DA	DA	
ERRF												DA/ FRMR TS	DA/ FRMR TS	DA/ FRMR TS	DA/ FRMR TS	DA/ FRMR TS	DA/ FRMR TS	DA/ FRMR TS	DA/ FRMR TS	DA/ FRMR TS	DA/ FRMR TS	DA/ FRMR TS	o/ TP
ERR			DA/ FRMR TS	DA/ FRMR TS	DA/ FRMR TS	DA/ FRMR TS	DA/ FRMR TS	DA/ FRMR TS	DA/ FRMR TS	DA/ FRMR TS	DA/ FRMR TS	DA/ FRMR TS	DA/ FRMR TS	DA/ FRMR TS	DA/ FRMR TS	DA/ FRMR TS	DA/ FRMR TS	DA/ FRMR TS	DA/ FRMR TS	DA/ FRMR TS	DA/ FRMR TS	DA/ FRMR TS	
ERRP	o/ DMF			DA/ FRMR F TS	DA/ FRMR F TS	DA/ FRMR F TS	DA/ FRMR F TS	DA/ FRMR F TS	DA/ FRMR F TS	DA/ FRMR F TS	DA/ FRMR F TS	DA/ FRMR F TS	DA/ FRMR F TS	DA/ FRMR F TS	DA/ FRMR F TS	DA/ FRMR F TS	DA/ FRMR F TS	DA/ FRMR F TS	DA/ FRMR F TS	DA/ FRMR F TS	DA/ FRMR F TS	DA/ FRMR F TS	o/ FRMR F TS

Table 3. State transition table for HDLC-BA protocol machine (2/2)

Initial state   [N, AA, AC, B01, B02, B04, B05, B11, B12, B14, B15, B41, B42, B44, B45, B51, B52, B54, B55, CA, CB, CC, DA]

     | busy clear

[N, AA, AC, B01, B02, B11, B12, B41, B42, B51, B52, CA, CB, CC, DA] [B41, B42, B51, B52] [B41, B42, B51, B52]

     | IP (R ⊀ N (S))

[N] [DA] [AA, AC, CA, CB, CC] [B02, B12, B42, B52] [B02, B12, B42, B52] [B42, B52] [B42, B52] [B42 B52] [B42, B52]

     | data transmission requested

[N] [DA] [AA, AC, CA, CB, CC] [B02, B42] [B12, B52] [B02, B42] [B12, B52] [B42] [B52] [B42] [B52] [B42] [B52] [B42] [B52]
              [B42] [B42]   [B42] [B42]

     | REJF

[N] [DA] [AA, AC, CC] [CB] [CC] [B02] [B02] [B12] [B02] [B02] [B02] [B12] [B02] [B02] [B02] [B02] [B02] [B02] [B02] [B02] [B02]
                      [B02] [B42] [B12] [B42] [B02] [B42] [B12] [B42] [B02] [B42] [B02] [B42] [B02] [B42] [B02] [B42]
                      [B42] [B42]   [B42] [B42]   [B42] [B42] [B42] [B42] [B42] [B42] [B42] [B42]

     | DM$\overline{F}$

[N] [AC] [AC] [AC, N] [CB] [N] [AC] [AC] [AC] [AC] [AC] [AC] [AC] [AC] [AC] [AC] [AC] [AC] [AC] [AC] [AC] [AC]

     | IP (R = N (S))

[N] [AC] [AC] [AC] [N] [CB] [N] [AC] [AC] [AC] [AC] [AC] [AC] [AC] [AC] [AC] [AC] [AC] [AC] [AC] [AC] [AC] [AC]

Fig. 3   Transient of state by the distinguish sequence

6. PRODUCT VALIDATION WHICH DOES NOT USE THE INPUTS FROM HIGHER LEVEL

CHARACTERISTICS OF THE PRODUCT VALIDATION NOT USING THE INPUT FORM HIGHER LEVEL

The product validation which does not use the inputs from higher level has the following problems.

(1) Even in the validation which uses only the external input, some inputs from higher level is indispensable for the validation. This includes the set up or the shut down of a data link. In an example to be described in this paper, for the validation of HDLC-BA protocol three inputs from higher level is used in the test sequence 3274 input signals.

(2) Even in a validation which does not use input from higher level, some input signal may be applied from higher level to HDLC level spontaneously. If the response to the spontaneous higher level input is erroneous, the validation procedure will be out of synchronization. Therefore, the protocol machine to be tested must be operated correctly to all the possible inputs from higher level. This is the basic assumption for the test.

(3) Consider the case that a state is obtained by applying an input sequence to an original state. If the original state cannot be attained from the state only by applying input from higher level, the machine cannot recover the original state in this validation procedure. Therefore the validation is performed by clustering the states into "external input strongly connected" states. The external input strongly connected states are defined as follows. The state s_i and s_j are said to be external input strongly connected if and only if there exist the external input sequences $\widetilde{x}$ and $\widetilde{x}'$ such that

$$s_i \xrightarrow{\widetilde{x}} s_j \quad \text{and} \quad s_j \xrightarrow{\widetilde{x}'} s_i .$$

The set of states in the protocol machine to be validated is partitioned into the external input strongly connected subsets and the protocol machine is only validated for the external input such that the next state obtained in response to the input is in the same subset.

(4) The distinguishing sequence should be composed of external inputs such that the next state obtained in response to the input is in the external input strongly connected subset to which the present state belongs. Above mentioned distinguishing sequence which is used for protocol validation using higher level inputs cannot be used in this case. In this protocol validation distinguish sequence is to be selected for each of state is called a D-set. The distinguishing sequence for a state should be composed so that the characteristic output sequence for the state may not be yielded when the distinguishing

```
X:  B  C    I < > P   DATA   REJF   DM      I = P   WAIT
Z:          DMF                             DMF              identification of state N

X:  B  C    I < > P   DATA   REJF   DM      I = P   UAF
Z:                           SABMP                          identification of state AA

X:  B  C    I < > P   DATA   REJF   DM      I = P
Z:                                                          identification of state AC

X: ⎡B  C    I < > P   DATA   REJF   DM      I = P⎤   UAF    I < > P
Z: ⎢        REJF   I              SABMP      ⎥            REJF
X: ⎢B  C    I < > P   DATA   REJF   DM      I = P⎥
Z: ⎨        REJF   IP     I       SABMP      ⎬
X: ⎢B  C    I < > P   DATA   REJF   DM      I = P⎥
Z: ⎣        REJF   IP     IP      SABMP      ⎦            identification of state B01

X: ⎡B  C    I < > P   DATA   REJF   DM      I = P⎤   UAF    B  H      RRF
Z: ⎢        RRF    I              SABMP      ⎥            RNRP
X: ⎢B  C    I < > P   DATA   REJF   DM      I = P⎥
Z: ⎨        RRF    IP     I       SABMP      ⎬
X: ⎢B  C    I < > P   DATA   REJF   DM      I = P⎥
Z: ⎣        RRF    IP     IP      SABMP      ⎦            identification of state B02

X: ⎡B  C    I < > P   DATA   REJF   DM      I = P⎤   UAF    B  H      I < >     RRF
Z: ⎢RRP     REJF   I      I        SABMP    ⎥            RNRP      (RNR)
X: ⎢B  C    I < > P   DATA   REJF   DM      I = P⎥
Z: ⎣RRP     REJF   I      IP       SABMP    ⎦            identification of state B04

X: ⎡B  C    I < > P   DATA   REJF   DM      I = P⎤   UAF    RNR
Z: ⎢RRP     RRF    I      I        SABMP    ⎥
X: ⎢B  C    I < > P   DATA   REJF   DM      I = P⎥
Z: ⎣RRP     RRF    I      IP       SABMP    ⎦            identification of state B05
```

Fig. 4   A part of test sequence for identification of states

X:		B C	I < > P	DATA	REJF	DM	I = P	UAF
Z:								

X:	FEND	B C	I < > P	DATA	REJF	DM	I = P	STAT
Z:	DISCP					DMF		SABMP

X:		B C	I < > P	DATA	REJF	DM	I = P	UAF
Z:								

X:	RR	B C	I < > P	DATA	REJF	DM	I = P
Z:			REJF	I		SABMP	
X:	RR	B C	I < > P	DATA	REJF	DM	I = P
Z:			REJF	IP	I	SABMP	
X:	RR	B C	I < > P	DATA	REJF	DM	I = P
Z:			REJF	IP	IP	SABMP	

X:		B C	I < > P	DATA	REJF	DM	I = P	UAF
Z:								

X:	RNR	B C	I < > P	DATA	REJF	DM	I = P
Z:			REJF			SABMP	

(a) A part of test sequence of transition from state B01

X:			B C	I < > P	DATA	REJF	DM	I = P	UAF
Z:									

X:	DATA	TOUT	B C	I < > P	DATA	REJF	DM	I = P
Z:	I	RRP		REJF	I	I	SABMP	
X:	DATA	TOUT	B C	I < > P	DATA	REFJ	DM	I = P
Z:	I	RRP		REJF	I	IP	SABMP	

(b) A part of test sequence of transition by time out from state B01

Fig. 5 A part of test sequence for validation of transitions

sequence is applied for the other state even if any input from the higher level is applied incidentally.

(5) When the input from the higher level is applied, it should be observed by the protocol tester. If the result is not observed, the protocol tester cannot know actual state of the protocol machine which is under the test.

THE TEST SEQUENCE FOR VALIDATION

The state of the HDLC-BA protocol machine which is given in the table 1 is partitioned into seven external input strongly connected subsets shown in Fig.6.

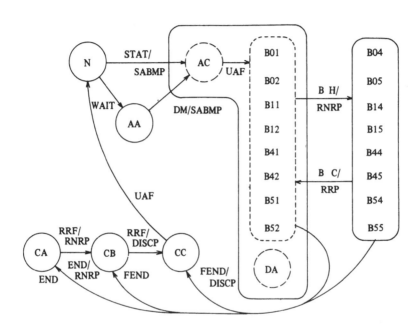

Fig. 6 External input strongly connected states of HDLC-BA protocol

$$S_N = \{ N \}, \quad S_{AA} = \{ AA \}$$
$$S_{B1} = \{ AC, B01, B11, B12, B41, B42, B51, B52, DA \}$$
$$S_{B2} = \{ B04, B05, B14, B15, B44, B45, B54, B55 \}$$
$$S_{CA} = \{ CA \}, \quad S_{CB} = \{ CB \}, \quad S_{CC} = \{ CC \}$$

The test sequence is composed for each of the subsets in the following way.

Validation is performed for each entry in the state transition table shown in table 3. An entry can be identified by the state and the input. If the transition and the output caused by the input can be confirmed the entry is validated. Before the validation of the entry, the present state should be confirmed. Since the present state may be changed by spontaneous inputs from higher level, if the transient cannot be observed from the protocol tester, some sensing frame may be needed to confirm the state for each of external input.

1) S_N

In state N, the protocol machine does not change state in response to any external input. As the distinguishing sequence for the state N, the input sequence

$$I = P \quad \text{(The characteristic output sequence is DMF.)}$$

can be used. Data link set up and wait input from higher level cause change to state N. The protocol tester an observe the data link set up input because this cause the protocol machine to transmit the SABM command with the p-bit on. However, the protocol tester cannot observe the result of wait input since the machine transmit no output frame. Therefore the protocol tester applies the $DM\overline{F}$ to the protocol machine to confirm that the protocol machine is in state N before the tester applies a series of external inputs to the protocol machine for the validation of state N. The test sequence for S_N is as follows:

$$\{ DM\overline{F}, \; x_i, \; I = P \} \quad x_i \text{: every external inputs.}$$

(2) S_{AA}

After applying the test sequence described in (1) the protocol machine to be validated is in state N. Therefore to transfer the state to AA, an input from higher level, i.e., wait input should be applied.

In state AA the protocol machine does not change the state for any external input except DMF. As the distinguishing sequence for state AA, the input sequence

$$I = P, \; DM\overline{F} \quad \text{(The characteristic output sequence is SABMP.)}$$

can be used. However, the state of the protocol machine is changed to AC in response to this input sequence. Therefore, the protocol machine is validated by applying every external input except $DM\overline{F}$ first and then applying the distinguish sequence to validate that the protocol machine is in state AA.

There is an input from higher level which change the state AA, i.e., forced data link shut down input, which transfer the state to N without output. Therefore, $I = P$ is applied to confirm that the protocol machine is in state AA before each external input is applied for the validation of state AA.

The test sequence for S_{AA} is therefore as follows:

$$\{ I = P, \; x_i \} \quad x_i \text{:every external input except } DM\overline{F},$$
$$I = P, DM\overline{F}, \text{ the distinguishing sequence for AC.}$$

(3) S_{B1}

As the distinguishing sequence for state AC, the input sequence

$$I = P, \; RRF, \; DMF, \; I = P, \; DM\overline{F}$$
(The characteristic output sequence is no output frames.)

can be used. To identify states B01 through B52, it is assumed that the protocol machine to be validated in loaded with the data to be transmitted and that it sends I frames in a burst as many as the maximum outstanding frame number. It is also assumed that the last frame of the burst has the p-bit on if the protocol machine can sent a p-bit-on frame.

As the distinguish sequence for state B01, B02, B41, or B42, the input sequence.

$$RR, \; I < > P, \; REJF$$

can be used, and for state B11, B12, B51, or B52, the input sequence

$$RNR, \; I < > P, \; REJF$$

can be used. And for state DA, the input sequence

$$I = P \text{ (The characteristic output sequence is FRMRF.)}$$

can be used.

For state AC, the response to all the external input and time out except DMF can be validated. For states B01 through B52 the response to all the external input, time out and data transmission requested input can be validated. For state DA the response to all the external input and time out can be validated.

For states B01, B02, B11, B12, B41, B42, B51, and B52 higher level inputs which change the state are data link shut down, forced data link shut down and busy. For state DA higher level input which change the state are reset and forced data link shut down. Input from higher level can be known by the protocol tester by observing RNR or DISC frame except data link shut down for state B41 through B51 and reset for state DA. The data link shut down and the forced data link shut down from states B41 through B52 can be observed by the REJF in the distinguish sequence. When the reset is applied to state DA, since the response to that is identical to the response for $\overline{DMF}$ and DMF, the identification is difficult.

The test sequence for S_{B1} is composed with the method described in chapter 3. The test sequence is shown in Fig.7, denoted in the same way as chapter 5.

(4) S_{B2}

To transfer the state to a state in subset S_{B2} busy input from higher level should be applied to state B01 as an example.

States B04, B14, B44, B54 in subset S_{B2} correspond to the states in which correct sequence number is received and states B05, B15, B45 and B55 correspond to the states in which incorrect sequence number is received. However in subset S_{B2} higher level of the protocol machine is busy. Hence the response to any external input is RNR irrespective of the correctness of the sequence number of received frames. These two groups of states can only be distinguishing sequence for states in S_{B2} cannot be composed only of external inputs. Therefore the protocol machine is assumed to be validated without separating these two states, As the distinguish sequence for state B04, B05, B44, or B45, the input sequence

$$RR, REJF$$

can be used, and for state B14, B15, B54, or B55, the input sequence

$$RNR, REJF$$

can be used.

The protocol machine is validated for every external input except DMF, DM, FRMRF, FRMF, ERR, and ERRP, and time out and data transmission requested input.

Data link shut down, forced data link shut down, and busy clear input from higher level change the states in S_{B2}. The response to forced data link shut down input states B04 through B55 and the data link shut down input are detected by the REJF in the distinguish sequence.

The test sequence for S_{B2} is composed in the same way as S_{B1} which is shown in Fig.8.

(5) S_{CA}

To transfer the state to AC, an input from higher level, i.e., data link shut down input should be applied in one of states B41 through B55.

As the distinguish sequence for state CA, the input sequence

$$I = P, \; RRF \text{ (The characteristic output sequence is RNRP.)}$$

can be used. But the state is transferred to CB by this distinguish sequence. Thus the validation sequence is composed of the external inputs that does not change the state and then the distinguish sequence.

X:	I = P	RRF	DM	I = P	DM	UAF	
Z:							identification of state AC

X:	RR	I < > P	REJF		RRF		
Z:	IP	REJF	IP				identification of state B01

X:	RR	I < > P	REJF		I =	RNRF	
Z:	IP	RRF	IP		(RR)		identification of state B02

X:	RNR	I < > P	REJF				
Z:		REJF					identification of state B11

X:	RNR	I < > P	REJF		I = P	REJ	
Z:		RRF			RRF	IP	identification of state B12

(a) A part of test sequence of state identification

X:	DATA		RR	I < > P	REJF	DMF
Z:	IP		I	REJF	IP	SABMP

X:	I = P	RRF	DM	I = P	DM	UAF
Z:						

X:	I =		RR	I < > P	REJF	DMF
Z:	(RR)		IP	REJT	IP	SABMP
X:	I =		RR	I < > P	REJF	
Z:	RRP		I	REJF	IP	
X:	I = P	RRF	DM	I = P	DM	UAF
Z:						

X:	I < >		RR	I < > P	REJF	DMF
Z:	REJ		IP	RRF	IP	SABMP
X:	I < >		RR	I < > P	REJF	
Z:	REJP		I	RRF	IP	

(b) A part of test sequence of transient from B01

Fig. 7 Test sequences for subset S_{B1}

The protocol machine is validated for the external inputs $I =, I <>, I = P, I <> P$, RR, RNR, REJ, UAF, DM. The test sequence for S_{CA} is as follows:

$$\{ x_i \} \quad x_i: \text{above mentioned 9 inputs,} \quad I = P, RRF$$

X:	RR	REJF		I <>	RRF	
Z:	IRNRP	IRNRP		(RNR)		identification of state B04

X:	RR	REJF		I =	RNRF	
Z:	IRNRP	IRNRP		(RNR)		identification of state B05

X:	RNR	REJF		I <> P		
Z:				RNRF		identification of state B14

X:	RNR	REJF		I = P	REJ	
Z:				RNRF	IRNRP	identification of state B15

X:	RR	REJF		I <>		
Z:	I	IRNRP		(RNR)		identification of state B44

(a) A part of test sequence of state identification

X:	DATA		RR	REJF		I <>	RNR
Z:	IRNRP		I	IRNRP		(RNR)	

X:	RNR	REJF		I =	RRF		
Z:		IRNRP		(RNR)			

X:	I =		RR	REJF		I <>	RNR
Z:	(RNR)		IRNRP	IRNRP		(RNR)	
X:	I =		RR	REJF			
Z:	RNRP		I	IRNRP			

X:	RNR	REJF		I =	RRF		
Z:		IRNRP		(RNR)			

X:	I <>		RR	REJF		RNR	
Z:	(RNR)		IRNRP	IRNRP			
X:	I <>		RR	REJF			
Z:	RNRP		I	IRNRP			

(b) A part of test sequence of transition from B04

Fig. 8 Test sequences for subset S_{B2}

(6) S_{CB}

As the distinguish sequence for CB, the input sequence

$$I = P, \ RRF \ \text{(The characteristic output sequence is DISCP.)}$$

can be used. The protocol machine change the state to CC by this distinguish sequence. The protocol machine is validated only by the external inputs which does not change the state. The external inputs for which state CB is validated are the same as state CA.

The test sequence for S_{CB} is follows:

$$\{ x_i \} \ x_i: \text{above mentioned}, \ ^{I = P, \ RRF}$$

(7) S_{CC}

As the distinguish sequence for CC, the input sequence

$$I = P, \ \text{time out} \ \text{(The characteristic output sequence is DISCP.)}$$

can be used. The external inputs for which the protocol is validated in CC are $I =$, $I <>$, $I = P$, $I <> P$, RRF, RRF^+, RR, $RNRF$, RNR, $REJF$, REJ and time out.

The test sequence for S_{CC} is composed of

$$\{ x_i \} \ x_i: \text{above mentioned 11 inputs}, \ ^{I = P, \ \text{time out}}$$

In summary the test sequence for HDLC-BA protocol machine is constructed with 3271 external inputs. In addition three inputs from higher level is needed to cause required state transitions.

7. EVALUATION OF THE PRODUCT VALIDATION SCHEMES

To evaluate the two product validation schemes, the validation ratio is introduced. The validation ratio R_V is defined as the percentage of total transition that can be validated, i.e.,

$$R_V = \frac{\text{number of the pairs of state and input in which the next state and output are validated.}}{\text{number of states} \times \text{number of inputs}}$$

For the product validation using the input from higher level,

$$R_{V1} = \frac{23 \times 29 - 13}{23 \times 29} = 0.98$$

and for the product validation which does not use the input from higher level,

$$R_{V2} = \frac{381}{23 \times 29} = 0.57$$

8. CONCLUSION

The product validation scheme based on automaton model was described in this paper. Inputs to the protocol machine are classified into three classes, i.e., external input, timer input and input from higher level. The first validation scheme used all the inputs and the second validation scheme used external input and timer input. Detail of the validation sequence was described for each of schemes and the completeness of the validation was evaluated.

[REFERENCES]

Kawaoka T., et.al. (1978). Specification and Verification of Protocols. Technical Group of IPS Japan, Software Eng. 8-5, Nov, 1978

Hennie F.C. (1964). Fault Detecting Experiments for Sequential Circuits. Proc. 5th Annual Symposium an Switching Theory and Logical Design, Nov. 1964

NTT (1978). Interface Condition of Packet Switching Service. Nippon Telegraph and Telephone Public Co., Nov. 1978

Kato T., et.al. (1979). A Verification Method for HDLC Protocol by means of Cascade Decomposition of Automata. Technical Group of IECE Japan, EC79-37, Nov. 1979

328

Apendix A

Test sequence for identification of states in the validation scheme using input
from higher level

```
B C   I<>P   DATA   REJF   DM     I=P        WAIT
      DMF                          DMF    identification of state N


B C   I<>P   DATA   REJF   DM     I=P
                           SABMP          identification of state AA


B C   I<>P   DATA   REJF   DM     I=P            UAF
                                          identification of state AC
```

```
⎧ B C   I<>P   DATA   REJF   DM     I=P ⎫      UAF   I<>P
⎪       REJF   I             SABMP       ⎪            REJF
⎪                                        ⎪
⎨ B C   I<>P   DATA   REJF   DM     I=P  ⎬
⎪       REJF   IP     I      SABMP       ⎪
⎪                                        ⎪
⎩ B C   I<>P   DATA   REJF   DM     I=P ⎭
        REJF   IP     IP     SABMP         identification of state B01
```

```
⎧ B C   I<>P   DATA   REJF   DM     I=P ⎫      UAF   B H   RRF
⎪       RRF    I             SABMP       ⎪            RNRP
⎪                                        ⎪
⎨ B C   I<>P   DATA   REJF   DM     I=P  ⎬
⎪       RRF    IP     I      SABMP       ⎪
⎪                                        ⎪
⎩ B C   I<>P   DATA   REJF   DM     I=P ⎭
        RRF    IP     IP     SABMP         identification of state B02
```

```
⎧ B C   I<>P   DATA   REJF   DM     I=P ⎫      UAF   B H   I<>    RRF
⎪ RRP   REJF   I      I      SABMP       ⎬            RNRP  (RNR)
⎪                                        
⎨ B C   I<>P   DATA   REJF   DM     I=P ⎭
⎩ RRP   REJF   I      IP     SABMP         identification of state B04
```

```
⎧ B C   I<>P   DATA   REJF   DM     I=P ⎫      UAF   RNR
⎪ RRP   RRF    I      I      SABMP       ⎬
⎪                                        
⎨ B C   I<>P   DATA   REJF   DM     I=P ⎭
⎩ RRP   RRF    I      IP     SABMP         identification of state B05
```

```
B C   I<>P   DATA   REJF   DM     I=P        UAF   I<>P   RNR
      REJF                 SABMP                   REJF
                                          identification of state B11


B C   I<>P   DATA   REJF   DM     I=P        UAF   B H    RNRF
      RRF                  SABMP                   RNRP
                                          identification of state B12
```

329

$$\left\{\begin{array}{llllll}
\text{B C} & \text{I<>P} & \text{DATA} & \text{REJF} & \text{DM} & \text{I≠P} \\
\text{RRP} & \text{REJF} & & \text{I} & \text{SABMP} & \\
\text{B C} & \text{I<>P} & \text{DATA} & \text{REJF} & \text{DM} & \text{I=P} \\
\text{RRP} & \text{REJF} & & \text{IP} & \text{SABMP} &
\end{array}\right\}$$

UAF B H I<> RNRF
   RNRP (RNR)

identification of state B14

$$\left\{\begin{array}{llllll}
\text{B C} & \text{I<>P} & \text{DATA} & \text{REJF} & \text{DM} & \text{I=P} \\
\text{RRP} & \text{RRF} & & \text{I} & \text{SABMP} & \\
\text{B C} & \text{I<>P} & \text{DATA} & \text{REJF} & \text{DM} & \text{I=P} \\
\text{RRP} & \text{RRF} & & \text{IP} & \text{SABMP} &
\end{array}\right\}$$

UAF B H B C
   RNRP RR

identification of state B15

$$\left\{\begin{array}{llllll}
\text{B C} & \text{I<>P} & \text{DATA} & \text{REJF} & \text{DM} & \text{I=P} \\
& \text{REJF} & \text{I} & \text{I} & \text{SABMP} & \\
\text{B C} & \text{I<>P} & \text{DATA} & \text{REJF} & \text{DM} & \text{I=P} \\
& \text{REJF} & \text{I} & \text{IP} & \text{SABMP} &
\end{array}\right\}$$

UAF B H B C I<>
   RNRP RR REJ

identification of state B41

$$\left\{\begin{array}{llllll}
\text{B C} & \text{I<>P} & \text{DATA} & \text{REJF} & \text{DM} & \text{I=P} \\
& \text{RRF} & \text{I} & \text{I} & \text{SABMP} & \\
\text{B C} & \text{I<>P} & \text{DATA} & \text{REJF} & \text{DM} & \text{I=P} \\
& \text{RRF} & \text{I} & \text{IP} & \text{SABMP} &
\end{array}\right\}$$

UAF B H
   RNRP

identification of state B42

$$\left\{\begin{array}{llllll}
\text{B C} & \text{I<>P} & \text{DATA} & \text{REJF} & \text{DM} & \text{I=P} \\
\text{RR} & \text{REJF} & \text{I} & \text{I} & \text{SABMP} & \\
\text{B C} & \text{I<>P} & \text{DATA} & \text{REJF} & \text{DM} & \text{I=P} \\
\text{RR} & \text{REJF} & \text{I} & \text{IP} & \text{SABMP} &
\end{array}\right\}$$

UAF B H I<>
   RNRP (RNR)

identification of state B44

$$\left\{\begin{array}{llllll}
\text{B C} & \text{I<>P} & \text{DATA} & \text{REJF} & \text{DM} & \text{I=P} \\
\text{RR} & \text{RRF} & \text{I} & \text{I} & \text{SABMP} & \\
\text{B C} & \text{I<>P} & \text{DATA} & \text{REJF} & \text{DM} & \text{I=P} \\
\text{RR} & \text{RRF} & \text{I} & \text{IP} & \text{SABMP} &
\end{array}\right\}$$

UAF B H B C RNR
   RNRP RR

identification of state B45

$$\left\{\begin{array}{llllll}
\text{B C} & \text{I<>P} & \text{DATA} & \text{REJF} & \text{DM} & \text{I=P} \\
& \text{REJF} & & \text{I} & \text{SABMP} & \\
\text{B C} & \text{I<>P} & \text{DATA} & \text{REJF} & \text{DM} & \text{I≠P} \\
& \text{REJF} & & \text{IP} & \text{SABMP} &
\end{array}\right\}$$

UAF B H B C I<> RNR
   RNRP RR REJ

identification of state B51

$$\left\{\begin{array}{llllll}
\text{B C} & \text{I<>P} & \text{DATA} & \text{REJF} & \text{DM} & \text{I=P} \\
& \text{RRF} & & \text{I} & \text{SABMP} & \\
\text{B C} & \text{I<>P} & \text{DATA} & \text{REJF} & \text{DM} & \text{I≠P} \\
& \text{RRF} & & \text{IP} & \text{SABMP} &
\end{array}\right\}$$

UAF B H RNR
   RNRP

identification of state B52

```
⎧ B C   I<>P   DATA   REJF   DM      I =P ⎫      UAF    B H   I<>    RNR
⎪ RR    REJF          I      SABMP        ⎪             RNRP  (RNR)
⎨                                         ⎬
⎪ B C   I<>P   DATA   REJF   DM      I =P ⎪      identification of state  B54
⎩ RR    REJF          IP     SABMP        ⎭


⎧ B C   I<>P   DATA   REJF   DM      I =P ⎫      UAF    B H   END
⎪ RR    RRF           I      SABMP        ⎪             RNRP
⎨                                         ⎬
⎪ B C   I<>P   DATA   REJF   DM      I =P ⎪      identification of state  B55
⎩ RR    RRF           IP     SABMP        ⎭


  B C   I<>P   DATA   REJF   DM      I =P         identification of state  CA
                     RNRP


  B C   I<>P   DATA   REJF   DM      I =P         STAT   UAF   FEND
                     DISCP          DMF           SABMP        DISCP
                                                 identification of state CB


  B C   I<>P   DATA   REJF   DM      I =P         STAT   UAF   FRMR
                                    DMF           SABMP
                                                 identification of state CC


  B C   I<>P   DATA   REJF   DM      I =P         identification of state  DA
       FRMRF                SABMP
```

Protection and Synchronisation in
a Message-Switched System

Jon Livesey* and Eric Manning+

*School of Information and Computer Science
Georgia Institute of Technology
Atlanta, Georgia, U.S.A.

+Department of Computer Science and CCNG
University of Waterloo
Waterloo, Ontario, Canada

ABSTRACT

We present a language, the Task Graph Language for the centralized representation of distributed control in the Mininet distributed
operating system. This context-free language allows a programmer to
specify the inter-process communication between a suite of distributed
processes in the form of a Task Graph (centralized representation) and
to have the constraints of the Task Graph enforced at run-time by
coöperating Token Lists, one at each task (distributed control).

The language allows the specification of connectivity (which
tasks can send messages to which), sequencing (which messages must
precede or follow one another), concurrency (which messages can be
sent without regard to order), and mutual exclusion (which message
sequences incident on a single task must be non-interfering).

1. Introduction

A great deal of work has been done in recent years on inter-
process communication between concurrent programs [LeLann 77], [Lam-
port 78], [Reed 78], [Hoare 74], [Chandy 79], [Peacock 79]. However,
synchronisation and protection algorithms have been implemented so
that their logic is distributed among the processes which use them.
This raises a problem similar to that encountered in single processor
systems using semaphores; when a coöperation mechanism is distributed

among its users, misuse of the mechanism by an individual process can affect the operation of other processes. Distributed algorithms exist which carry out synchronisation correctly [LeLann 77], [Lamport 78], [Reed 78], [Peacock 79], but only if they are used correctly. Their correct use depends on correct understanding of the algorithm, and on voluntary coöperation between the participating processes at runtime. In order to be a robust synchronisation algorithm, an algorithm must also be a protection algorithm; that is; it must continue to enforce the user-defined synchronisation on its constituent processes, even in the face of misuse by some of these processes.

This problem was tackled in single-processor systems by the introduction of monitors, [Hoare 74], and path expressions [Habermann 75], [Campbell 74], and [Andler 79]. Synchronisation between users of a resource is enforced by code in the resource itself. Since the synchronisation code is inside a single process (the resource) it can be guaranteed that misuse by one process cannot affect other user processes[*]. We cannot embed synchronisation code for distributed resources in any one process, else this process becomes a non-distributed controller for the whole subsystem. Synchronisation code for distributed resources has to be distributed, yet designers typically want to verify their systems, and they want to verify them as complete systems, not piecemeal as individual processes. This implies that, even if they are implemented in a distributed fashion, algorithms should be specified centrally. In a distributed system one wants a distributed implementation but a centralised specification. In this paper, we describe the justification and principles of such a system. We have also [Livesey 80] described its implementation as part of the Mininet System.

---

[*] The synchronisation which can be enforced may be simple (monitors [Hoare 74]), complex (path expressions [Habermann 75]), or very complex (predicate path expressions [Andler 79]).

1.1. The Mininet System

Message switched operating systems are those in which the main method of inter-process communication (IPC) is by switching messages from one process to another. The Mininet system, [Manning 80][Peebles 74], which was implemented by the first author [Livesey 77] is an example of a purely message-switched system.

The analogue of the process in Mininet is the task. Tasks run in their own, mutually disjoint address spaces, and message switching is the only allowed method of inter-process communication. The processing of a transaction is specified by a rooted, directed graph, the task graph, whose nodes represent tasks and whose directed edges represent message flows among tasks.

1.1.1. Task Structure in Mininet

A task in Mininet is an independently schedulable, executable object. Each task is defined by a Task Queue Entry (TQE), containing pointers to a code module and a data module. A module is a collection of related code or data segments, where a segment is a section of physically contiguous memory. The code module of a task is its executable part, and when a task is active and eligible to run, all its code segments are loaded into memory together. A task cannot manipulate its code segments individually. (We will use the terms process and task interchangeably in this paper, where the meaning is clear from the context.)

A task's data module consists of data segments which can be manipulated individually by the task programmer. It contains the task's stack segment, initialised and un-initialised data segments, and its working storage including message segments. Working segments may be created and written or read by the task for its own use, and may be sent to other tasks as messages. Message segments are simply data segments which have the attribute message, and can therefore be sent to another task using the send command.

For each active task, there is a hardware-imposed limitation of eight code and eight data segmentation registers. Therefore, each task may have up to a maximum of eight code segments, and up to eight immediately addressable, or active, data segments. (A task may own an unbounbed number of inactive data segments. Inactive segments are not immediately addressable, until they have been activated.)

1.1.2. Segment Handling

The task programmer has explicit control over the data segments of his task, including messages. He is allowed to create, destroy, activate and deactivate his own segments, and alter his allowed access to them.

The same segment may be activated and deactivated many times, as the programmer 'time-shares' his eight active segment registers among the segments which he wishes to access from time to time. (To activate a segment means to have the system enter the segment's address, length and access permission bits into one of the machine's hardware segmentation registers, making the segment directly accessible to the code of the task. Conversely, a segment which is not currently needed can be deactivated.)

1.1.3. Inter-Process Communication

The only method of inter-process communication, message sending, is carried out using the send command:

        send (from, to, msg, r_option, s_option);

This call moves the message segment msg from task from to task to. If r_option is APPEND, then to must be the identifier of an existing task, and _msg_ is appended to it. If _r option_ is CREATE, then _to_ must be the identifier of a code module, also known as a _software machine_, from which a new task is created before _msg_ is appended to it.   The identifier of the new task is returned to the sender.   If _s option_ is DESTROY, then _from_ dies as soon as _msg_ has been sent suc-cessfuly, while if _s option_ is PRESERVE, _from_ stays in existence.

There is no explicit _receive_ command corresponding to _send_.   A task which wishes to receive a message must create a special null seg-ment, called a _message-receiving segment_, which ran be taqqed for receipt of a message from a particular sending task, or open to any task. If and when a message segment does arrive, its details are copied into the message-receiving segment's segment table entry, which then becomes the segment table entry of the newly arrived seqment, (which can be _activated_ and then read or written as any other data segment). The segment details are deleted from the message seqment's segment table entry in the sending task, and ownership of the seqment passes from the sending to the receiving task. The receiving task is notified of message arrival by a software _signal_ which causes a transfer of control to a designated address in the task.

The mechanics of message transmission are handled by a privileged task, the Switch, one copy of which runs in each host in the system. This task owns the tables which define tasks and segments, and per-forms the changes to the segment table entries described above. For message transmission to a task in a remote host, the local Switch takes charge of the message segment, and passes it to a local communi-cations processor, the _Communications Device_ (_CD_), which breaks the message down into packets and transmits it to the CD of the remote host across the communications subnetwork. At the remote CD, the packets are reassembled into a complete message which is then handed to the remote Switch for transmission to the receiving task.

2. Message-Switched Inter-Process Communication

2.1. Advantages

In another paper [Manning 80] we discussed what we believe to be the advantages of message-switched systems over procedure oriented systems. We also believe that Mininet has several advantages over other message-switched operating systems; for the purposes of this paper, the principal of these is Mininet's non-blocking receive primitive.

However, message-switched systems have some problems, which we discuss now.

2.2. Code Fragility

We have discovered by experience that in programming an unstructured message-passing system, the programmer encounters several practical difficulties: the need to keep in mind the properties and characteristics of other tasks when programming his own; uncertainty about which tasks in the system are still alive and which have died; uncertainties over the exact sequence of events in the system; detection of such bugs as, a sender task sending a message to the wrong receiver; and, in general, needing to know 'too much' about the exact assignment of function to task, in the system. These difficulties conspire to cause process code to be 'fragile' with respect to changes in inter-process communication. Hence we have

> Problem 1.1: How, in a message-oriented system, do we represent the processing of transactions so to avoid the fragility of code predicted by the difficulties mentioned above?

2.3. Redundancy

In order to have some confidence that a specification correctly expresses the intent of a task, it is often useful to have two mutually redundant specifications. In designing software, if we can arrange to have our intent executed in two mutually redundant ways, with checking between them, our confidence in the outcome is increased.

Problem 1.2: Can we find a simple and effective means of specifying system behaviour, suitable for a run-time redundancy check on that behaviour?

The method chosen must implement several kinds of redundancy check on the run-time behaviour of tasks.

1.   Correct sender and receiver for each message.

2.   Correct sequencing of message passing.

3.   Detection of unauthorised message passing.

4.   Detection of missing messages.

5.   Detection of tasks which die prematurely.

6.   Detection of message transmissions which time out.

7.   Detection of other hardware and software malfunctions.

On the other hand, we can identify several factors which are not checked by a run-time enforcement scheme:

1.   Internal actions of tasks, not involving message passing.

2.   The relative execution speeds of tasks, or changes in execution speed, except where this is synchronised by message passing.

3.   Speed of inter-process communication between pairs of tasks, for instance, between tasks inside one processor, or between tasks in different processors.

4.   Changes in allocation of tasks to hardware hosts.

5.   Changes in hardware configuration, over and above a certain specified minimum, at a host.

2.4. Inter-Task Communication

Since inter-process communication is by means of message passing, we need to ensure that these messages have the correct sequence. Hence:

Problem 1.3: How do we control the sequence of messages

emitted by a single task?

Since system resources, such as files, directories, peripherals and the like, are guarded by resource tasks, and since message passing is the only allowed mode of inter-task communication, the problem of enforcing prescribed access by tasks to system resources reduces to the problem of controlling message transmission among tasks.

> Problem 1.4: Impose a control structure which will ensure that messages between pairs of tasks go from the planned sender to the planned receiver, and in the planned sequence.

We have to impose a structure on the subnets of tasks which make up system resources. We previously said that all system resources were tasks. Now we wish to introduce higher-level objects called task graphs (see sec 1.1) containing more than one task, which can be treated as tasks. Rather than seeing individual tasks in a system, we wish to see resources, made up of coöperating subnets of tasks, whose interactions can be planned in advance. If a resource is made up of, say, directory, file, and device driver tasks, we wish to ensure that user tasks send request messages only to the directory task, and not straight to the device driver tasks.

> Problem 1.5: Introduce a control system which will allow the imposition of a structure onto the subnets of tasks making up system resources, so that these structures look like single resource tasks. The system adopted must impose a control on the access to these resources by message passing, and on the interactions among the resource's constituent tasks. We call this sequence control inside resources.

We may have several user tasks accessing the same resource, and in this case we wish to control their sequence of access to it (for instance, the reader-writer problem, or the mutual exclusion problem).

> Problem 1.6: Introduce a control system which will allow control of the sequence of use of these resources, by message passing. We call this sequence control outside resources.

2.5. Internal Task Structure

Problems arise from internal task structure, which is intimately connected with inter-process communication (IPC). Fig 1.1 represents a typical Mininet task, with message-handling routines R1,...., each of which is specialised to handle one type of input message. (The In-1,...In+2 are incoming messages, and the On-1,...On+2 are outgoing messages.) Since we employ a non-blocking receive primitive, these input messages can arrive in indeterminate order. This increases the potential parallelism exhibited by the task, since it does not have to wait for any particular message, but can simply serve them first-come first-served. However, this very flexibility may create difficulties. If an internal shared variable X of the task is accessed by routines Rn and Rn+1, say, then we have a potential internal critical section.

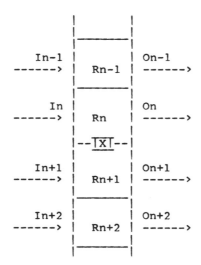

Fig 1.1 - Event-Driven Task Model

In fact, we may have two problems.

1. The arrival of message In+1 may interrupt the processing of message In while Rn is accessing the shared variable X. If Rn+1 then changes X, the results of Rn's computation may be in error. (the critical section problem).

2. The sequencing of access of Rn, Rn+1, to the shared variable X may be important. We might wish to demand that the sequence of access to X be <Rn, Rn+1>, for instance. (The shared variable

access sequence problem).

Any task which has two or more message-handling routines adding messages to a common queue will have the critical section problem, and any task which has a resource allocation routine Rn, and a resource allocation release routine Rn+1 will face the access sequence problem. In either of these cases, we can easily solve the problem by introducing code inside the task. In the first case, this internal code would have to ensure mutual exclusion on X, between Rn and Rn+1. In the second case, the internal code would have to enforce the correct sequence of access to X by Rn and Rn+1.

However, if we adopt this approach, mutual exclusion and/or access sequence code will be duplicated in every task with internally shared data. It would be preferable, from the point of view of task size, and also from that of task simplicity, (and therefore verifiability) if we could handle these problems outside tasks, by controlling message sequencing there.

Problem 1.7: How can we control message sequencing outside tasks in order to avoid critical sections and access sequence problems inside them?

3. Current Solutions

In this section we mention some current work in message-switched and procedure-oriented operating systems which is intended to solve some of these problems.

Problem 1.1: The problem of transaction representation is the subject of considerable interest, and we might mention the work of Lessor [Lessor 79] and Cook [Cook 79], in which resource structure is reflected in a process source language which includes communication connectivity (but not message sequencing). Mininet introduced the idea of a task graph [Manning 78] in order to represent transaction processing. System 250 [Cosserat 72], [England 72] set up domain structures, controlled by capability lists, to represent resources, and a similar idea is used in CAL, [Lampson 76], and also CAP, [Wilkes 79], but in all these systems, we must rely on the code inside resource processes to use the capabilities they own in the correct sequence.

Problem 1.2: The problem of run-time redundancy checks has been considered by Devy [Devy 79].

Problem 1.3: The sequencing of message emission from a single process is handled inside processes in most contemporary programming languages for distributed processing, (Communicating Sequential Processes [Hoare 78], PCL [Lessor 79], Communication Port [Mao 79], and *MOD [Cook 79], for example) but in this research we shall concentrate on ways to enforce this sequence from outside the task.

Problem 1.4: The question of process name discovery and of checking that messages are sent to the correct process is a very large one, and it is implied in apparently unrelated work such as that on capablilities [Dennis 66], process renaming [Cheriton 78], and bidding systems [Farber 77]. In the field of message-switched systems, the Distributed Computer Network employs named ports, which can be granted and revoked by their owning processes, in order to ensure that messages pass between the intended processes [Mills 76]. However, in DCN, these ports are treated more or less as capabilities, and no sequence of use is imposed. Milner [Milner 79] also considers named ports, which can only be con- nected if they have converse names (port a leads to port a'), when dealing with sender and receiver processes. In DCS ⌐Farber 73⌐ an exchange of bids between requesting and serving process ensures correct sender and receiver for subsequent messages, while in HXDP [Jenson 78] and DLCN [Reames 76], this appears to depend on the logic of the sender and receiver process. The rendevous table of the KOCOS system [Kamibayashi 78] might be useful here, since it can be used to set up a form of virtual channel between processes. The channels of DEMOS [Baskett 79] are similar, and all have the same defect; that they require the voluntary cooperation of sender and receiver, rather than having correct sender and receiver enforced from outside. The TANDEM system ⌐Tandem ⌐, provides some hardware assistance in inter-process communication, allowing the programmer to view the entire system as a field of process names, ignoring the physical location of processes. Its hardware- controlled message transmission facility also has the potential for supervising message transmission.

Problem 1.5: The link construction of the DEMOS system [Baskett 79] has some potential for aiding in the introduction of control structure inside resource subnets, since links can be created and deleted dynamically. The same can be said for port and capability structures, if we add sequencing information. Cheriton [Cheriton 78] presents a static system for discovering deadlocks in resource subnets. The classic capability systems

[England 72], [Needham 79], trust system resource programs to use capablities correctly according to the resource structure that they represent, while Hydra [Cohen E 75] appears to rely on a proliferation of capability types to guard against malfunction by system resource processes.

Problem 1.6: Sequence control inside a single process (or resource) has been well studied by Hoare [Hoare 74], Brinch Hansen [Brinch Hansen 77], Habermann [Habermann 75] and Andler [Andler 79]. The methods proposed range from P and V operations, via compiler checks [Brinch Hansen 77], to Path Expressions [Habermann 75]. The crucial point here is the separation of the implementation of the resource from the enforcement of the synchronisation [Andler 79]. Sequence control between resources has been examined by Farber and Pickens [Farber 4], and by Cheriton [Cheriton 78]. Path expressions [Habermann 75], [Campbell 74], [Andler 79], appear to be the best current method of representing sequence control, but have so far been applied only to single processes.

Problem 1.7: The related problem of critical section avoidance has been dealt with at length by Hoare [Hoare 74], and for message-switched systems, by Cheriton [Cheriton 78]. However, both of these authors have treated the avoidance of critical sections as an attribute of the individual process, (Cheriton, for instance, by enforcing strict sequentiality on message reception) rather than as a property of the message sequence between processes.

The component problems discussed above have already received conderable attention. (see bibliography). However, as far as we know, e integration of solutions to all of the above problems into one n-time system has never yet been accomplished.

4. Task Graph

We now describe our own method of inter-process communication enforcement. We chose a graphical representation for our system in which nodes represent processes (tasks) and directed edges represent message flows between the tasks (message edges). We refer to this model as the Task Graph [Manning 78], [Livesey 78]. The user programmer can specify protection and synchronisation constraints through a Task Graph of his own subsystem; there are four choices in representing processing as graphs.

1. Employ a graph language directly. This involves representing the graph nodes and edges step by step at the source coding level. In Mininet, this would involve the direct use of the tokens which we employ to control message sequencing (see section 5.) This is the equivalent of assembly-language programming, and is inappropriate in a system in which the nodes (tasks) are themselves fairly complex.

2. Extract a graphical structure from an existing programming language, such as FORTRAN or Pascal. This approach is very hard, and not relevant where much of the node (task) code is already written.

3. Use an existing concurrent language, such as concurrent Pascal. Several authors, such as Brinch, Hansen, Cook, Mao and Lessor [op.cit.] have taken the approach of integrating communication between concurrent processes into the source language in which these processes are written. In our opinion, this approach, while valuable, has some significant defects:

   i. It leads to the integration of processes into a particular set associated with a particular transaction (in Mininet, a given task can take part in several different transactions, by being invoked in their several Task Graphs).

ii.   It prevents the writing of tasks in several source languages, each suitable for tasks of a particular kind (mathematical, character handling, symbol manipulation, etc).

iii. The compiler for a language including both the task source language and the message-passing control language is likely to be very large. Moreover, the elapsed time to complete such a compiler is likely to be larger than that required to write a compiler for the task source language and the message-passing control language in parallel.

iv. Most important, it discards a valuable redundancy between the source program and the system level.

4.   As a final option, introduce a new language specifically to represent inter-process communication.

We have chosen the fourth alternative, and in order to allow the automatic generation of protection and synchronisation code from the Task Graph, we introduce a context-free language, the Task Graph Language [Livesey 80].

The language allows the specification of connectivity (which tasks can communicate), sequencing (which messages must precede or follow one another), concurrency (which messages can be sent without regard to order), and mutual exclusion (which message sequences incident on a single task must be non-interfering). A compiler parses a program written in this language, a Task Graph Program, to generate so-called Token Lists. Token lists are a distributed representation of the task graph in the form of mini-task graphs, one per process, each mini-task graph containing just the information needed to synchronise the message sending operations of that process with those of its neighbours in the task graph (the processes with which it exchanges messages).

4.1. Example I

To explain the token-based enforcement mechanism used in Mininet and to illustrate the importance of correct sequencing of message-sending activity at run-time, we can consider the transaction represented in Fig 1.2. The tasks in the Task Graph are as follows:

T1 - User's record update task

T2 - File task

T3 - Disc task

T4 - Error report task

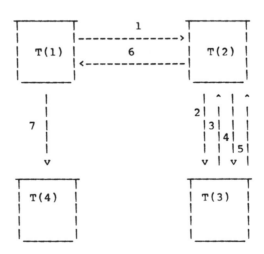

Fig 1.2 - Task Graph

The whole Task Graph could represent a request from task T1 for T2 to read a file record consisting of two disc blocks, whose block numbers, or a pointer to them, are in the first message, the read request (edge e1). (The subgraph consisting of T2, T3 is the resource consisting of the file and driver tasks.) T2 then issues two disc block read requests to T3, and when the data blocks are returned by

T3, T2 unites them and sends them back to T1 as a single message. The message sending activity represented by the edges e1 to e7 might be as follows:

e1 — <u>read</u> a record (block(m), block(n))

e2 — <u>read</u> a block (m)

e3 — data block (m)

e4 — <u>read</u> a block (n)

e5 — data block (n)

e6 — record data = concat (n, m)

e7 — error notification message

In addition to enforcing correct sender and receiver identities for each message, we want to ensure that the messages are sent in the specified order at run-time. For instance, it is essential that e2 is not executed before e1, else e2's message must contain a fictitious block number. Equally, we have to ensure that all of e2 to e5 take place before e6, else e6 must contain fictitious record data. On the other hand, there is potentially some parallellism to be exploited among the edges e2 to e5, allowing, for instance, both 'read block' requests to be dispatched before the return of any disc block from the disc driver task. The disc driver task T3 might also reorder the requests in e2, e4 in order to deal with them in a sequence which would, for instance, optimize head movement, so the order of e3, e5 might be reversed as a result. Finally, we should take care that e6 takes place within some predetermined time, else T1 will be hung up waiting for it. This in turn implies that T2 should not wait for e3 or e5 indefinitely.

We also want to repeat the request <u>while</u> T1 successfully executes e1, and to check for the failure of message transmissions; we will send message e7 if any occur.

4.2. Task Graph Description Language

```
begin
    /*  the files holding the software machines */

    sm      sm1     ==      "/sw/sm/update";
    sm      sm2     ==      "/sw/sm/file";
    sm      sm3     ==      "/sw/sm/disc";
    sm      sm4     ==      "/sw/sm/error";

    /*  the tasks in terms of software machines */

    task    task1   == sm1;
    task    task2   == sm2;
    task    task3   == sm3;
    task    task4   == sm4;

    /* declare task1 to be of type 'root' */

    root: task1;

    /* declare task3 to be of type 'perm' */

    perm: task3;

    /* declare task2 etc to be of type 'trans' */

    trans:  task2,  task4;

    /* e1 etc are of type 'edge' */

    edge:   e1,     e2,     e3;
    edge:   e4,     e5,     e6,     e7;

    /* declare the sender and receiver of each edge */

    e1      := task1 creates task2;
    e2      := e4    := task2 -> task3;
    e3      := e5    := task3 -> task2;
    e6      := task2 -> task1;
    e7      := task1 creates task4;

    ( while
    ( e1 ) do (if ( send_err (
            ( [ e2 < e3¯] ^ [ e4 < e5 ] ) < e6  ))
                then e7 ));

end
```

Fig 1.3 - Task Graph Description Program

We show the Task Graph Language representation of this task graph in figure 1.3. In the next section, we introduce the semantics of the language.

4.3. Semantics

In this section we give semantic definitions of the Task Graph Language constructs.

Software Machine definition;

$$sm:\quad sml\ ==\ "/sw/sm/update";$$

This allows us to associate the name of a software machine (actually, a pathname of the file system) with the task whose code part it will be.

Task declaration;

$$task:\qquad taskl\ ==\ sml;$$

This allows us to declare certain named objects as tasks; in other words, nodes of the graph, and associate them with their software machines.

Type declaration;

This allows us to declare the type of certain named objects as edge.

$$edge:\qquad el,\quad e2,\quad e3;$$

Tasks can also be declared as being of type perm, meaning that they were not created in this task graph.

Edge definition;

$$el\quad :=\ taskl\ ->\ task2;$$

This allows us to give the sending and receiving task of each edge.

Edge sequencing;

$$el\ <\ e2$$

This has execution order:

$$e1; \quad e2$$

Edge Parallelism;

$$e1 \; \hat{} \; e2$$

This has execution orderings:

$$e1; \; e2 \qquad or \qquad e2; \; e1$$

For sequencing and parallelism, edges e1, e2, can be replaced by series/parallel collections of edges:

$$(e1 < e2) \; \hat{} \; (e3 < e4)$$

The possible execution orderings* specified by this expression are:

$$e1; \; e2; \; e3; \; e4$$
$$e1; \; e3; \; e2; \; e4$$
$$e1; \; e3; \; e4; \; e2$$
$$e3; \; e4; \; e1; \; e2$$
$$e3; \; e1; \; e4; \; e2$$
$$e3; \; e1; \; e2; \; e4$$

A transaction will not be executed in exactly the same way every time it is invoked; events such as the following may take place to change the execution sequence.

1. Hardware or software errors.

    The hardware provides error codes for some common program malfunctions (address error, arithmetic error, etc.). In order to redirect processing when these occur, we need a set of functions which detect hardware-generated errors, for example:

$$if \; address\_error \; () \; then \; S1;$$

2. Erroneous message transmission (wrong receiver, non-existent

---

* Please see 3.5 for a more restrictive form of parallelism.

message, receiver not ready, etc.) and failures in the message transmission mechanism.

The Switch returns a value for each successful or unsuccessful Switch call. This value (identifier of newly created task, address of newly activated segment, ERROR, etc) is already supplied to the calling task. We have proposed a set of functions which detect return values from system calls, for example:

if system_error() then S1 else S2;

3. Changes in data values read during processing, in particular data errors and exceptions.

A function

assign_to_task_graph()

which can be invoked at the user task level, allows this restricted data assignment. At the Task Graph level we examine the result of the latest such assignment using:

if user_data() then S1 else S2;

4. Changes in data values in messages. We have experimented with typed messages, messages which carry data, along with a standardized description of the data; data field locations, types, and range checks, along with system information such as Task Graph and edge identifier. At run-time, the Switch has access to the message itself, because the Switch is responsible for transferring it from sender to receiver task, and so we can write Task Graph procedures which examine the contents of any message which conforms to this standardized format. To ensure this, we could enforce the message format as a system standard.

choice

The semantics of the choice construct:

$$\text{if} \text{ <exp> } \underline{then} \text{ S1 } \underline{else} \text{ S2 } \underline{fi};$$

are that the expression <exp> is evaluated at runtime, and the result used to control which of S1, S2, will be executed. The expression can be any statement in the language which returns a logical value.

Iteration

$$\text{while} \text{ <exp> } \underline{do} \text{ S1 } \underline{end}$$

We execute statement S1 while <exp> remains true.

4.4. Binding

It can happen that we wish a sequence of edges to be treated as a unit, so that either all are executed, or, if some edge fails, all subsequent edges in the unit are aborted. For the 'bound' construct:

$$[\text{ e1 } < \text{ e2 } < \text{ ...... } < \text{ en }]$$

we introduce the convention that as soon as an edge in a bound sequence fails, the entire bound construct fails, and we jump forward to the end of binding ']'. If a bound edge sequence has begun to execute, its execution cannot be interleaved with the execution of other edges (provided preceedence between the edges can be enforced). For the following example:

$$([\text{ e1 } < \text{ e2 }] \text{ ^ } [\text{ e3 } < \text{ e4 }])$$

we have two bound constructs:

$$[\text{ e1 } < \text{ e2 }]$$
$$[\text{ e3 } < \text{ e4 }]$$

The edges in these constructs can be executed in either order as pairs, but cannot interleave with one another. The possible execution orders are therefore:

```
el; e2; e3; e4;

e3; e4; el; e2;
```

This is a form of mutual exclusion on the two message sequences el < e2 and e3 < e4; they can be executed in either order, but may not interfere with one another. We have therefore introduced a restriction, compared to an ordinary concurrent construct:

$$(el < e2) \; \char`\^ \; (e3 < e4)$$

in which there are four other possible execution orders:

```
el; e3; e2; e4;
el; e3; e4; e2;
e3; el; e2; e4;
e3; el; e4; e2;
```

The convention that a bound edge sequence jumps forward to the terminating ']' if one of its edges fails, effectively prevents it from causing a livelock in a Task Graph [1]. In an if-then-else, the condition expression <exp> can be a statement of the form:

$$[\; el < e2 < e3 \;]$$

In this case, all of [el < e2 < e3] would be executed, and the final result used. By the 'final' result we mean success, if all the edges execute successfully, or if any of el, e2 or e3 fail, then the entire bound construct fails, and the final error status is the error status of the edge which failed.

4.5. Create and Die Edges

Since task creation in Mininet is associated with message passing, certain edges in a Task Graph are distinguished as create edges.

```
edge1      := task1 creates --> task2;
```

---

[1] If we did not terminate a bound construct whenever one of its edges failed, then it could hold up subsequent, or concurrent, Task Graph edges.

Such edges represent the sending of one message, and also the associated creation of a task. Only certain tasks will be created during the execution of a Task Graph; others will exist permanently [2]. Similarly, task death is associated with message sending, so we can have a message edge:

edge1 := task1 dies --> task2;

indicating that task 1 dies if it successfully transmits its message to task2.

4.6. Non-Message Synchronisation

It is possible for two edges in a Task Graph to have their order specified without there being an exchange of information inside the Task Graph to which they belong. For instance, if we have a Task Graph:

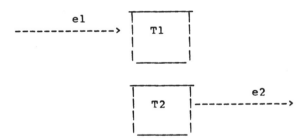

then it would be possible for task T1, upon the arrival of edge e1, to invoke some other Task Graph which changes some data value external to this Task Graph, perhaps in a file. Meanwhile, task T2 invokes some third Task Graph which examines the data value, and T2 does not execute edge e2 until the data value is changed by T1. We

---

[2] Examples of such tasks are resource-hiding tasks such as peripheral controller tasks, file-open tasks, and so on. There must only be one copy of such tasks, so as to ensure exclusive access to the resource which they hide. Requests for access to these resources all come to the same task, which then services them. A resource-managing task can therefore not be created by any one task graph handling a transaction, but must be created centrally, so as to ensure that one and only one task with access to the resource exists.

therefore have an effective synchronization of the edges el, e?, without information about the arrival of el or the sending of e?, being exchanged <u>inside</u> the Task Graph.

Consequently we allow non-message edges, which are defined in the Task Graph program as

```
edgel := taskl signals task2;
```

5. Example 1 Revisited

We return to figure 1.3, and point out some details which may not be obvious. First, two edges, e1 and e7, are declared to be <u>create</u> edges, a side-effect of which is to create the tasks declared as their receiver tasks, which do not exist before their execution. The tasks created are task2 and task4, while tasks task1 and task3 are assumed already to exist, for different reasons. Task task3 is a permanent task, already existing outside the Task Graph. In fact task3 is a <u>resource task</u>, a disc driver, which is permanently in existence, accepting requests from many user tasks and in this case from task2, the file task created by this Task Graph. Task task1 is the 'root' task of this Task Graph, created, not by a create edge within the Task Graph, but by the Task Graph Supervisor in the invocation of the Task Graph. Tasks declared as 'perm' or as 'root' are assumed to exist before the Task Graph is executed, while tasks declared as 'task' must appear as the receiver task of some <u>create</u> edge <u>before</u> they can be used as the sender or receiver of any non-create edge in the Task Graph.

In this Task Graph, we intend to execute the sequence of edges inside the condition of the if-then-else as long as e1 is executed successfully by task T1. The if condition is a function call send_err() which returns the value <u>true</u> if any of the edges in its parameter list causes an error in execution. If any edge in this sequence fails, then the edge e7 will be executed, and not otherwise. It is not quite realistic to have the error message edge e7 executed always by task T1, but this simplification should make the Task Graph easier to understand. Note that within the edges which make up this parameter list:

$$(([e2 < e3] \hat{} [e4 < e5]) < e6)$$

we have two bound constructs:

$$[\ e2 < e3 \ ]$$
$$[\ e4 < e5 \ ]$$

The edges in these constructs can be executed in either order <u>as</u> <u>pairs</u>, but cannot interleave with one another. We therefore have mutual exclusion on task task3 ("disc") with respect to [e2 < e3] and [e4 < e5]. Put another way, tasks serves requests in a strictly serial manner. The possible execution orders are therefore:

$$e2; \ e3; \ e4; \ e5; \ e6$$
$$e4; \ e5; \ e2; \ e3; \ e6$$

We now describe the mechanism by which this task graph is enforced at run-time.

6. Enforcement Mechanism

The Task Graph has to act as a check on the operations of the Switch. There should therefore be a redundancy check between the Switch, which tries to execute what the user tasks request, and the required mechanism, which checks message passing requests made by user tasks against the Task Graph. The sequencing of message passing is specified by the Task Graph, and we need to ensure that this sequence is preserved at run-time. We considered three mechanisms for this. All three involve one form or another of a task called a Task Graph Supervisor.

6.1. Enforcement Through the Task Graph Supervisor

Under the first mechanism considered, the Switch invokes the Task Graph Supervisor whenever a task requests the Switch to send a message. The Task Graph Supervisor holds a representation of the task graph in a data segment and can therefore determine whether the proposed message sending or task creation activity corresponds to the task graph. All message passing, task creation and task destruction take place through the Switch. This ensures that the Task Graph Supervisor is consulted about every such action, assuming correct behaviour on the part of the Switch.

The main objection to this method is that each message sent would involve invoking an additional task, and, as a result of this, message passing overheads would rise unacceptably. We have a message transmission time of about one millisecond; but invocation of the Task Graph Supervisor for each message send would multiply this time by a factor of at least two. (Each message send would involve sending the message first to the Task Graph Supervisor, loading and executing the Task Graph Supervisor to check if the proposed message send is allowed, and then forwarding the message to its intended receiver task.) A similar objection seems to be valid in the case of the Petri

Net system of Ayache [Ayache 1].

6.2. Through the Switch

In the second proposal the Task Graph Supervisor would check the Task Graph for validity and then pass it to the Switch, so that the Switch could check the progress of transaction processing against the Task Graph.

The objections to this are, first, that the Switch would have to hold many Task Graphs, one for each currently active transaction. As a result the Switch virtual address space would tend to fill up. Secondly, the Switch would have taken over some of the functions of the Task Graph Supervisor, contrary to the principle of separating functions into tasks. The Task Graph would no longer be under the control of the Task Graph Supervisor. We would therefore lose the redundancy between Switch and Task Graph Supervisor that the Task Graph is intended to preserve. Finally, who would hold the Task Graph for a transaction if its processing were spread over more than one machine?

6.3. The Token List Mechanism

In this method the Task Graph Supervisor holds the Task Graph in its own user address space, but distributes information corresponding to the Task Graph in a non-graphical form to the individual tasks, for use at run-time.

Briefly, each task has a token list, where its tokens are stored, and from which the Switch can retrieve them. On the basis of the graph, tokens are distributed by the Task Graph Supervisor to the tasks in the graph. They are later used by those tasks to 'pay for' system services, such as message sending and task creation. The token list is inaccessible to the user task, and can only be accessed by the Switch when it checks a token which has been offered to pay for a send.

On the basis of the nodes and edges in the task graph, the task graph supervisor distributes tokens to the tasks in its task graph which are currently active. Send tokens are rights to pass a message to a designated receiving task, receive tokens are rights to receive the corresponding message, while create tokens are rights to create a task from a designated code module. There are also control tokens which redirect processing inside a task graph, and which are generated automacally by the task graph language compiler to represent choice and iteration statements in the task graph source program.

Each directed edge which represents a send operation is represented at run-time by two tokens; a send token owned by the sender, and a receive token owned by the receiver. At run-time these two tokens have to be used up as a pair. For a send action to take place, there must be a send token at the sender task, and a corresponding receive token at the receiver, and each of these two tokens must be the next unused token of their respective token lists.

In order to carry out their message sending and task creating activities, the tasks in the task graph must present their send, receive, and create tokens to the Switch when they make the corresponding system calls. Thus the Switch will guarantee to check that all message sending and task creating activity of a transaction is validated by the appropriate tokens previously given out by the task graph supervisor. (The tokens of each task reside in its control segment, which is inaccessible to the task.)

The send system call

send (from, to, msg, R_option, S_option)

is trapped by the Switch, whose job it is to make the changes in table entries necessary to transfer the segment msg from task from to task <u>to</u>. The Switch first verifies the existence of <u>from</u>, <u>to</u>, and <u>msg</u> in the proper form, and then checks the token lists of <u>from</u> and <u>to</u>, to ensure that they have the correct <u>send</u> and <u>receive</u> tokens. The discipline which is enforced on the use of tokens is that the most recently received token at a task which is as yet unused is the one which must be used next. No <u>send</u> command is allowed to be carried out at run-time unless the sending and the receiving tasks both have the correct tokens as their latest unused tokens.

This method has the following advantages:

1.   It imposes very little extra load on the Switch at runtime, (less than 10% extra on any single <u>send</u>) since the tokens are located in data structures which are accessed by the Switch in the normal course of message sending.

2.   It allows distribution of control information, even over several machines. Hence it is amenable to distribution of processing, a requirement for those Mininet transactions which violate locality of reference.

3.   This distribution ensures that a task, even if it should get access to its own token list, can make very few deductions about the processing of the whole Task Graph. When Task Graph information is held centrally, as in the methods above, a task which obtains access to it can see how the whole transaction is processed.

4.   It maintains separation of function between Switch and Task Graph Supervisor.

5.   It allows changes at run-time to transaction execution.

1.4. Example I - Token Lists

The token lists corresponding to part of the task graph in Fig 1.1 are shown in Fig 1.4. We concentrate here on the simplified sequence of edges:

```
Task 1            Task 2             Task 3
------            ------             ------

send t2           receive t1         par_begin
receive t2        par_begin           ser_begin
                    ser_begin          receive t2
                      send t3           send t2
                      receive t3      ser_end
                    ser_end           ser_begin
                    ser_begin          receive t2
                      send t3           send t2
                      receive t3      ser_end
                    ser_end           par_end
                  par_end
                  send t1
```

<u>Fig 1.4 - Token Lists for Tasks T1, T2, T3.</u>

e1 < ((e2 < e3) ^ (e4 < e5)) < e6;

    with the same senders and receivers as the same edges in fig 1.1.
(The token list for the complete task graph is too complicated to be
shown here. We explain the token lists generated for <u>choice</u> and
<u>iteration</u> statements in [Livesey 80]) Token lists are linked lists of
token values, each list having an associated pseudo P-counter (Token
Counter), and at run-time the tokens in them are used up in the following sequence. The next token on the list of any task attempting a
message-sending operation (that currently pointed to by the token
counter for that task) is examined, and compared with the current
token on the list of the proposed receiving task. Tokens which make
up matched pairs, with matching operations and objects, are able to be
executed. In Figure 1.4, at the beginning of the transaction the only
valid pair of <u>send-receive</u> tokens is the pair <send t2, rec t1> which
is next on the token lists of the tasks T1 and T2. This pair of
tokens corresponds to the edge numbered e1 in Fig 1.2. After this
edge is executed the token counters for the two tasks (T1,T2) are
moved on to the next tokens in their token lists, and then matched
token pairs are sought again. We can ignore the (rec t2) token at

task T1 since it matches with the (send t1) token which is at the bottom of task T2's token list, and therefore inaccessible. These two cannot yet make a valid send-receive pair.

Looking at tasks T2 and T3, the pseudo-token par begin indicates the beginning of a section of the task's token list containing tokens or sequences of tokens, which can be used concurrently. That is, two tokens enclosed by a par begin-par end pair may be used as though either of them was the latest token. A ser begin pseudo-token indicates the start of a strict serial group of tokens within a concurrent series. That is, if we have tokens enclosed by a ser begin-ser end pair then only the next token in the group can be used concurrently with other tokens in the enclosing par begin-par end pair which holds this ser begin-ser end group.

In Fig 1.4 we can use the next tokens in either of the ser begin-ser end groups inside the outermost par begin-par end grouping. This implements the parallellism in the task graph in fig 1.1, which allows either of edges e2 or e4 to proceed next at run-time. It also prevents edges e3 or e5 from being executed until either edges e2 or e4 have been executed, preserving the precedence relation between edges e2 and e3 and between edges e4 and e5. Finally, edge e6 can only be executed when the pair <send t1, rec t2> are the next tokens on the token lists of tasks T1 and T2, and this can only happen after all task T2's other tokens have been marked 'used', that is, when edges e2, e3, e4 and e5 have been executed. This enforces the final precedence relation in Fig 1.3, that which says that both the pair (edge e2 < edge e3) and the pair (edge e4 < edge e5) precede edge 6.

5. Compilation

We compile the representation of a task graph in the Task Graph Language into token lists automatically. In compilation, we follow the path:

1. Compose the task graph in the Task Graph Language. (done manually)

2. Parse the task graph, and find syntactic errors.

3. Build a precedence graph. This graph shows the precedence relation between the edges in the task graph.

4. Generate token lists from the precedence graph, and save them in a file for this task graph.

5. The Task Graph Supervisor program reads the file, containing the token list representation of the precedence graph, at run-time when a transaction enters the system, and distributes tokens to the tasks which are created to process the transaction.

6. The token lists are used for run-time enforcement.

These steps are described in detail in [Livesey 80]. A prototype version of the software to achieve steps 1. to 6. is operational.

7. Solutions

In this section, we examine how successful our chosen control method is in solving the problems raised in the last chapter.

__Problem 1.1__: Task graphs impose a structure on message-passing.

__Problem 1.2__: Task Graphs allow a useful redundancy between the message passing defined inside tasks, and that defined in the task graph.

__Problem 1.3__: Task Graphs allow the sequencing of messages emitted by a single task.

__Problem 1.4__: Task graphs impose a control structure which ensures that messages between pairs of tasks go from the planned sender to the planned receiver, and in the planned sequence.

__Problem 1.5__: Task Graphs allow a structure to be imposed on the tasks which jointly make up a resource, and they impose sequencing on the interactions between these tasks. A single resource task can appear in several task graphs.

__Problem 1.6__: Task graphs allow a time sequence to be imposed on the accesses made to a resource by user tasks.

__Problem 1.7__: Task graphs allow sequencing to be imposed on messages arriving at tasks, to avoid the programming of critical sections inside the tasks.

__Problem 1.8__: Task graphs allow the same task to behave as a blocking or non-blocking task, depending on the sequence imposed on messages to it.

Acknowledgements

We wish to acknowledge the contributions of other members of the ininet project at Waterloo. The financial support of the Natural cience and Engineering Research Council of Canada is gratefully acknowledged.

9. Bibliography

Andler 79 Andler S. Predicate Path Expressions. Proc. Sixth Annual ACM Symposium on Principles of Programming Languages. A.C.M. Jan 1979.

Baskett 79   Baskett F., J.H. Howard, and J.T. Montague Task Communication in DEMOS. Proc. 6th ACM Symposium on O.S. Principles. 1979.

Brinch Hansen 77   Brinch Hansen P. The Architecture of Concurrent Programs. Prentice Hall. 1977.

Campbell 74   Campbell R.H. and A.N. Habermann The Specification of Process Synchronization by Path Expressions. Lecture Notes in Computer Science. Springer-Verlag, Vol 16, 1974.

Cheriton 78   Cheriton D.R. Multi-Process Structure and the THOTH Operating System. PhD Thesis. University of Waterloo, August, 1978.

Chandy 79 Chandy K. M. and J. Misra Distributed Simulation: A Case Study in the Design and Verification of Distributed Programs. IEEE Trans. on Software Engineering. SE-5, No. 5, Sept 1979.

Cohen 75 Cohen E., and D. Jefferson Protection in the Hydra Operating System. 5th Symposium on Operating System Principles. Texas 1975.

Cook 79   Cook R.P. *MOD - A Language for Distributed Computing. Proc. 1st. International Conference on Distributed Computer Systems. IEEE. Oct. 1979.

Cosserat 72   Cosserat D.C. A Capability oriented Multiprocessor System for Real-time Applications. I.C.C. Conference, Washington, Oct 1972.

Dennis 66 Dennis J.B. and E.C. Van Horn Programming Semantics for multiprogrammed computations. Comm. ACM 9, March 1966.

Devy 79   Devy M. and M. Diaz Multilevel Specification and Validation of the Control in Communication Systems. Proc. 1st. International Conference on Distributed Computer Systems. IEEE. Oct. 1979.

England 72   England D.M. Operating System of System 250. International Switching Symposium. Cambridge, Mass., June 1972.

Farber 73 Farber D. J. and K.C. Larsen The System Architecture of the Distributed Computer System - The Communications System. Proc. NCC. June 1973.

Farber 76 Farber D.J. and J.R. Pickens The Overseer, a Powerful Communications Attribute for Bebugging and Security in thin-wire Connected Control Structures. Proc. ICCC 1976. October 1976.

Habermann 75   Habermann A.N. Path Expressions. Tech. Report Dept. of Computer Science. Carnegie-Mellon University. June 1975.

Hoare 74   Hoare C.A.R. Monitors, an Operating Systems Structuring Concept. CACM Oct 74.

Hoare 78   Hoare C.A.R.   Communicating Sequential Processes.   C.A.C.M.
    21, 8.   August 1978.

Jensen 78 Jensen E.D.   The Honeywell Experimental Distributed Proces-
    sor - An Overview.   Computer 11, 1.   Jan 1978.

Kamibayashi 78 Kamibayashi N. et al.   Distributed Processing Oriented
    Interprocess Communication Facility for KOCOS.   Proc. 3rd
    USA-Japan Computer Conference.   AFIPS.   Oct 1978.

Lamport 78   Lamport L.   Time, Clocks and the Ordering of Events in
    a Distributed System.   C.A.C.M. 21, 7.   July 1978.

Lampson 76   Lampson B.W. & Sturgis H.E.   Reflections on an Operat-
    ing System Design.   CACM 19, 5 (May 1976) pp 251-265.

Lelann 77 Lelann G.E.   Distributed   Processing - Towards a Formal
    Approach.   Proc. IFIP 1977.

Lessor 79 Lessor V., Serrain D. and Bonar J.   PCL: A Process Oriented
    Job Control Language.   Proc. 1st. International Conference on
    Distributed Computer Systems.   IEEE.   Oct. 1979.

Livesey 77 Livesey N. J.   A Hybrid Implementation of Capabilities.   M.
    Math. Thesis.   University of Waterloo.   April 1977.

Livesey 78 Livesey N.J. and Eric Manning Run-time Supervision in Tran-
    saction Processing.   Seventh Texas Conference on Computing
    Systems October 1978.

Livesey 78a Livesey N. J. and Eric Manning What Mininet has Taught us
    about Programming Style.   Proc. COMPSAC 78.   I.E.E.E.   October
    1978.

Livesey 78b Livesey N. J.   Contribution to: Enslow, P, Ed.   Workshop
    on Interprocess Communication in Highly Distributed Systems.
    Atlanta, Georgia.   November 20-22, 1978.

Livesey 79 Livesey N. J.   Inter-process Communication and Naming in
    the Mininet System.   Proc. COMPCON 79.   I.E.E.E.   February
    1979.

Livesey 80 Livesey N. J.   Run-Time Control in a Transaction-Oriented
    Operating System.   PhD Thesis.   University of Waterloo.   April
    1980.

Manning 78   Manning Eric and R. W. Peebles.   A Homogeneous Network
    for Data Sharing: Communications. Computer Networks, April
    1978.

Manning 80   Manning Eric, Livesey N.J. and H. Tokuda.   Inter-
    Process Communication in Distributed Systems: One View.   IFIP
    '80, To appear.

Mao 79   Mao T. W. and R.T. Yeh Communications Port - A Language
    Concept for Concurrent Programming.   Proc. 1st. International
    Conference on Distributed Computer Systems.   IEEE.   Oct. 1979.

Milner 79 Milner R.   Flowgraphs and Flow Algebras.   J.A.C.M., 26, 4.
    Oct. 1979.

Mills 76 Mills D.L.   The Basic Operating System for The Distributed
    Computer Network.   Tech. Report TR 416.   University of

368

Maryland. Jan. 1976.

Peacock 79a   Peacock J. K., J.W. Wong and Eric Manning. A Distributed Approach to Queuing Network Simulation. Proc. Winter
Simulation Conference. San Diego 1979.

Peacock 79b   Peacock J. K., J.W. Wong and Eric Manning. Distributed
Simulation Using a Network of Processors. Computer Networks,
3, 1. February 1979.

Peacock 80   Peacock J. K., Eric Manning and J.W. Wong. Synchronization of Distributed Simulation Using Broadcast Algorithms.
Computer Networks 4, 1. February 1980.

Peebles 74   Peebles R.W. and Eric Manning. A Homogeneous Network
for Data Sharing - Software Architecture and Data Management.
CCNG Report E-16. University of Waterloo. 1974.

Reed 78   Reed D.P. and R.K. Kanoida. Synchronisation with Event
Counts and Sequencers. Proc. SOSP-6. Nov. 1977.

Tandem Tandem Corporation. Tandem 16 System Introduction. Undated.

Wilkes 79 Wilkes M.V and R.M. Needham. The Cambridge CAP Computer and
its Operating System. North Holland. 1979.

Zave 76   Zave P. On the Formal Definition of Processes. Proc 1976
International Conference on Parallel Processing. IEEE Computer Society. 1976.

ON THE PROGRESS OF COMMUNICATION
BETWEEN TWO MACHINES

M. G. Gouda[1], E. G. Manning[2], Y. T. Yu[1]

ABSTRACT

We consider the following problem concerning any two finite state machines M and N which exchange messages via two one-directional channels. "Is there a positive integer K such that M and N with K-capacity channels never reach a nonprogress state?" The problem is shown to be undecidable in general. For a reasonable class of communicating machines, the problem is shown to be decidable; and the decidability algorithm is polynomial. We also discuss some sufficient conditions for the problem to have a a positive answer; these sufficient conditions can be checked for the given M and N in polynomial time.

Keywords: Bounded communication, communicating finite state machine, communication deadlock, communication protocol, progress, unspecified reception.

[1]Department of Computer Sciences, University of Texas at Austin.

[2]Department of Computer Sciences, University of Waterloo.

Table of Contents

I. INTRODUCTION

The model of communicating finite state machines is an abstraction of sequential processes which communicate exclusively by exchanging messages. The abstraction is achieved by suppressing the local data structures and internal operations of the processes, and representing each of them only by its sending and receiving operations with other processes. This abstract model has been useful in the specificaton [4, 8], analysis [1, 9, 10], and synthesis [6, 11] of communication protocols. But its major impact has been in characterizing some communication progress properties such as boundedness, and freedom of deadlocks and unspecified receptions [2, 11].

In this paper, we consider the general problem of communication progress between two machines, and discuss its relationship to the above progress properties. We also show that the problem is undecidable in general and present some special cases for which the problem is decidable by polynomial algorithms.

The paper is organized as follows. The communication progress problem is defined in Section II, and equivalent forms for the problem are presented in Section III. In Section IV, the problem is shown to be undecidable in general; and in Section V, it is shown to be decidable by a polynomial algorithm for a special class of communicating machines called alternating machines. In Section VI, we discuss a set of sufficient conditions to ensure that the problem has a positive answer; these conditions can be checked by a polynomial-time algorithm. A summary of the results is given in Section VII.

II. THE COMMUNICATION PROGRESS PROBLEM

A communicating machine M is a directed labelled graph with two types of nodes – sending and receiving nodes. One of the nodes in M is identified as its initial node; and each node in M is reachable by a directed path from the initial node.

Each node in M has at least one output edge. An output edge of a sending (or receiving) node is called a sending (or receiving) edge, and is labelled send(g) (or receive(g) respectively) for some message g from a finite set S of messages. No two outputs of the same node in M have identical labels.

Let M and N be two communicating machines with the same set S of messages and let K be a positive integer, $K > 0$. A state of M and N with K-capacity channels is a four-tuple [m,n,x,y] where m and n are two nodes in M and N respcetively and x and y are two strings of messages from the set S such that $|x| \leq K$ and $|y| \leq K$ where $|x|$ and $|y|$ are the numbers of messages in x and y respectively. Informally, a state [m,n,x,y] means that the execution of M has reached node m, and the execution of N has reached node n, while the input channel of M has the message sequenc x, and the input channel of N has the message sequence y.

The <u>initial</u> <u>state</u> of M and N with K-capacity channels is $[m_0, n_0, E, E]$ where m_0 and n_0 are the initial nodes of M and N respectively, and E is the empty string.

A state $[m, n, x, y]$ of M and N with K-capacity channels is called an <u>overflow</u> <u>state</u> iff either m is a sending node and $|y|=K$ or n is a sending node and $|x|=K$.

Let $s=[m, n, x, y]$ be a state of M and N with K-capacity channels and let e be an output edge of node m or n. A state s' of M and N with K-capacity channels is said to <u>follow</u> s <u>over</u> e, denoted $s--e-->s'$, iff s is not an overflow state and the following four conditions are satisfied:

i. <u>If</u> e is from m to m' in M <u>and</u> is labelled send(g),
   <u>then</u> $s'=[m', n, x, y \cdot g]$, where "." is the concatenation operator.

ii. <u>If</u> e is from n to n' in N <u>and</u> is labelled send(g),
    <u>then</u> $s'=[m, n', x \cdot g, y]$.

iii. <u>If</u> e is from m to m' in M <u>and</u> is labelled receive(g),
     <u>and</u> $x=g \cdot x'$,
     <u>then</u> $s'=[m', n, x', y]$.

iv. <u>If</u> e is from n to n' in N <u>and</u> is labelled receive(g),
    <u>and</u> $y=g \cdot y'$,
    <u>then</u> $s'=[m, n', x, y']$.

Let s and s' be two states of M and N with K-capacity channels, s' <u>follows</u> s if there is a directed edge e in M or N such that $s--e-->s'$.

Let s and s' be two states of M and N with K-capacity channels. s' is <u>reachable</u> <u>from</u> s if either $s=s'$, or there exist states $s_1, \ldots, s_r$ such that $s=s_1$, $s'=s_r$, and s_{i+1} follows s_i for $i=1, \ldots, r-1$.

A state s of M and N with K-capacity channels is <u>reachable</u> if it is reachable from the initial state of M and N. The set R_K of all reachable states of M and N with K-capacity channels is called the <u>reachable</u> <u>set</u> of M and N with K-capacity channels.

A state s of M and N with K-capacity channels is said to be a <u>nonprogress</u> <u>state</u> if no state follows s. For instance, an overflow state is a nonprogress state.

In this paper, we address the following <u>communication</u> <u>progress</u> <u>problem</u>. "Given two communicating machines M and N, is there a positive integer K such that the reachable set R_K of M and N with K-capacity channels has no nonprogress states?" If an instance of this problem has a positive answer, then it is possible to determine the smallest K, denoted K_{min}, for which this instance has a positive answer. This is because, in this case, the set $R = \underset{K \geq 1}{U} R_K$ is finite as can be shown from Theorem 2 (below). Therefore K_{min} can be computed as follows.

$$K_{min} = \underset{[m, n, x, y] \text{ in } R}{max} (|x|, |y|).$$

In the next section, we discuss two other equivalent forms for the communication progress problem; then in section IV, we prove that one of these forms, and hence all of them, are undecidable.

III. OTHER FORMS FOR THE COMMUNICATION PROGRESS PROBLEM

Let M and N be two communicating machines. A state $s=[m,n,x,y]$ of M and N with K-capacity channels is a <u>deadlock state</u> if m and n are two receiving nodes in M and N respectively and $|x|=|y|=0$.

A state $s=[m,n,x,y]$ with K-capacity channels is an <u>unspecified reception state</u> if one of the following two conditions is satisfied

    i. $x=g_1 \cdot g_2 \cdot \ \cdots \ \cdot g_k$, for some $k \geq 1$ and m is a receiving node with no output labelled receive(g_1) in M.

    ii. $y=g_1 \cdot g_2 \cdot \ \cdots \ \cdot g_k$, for some $k \geq 1$ and n is a receiving node with no output labelled receive(g_1) in N.

An overflow or a deadlock state is a nonprogress state; but an unspecified reception state is not necessarily a nonprogress state. Nevertheless, the following theorem implies that an unspecified reception state always leads to a nonprogress state.

Theorem 1: Let M and N be two communicating machines; and let R_K be the reachable set of M and N with K-capacity channels. R_K has a nonprogress state iff R_K has an overflow state, a deadlock state, or an unspecified reception state.

Proof: If Part: According to the definition of "follow", a deadlock state or an overflow state is a nonprogress state. It remains to show that an unspecified reception state leads to a nonprogress state. Assume that an unspecified reception state $s=[m,n,x,y]$ is in R_K. There are two cases to consider:

    i. $x=g_1 \cdot g_2 \cdot \ \cdots \ \cdot g_k$, for some $k \geq 1$ and m is a receiving node with no output labelled receive(g_1) in M.

    ii. $y=g_1 \cdot g_2 \cdot \ \cdots \ \cdot g_k$, for some $k \geq 1$ and n is a receiving node with no output labelled receive(g_1) in N.

Since the proofs for the two cases are similar, only case i is considered. If a state s' is reachable from s then there exist states $s_1, \ldots, s_r$, such that $s=s_1$, $s'=s_r$ and $s_i--e_i-->s_{i+1}$, where e_i is an edge in N, for $i=1, \ldots, r-1$. (Notice that no e_i is in M from case i).

Let the number of sending (or receiving) edges in $\{e_i | i=1, \ldots, r-1\}$ be S (or R respectively). Therefore, $S \leq K-|x|$ and $R \leq |y|$. In other words, the number of states reachable from s is finite; and a nonprogress state must be reachable from s.

Only If Part: Assume that a nonprogress state $s=[m,n,x,y]$ is in R_K. There are two cases to consider.

i. Both m and n are receiving nodes: If x and y are empty then s is a deadlock state. Otherwise, let $x=g_1 \cdot \ldots \cdot g_k$. Since $s=[m,n,x,y]$ is a nonprogress state, then no output of m is labelled receive(g_1); and s is an unspecified reception state.

ii. Either m or n is a sending node: If m (or n) is a sending node and $|y|<K$ (or $|x|<K$ respectively) then there is a state following s; contradiction. Therefore, $|y| \geq K$ (or $|x| \geq K$ respectively) and s is an overflow state.   []

From Theorem 1, the communication progress problem can be equivalently stated as follows. "Given two communicating machines M and N, is there a positive integer K such that the reachable set R_K of M and N with K-capacity channels has no overflow, no deadlock, and no unspecified reception states?". This proves that overflows, deadlocks, and unspecified receptions are the causes of nonprogress between two machines which communicate via finite-capacity channels. Next we discuss a third equivalent form for this same problem.

Let M and N be two communicating finite state machines with the same set S of messages. A state of M and N with infinite-capacity channels is a four-tuple $[m,n,x,y]$ where m and n are two nodes in M and N respectvely and x and y are two strings of messages from the set S. Notice that in this definition the length of x or y is not required to be bounded by any constant. Hence, the concept of an overflow state is not present in this case.

The initial state of M and N with infinite-capacity channels is $[m_0,n_0,E,E]$ where m_0 and n_0 are the initial nodes of M and N respectively, and E is the empty string.

Let $s=[m,n,x,y]$ be a state of M and N with infinite-capacity channels and let e be an output edge of node m or n. A state s′ of M and N with infinite-capacity channels is said to follow s over e, denoted s--e-->s′, iff the four conditions i, ii, iii, and iv of the above "follow-over" definition for K-capacity channels are satisfied.

From this "follow-over" definition, the definitions of "follow", "reachable from", "reachable", and "reachable set" for infinite-capacity channels are similar to their counter parts for K-capacity channels. Also the definitions for a "nonprogress state", a "deadlock state" and an "unspecified reception state" are defined for infinite capacity channels in a similar way as for K-capacity channels.

Let R be the reachable set of M and N with infinite-capacity channels; and let K be a positive integer. The communication between M and N is said to be bounded by K iff each state $[m,n,x,y]$ in R is such that $|x| \leq K$ and $|y| \leq K$; the communication is bounded iff it is bounded by K, for some positive integer K. The communication between M and N is said to be deadlock-free iff R has no deadlock states. The communication between M and N is said to be without unspecified receptions iff R has no unspecified reception states.

Theorem 2: Let M and N be two communicating machines, and let R_K be the reachable set for M and N with K-capacity channels. The following two statements are equivalent.

    i. There is a positive integer K such that R_K has no overflow, deadlock, or unspecified reception states.

    ii. The communication between M and N is bounded, deadlock-free, and without unspecified receptions.

Proof: i-->ii: Let K be a positive integer such that R_K has no overflow, deadlock, or unspecified reception states. Since R_K has no overflow states, each state in R is in R_K; and the communication between M and N is bounded by K. Also, no deadlock state or unspecified reception state is in R ; and the communication between M and N is deadlock-free and has no unspecified receptions.

ii-->i: The communication between M and N is bounded; so there is a positive integer K such that for each state [m,n,x,y] in R , $|x| \leq K$ and $|y| \leq K$. We show by contradiction that R_K has no overflow, deadlock, or unspecified reception states. Let s=[m,n,x,y] be an overflow state in R_K; i.e. m is a sending node and $|y|$=K. Since each state in R_K is also in R, there is a state s'=[m',n',x',y'] which follows s in R such that $|y'|$=K+1; contradiction. Therefore, R_K has no overflow state. Similarly, we can show that R_K has no deadlock or unspecified reception states. []

From Theorem 2, the communication progress problem can be equivalently stated as follows. "Given two communicating machines M and N, is their communication bounded, deadlock-free, and without unspecified receptions?" In the next section we prove that this problem is undecidable.

IV. UNDECIDABILITY OF THE COMMUNICAION PROGRESS PROBLEM

To prove the undecidability of the communication progress problem, we need first to establish a mapping from Post machines into pairs of communicating finite state machines. (A similar mapping from Turing machines into a slightly different model of communicating machines is discussed in [2].)

Theorem 3: For any Post machine P there are two communicating machines M and N which satisfy the following two conditions:

  i. There is a node f in N such that P halts over the empty string iff there is a state of the form [m,f,x,y] in the reachable set R of M and N with infinite-capacity channels.

  ii. For any state s in R, if s is not of the form [m,f,x,y], then s is neither a deadlock nor an unspecified reception state. (Informally, this implies that M and N cannot reach a deadlock or an unspecified reception state before the execution of N reaches node f.)

Proof: A Post machine P is a finite directed graph with one variable z, whose value can be any string over the symbols {0,1,#} [7]. Each vertex in the graph corresponds to a statement which has one of the forms shown in Figure 1.

The ASSIGNMENT statements allowed in P are to concatenate a symbol, namely 0, 1, or # to the right of z.

The TEST statement checks the leftmost symbol of z, namely head(z), and deletes it after making the decision.

A Post machine is said to halt over the empty string iff the computation of P starting with z=E (where E denotes the empty string) eventually reaches the HALT statement.

Given a Post machine P, we show how to construct two communicating machines M and N with the set {0,1,#,$} of messages such that conditions i and ii are satisfied. Machine M is shown in Figure 2. Informally, machine M sends every message it receives. Notice that the nodes of machine M are labelled 0, 1, #, and E (for the empty string); later we prove that variable z of P can be written as a string y.m.x where y and x are two strings over {0,1,#,$} and m is a lebel of a node in M.

Machine N is the finite labelled directed graph constructed by applying four

377

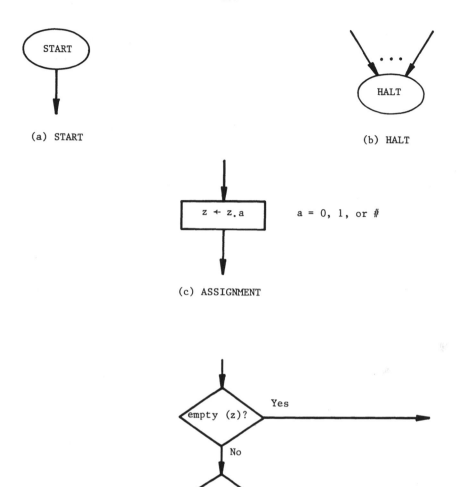

(a) START

(b) HALT

(c) ASSIGNMENT

$a = 0, 1, \text{ or } \#$

(d) TEST

Figure 1. Different types of statements in a Post machine.

transformation <u>rules</u> to the different types of vertices in the given Post machine P.

Rule T_1, illustated in Figure 3a, transforms the START statement in P to an arrow which indicates the initial node in N.

Rule T_2, illustrated in Figure 3b, transforms the HALT statement in P into the special node f in N. Notice that node f can be selected later as a sending or a receiving node.

Rule T_3, illustrated in Figure 3c, transforms an assignment z<--z.a, where "a" is in {0,1,#}, into a sending node with an output labelled send(a) in N.

Rule T_4 is illustrated in Figure 3d. Informally, N simulates the test empty(z)? by sending the special symbol $ to M, then it waits to receive from M. If it receives the same symbol $, it recognizes that z is empty. If it receives 0, 1, or #, then it recognizes that z is not empty. In this case, M removes the symbol $ then waits to receive the next symbol and depending on its type, the execution of N proceeds along one of the three output branches.

Let T(v) be the resulting subgraph after applying the approciate transformation rule T to a vertex v in P. And let the entry node of the subgraph T(v) in N be labelled v also.

Using induction, the following statement can be proven from the transformation rules T_1 to T_4. A vertex v in P is reached with the value of z being w iff a state [m,v,x,y], where y.m.x=w, is in the reachable set R of M and N with infinite-capacity channels. From this statement, conditions i and ii can be proven as follows:

i. Node f in N is the one which corresponds to the HALT satement in P. So, P halts over the empty string iff there is a state [m,f,x,y] in the reachable set R.

ii. Since each receiving node in M or N, except possibly node f, has an output labelled receive(g) for each message g in {0,1,#}, then if [m,n,x,y] is in R and n≠f then [m,n,x,y] cannot be an unspecified reception state. Also, since the Post machine P only stops at the HALT statement, so if [m,n,x,y] is in R and n≠f then [m,n,x,y] is not a deadlock state. []

Since the halting problem for Post machines is undecidable [7], the communication progress problem is also undecidable as shown in the next theorem.

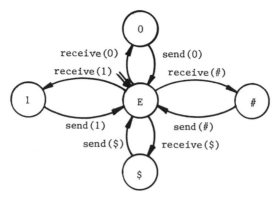

Figure 2.   Communicating machine M.

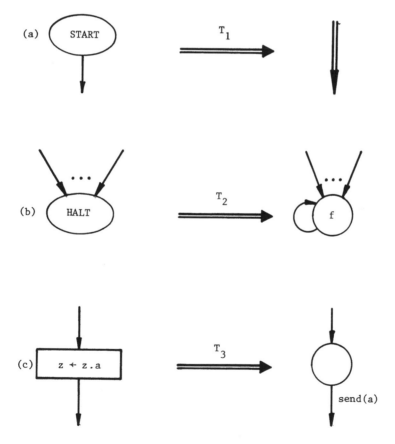

Figure 3.   Transformation rules from Post machine P to
communicating machine N.

380

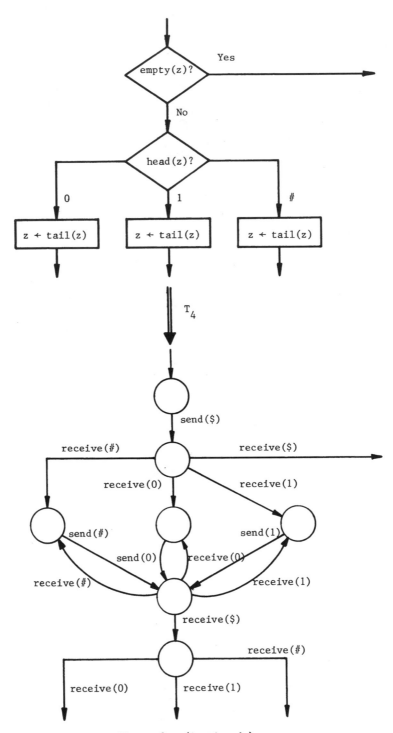

Figure 3.   (Continued.)

Theorem 4: Given two communicating machines; the problem of whether their communication is bounded, deadlock-free, and without unspecified receptions is undecidable.

Proof: (by contradiction) Assume that there is an algorithm, say algorithm A, to decide whether the communication between two given machines is bounded, deadlock-free, and without unspecified receptions. We show that algorithm A can be used to decide whether any Post machine halts over the empty string.

Let P be a Post machine; and let M and N be the two communicating machines constructed from P as discussed in Theorem 3. Also let R be the reachable set of M and N with infinite-capacity channels. From Theorem 3, P halts over the empty string iff a state [m,f,x,y] is in R, where f is the special node in N, discussed in Theorem 3.

Let N' be the resulting machine from N by replacing node f by a construct shown in Figure 4 which continuously receives a message then sends it. Clearly, the communication between M and N' is deadlock-free and without unspecified receptions. Apply algorithm A to machines M and N' to decide whether their communication is bounded, deadlock-free, and without unspecified receptions. If the answer is "no" implying that the communication between M and N is unbounded, then no state of the form [m,f,x,y] is in R and P does not halt over the empty string. On the other hand, if the answer is "yes" implying that the communication between M and N is bounded, then the set R is finite and all its states can be generated to check whether or not it has a state of the form [m,f,x,y]; this in turn can decide whether or not P halts over the empty string. []

From Theorem 4, there is no algorithm to answer the communication progress problem in general. Still, there are two approaches to bypass this negative result. First, identify special classes of communicating machines for which the problem is decidable. One example of this approach is discussed in the next section. The second approach is based on the observation that in most instances one is more interested in proving a positive answer for the problem. Therefore, in section VI we discuss some sufficient conditions which if satisfied by two communicating machines then the communication progress problem for them has a positive answer.

V. ALTERNATING COMMUNICATING MACHINES

A communicating machine M is called <u>alternating</u> if each sending node in M is immediately followed by receiving nodes only. We show in the next two theorems that the communication progress problem for alternating machines is decidable, and that its decidability algorithm is polynomial.

Theorem 5: The communication between any two alternating machines is bounded by two.

Proof: Let M and N be two alternating communicating machines and let R be the reachabl set of M and N with infinite-capacity channels. We prove that the communication between M and N is bounded by two. Let $[m_0, n_0, E, E]$ be the initial state. there are four cases to consider:

i. m_0 and n_0 are receiving nodes: R contains only the initial state. Therefore the communication is bounded by one (and so by two).

ii. m_0 is a sending node and n_0 is a receiving node: As shown in Figure 5a, if the initial state is of the form $[s, r, E, E]$, where s (or r) denotes a sending (or receiving respectively) node, then any state in R is in any one of the following five forms: $[s, r, E, E]$, $[r, r, E, E]$, $[r, s, E, E]$ $[r, r, g, E]$ or $[r, r, E, g]$, where g denotes a string which consists of only one message. In this case, the communication is bounded by one (and so by two).

iii. m_0 is a receiving node and n_0 is a sending node: Using an argument similar to that in case ii, it can be shown that the communication is bounded by one (and so by two).

iv. m_0 and n_0 are sending nodes: As shown in Figure 5b, the initial state is of the form $[s, s, E, E]$, where s denotes a sending node, then any state in R is in any one of the 13 forms in Figure 5b, where r denotes a receiving node, g denotes a string which consists of one message, gg denotes a string which consists of two messages. In this case, the communication is bounded by two. []

Theorem 6: There is a polynomial-time algorithm to solve the communication progress problem for any two alternating communicating machines.

Proof: Let M and N be two alternating communicating machines over a set S of messages. And let R be the reachable set of M and N with infinite-capacity channels. From Theorem 5, any state $[m, n, x, y]$ in R is such that $|x| \leq 2$ and $|y| \leq 2$. Thus, the number of states in R is $O(uvw^4)$, where u is the number of nodes in machine M, v is

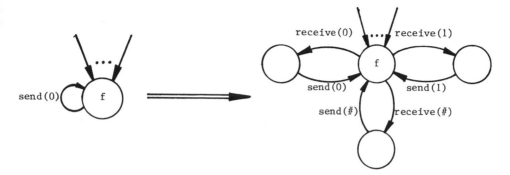

Figure 4.   Proof of Theorem 4.

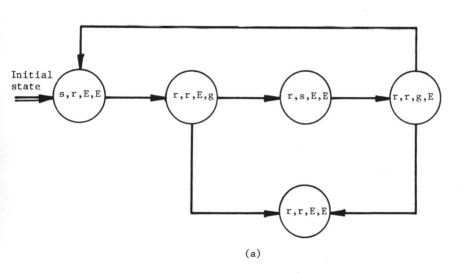

(a)

Figure 5.   Proof of Theorem 5.

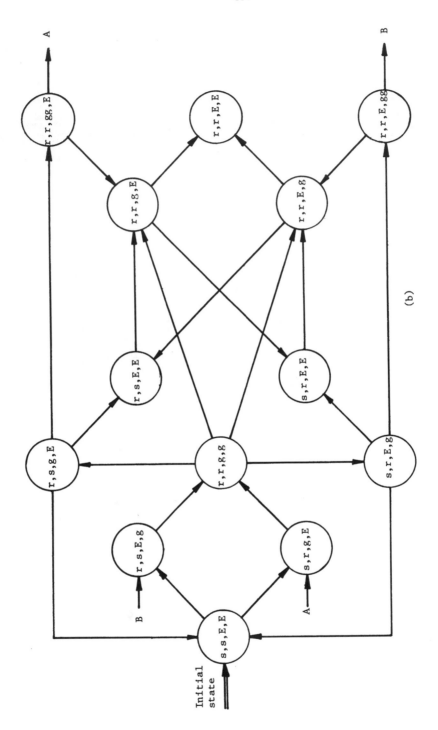

384

Figure 5. (Continued.)

(b)

the number of nodes in machine N, and w is the number of messages in set S. Therefore, each state in R can be generated and checked for being a deadlock or an unspecified reception state. Clearly, this algorithm can solve the communication progress problem for M and N and it requires polynomial time.   []

In the next section, we discuss a set of sufficient conditions to ensure that the communication progress problem has a positive answer.

VI. COMPATIBLE COMMUNICATION

Let M and N be two communicating machines; and let p and q be two directed paths which start with the initial nodes in M and N respectively. Paths p and q are said to be __compatible paths__ if for i=1,2,..., the ith edge in p is labelled send(g) (or receive(g)) and the ith edge in q is labelled receive(g) (or send(g) respectively). The communication between M and N is said to be __compatible__ if for any directed path p which starts with the initial node in M, there exists exactly one directed path q which starts with the initial node in N, and vice versa, such that p and q are compatible.

The reason for our interest in compatible communication is two fold. First, compatibility is a sufficient condition to ensure that the communication is deadlock-free and without unspecified receptions as we prove in Theorem 7. Second, it is decidable whether the communication between two machines is compatible, as we prove in Theorem 8.

Theorem 7: Let M and N be two communicating machines. If the communication between M and N is compatible then it is deadlock-free and without unspecified receptions.

Proof: Let M and N be two machines whose communication is compatible. And let R be the reachable set of M and N with infinite-capacity channels. We show by contradiction that no nonprogress state is in R. Assume that a nonprogress state s is in R, there are two cases to consider; each of which leads to a contradiction:

1. __s is a deadlock state__: Since s is in R, there exist states $s_0,...,s_r$, such that s_0 is the initial state, $s_r = s$, and $s_{i-1} - e_i \to s_i$ for i=1,...,r. The set of edges $\{e_i | i=1,...,r \text{ and } e_i \text{ is in M}\}$ corresponds to a directed path p which starts with the initial node in M. Similarly, the set of edges $\{e_i | i=1,...,r \text{ and } e_i \text{ is in N}\}$ corresponds to a directed path q which starts with the initial node in N. Since s is a deadlock state, then $|p| = |q|$. There are two cases to consider:

a. p and q are compatible: In this case, if path p is extended in any way into p' in M, then no directed path q' which starts with the initial node in N is compatible with p'. This contradicts the assumption that the communication between M and N is compatible.

b. p and q are not compatible: Since the communication between M and N is compatible, there is a directed path $\bar{p}$ which starts with the initial node in N such that p and $\bar{p}$ are compatible. Clearly, $|q|=|p|=|\bar{p}|$ and pathes q and $\bar{p}$ are not identical. let e and $\bar{e}$ be the first different edges in q and $\bar{p}$ respectively. Edges e and $\bar{e}$ have the same tail node; and they are either the ith sending edges or the ith receiving edges in their respective paths. Therefore, they correspond to the ith receiving edge or the ith sending edge of path p in M; i.e., they have identical labels; this contradicts the fact that no two outputs of the same node in N have identical labels.

ii. s is an unspecified reception state: Using a similar argument as in case i can lead to a contradiction. []

Theorem 8: There is a polynomial-time algorithm to decide whether the communication between two communicating machines is compatible.

Proof: Let M and N be two communicating machines with a set S of messages. Construct machine $\bar{N}$ from N by replacing each sending node by a receiving node and vice versa, and by replacing each label "send(g)" by "receive(g)" and vice versa. View machine M and $\bar{N}$ as two finite automata over the alphabet {send(g),receive(g)|g is in S}; and assume that each node in M or $\bar{N}$ is an accepting state. Each path p (or q) which starts with the initial node in machine M (or $\bar{N}$) corresponds to a word in the regular language L(M) (or L($\bar{N}$)) accepted by the automaton M (or $\bar{N}$ respectively). Therefore, the communication between M and N is compatible iff L(M)=L($\bar{N}$). Since whether L(M)=L($\bar{N}$) is decidable in polynomial time [5], the problem of whether the communication between M and N is compatible is decidable in polynomial time. []

From Theorem 7, compatibility guarantees freedom of deadlocks and unspecified receptions; however, it does not guarantee boundedness. Therefore, compatibility alone does not ensure a positive answer to the communication progress problem; and an additional condition is needed for that purpose.

Theorem 9: Let M and N be two communicating machines. Assume that the communication between M and N is compatible and that each directed cycle in M or N has at least one sending and one receiving nodes. Then, there is a positive integer K such that the reachable set R_K for M and N with K-capacity channels has no nonprogress states.

Proof: Since any directed cycle in M or N contains at least one sending and one receiving nodes, define K to be the maximum number of successive nodes of the same type (sending or receiving) in M or N. We show that any reachable state s=[m,n,x,y] of M and N with infinite-capacity channels satisfies the following three conditions:

   i. s is not a deadlock state.

   ii. s is not an unspecified reception state.

   iii. $|x| \leq K$ and $|y| \leq K$.

Conditions i and ii are satisfied since the communication between M and N is compatible (Theorem 7). It remains to prove condition iii. Let p and q be two compatible infinite paths in M and N respectively. Neither p nor q contains an infinite number of successive sending nodes or an infinite number of successive receiving nodes. Therefore, p or q consists of a finite number of sending nodes followed by a finite number of receiving nodes, followed by a finite number of sending nodes, etc. All these numbers are bounded by K. Without loss of generality, assume that p begins with a number of sending nodes; hence q begins with the same number of receiving nodes. p can send up to K messages before q receives any of them. Then p waits until q receives all of them and starts sending to p. In this case, q can send up to K messages, and then it waits until p receives all these messages and starts sending to q. The same argument can be applied to the rest of p and q. Therefore any reachable state [m,n,x,y] along p and q is such that $|x| \leq K$ and $|y| \leq K$. Since any state must be reached along compatible paths, any reachable state [m,n,x,y] is such that $|x| \leq K$ and $|y| \leq K$. This completes the proof that $R_K = R$ and that no state in R_K is a nonprogress state.   []

VII. SUMMARY OF RESULTS

We have addressed the following communication progress problem. "Given two communicating machines M and N, is there a positive integer K such that the reachable set of M and N with K-capacity channels has no nonprogress states?" We have shown the following

i. Nonprogress between two machines which communicate via finite-capacity channels is caused by overflows, deadlocks, or unspecified receptions (Theorem 1).

ii. The communication progress problem is equivalent to the problem, "Is the communication between M and N bounded, deadlock-free, and without unspecified receptions?" (Theorem 2).

iii. The problem is undecidable in general (Theorem 4).

iv. The problem is decidable for a special class of communicating machines called atternating machines; and the decidability algorithm is polynomial (Theorem 6).

v. The problem has a positive answer if the communication between M and N is compatible and each directed cycle in M or N has at least one sending and one receiving nodes (Theorem 9). These two conditions can be detected in polynomial time (Theorem 8).

We have also derived two results concerning K_{min}, the smallest K for which the problem has a positive answer if at all.

i. If the given M and N are alternating machines then $k_{min}=2$ (Theorem 5).

ii. If the given M and N satisfy the two cited conditions in Theorem 9 then K_{min} = the maximum number of successive nodes of the same type (i.e., sending or receiving) in M or N (Theorem 9).

Other results related to the communication progress problem have appeared in [3,6]. In [3], the communication progress problem is shown to be decidable if M and N exchange one type of messages. The complexity of this decidability algorithm is yet to be determined. In [6], a synthesis approach to the problem is taken; in particular, the following problem is addressed. "Given one communicating machine M, it is required to synthesize another communicating machine N such that the communication progress problem for M and N has a positive solution." A synthesis algorithm is discussed in [6] along with an algorithm to compute K_{min} for M and N. Both algorithms are polynomial in the number of nodes in M and N.

REFERENCES

[1] G. V. Bochmann, "Finite state description of communication protocols," Computer Networks, Vol. 2, 1978, pp. 361-371.

[2] D. Brand and P. Zafiropulo, "On communicatin finite-state machines," IBM Research Report, RZ1053(#37725), Jan. 1981.

[3] P. R. Cunha and T. S. Maibaum, "A synchronization calculus for message oriented programming," Res. Rep. CS-80-43, Dept. of Comp. Sc., Univ. of Waterloo, Sep. 1980.

[4] A. Danthine, "Protocol representation with finite state models," IEEE Trans. Comm., Vol. COM-28, No. 4, April 1980, pp. 632-643.

[5] M. R. Garey and D. S. Johnson, Computers and interactability, a guide to the theory of NP-completeness, W. H. Freeman and Company, San Francisco, 1979.

[6] M. G. Gouda and Y. T. Yu, "Designing deadlock-free and bounded communication protocols," Tech. Rep. 179, Dept. of Comp. Sc., Univ. of Texas at Austin, June 1981. submitted to IEEE Trans. on Comm..

[7] Z. Manna, Mathematical theory of computation, McGraw-Hill Book company, 1974.

[8] C. A. Sunshine, "Formal modeling of communication protocols," USC/Inform. Sc. Institute, Res. Rep. 81-89, March 1981.

[9] C. H. West, "An automated technique of communication protocol validation," IEEE Trans. Comm., Vol. COM-26, pp.1271-1275, Aug. 1978.

[10] Y. T. Yu and M. G. Gouda, "Deadlock-detection for a class of communicating finite state machines," Tech. Rep. 193, Dept. of Computer Sciences, Univ. of Texas at Austin, Feb. 1982. Submitted to IEEE Trans. on Comm..

[11] P. Zafiropulo, et. al., "Towards analyzing and synthesizing protocols," IEEE Trans. Comm., Vol. COM-28, No. 4, April 1980, pp. 651-661.

Part VII.

Development Process and Tools

It is widely recognized that tools are a very important
ingredient of software engineering. Particularly, an
efficient and powerful tool to handle design data is essential.
The first paper by H. Kitagawa and T. L. Kunii proposes
"Nested Table Data model (NTD)," which enables users freely
and dynamically to specify application oriented nested
tables. The users can have nests of columns and/or rows, as
user views. An important problem in introducing nested
structures is the reversibility of nesting processes. The
paper defines four operators for dynamic nesting and assures
the reversibility of the nesting processes based on them.
The second paper by T. Hirota, K. Tabata and Y. Ohno proposes
a technique for the design of concurrent process systems.
The design of concurrent systems must treat the problems
particular to concurrent processing such as mutual exclusions,
process synchronizations and system deadlocks. The proposed
technique can show the designers several desirable execution
sequences for each process, when the specification of each
process is given as a set of processing steps and a partial
order on the set. After an execution sequence for each
process is selected by the designer, the technique establishes
critical regions and constructs a design proposal. Most of
the technique is mathematical operations on partial ordered
sets and can be automated. The proposed technique should be
a great help for designers, especially in an early stage of
design for a concurrent process system.

FORM TRANSFORMER

- A FORMALISM FOR OFFICE FORM MANIPULATION -

Hiroyuki Kitagawa and Tosiyasu L. Kunii
Department of Information Sceince
Faculty of Science
The University of Tokyo
7-3-1 Hongo, Bunkyo-ku
Tokyo 113, Japan

ABSTRACT

The nested table data model (NTD) is proposed as a powerful office data modeling tool, and basic aspects of data handling in NTD are discussed. Nested tables are introduced as straightforward and uniform office data representation forms, and four form transformer operators are defined for manipulating nested tables. Then, reversibility and commutability of the form transformer operators are examined.

1. INTRODUCTION

In the last few years, there has been an increasing demand for computer systems to directly support both routine and casual office information handling activities. Needless to say, office workers are manually manipulating volumes of data specified in varieties of office forms. Therefore, to properly automate or semi-automate their activities, machine processing of the conventional office forms is essential. To achieve this goal, an office form modeling technique is initially necessary for their systematic manipulation.

We have proposed a new data model named the nested table data model (NTD) [5, 6, 7, 8] as a powerful office form modeling tool. NTD features (1) straightforward and (2) uniform modeling of the office forms. The first feature, namely the straightforwardness, is important, since most users of office information systems are usually end-users, though they are specialists in their own works. Even administrative users have rather limited background in computer systems What they want to do is to manipulate office data in computer systems, without additional training or education, as if they were handling conventional office forms. Therefore, the mapping between the office form model and the conventional representation of office forms should be as straightforward as possible.

The second feature, namely the uniformily, is required from a managerial viewpoint. It is usually the case that varieties of office forms are used in an organization, and that their cross-references and re-formings are necessary for statisfying various office data processing needs. Such cross-references and re-formings are impossible, unless data are uniformly managed in the system.

In NTD, nested tables are used as canonical office data representation forms. A nested table is a table with nests of columns and/or rows. An example of a nested table is shown in Fig. 1. Nested tables are end-user friendly data representation forms, since they are often used for tabulating data in our daily life. Therefore, office users can readily get accustomed to using nested tables. In addition, conventional office forms usually have such nests of columns and/or rows, and data specified in currently used office forms can be directly transformed into nested tables. For example, data specified in an example office form shown in Fig. 2 can be represented by a row of the sample nested table shown in Fig. 1. Texts and images as well as those formatted data are also allowed as data items of nested tables. Thus, nested tables are suitable for handling a variety of conventional office data in a unified way, and they serve as a powerful data modeling tool

*PART-SUPPLY-FORM							
SID	PART		*SLIST				
	PID	TYPE	QTY	DATE			
				YEAR	MONTH	DAY
1	1	A	50	80	MAY	15
			60	80	JUN	3
1	2	A	30	80	JUN	3
1	3	B	20	80	MAY	24
2	3	B	100	80	MAY	15
			50	80	JUN	3
3	2	A	10	80	MAY	24
			50	80	JUN	3
⋮	⋮	⋮	⋮	⋮	⋮	⋮

Fig. 1   NESTED TABLE *PART-SUPPLY-FORM

PART-SUPPLY-FORM			
SID(SUPPLIER-ID)			1
PART	PID(PART-ID)		1
	TYPE		A
SLIST(SUPPLY-LIST)			
QTY(QUANTITY)	DATE		
	YEAR	MONTH	DAY
50	80	MAY	15
60	80	JUN	3

Fig. 2 OFFICE FORM PART-SUPPLY-FORM

*YET-ANOTHER-PART-SUPPLY-FORM						
*SLIST-PER-DATE				DATE		
	*SLIST-PER-SUPPLIER					
SID	PART		QTY	YEAR	MONTH	DAY
	PID	TYPE				
1	1	A	50	80	MAY	15
2	3	B	100			
1	3	B	20	80	MAY	24
3	2	A	10			
1	1	A	60	80	JUN	3
	2	A	30			
2	3	B	50			
3	2	A	50			
⋮	⋮	⋮	⋮	⋮	⋮	⋮

Fig. 3 NESTED TABLE *YET-ANOTHER-PART-SUPPLY-FORM

in supporting office information processing activities.

NTD provides a set of algebraic, highly abstract operators for
freely transforming   nested tables.   They are named <u>nested table</u>
<u>operators</u> [7], and include projection, selection, join, form transformer,
and table updation operators.   Daily and ad-hoc office form manipulation activities in offices can readily be modeled in terms of the nested
table operators.

In this paper, we discuss some operational properties of NTD.
Those properties are useful for automatically detecting data manipulation anomalies and for designing well-structured nested tables.
Because of limitations of space, we consider only basic properties of
some of the nested table operators in this paper, but the same approach
is applicable to the other operators.   Four types of operators are
considered.   They are used for changing nests of columns and/or rows
in nested tables, for instance, from table *PART-SUPPLY-FORM shown in
Fig. 1 to table *YET-ANOTHER-PART-SUPPLY-FORM shown in Fig. 3, and vice
versa.   They are generically referred to as <u>form transformer</u> operators.
In section 2 of this paper, nested tables and some related concepts
are introduced.   In section 3, the form transformer operators are
defined.   In section 4, sample usages of those operators are shown.
In section 5, thier basic operational properties are examined.   Section
6 concludes the paper.

2. NESTED TABLE

A <u>nested table</u> is a table with nests of columns and/or rows.
Columns of nested tables are called <u>fields</u>.   The top-level field in
the hierarchy is called the <u>root</u> and gives the table name.   In nested
table *PART-SUPPLY-FORM shown in Fig. 1, the root has three fields
SID, PART, and *SLIST as its <u>components</u>.   Fields PART and *SLIST have
their components PID and TYPE, and QTY and DATE, respectively.   Furthermore, field DATE has three components YEAR, MONTH and DAY.   Fields
which have at least one component are called <u>group</u> fields, and the
others are called <u>simple</u> fields.   In case a field A is a component of
a field B, A is also referred to as a <u>child</u> of field B, and B is
referred to as A's <u>parent</u>.   Data values actually appearing in the table
contents are called <u>occurrences</u>.   In the example shown in Fig. 1,
occurrences of simple fields SID and TYPE are integers 1,1,1,2, ...
and characters A,A,B,B,..., respectively.   Occurrences of group field
PART are tuples such as (1,A),(2,A), and (3,B).   In case of group field
*SLIST, two types of occurrences are to be considered.   Occurrences

of one type are sets of tuples† such as {(50,(80,MAY,15)),(60,(80,JUN, 3))} and {(30,(80,JUN,3))}††. They are called set occurrences. Occurrences of the other type are tuples such as (50,(80,MAY,15)), (60,(80,JUN,3)), and (30,(80,JUN,3)). Occurrences of this type are called elementary occurrences. Fields which have set occurrences are called repeating fields, and the others are called non-repeating fields. Repeating fields are tagged with asterisks. In the following part of this paper, set occurrences are simply referred to as occurrences for repeating fields. The root must be a repeating group field. Note that a set occurrence of the root gives the whole table contents. Thus, each field is either simple or group, and is either non-repeating or repeating. Fields of nested table *PART-SUPPLY-FORM are classified as follows:

(1) non-repeating simple fields: SID, PID, TYPE, QTY, YEAR, MONTH, DAY,

(2) repeating simple fields: none,

(3) non-repeating group fields: PART, DATE,

(4) repeating group fields: *PART-SUPPLY-FORM,*SLIST.

Formally, each field F has a domain dom(F) of its occurrences. Domains must obey the following constraints:

(1) if F is a non-repeating simple field, dom(F) is a set of atomic data items (e.g., integers, character strings, texts, and images),

(2) is F is a repeating simple field, dom(F) is the power set of a set of atomic data items,

(3) if F is a non-repeating group field, and $C_1,...,C_N$ are its components, then

$dom(F) \subseteq CP(C_1,...,C_N)$, and

(4) if F is a repeating group field, and $C_1,...,C_N$ are its components, then

$dom(F) \subseteq 2^{CP(C_1,...,C_N)}$ (the power set of $CP(C_1,...,C_N)$).

Here, $CP(C_1,...,C_N)$ denotes the Cartesian Product of sets $dom(C_1),...,$ $dom(C_N)$. Elements of $CP(C_1,...,C_N)$ are called tuples. An occurrence of field C_i in a tuple t is denoted by $t[C_i]$. This notation is also used for a set of fields $X \subseteq \{C_1,...,C_N\}$.

Our nested tables are in some points similar to the forms purposed by Housel, Shu, et al. [4, 9, 12] as tabular representations of hierarchical data structures. However, at least two differences are

---

† Each of these tuples (e.g., (50,(80, MAY,15))) is composed of an integer (e.g., 50) and a tuple (e.g., (80,MAY,15)).

†† From a practical viewpoint, duplication and ordering of set element have to be considered. However, these points are neglected for the logical simplicity of this paper.

identified. Namely, in forms,

(1) non-repeating group fields and repeating simple fields are not explicitly considered, and

(2) every repeating group field is implicitly assumed to have at least one non-repeating component.

Therefore, regarding the above two points, our nested tables are more general than the forms.

3. FORM TRANSFORMER OPERATORS

In this section, four operators for 'ennesting' and 'denesting' columns and/or rows are defined. They are Column Ennest (CE) operator, Column Denest (CD) operator, Row Ennest (RE) operator, and Row Dennest (RD) operator. The first two operators handle column nesting, and the latter two handle row nesting; the 'ennest' operators nest columns or rows, and the 'denest' operators reduce the nests. These four operators are generically referred to as FT (Form Transformer) operators. The language CONVERT [4, 12] includes some operators for handling structures of forms. However, our FT operators do support basic column/row nesting, and are more primitive than those CONVERT operators. Therefore, the CONVERT operators are represented as combinations of the FT operators.

Definitions of the FT operators are as follows. Their functions are illustrated in Fig. 4.

(1) Column Ennest: $CE[F_1, \ldots, F_N \text{ INTO } H]$

Let $F_1, \ldots, F_N$ $(N \geq 1)$ be fields which are components of some group field G. For simplicity, let $F_1, \ldots, F_N, F_{N+1}, \ldots, F_M$ $(M \geq N)$ be all components of G. An occurrence of G is a tuple of $CP(F_1, \ldots, F_N, F_{N+1}, \ldots, F_M)$ (in case G is a non-repeating group field) or a set of such tuples (in case G is a repeating group field). This operator creates a new non-repeating group field H as a component of G, and changes $F_1, \ldots, F_N$ into components of H. (Fields $F_{N+1}, \ldots, F_M$ remain components of G.) At the same time, every above mentioned tuple, say $t=(t[F_1], \ldots, t[F_N], t[F_{N+1}], \ldots, t[F_M])$, is replaced by $((t[F_1], \ldots, t[F_N]), t[F_{N+1}], \ldots, t[F_M])$. Note that tuple $(t[F_1], \ldots, t[F_N])$ becomes an occurrence of field H.

(2) Column Denest: $CD[H]$

Let H be a field which is a non-repeating group component of some group field G. Let $F_1, \ldots, F_N$ $(N \geq 1)$, and , for somplicity, $H, I_1, \ldots, I_M$ $(M \geq 0)$ be all components of H and G, respectively. An occurrence

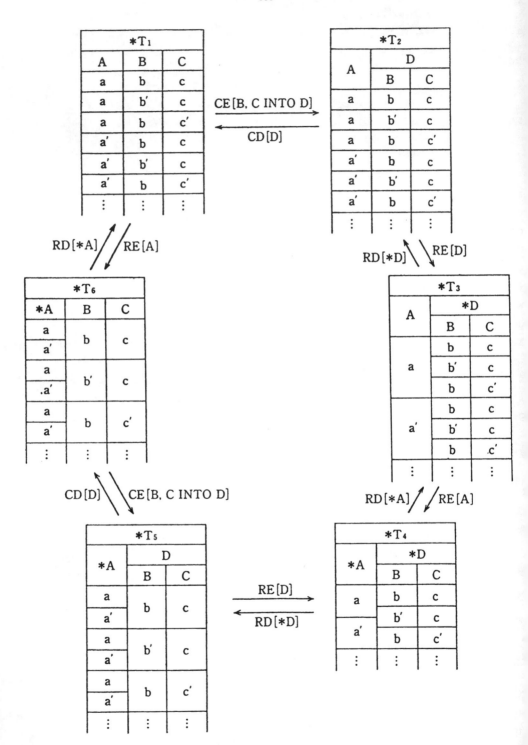

Fig. 4 FORM TRANSFORMER OPERATORS

of G is a tuple of $CP(H,I_1,\ldots,I_M)$ (in case G is a non-repeating group field) or a set of such tuples (in case G is a repeating group field). This operator erases field H, and changes $F_1,\ldots,F_N$ into components of G. At the same time, every above mentioned tuple, say $t=(t[H],t[I_1],\ldots,t[I_M])$, is replaced by $(t[H][F_1],\ldots,t[H][F_N],t[I_1],\ldots,t[I_M])$. Note that occurrence $t[H]$ is a tuple of $CP(F_1,\ldots,F_N)$.

(3) Row Ennest: RE[F]

Let F be a field which is a non-repeating component of some repeating group field G. For simplicity, let $F,H_1,\ldots,H_N(N \geq 0)$ be all components of G. Since G is a repeating group field, each occurrence of G is a set of tuples of $CP(F,H_1,\ldots,H_N)$. This operator changes non-repeating field F into a repeating field *F, and replaces every occurrence R of field G by the following R':
$$R'=\{(S(t),t[H_1],\ldots,t[H_N])\mid t \in R\}$$
where
$$S(t)=\{s[F]\mid s \in R \wedge s[H_1]=t[H_1] \wedge \ldots \wedge s[H_N]=t[H_N]\}.$$
Note that set $S(t)$ becomes an occurrence of repeating field *F.

(4) Row Denest: RD[*F]

Let *F be a field which is a repeating component of some repeating group field G. For simplicity, let $*F,H_1,\ldots,H_N(N \geq 0)$ be all components of G. This operator changes repeating field *F into a non-repeating field F, and replaces every occurrence R of field G by the following R':
$$R'=\{(s,t[H_1],\ldots,t[H_N])\mid t \in R \wedge s \in t[*F]\}.$$
Note that occurrence $t[*F]$ is a set.

4. EXAMPLE

The FT operators are used to re-form a given column/row nesting into another one most appropriate for application data use in data retrieval, report generation and so on. In our NTD-based office form management system, the users can either define the resultant new table as a user view of the original table or actually store it into the database as a snapshot. In this section, usages of the FT operators are illustrated with an example. Suppose nested table *PART-SUPPLY-FORM (Fig. 1) is given. This nested table fits data usages such as

usage 1) find the date(s) when the supplier X supplied the part Y,

usage 2) find the combination(s) of a supplier and a part such that the supplier has supplied the part more than X times, and

usage 3) find the combination(s) of a supplier and a part such that the quantity of part supply is always greater than X.

These queries are easily formulated as the selection operator applied to the nested table *PART-SUPPLY-FORM. However, if data usages are of the following types, nested table *YET-ANOTHER-PART-SUPPLY-FORM (Fig. 3) is suited both for a user view on which queries are formulated and for a report form:

(usage 4)   for each day, find the part supply of each supplier,

(usage 5)   find the date(s) when each supplier supplied all kinds of part, and

(usage 6)   find the date(s) when the total quantity of parts supplied by each supplier is greater than X.

Table *YET-ANOTHER-PART-SUPPLY-FORM is derived from table *PART-SUPPLY-FORM by the following sequence of the FT operators:

RD[*SLIST];

CD[SLIST];

CE[PART, QTY INTO SLIST-PER-SUPPLIER];

CE[SID, SLIST-PER-SUPPLIER INTO SLIST-PER-DATE];

RE[SLIST-PER-DATE];

RE[SLIST-PER-SUPPLIER].

Of course, there are some other sequences of the FT operators to get the same result. Reversibility and commutability of the FT operators are discussed in section 5.

5. OPERATIONAL PROPERTIES OF FORM TRANSFORMER

In this section, properties of the FT operators are examined. First, functional dependency and multivalued dependency in nested tables are formulated. They serve as convenient tools in expressing basic semantics of table contents. Then, we show some basic properties of the FT operators.

5.1 DEPENDENCIES

An extension of functional dependency and multivalued dependency [2, 3] to unnormalized relations was first shown by Makinouchi [10]. Here, we reformulate his definition in our formalism.

In the following part of this paper, when dependencies in nested tables are considered, all non-repeating group fields are virtually regarded as pseudo fields giving naming conventions. For example, when dependencies in table *PART-SUPPLY-FORM shown in Fig. 1 are considered, non-repeating group fields PART and DATE are simply regarded as names given to groups of fields for naming convenience. Then, in the following formalism, fields SID, PID, TYPE, and *SLIST are conside:

components of the root *PART-SUPPLY-FORM, and fields QTY, YEAR, MONTH, and DAY are considered components of field *SLIST. This interpretation simplifies the definition of dependency concepts in nested tables.

Let G be a repeating group field of a nested table T, and let C be the set of its components in the above mentioned sense. Then, $dom(G) \subseteq 2^{CP(C)}$, as mentioned in section 2. Therefore, each occurrence R of G is a set of tuples of CP(C).

Definition 1. Let X and Y be subsets of C. A <u>functional dependency</u> $X \to Y$ holds in R, iff, for every tuple t_1 and t_2 in R, $t_1[X]=t_2[X]$ implies $t_1[Y]=t_2[Y]$. Iff $X \to Y$ holds in every occurrence of G, $X \to Y$ holds in nested table T.

The projection of R over $X \subseteq C$ is denoted by R[X], that is
R[X]={t[X]|t ∈ R}.
The projection of R over $Y \subseteq C$ with an X-value $x \in CP(X)$ is denoted by $R_x[Y]$, that is
$R_x[Y]=\{t[Y]|t \in R \wedge t[X]=x\}$.
Similarly, for $x \in CP(X)$ and $z \in CP(Z)$ ($Z \subseteq C$), $R_{xz}[Y]$ is defined as
$R_{xz}[Y]=\{t[Y]|t \in R \wedge t[X]=x \wedge t[Z]=z\}$.

Definition 2. Let X and Y be subsets of C, and let Z=C-X-Y. A <u>multivalued dependency</u> $X \to\to Y$ holds in R, iff, for every x and z such that t[X]=x and t[Z]=z for some $t \in R$,
$R_{xz}[Y]=R_x[Y]$.
Iff $X \to\to Y$ holds in every occurrence of G, $X \to\to Y$ holds in nested table T.

4.2 OPERATIONAL PROPERTIES

Now we discuss basic properties of the FT operators. Here, we concentrate our discussion on reversibility and commutability of the FT operators. First, we consider the reversibility of CE and CD operators.

Proposition 1. Given a nested table T, let $F_1 \ldots, F_N$ be components of some group field G, and let $T'=CE[F_1, \ldots, F_N \text{ INTO } H](T)$. Then, $T=CD[H](T')$.

Proposition 2. Given a nested table T, let H be a non-repeating group field with its component set C, and let $T'=CD[H](T)$. Then, $T=CE[C \text{ INTO } H](T')$.

	*T₁		
*A	B	C
a			
a′	b	c
a″	b	c

$\xrightarrow{\text{RD}[*A]}$

	*T₂		
A	B	C
a	b	c
a′	b	c
a″	b	c

$\xrightarrow{\text{RE}[A]}$

	*T₃		
*A	B	C
a			
a′	b	c
a″			

Fig. 5   IRREVERSIBLE TRANSFORMATION

These propositions are trivially proved from the definitions of CE and CD operators. Therefore, every transformation by CE and CD operators is assured to have a reverse transformation by CE and CD operators.

<u>Proposition 3</u>. Given a nested table T, let F be a non-repeating component and let T'=RE[F](T). Then, T=RD[*F](T'). (Field *F is a repeating field of T' corresponding to field F of T.)

This proposition assures that every transformation expressed by RE operators have a reverse transformation expressed by RD operators. However, transformations by RD operators are not always reversible. A sample case is illustrated in Fig. 5. Operator RD[*A] is applied to table *T₁ to get table *T₂, and then RE[A] is applied to *T₂. Table *T₃ is obtained as the result, and the contents of *T₃ are different from those of *T₁. Thus, the transformation from *T₁ to *T₂ is not reversible. To attain the reversibility, the following functional dependency has to hold in *T₁.

<u>Proposition 4</u>. Given a nested table T, let *F be a repeating component of a repeating group field G, and let C be the component set of G. Then, let T'=RD[*F](T). Iff C-*F→*F[†] holds in T, T=RE[F](T'). (Field F is a non-repeating field of T' corresponding to field *F of T.

(Sketch of Proof) Let T"=RE[F](T'), and let R, R' and R" be correspond-ing occurrences of G in T, T', and T", resepctively. For any tuple t"∈ R",

$$t''[*F]=R'_{t''[C-*F]}[F] \quad (=\{t'[F] \mid t'\in R' \wedge t'[C-*F]=t''[C-*F]\}),$$

[†] For simplicity, C-{*F}→{*F} is shortly denoted by C-*F → *F, since there is no possibility of confusion. Such a shorthand is used in the following part of the paper.

and

$$R'_{t''[C-*F]}[F] = \bigcup_{\substack{t \in R \ \land \\ t[C-*F] = t'[C-*F]}} t[*F].$$

Thus,

$$t''[*F] = \bigcup_{\substack{t \in R \ \land \\ t[C-*F] = t'[C-*F]}} t[*F].$$

Therefore, R=R", iff there exists just one t such that t $\in$ R and t[C-*F]=t"[C-*F]. The condition that C-*F $\rightarrow$ *F holds in T is obviously necessary and sufficient for this. □

Note that BC $\rightarrow$ *A does not hold in *T_1, since there are two tuples, ({a,a'},b,c) and ({a"},b,c), which have identical occurrences for fields B and C. If BC $\rightarrow$ *A holds in *T_1, the reversibility is assured. For constructing nested tables from flat tables, the following two corollaries are useful.

Corollary 1. In case a nested table is constructed by applying CE and RE operators to some flat table, this form transformation, that is the construction process, has a reverse transformation expressed by CD and RD operators.

Corollary 2. Suppose T be a nested table obtained by applying CE and RE operators to some flat table U. If T is updated (i.e., tuples are inserted, deleted, and/or modified) under the constraint that N $\rightarrow$ *F always holds in T for any repeating component *F, all updates of T can be properly relected on the source flat table U. (N denotes the non-repeating simple components of *F's parent.)

Corollary 2 assured that nested table T can be supported as a user view of the flat table U without the view update problems [1, 11].

On commutability and incommutability of the FT operators, there are many points to be discussed. Here, one case is discussed as an example. Two successive applications of RE operators are not always commutative as illustrated in Fig. 6, although the resultant tables have the same nested structures of fields. The next proposition gives a sufficient condition for the commutability in such cases.

Proposition 5. Given a nested table T, let G be a repeating group field with its component set C, and let H and I be distinct non-repeating components of G. If C-H-I $\rightarrow\rightarrow$ H holds in T, then RE[I](RE[H](T))=RE[H](RE[I](T)).

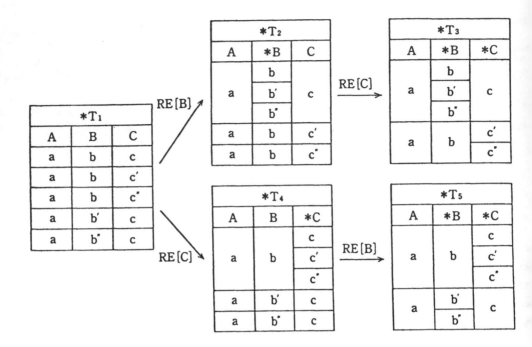

Fig. 6   INCOMMUTABILITY OF RE OPERATORS

(Sketch of Proof)   Let D=C-H-I, and let R, R'_α, and R''_α be corresponding occurrences of G in T, RE[H](T), and RE[I](RE[H](T)), respectively. For any tuple $t \in R''_\alpha$ with a D-value $d \in CP(D)$,

$$t[*I]=\{u[I]\,|\,u \in R'_\alpha \wedge u[D]=d \wedge u[*H]=t[*H]\},$$

and, for any tuple $u \in R'_\alpha$ with a D-value d,

$$u[*H]=\{v[H]\,|\,v \in R \wedge v[D]=d \wedge v[I]=u[I]\}=R_{du[I]}[H].$$

Since D $\rightarrow\!\!\rightarrow$ H holds in T,

$$R_{du[I]}[H]=R_d[H].$$

Therefore,

$$t[*H]=R_d[H],$$

and

$$t[*I]=R_d[I].$$

Similarly, let R, R'_β, and R''_β be corresponding occurrences of G in T, RE[I](T), and RE[H](RE[I](T)), resepctively. Then, for any tuple $w \in R''_\beta$ with a D-value d, we obtain

$$W[*H]=R_d[H],$$

and

$$W[*I]=R_d[I].$$

Therefore,

$$R_\alpha''=R_\beta'',$$

and then

$$RE[I](RE[H](T))=RE[H](RE[I](T)). \qquad \Box$$

6. CONCLUSION

In this paper, NTD was presented as a powerful office form modeling tool, and some basic properties of data manipulation in NTD were discussed. First, nested tables were defined, and four FT operators for the form transfofmation were intorduced. Then, sample usages of the FT operators were shown, and some propositions and corollaries on their basic properties were given. Particular emphasis was placed on the assurance of the reversibility and commutability of the form transformation. It was also clarified that, on a certain condition nested tables can be supported as user views to flat tables without tedious veiw update problems.

We are currently developing a prototype form handling system based on NTD especially aiming at automation of software management offices [6].

REFERENCES

[1] Chanberlin, D.D., 'Views, Authorization, and Locking in a Relational Data Base System,' Proc. AFIPS National Computer Conference, NCC '75, Anaheim, May 1975, pp. 425-430.

2] Codd, E.F., 'Further Normalization of the Data Base Relational model,' in 'Data Base Systems,' Rustin R., Ed., Prentice-Hall, 1972, pp.33-64.

3] Fagin, R., 'Multivalued Dependencies and a New Normal Form for Relational Databases,' ACM Trans. on Database Systems, Vol.2, No.3, September 1977, pp.262-278.

4] Housel, B.C., and Shu, N.C., 'A High-Level Data Manipulation Language for Hierarchical Data Structures,' Proc. Conf. on Data Abstraction, Definition and Structure, Salt Lake City, March 1976, pp. 155-168.

5] Kitagawa, H., Kunii, T.L., Harada, M., Kaihara, S., and Ohbo, N.,

'A Language for Office Form Processing (OFP) - with Application to Medical Forms -,' Proc. 3rd World Conf. on Medical Informatics, Tokyo, September 1980, pp. 713-718.

[6] Kitagawa, H., Kunii, T.L., Azuma, M., and Mizuno, Y., 'User- and Administrator- Friendly Architecture for Interactive Software Devleopment,' Proc. Intl. Cong. Applied Systems Research and Cybernetics, Acapulco, Mexico, Dec. 1980.

[7] Kitagawa, H., and Kunii, T.L., 'APAD: Application-Adaptable Database System - Its Architecture and Design -' in 'Data Base Design Techniques,' Yao, S.B. and Kunii, T.L., Eds., Springer Verlag, Lecture Notes in Computer Science, 1981.

[8] Kitagawa, H. and Kunii, T.L., 'Design and Implementation of a Form Management System APAD Using ADABAS/INQ DBMS,' Proc. IEEE Computer Society's 5th Intl. Computer Software and Applications Conf., Chicago, Nov. 1981.

[9] Luo, D., and Yao, S.B., 'Form Operation by Example - a Language for Office Information Processing,' Proc. Intl. Conf. on Management of Data, Ann Arbor, 1981.

[10] Makinouchi, A., 'A Consideration on Normal Form of Not-Necessaril Normalized Relation in the Relational Data Model,' Proc. 3rd Intl Conf. on VLDB, Tokyo, October 1977, pp. 447-453.

[11] Osman, I.M., 'Updating Defined Relations,' Proc. AFIPS National Computer Conference, NCC '79, New York, June 1979, pp.733-740.

[12] Shu, N.C., Housel, B.C., and Lum, V.Y., 'CONVERT: A High Level Translation Definition Language for Data Conversion,' Comm. ACM, Vol.18, No.10, October 1975, pp. 557-567.

AUTOMATED DESIGN OF CONCURRENT PROCESS SYSTEMS

Toyohiko Hirota, Yutaka Ohno
Kyoto University, Kyoto, 606 JAPAN
Koichi Tabata
University of Library and Information Science
Yatabe-chou, 305 JAPAN

ABSTRACT

We have developed a computer-aided design technique for a concurrent
process system. A concurrent process system is a system that several
processes concurrently access some common variables. In designing
such a system, a designer must pay attention to mutual exclusion of
common variable access, synchronization between processes, and
prevention of deadlock. Our design technique helps a designer to
solve these problems. In our design technique, a designer describes
formally some processing requirements of an object system. In this
description, each process in the system is specified as a set of
processing steps and a partial order on the set. Then our design
technique proposes to the designer some proper execution sequences
for each process. After an execution sequence for each process is
selected, our design technique establishes several critical regions
and constructs a design proposal, based on the designer's
requirements about mutual exclusion and consistency of common
variable access. Because for the most part our design technique is
mathematical operations on partially ordered sets, our design
technique can be greatly aided by a computer, and then a designer can
get a valid design proposal for a concurrent process system by using
our design technique.

1. INTRODUCTION

In designing a concurrent process system in which several processes
access common variables, a designer must pay attention to mutual
exclusion of common variable access, synchronization between
processes, and prevention of deadlock. To help a designer in such
problems, we have developed a computer-aided design technique, which
is mainly for software design of an on-line system [Hirota (1978)].

In this paper, we will present a modified version of our design technique so as to apply it to the design of a concurrent process system.

Several design techniques, such as modularization by Parnas [Parnas (1972)], composite design [Myers (1978)], and usage of data abstraction [Liskov (1975)], give us some useful guidelines for designing modular software, but they do not deal with the problems of concurrent process. On the other hand, Concurrent Pascal [Hansen (1975)] is a powerful programming language for a concurrent process system, but it does not help much at the design stage.

In our design technique, a designer describes formally some processing requirements of an object system. In this description, each process in the system is specified as a set of processing steps and a partial order on the set. First an execution sequence, a total order of processing steps, should be selected for each process. Our design technique has two guidelines for selection, i.e., localization and similarization. Then the designer has only to consider the proposed execution sequences without checking all the possibilities contained in the original processing requirements.

After the selection of an execution sequence, our design technique establishes several critical regions and constructs design proposal. At this stage, the designer has only to describe some requirements about mutual exclusion and consistency of common variable access.

Because for the most part our design technique is mathematical operations on partially ordered sets, our design technique can be greatly aided by a computer. Therefore, the designer can easily get a valid design proposal for a concurrent process system by using our design technique.

2. PRELIMINARY CONCEPTS

A concurrent process system is a system that several processes concurrently access some common variables, and we call each process in such a system a concurrent process. In this chapter, we will discuss some important features of concurrent process.

It is usually difficult to check the validity of concurrent process. For an independent process, we can validate an execution of a certain statement by checking the relations between some variables before and after the execution of the statement. Such a validation is not always applicable for concurrent process. Then we introduce an execution environment and serializability [Bernstein (1978)] to explain the validity of concurrent process.

The execution environment of a process is the set of the states of some parts of the system. If the execution of a process is closely connected with a certain part S at a time T of the system, the state S(T) of the part S at the time T is an element of the execution environment of that process.

If an execution environment of a concurrent process is equivalent to a certain other execution environment where the process is serially executed, we call the former environment serializable. Fig.1 shows an example of a serializable execution environment. In this case, the process Y accesses the variable F1 immediately after the process X finishes the access to the variable F1. The execution environment of X is {F1(T1),F2(T3)} and that of Y is { F1(T2), F2(T4) }. On the other hand, in serial execution, the execution of Y should be executed as Y' in Fig.1. Then the execution environment of Y and that of Y' are the same because both of those environments consist of the contents of the variables after the process X accesses them. Therefore the execution environment of Y is serializable. Fig.2 shows an example, in which the execution environments of

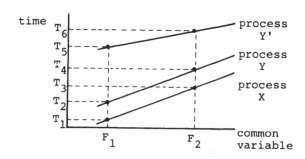

Fig.1 Serializable Execution Environment

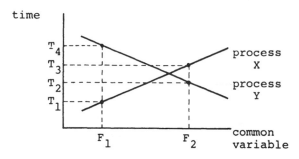

Fig.2 Unserializable Execution Environment

the processes, X and Y, are not serializable.

We suppose that concurrent processes would be validly executed under serializable execution environments, and we would like to execute many processes concurrently. Therefore we will need some mechanisms for synchronization between processes to prepare a serializable execution environment (as shown in Fig.1) for each process in the system.

3. PROCESSING REQUIREMENTS DESCRIPTION

For our design technique, a designer must prepare a processing requirements description PRD. PRD is to show what common variables should be accessed and in what sequence those common variables should be accessed in each process.

In PRD, each process is described as a set of processing steps and a partial order on the set. A processing step is an elementary unit of a process, which contains an access to a common variable.

[Definition 1] A processing step is specified by a step identifier i and a common variable d:

$u = \langle i, d \rangle$

[Definition 2] Processing requirements P^t of a process t are specified by a set U^t of processing steps and a partial order R^t on U^t (See Appendix 1):

$P^t = \langle U^t, R^t \rangle$

U = a set of processing steps for a process t

$R = \{ \langle u_i, u_j \rangle \mid u_i, u_j \in U^t \}$

[Definition 3] A processing requirements description PRD of a concurrent process system is defined as follows:

$PRD = \langle T, D, TP \rangle$

T = a set of processes

D = a set of common variables

$TP = \{ P^t \mid$ processing requirements of a process t $(\in T) \}$

The designer should take care of a partial order R in PRD. He should describe a necessary and sufficient set of the ordered pairs

of processing steps as a partial order. If the set is not
sufficient, the design procedure might produce a wrong result. On
the other hand, if it contains some unnecessary pairs, the result
would be inefficient.

4. SELECTION OF EXECUTION SEQUENCE

In a processing requirements description, the relations between the
processing steps are specified as a partial order, which is usually
satisfied by many execution sequences, i.e., total orders of the
processing steps. As a first step of our design technique, we select
proper execution sequences which satisfy the validity condition for
a concurrent process system or require only minimal modification to
satisfy the condition.

For selecting proper execution sequences, we have two procedures,
localization which is applied to each process separately, and
similarization which is applied to all the processes together.

Localization

For the performance of the object system, it is desired that many
processes, if possible, be concurrently executed. But, while one
process is accessing a certain common variable, other processes
should not access the variable. For guaranteeing this mutual
exclusion, common variable access of a process should be executed in
a critical region. Evidently the processing in a critical region
should not contain any irrelevant processing. Localization is a
procedure to eliminate the execution sequences in which the process
executes any irrelevant processing steps during the accesses to a
certain common variable. The localization procedure for each process
t is as follows.

First, the set U^t of the processing steps is partitioned into
subsets so as to satisfy the following conditions:
  (1) $U^t = \bigcup LB_i^t$, $LB_i^t \cap LB_j^t = \emptyset$ if $LB_i^t \neq LB_j^t$
  (2) if there exists u such that $u \in LB_i^t$ and $u \in M_d^t$
        ($M_d^t = \{u | u = <i,d>, u \in U^t\}$),
      then $u \in LB_i^t$ for all $u \in M_d^t$
  (3) for each LB_{ki}^t $(i=1,\ldots,n)$,

if there exist u_{ki1}, u_{ki2} in LB_{ki}^t and

$\quad$ $\langle u_{ki2}, u_{k2i} \rangle$, $\langle u_{k22}, u_{k3i} \rangle$, ..., $\langle u_{kn2}, u_{ki1} \rangle \in R^t$,

then $LB_{k1}^t = LB_{k2}^t = \cdots = LB_{kn}^t$

The conditions, (2) and (3), mean that there are no bidirectional relations between LB_i^t's. On the set $\{LB_i^t\}$, we define a relation LR as follows:

$\overline{LR}^t = \{ \langle LB_i^t, LB_j^t \rangle \mid {}^{\exists} u_1 \in LB_i^t, {}^{\exists} u_2 \in LB_j^t, \langle u_1, u_2 \rangle \in R^t \}$

LR^t = a transitive closure of $\overline{LR}^t$ (See Appendix 2)

In short, this LR^t shows the sequence of the common variable accesses in a process t.

[Theorem 1] LR^t is a partial order on the set $\{LB_i^t\}$.

With this partial order LR^t, we construct a new relation R_{loc}^t from the original R^t:

$\overline{R}_{loc}^t = R^t \cup \{ \langle u_1, u_m \rangle \mid u_1 \in LB_i^t, u_m \in LB_j^t,$

$\quad\quad\quad$ while $LB_i^t \neq LB_j^t$ and $\langle LB_i^t, LB_j^t \rangle \in LR^t \}$

R_{loc}^t = a transitive closure of $\overline{R}_{loc}^t$

[Theorem 2] R_{loc}^t is a partial order on U^t.

[Corollary] R_{loc}^t does not contain any ordered pairs inconsistent to R^t.

The partial order R_{loc}^t obtained by the above procedure is a restricted one of R^t, and improper execution sequences are eliminated from R^t based on the viewpoint of localization.

Similarization

To maitain the consistency between common variables, the processes which access these variables should be synchronized as shown in chapter 2. For efficient synchronized execution, it is desired that those processes access the variables in the same sequence. Similarization is a procedure to analyze the accesses to common variables in the execution sequence of each process, and to select proper execution sequence, if possible, toward the unification of all the sequences of common variable accesses.

Based on the processing requirements of all the processes, we construct a relation DR on the set D of common variables as follows:

$\overline{DQ} = \{<d_i, d_j> | d_i, d_j \in D$ and $(^{\exists}t \in T, {}^{\exists}u_i \in M_{d_i}^t, {}^{\exists}u_m \in M_{d_j}^t$

such that $<u_i, u_m> \in R^t)\}$, (See 4.1 about $M_{d_i}^t$)

$DQ =$ a transitive closure of $\overline{DQ}$

$DR = \{<d_i, d_j> | d_i = d_j$, or $<d_i, d_j> \in DQ$ and $<d_j, d_i> \notin DQ\}$

[Theorem 3] DR is a partial order on the set D.

DR is constructed from the common or consistent ordered pairs of common variable access specified in the requirements of all the processes. From DR, we can get a new partial order R_{sim}^t for R^t of a process t:

$\overline{R}_{sim}^t = R^t \cup \{<u_i, u_j> | u_i \in M_{d_l}^t, u_j \in M_{d_m}^t (d_l \neq d_m)$ and $<d_l, d_m> \in DR\}$

$R_{sim}^t =$ a transitive closure of $\overline{R}_{sim}^t$

[Theorem 4] R_{sim}^t is a partial order on U^t.

[Corollary] R_{sim}^t does not contain any inconsistent ordered pairs to R^t.

Localization and similarization can be applied not only to R^t but also to any partial order on U^t. Therefore we can first get R_{loc}^t by localization, and apply similarization to this R_{loc}^t to get R_{sim}^t.

5. CONSTRUCTION OF CRITICAL REGION

As the second step of our design technique, we establish several critical regions and construct a design proposal. Though there are generally several possible execution sequences for each process, the second step can be applied independently to any set in which one and only one execution sequence is contained for each process. Then the designer can select one of those sets by comparing one design with another, which will be derived from those sets by the second step.

The second step has three substeps, i.e., mutual exclusion, prevention of deadlock, and mutual consistency. We will describe each procedure after an introductory explanation of an execution sequence and several types of critical regions.

Execution Sequence and Critical Region

An execution sequence Q^t of a process t is a set of ordered pairs of the elements in U^t:

$$Q^t = \{<u_i, u_j> | u_i, u_j \in U^t\}$$

Q^t is a total order, that is, it must satisfy the conditions for a partial order and, for any pair of elements u_i and u_j, there necessarily exists $<u_i, u_j>$ or $<u_j, u_i>$ in Q^t.

As the design progresses, some flow-control steps (described below) may be added to the set U^t, we denote such an extended set of processing steps by $\widetilde{U}^t$ and a total order on $\widetilde{U}^t$ by $\widetilde{Q}^t$. Unlike U^t or Q^t, $\widetilde{U}^t$ and $\widetilde{Q}^t$ can vary with the progress of the design.

We use critical regions [Hansen (1973)] for mutual exclusion of common variable access and synchronization between processes. We assume a critical region satisfies the following conditions:

   (1) A critical region accepts one process at a time and in FCFS (First Come First Served).
   (2) A process remains inside a critical region for a finite time only.
   (3) Different critical regions can be executed concurrently.

In our design technique, we use two types of critical regions, i.e., basic critical regions and flow-control critical regions.

A basic critical region M_d is related to a specific common variable d and defined as the set of the processing steps in which a process accesses the variable:

$$M_d = \bigcup M_d^t = \{u | \exists t \in T, u = <i, d> \in U^t\} \quad (d \in D)$$

The construction of basic critical regions are uniquely specified for an execution sequence based on the definition.

A flow-control critical region is one which contains several critical regions in itself, and is defined as the set of flow-control steps for "enter" and "depart":

$$M_c = F_c \cup G_c \quad (c: identifier)$$
$$= \{f | \exists t \in T, f \in \widetilde{U}^t\} \cup \{g | \exists t \in T, g \in \widetilde{U}^t\}$$

   (f denotes a flow-control step for "enter" and g denotes one for "depart")

In the second step of our design technique, we begin with the construction of the basic critical regions, check whether all the processes are validly executed, and insert some flow-control critical regions if necessary. These operations will be described in detail in the following sections.

Mutual Exclusion

Mutual exclusion is required for processing on a common variable. For example, when a process enters a basic critical region, at two times (before and after the execution in another critical region), this critical region should not accept any other process during that period, in order to keep the consistency of the variable in itself. In such a case, a common variable should be accessed in a flow-control critical region. Then, because mutual exclusion is not always required for any variable, the designer should specify mutual exclusion requirements ER as follows:

ER={ data sets which require mutual exclusion } (ER $\subseteq$ D)

For any element d in ER, the following condition EC(d) is true if and only if the mutual exclusion on the variable d is established:

$$EC(d) = \neg(\exists t \in T, \forall u_i, \forall u_j \in M_d^t, \exists u_k \notin M_d^t,$$
$$(\langle u_i, u_k \rangle \in \widetilde{Q}^t) \wedge (\langle u_k, u_j \rangle \in \widetilde{Q}^t))$$
$$\vee(\exists c \in CR, \forall t \in T, \exists f \in F_c, \exists g \in G_c, \forall u \in M_d^t,$$
$$(\langle f, u \rangle \in \widetilde{Q}^t \wedge \langle u, g \rangle \in \widetilde{Q}^t))$$

If all processes access continuously a variable d ($\in$ ER), or if all the accesses to d are performed in a critical region c, EC(d) becomes true.

The design procedure is as follows: we check the first term of EC(d) for any d in ER, and if it is false, insert some flow-control steps into the execution sequence of each process to satisfy the second term of EC(d). The following theorem shows this procedure cannot fail.

[Theorem 5] For any d in ER, there exist $\widetilde{U}^t$ and $\widetilde{Q}^t$ for each process t which satisfy EC(d).

Prevention of Deadlock

All EC(d)'s can becomes true by using only one flow-control critical region, but this means, in fact, that processes are serially executed. Using a separate flow-control critical region for each d in ER, processes might be concurrently executed, which would improve the performance. When more than one flow-control critical region is used, however, a deadlock might occur. Therefore we must use some means for preventing a deadlock. We adopt an idea of introducing a partial order among flow-control critical regions to exclude the possibility of a circular waiting.

We define a relation FR on a set FM of flow-control critical regions:

$$\overline{FR}=\{<M_a,M_b>|M_a, M_b \in FM, \exists t \in T,$$
$$\exists f_a, \exists g_a, \exists f_b, \exists g_b \in \widetilde{U}^t,$$
$$(<f_b,f_a> \in \widetilde{Q}^t) \wedge (<f_a,g_b> \in \widehat{Q}^t)\}$$

FR= a transitive closure of $\overline{FR}$

For preventing a deadlock, FR should satisfy the following condition DC:

$$DC=(\ ^\forall M_a, \ ^\forall M_b \in FM, \ M_a \neq M_b, \ <M_a,M_b> \in FR \rightarrow <M_b,M_a> \notin FR)$$

FR does not always satisfy it. When it does not , we construct a new relation FRdp according to the following conditions.

(1) $<M_a,M_b> \in FR \wedge <M_b,M_a> \notin FR \rightarrow <M_a,M_b> \in FR_{dp}$

(2) $<M_a,M_b> \in FR \wedge <M_b,M_a> \in FR \rightarrow$
$$<M_a,M_b> \in FR_{dp} \vee <M_b,M_a> \in FR_{dp}$$

(3) $<M_a,M_b> \in FR_{dp} \rightarrow <M_b,M_a> \notin FR_{dp}$

(4) FR $_{dp}$ satisfies the transitive law.

These conditions mean that we construct a partial order FR $_{dp}$ from FR by cutting all loops, if any, in FR.

Based on FRdp , we construct a candidate $\widetilde{Q}^t_{dp}$ for each execution sequence of a process t:

$$\widetilde{Q}^t_{dp} =\{<u_i ,u_j >|u_i ,u_j \in U^t \bigcup \{g_a| \ \exists M_a \in FM, \ g_a \in \widetilde{U}^t\}$$
$$\text{and} \ <u_i ,u_j> \in \widehat{Q}^t\}$$
$$\bigcup\{<f_a,f_b>| \ ^\forall M_a, \ ^\forall M_b \in FM,$$
$$\exists f_a, \exists f_b, \exists g_a, \exists g_b \in \widetilde{U}^t,$$
$$(<f_a,f_b> \in \widehat{Q}^t \wedge (<M_b,M_a> \in FR_{dp} \vee a=b))$$
$$\vee (<f_a,f_b> \in \widehat{Q}^t \wedge <g_a,g_b> \in \widehat{Q}^t)$$
$$\vee (<M_b,M_a> \in FR_{dp} \wedge <f_b,f_a> \in \widehat{Q}^t \wedge <f_a,g_b> \in \widetilde{Q}^t)\}$$

$$\bigcup \{<u,f_a> \mid (\text{for } {}^\forall M_a \in FM, {}^\exists f_a \in \tilde{\tilde{U}}^t, {}^\exists u \in U^t,$$
$$<u,f_a> \in \tilde{Q}^t)$$
$$\wedge(\text{for } {}^\forall M_b \in FM, {}^\exists f_b, {}^\exists g_b \in \tilde{\tilde{U}}^t,$$
$$<M_b,M_a> \in FR_{dp} \wedge <u,f_b> \in \tilde{Q}^t \wedge <f_a,f_b> \in \tilde{Q}^t$$
$$\wedge <g_b,f_a> \in \tilde{Q}^t)\}$$
$$\bigcup \{<f_a,u> \mid \text{for } \forall M_a \in FM, {}^\exists f_a \in \tilde{\tilde{U}}^t, {}^\exists u \in \tilde{\tilde{U}}^t,$$
$$(<f_a,u> \in \tilde{Q}^t)$$
$$\vee ({}^\exists M_b \in FM, {}^\exists f_b, {}^\exists g_b \in \tilde{\tilde{U}}^t,$$
$$(<M_a,M_b> \in FR_{dp} \wedge <f_b,f_a> \in \tilde{Q}^t$$
$$\wedge <f_a,g_b> \in \tilde{Q}^t \wedge <f_b,u> \in \tilde{Q}^t))\}$$

$\tilde{Q}^t_{dp}$ is the same total order as $\tilde{Q}^t$ except that $\tilde{Q}^t_{dp}$ does not contain any ordered pair inconsistent to FR_{dp}, and the following theorem are established on $\tilde{Q}^t_{dp}$.

[Theorem 6] $\{\tilde{Q}^t_{dp} \mid {}^\forall t \in T\}$ makes DC true.

[Theorem 7] $\{\tilde{Q}^t_{dp} \mid {}^\forall t \in T\}$ makes EC(d) true for any d in ER.

[Theorem 8] $\tilde{Q}^t_{dp}$ is a total order on $\tilde{\tilde{U}}^t$.

According to these theorems, we can adopt $\tilde{Q}^t_{dp}$, as an execution sequence, instead of $\tilde{Q}^t$, and both mutual exclusion and deadlock prevention are provided by $\tilde{Q}^t_{dp}$.

Mutual Consistency

If the contents of several variables have some relations with one another, the processes which access them should be synchronized as discussed in chapter 2, or those variables must be accessed in one critical region. For checking these requirements, the designer must specify mutual consistency requirements MR:

MR= a set of variables the contents of which are mutually related
(MR ⊆ D)

If several MR's are required, the following procedure is applied to each of them respectively.

Using MR, we extract the relevant processes and the relevant parts of their execution sequences as follows:

MT= $\{t \mid t \in T, {}^\exists u=<i,d> \in U^t \text{ for } {}^\forall d \in MR\}$

$MU = \{u \mid \exists d \in MR, u \in M_d^t\}$

$\qquad \bigcup \{u \mid \exists M_a \in FM, \exists f_a, \exists g_a \in \tilde{U}^t, \exists u_d \in M_d^t (d \in MR),$

$\qquad\qquad u \in \tilde{U}^t \wedge \langle f_a, u \rangle, \langle u, g_a \rangle, \langle f_a, u_d \rangle, \langle u_d, g_a \rangle \in \tilde{Q}^t\}$

$MQ = \{\langle u_i, u_j \rangle \mid u_i, u_j \in MU^t \text{ and } \langle u_i, u_j \rangle \in \tilde{Q}^t\}$

For checking an execution sequence of a relevant process t, we define a mapping G^t from the processing steps to the critical regions:

$G^t(u) = M_d \quad (u \in M_d)$

$\qquad$ when $(\langle u, f_a \rangle \in MQ^t \text{ or } \langle g_a, u \rangle \in MQ^t)$

$\qquad\qquad$ for $\forall M_a \in FM$

$G^t(u) = M_a$

$\qquad$ when $\exists M_a \in FM, \langle f_a, u \rangle \in MQ^t,$

$\qquad\qquad$ and $(\langle f_a, f_b \rangle \in MQ^t \text{ or } \langle g_b, u \rangle \in MQ^t)$

$\qquad\qquad$ for $\forall M_b \in FM$

An inter-region sequence NP^t of a process t is specified based on G^t:

$NP^t = \langle NU^t, NQ^t \rangle$

$NU^t = \{M_i \mid \exists u \in MQ^t, G^t(u) = M_i\}$

$NQ^t = \{\langle M_i, M_j \rangle \mid \exists u_k, \exists u_l \in MU^t, \langle u_k, u_l \rangle \in MQ^t,$

$\qquad\qquad\qquad G^t(u_k) = M_i, G^t(u_l) = M_j\}$

[Theorem 9] NU^t is a total order on NQ^t.

A mutual consistency among variables which MR specifies is checked by the following condition:

$MC(MR) = (\forall t_i, \forall t_j \in MT, NQ^{t_i} = NQ^{t_j})$

This condition becomes true not only when all the NP^t's are the same, but also when the relevant variables are accessed in one critical region, which is concluded from the definition of G^t.

The design procedure for mutual consistency requirements MR is as follows. First we extract $\langle MU^t, MQ^t \rangle$ for any t in MT, and construct an inter-region sequence $\langle NU^t, NQ^t \rangle$ by applying G^t. Then we can check MC(MR). To make MC(MR) true, we might insert some dummy step in the execution sequence of a certain process. But if the process has already had a processing step which accesses the same variable as the dummy step does, the insertion is not permitted because it may destroy a mutual exclusion for that variable. Therefore we usually introduce a new flow-control critical region, if necessary, and insert properly some flow-control steps to the relevant execution sequences to establish MC(MR). This insertion satisfies the following theorems.

[Theorem 10] Insertion of flow-control steps does not destroy a mutual exclusion for any data set.

[Theorem 11] Insertion of flow-control steps does not affect a deadlock condition DC if it varies an inter-region sequence NP .

6. EXAMPLE

To illustrate our design technique, we will show an example, which contains 3 processes, X_1, X_2, and X_3, and 6 common variables, TIN, TOUT, F_a, F_b, F_c, and F_d. The processing requirements description PRD of this example is described as the precedence graphs in Fig.3.

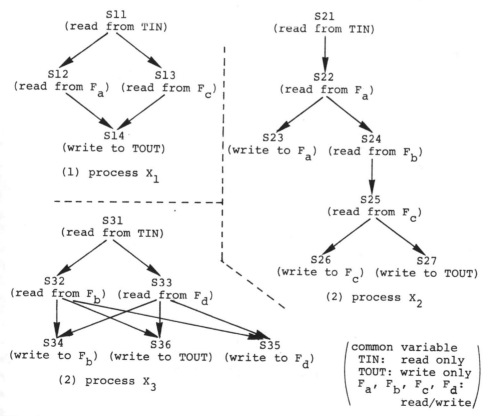

Fig.3 Processing Requirements Description of the Example

In the first step of the design, localization and similarization are applied to the PRD. Fig.4 shows $\{LB_i^t\}$, LR^t, and the result of the localization, and Fig.5 shows DR and the result of the similarization. The final result of the first step (Fig.6) indicates that only one execution sequence is specified for X_1 or X_2, and that several execution sequences are possible for X_3.

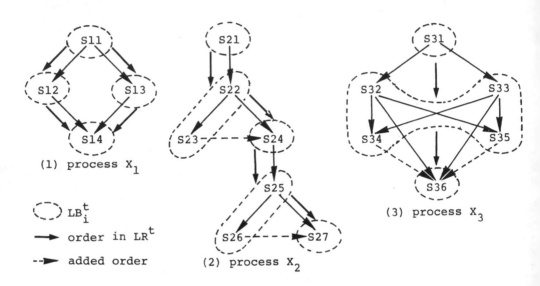

Fig.4 Localization

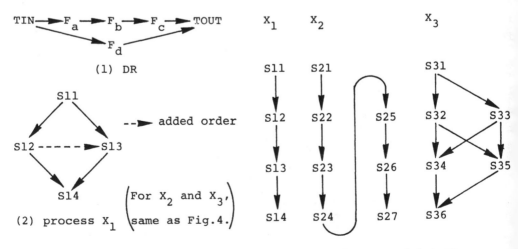

Fig.5 Similarization

Fig.6 Result of 1st Step

In the second step, we will explain the specific set of execution sequences shown in Fig.7.

We assume mutual exclusion requirements ER is as follows:

ER={F_a,F_b,F_c,F_d}

Because EC(F_d) becomes false, one flow-control critical region is needed for the mutual exclusion of F_d and flow-control steps are inserted as shown in Fig.8. In this case, the condition DC for a deadlock prevention is clearly true.

As mutual consistency requirements, we assume the following set:

MR={F_a,F_c}

The set MT which contains the relevant processes to MR is as follows:

MT={X_1,X_2}

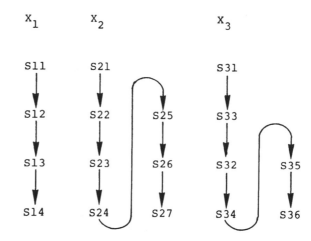

Fig.7 Execution Sequence for 2nd Step

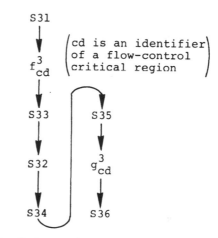

Fig.8 Insertion of Flow-Control Step for X_3

The inter-region sequence NP^+ are computed as shown in Fig.9. By using a heuristic method, we can find the best solution, that is, the insertion of a dummy step for a process X_1 (Fig.10).

X_1 $M_{Fa} \longrightarrow M_{Fc}$

X_2 $M_{Fa} \longrightarrow M_{Fb} \longrightarrow M_{Fc}$

Fig.9 Inter-Region Sequence of X_1 and X_2

S11 $\longrightarrow$ S12 $\longrightarrow$ S15 $\longrightarrow$ S13 $\longrightarrow$ S14

$\begin{pmatrix} \text{S15: dummy step,} \\ \text{request for } F_b \end{pmatrix}$

Fig.10 Insertion of Dummy Step for X_1

The resulting design proposal is shown in Fig.11 (textual form) and Fig.12 (pictorial form). This proposal is one based on the specific set of execution sequences shown in Fig.7. Thus the designer should examine another design proposal based on another set of execution sequences which will be derived from Fig.6.

7. CONCLUSION

Our design technique can help a designer especially at an early stage of design for a concurrent process system, because it requires only the information about common variable access of processes. The design proposal produced by our design technique can be used as a basis for detailed design, performance prediction, or the like.

For our previous design technique for an on-line system, we have already implemented an experimental software which generates automatically a design proposal from processing requirements description. And according to the design technique described in this paper, we are now developing a new software for the design of a concurrent process system.

REFERENCES

Bernstein P.A., et al. (1978). The Concurrency Control Mechanism of SDD-1: A Sytem for Distributed Database

```
process X1;
begin
  region MTIN do S11;
  region MFa do S12;
  region MFb do S15;
  region MFc do S13;
  region MTOUT do S27
end;

process X2;
begin
  region MTIN do S21;
  region MFa do begin
    S22;
    S23
  end;
  region MFb do S24;
  region MFc do begin
    S25;
    S26
  end;
  region MTOUT do S27
end;

process X3;
begin
  region MTIN do S31;
  region Mcd do begin
    f3cd;
    region MFd do S33;
    region MFb do begin
      S32;
      S34
    end;
    region MFd do S35;
    g3cd
  end;
  region MTOUT do S36
end;
```

Fig.11 Design Proposal for the Example (1)

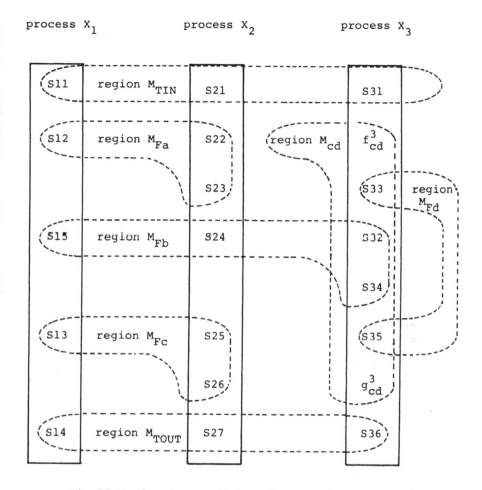

Fig.12 Design Proposal for the Example (2)

(The Fully Redundant Case). IEEE Trans. Software Eng., Vol.SE-4, No.3, May 1978.

ansen P.B. (1973). Operating System Principles. Prentice-Hall, 1973.

ansen P.B. (1976). The Programming Language Concurrent Pascal. IEEE Trans. Software Eng., Vol.SE-1, No.2, June 1975.

irota T., Tabata K. and Ohno Y. (1978). Computer-Aided Design of oftware Module: Validity of Concurrent Processing on On-Line File. rd USA-JAPAN Computer Conference, Oct. 1978.

Liskov B.H.,   et al.   (1975) Specification Techniques for Data
Abstraction. IEEE Trans. Software Eng., Vol.SE-1, No.1, March 1975.

Myers G.J. (1978). Composite/Structured Design. Litton Educational
Publishing, 1978.

Parnas D.L.   (1972).   A Technique for Software Module Specification
with Examples. CACM, Vol.15, No.15, May 1972.

APPENDICES

1. PARTIAL ORDER

A partial order R on a set U is:
  $R=\{<u_i,u_j>|u_i,u_j \in U\}$
and satisfies the following conditions:
  (1) reflexive law: $<a,a> \in R$ $(a \in U)$
  (2) asymmetric law: if $<a,b> \in R$ and $<b,a> \in R$, then a=b
      $(a,b \in U)$
  (3) transitive law: if $<a,b> \in R$ and $<b,c> \in R$, then $<a,c> \in R$
      $(a,b,c \in U)$

2. TRANSITIVE CLOSURE

R is called a transitive closure of $\bar{R}$ if R is constructed by adding
several ordered pairs to $\bar{R}$ which is in turn a set of ordered pairs.
If $\bar{R}$ satisfies the reflexive law and does not contain any loops of
ordered pairs, R becomes a partial order.

Part VIII.

Data Flow Machines

Data flow machines and functional programming are under keen
attention. The first paper by R. E. Bryant and J. B. Dennis
reviews three major approaches to concurrent programming and
indicates that data flow languages are very promising for
expressing computations for concurrent execution. It is
also indicated that data flow languages permit modular
programming and allow programmers to explicitly limit the
sources of nondeterminacy. Functional programming as such
offers numerous advantages for parallel and distributed
processing. However, purely functional languages lack the
power to express manipulation of shared objects. In order
to remedy this, the second paper by Arvind and J. Dean Brock
proposes the "manager" construct which embodies the concept
of "stream."

CONCURRENT PROGRAMMING[1]

R. E. Bryant

California Institute of Technology

J. B. Dennis

Massachusetts Institute of Technology

1. Introduction

Concurrency of activities has long been recognized as an important feature in many computer systems. These systems allow concurrent operations for a number of reasons of which three are particularly common. First, by executing several jobs simultaneously, multiprogramming and time-sharing systems can make fuller use of the computing resources. Second, real-time transaction systems, such as airline reservation and point-of-sale terminal systems, allow a number of users to access a single database concurrently and to obtain responses in real-time. Finally, high speed parallel computers such as array processors dedicate a number of processors to the execution of a single program to speed up completion of a computation.

In developing the software for some of the early multiprogramming systems, programmers soon discovered a need for an abstract and machine-independent means of expressing the behavior of systems which involve concurrent activities. They found that machine level programming was tedious and very difficult to do correctly. When many tasks are to proceed concurrently, the problems of allocating system resources, of scheduling the order in which tasks are performed, and of preventing concurrent activities from disastrously interfering with one another are difficult to deal with without assistance from a high level programming language.

One of the first concepts to emerge in an attempt to satisfy this need for a more abstract view of concurrent systems was the process concept. In this view, the sequence of actions performed during execution of a sequential program is viewed as an abstract entity called a process, and details such as which physical processor is used and the time of execution are ignored. For example, in a typical

1. This paper is a revised version of one published in Research Directions in Software Technology , P. Wegner, editor. This research was supported by the National Science Foundation under grant DCR75-04060 and by the Advanced Research Projects Agency of the Department of Defense, monitored by the Office of Naval Research under contract number N00014-75-C-06661.

multiprogramming system the different user jobs, the interrupt routines, and the I/O channel program executions may be viewed as separate processes. During system operation, the processors and memory may be switched among the processes, so all processes are carried forward, even though no process retains exclusive control of all the resources it needs nor runs in one continuous sequence.

Traditional high level programming languages such as Fortran, Algol, and Cobol express computations as independent, noninteracting processes. The processes in a concurrent system, however, may interact with each other for several reasons. First, one process may convey data to another. This is called communication. Second, processes may interact to ensure a correct sequencing of events. Process interaction which serves to control the order in which processes execute is called synchronization. These synchronization operations may be required for several different reasons, of which two are particularly common. First, if one process must perform some task before a second can proceed, there is a precedence constraint between the two processes. For example, the second process may need data which is computed by the first. Conversely, if one process produces data to be used by another, then the producer process cannot produce more data than the buffer between them can hold until the consumer process has used some of the old data. Hence, precedence constraints can exist in both directions between producers and consumers of data. Second, processes which share common resources such as processors, memory locations, or input/output devices require synchronization so the resources will be allocated in a systematic way. This allocation may be a simple form of mutual exclusion, in which a process retains exclusive control of a resource until the process voluntarily releases it, at which time the resource is granted to any process waiting for the resource. More complex allocation schemes can involve such features as allowing several processes to use a resource simultaneously, assigning different priorities to processes contending for a resource, or allowing one process to forcibly remove a resource from the control of some other process. Traditional programming languages are not powerful enough to express these types of interactions. Instead, a program must invoke operating system routines to perform the necessary communication and synchronization with other processes in the system.

Besides the inability to express the interactions between processes, traditional high level languages cannot express nondeterminate computations. That is, they can only express computations whose output values depend only on the values of inputs. In a nondeterminate computation, on the other hand, output values can depend on other factors, such as the times at which events occur in the system. For example, suppose agents at two different remote terminals of an airline reservation system both request the last seat on the same flight. One will be granted this seat and one will not, but which one receives which response depends on the relative order in which the requests are received and processed. Nondeterminacy is essential in many concurrent systems.

The need for high level programming languages which can express the operation of a system of concurrent processes has led to the development of programming constructs with which one can express these communication and synchronization operations. Some of these approaches, such as semaphores [13] and monitors [6,7,19], suppose systems in which all processes have access to a single, shared memory. Others assume that processes communicate by sending messages to one another [4,20,24]. Languages based on actor semantics [15,16,17] carry the message-passing concept even further by considering all primitive operations to be carried out by separate, message-passing processes. Other approaches to concurrent programming have been developed which, instead of viewing a system as a number of communicating, sequential processes, view a program as an unordered set of instructions and permit an instruction to be executed any time its operands are ready. This form of program execution can potentially achieve a higher degree of concurrency than is possible with sequential processes. Languages based on this approach are called data flow languages [1,2,11,25,27].

Several issues must be considered when designing programming languages to support concurrent computation. Of primary importance is expressive power. The expressive power of a language, in the context of concurrent systems, means the forms of concurrent operations, and the types of communication, synchronization, and nondeterminacy which can be expressed in the language. A language which lacks expressive power will force the programmer to rely on a suitable set of operating system routines to implement desired behaviors. A properly designed language, on the other hand, should have sufficient richness to express these functions directly. Furthermore, if the language lacks expressive power, a programmer may need to resort to awkward or inefficient programming techniques to achieve desired results.

A second issue in the design of a language for concurrent programming is the clarity of programs written in the language, that is, how easily the effect of executing a program can be understood by looking at the program. A properly designed language can provide a programmer with the tools needed to write clear and concise programs. To meet this goal, the language must allow programs to be written in a modular fashion, so that the sections of the program can be viewed independently of one another. This property is critical in concurrent system design, since the sections of the programs which are executed concurrently can often affect each other in subtle ways, and these effects can ultimately lead to deadlocks, hazards, or other forms of incorrect behavior. Furthermore, these effects may cause problems only under relatively rare combinations of circumstances, and as a result the errors may remain undetected even after a long period of system operation. Hence, a modular program in which it is quite clear how the concurrent activities in the system can affect each other would be of great value to the programmer, and to anyone who wishes to modify the program later. A programming language can also help the programmer write clear and concise programs by providing high level constructs to express the synchronization, communication, and nondeterminacy within the system. This will not only make programming less tedious, it will reduce the chance of error and make the programs more readable.   If concurrent programming languages are to describe the operation of large and complex systems, it is important for these languages to have a clarifying rather than an obscuring effect on the programs.

Ultimately, one must be concerned with implementation issues. These include the ease of implementation of the language -- whether it can be implemented on existing computer systems, whether slight modifications to an existing system will be sufficient, or whether it will require a whole new approach to computer design. A second factor in implementation is its efficiency, that is whether concurrency expressed in programs can be exploited without undue overhead. This desire for a language which is easy to implement, yet runs efficiently, often seems in conflict with the goals of expressive power and clarity of programs, and these two goals can themselves conflict with each other. Inevitably, trade-offs must be made, and hence the decision of which approach to use depends to a large degree on design priorities.

In this paper, the main approaches to constructing concurrent programs will be presented and compared. As a basis for comparison, two examples of systems incorporating concurrent operations have been chosen, and programs for these examples will be presented using the different approaches to concurrent programming. Of particular interest are the semantic issues in language design, i.e. how the computation is expressed, rather than the detailed syntax of the languages. Hence, in the interest of uniformity, the example programs will be written in PASCAL [22], modified to include the necessary constructs. As will be seen, the different approaches to concurrent programming differ greatly in their expressive power, clarity of expression, and ease and efficiency of implementation.

. Example Systems

Two examples have been chosen as representative of systems for which concurrent programming is required. The first is an airline reservation system, in which a number of users (agents) can perform transactions interactively with a single database.   In such a system concurrency in processing transactions is required to enable sharing of data, reasonable throughput, and real-time, interactive use. The second example is an input/output buffer system in which several input devices can read different files and send these files, via a buffer, to any of several output devices. By allowing the input and output devices to operate concurrently, this system can utilize hardware resources more effectively than would be possible otherwise.

The examples have been chosen to convey the basic features of concurrent systems. They have been simplified considerably to avoid the large amounts of detail typically required in real-life systems. For example, neither system has any form of error-checking, nor is there any provision for terminating system operation. Of course, it is difficult to draw conclusions about the merits of programming language features on the basis of such simple examples. In considering these programs, one must also consider how difficult it would be to add more sophistication to the system designs.

The database for the airline reservation system contains information about the flights for a single airline. Initially, each flight has 100 seats available. The system can accept two types of commands. To reserve seats on a flight, an agent gives the command ('reserve',f,n). If at least n seats are available on flight f, the seats will be reserved, and the system will respond with the message true. If that many seats are not available, no seats will be reserved, and the system will respond with the message false. To find out how many seats are available on flight f, a system user gives the command ('info',f). The system will respond with the number of seats which are available on the flight at the time the command is processed.

The input/output buffer system contains input devices input1, input2, ..., inputj, output devices output1, output2, ..., outputk, and a single buffer. During operation, the input devices read their respective blocks of data concurrently. Once a block has been read in, it is loaded into the buffer, at which time the input device can begin reading a new block. The block in the buffer is then moved to the local storage of one of the output devices and written out. Each output device is capable of writing any of the output blocks; hence a block in the buffer can be transferred to the first available output device rather than to a particular, predetermined one. The buffer can hold only one block at a time; hence the readers must contend with each other for use of the buffer. Similarly, each block is to be written out by only one output device; hence the output devices must contend for the output blocks. It is assumed that the buffering operations (i.e. moving a block from the input device to the buffer and from the buffer to the output device) are much faster than the input and output operations, so the buffer will not form a bottleneck in the system.

3. Processes Executing Within a Global Environment

The earliest organized approach to concurrent programming was to view a system as a number of sequential processes which execute concurrently in a common, global environment. This view is a natural abstraction of the operation of a multiprogramming system, which typically contains one or more central processing units and several input/output processors, all of which can access a single, shared memory. The processors communicate with one another by reading or writing mutually agreed upon memory locations according to some convention. Thus, we can view execution of a set of instructions by a processor as an abstract process and the common memory locations as the global environment for these processes. Assignment statements with global variables on either the left- or the right-hand side express the communication between processes.

Some mechanism is required to synchronize accesses to the global variables. In practice this is done using the program interrupt facility of the hardware. Examples of abstract synchronization mechanisms include the semaphores of Dijkstra [13] and the monitors of Brinch Hansen [6,7] and Hoare [19]. Other synchronization mechanisms have been developed [9], but none have received as much attention as semaphores and monitors. A semaphore is a special type of shared variable upon which several primitive synchronization operations can be performed. A monitor, on the other hand, is a set of programmer-defined procedures which can be called by the processes to gain access to global variables.

3.1. Process Synchronization by Semaphores

A semaphore S is an integer variable initialized to some value. Associated with the semaphore is a queue which holds names of processes. Two operations are defined on the semaphore: wait(S) and signal(S) (Dijkstra called these P and V, respectively.) If a process P executes wait(S), then the value of S is decremented. If this new value is negative, the name of P is placed on the queue associated with the semaphore, and P is blocked from executing. If, on the other hand, S is nonnegative, P is allowed to continue. If a process P executes signal(S), then the value of S is incremented. If the new value of S is less than or equal to zero, then the name of one process is removed from the queue, and this process is allowed to resume execution.

Semaphores provide a means to suspend execution of a process until certain conditions are satisfied. If processes perform semaphore operations in conjunction with their accesses to the global variables, the necessary synchronization in the system can be achieved. For example, a semaphore with initial value 1 can be used to maintain mutual exclusion of processes accessing a shared variable. A process which is updating the database in the airline reservation system, for instance, must have exclusive control of the database so that the database will remain in a consistent state during each transaction. Hence, to reserve n seats on flight f, a process would execute the following code segment:

```
wait(mutex);
if available[f] <= n
then begin
    available[f]:= available[f] - n;
    success:= true
end
else success:= false;
signal(mutex);
```

In the above program, mutex is a semaphore with initial value 1, and the array available is a global variable which represents the shared database.

If several processes wish to access the database without changing the database state, these accesses can proceed concurrently. Furthermore, if a process wants to read only one word in the database, there is no danger of finding the database in an inconsistent state, hence this access can proceed even while other processes are updating the database. To find out how many seats are available on the flight, a process would simply execute the statement

$$n:= available[flight].$$

Of course, in a more realistic airline reservation an agent would want to know more about a flight than the number of seats available. Hence, processing an 'info' request would require reading several words of memory. If the database is altered in the middle of these reads, the information returned to the agent may contain inconsistencies. To program a more sophisticated reservation system, we would divide the types of transactions into two classes: those which only read the database (the readers), and those which alter the database (the writers.) A number of readers can proceed concurrently, but a writer must have exclusive control of the database. Programs which solve the readers-writers problem [10,16,19] are considerably more complex than our simple example.

Semaphores can also be used to control the order in which processes access resources. For example, the input and output processes in the input/output buffer system would execute codes as follows:

```
Input[j]                              Output[k]

while true do                         while true do
begin                                 begin
    read(inj,infilej);                    wait(loaded);
    wait(free);                           outk:= buffer;
    buffer:= inj;                         signal(free);
    signal(loaded)                        write(outk,outfilek)
end                                   end
```

Initial values: free = 1, loaded = 0.

In the above program, the global variable buffer serves as the buffer between the input and output processes. The semaphores free and loaded are used to maintain correct sequencing between input and output processes. Furthermore, the semaphore free is used to guarantee that only one input process can load a value into the buffer at a time, and the semaphore loaded guarantees that only one output process will print a particular buffer value. Thus, the two semaphores enforce both precedence constraints and mutual exclusion in the system.

The semaphore construct is sufficient to solve a wide variety of process synchronization problems, although sometimes with great difficulty. Two concepts which are found in many computer systems, however, are noticeably lacking. The first is the concept of the time at which events occur. For example, a process cannot pause for a specified amount of time before continuing execution. The second is that one process cannot force another process to stop execution. These two features were left out intentionally, since the process abstraction removes the time at which events actually occur in the system from the programmer's control, and a process can be affected by other processes only when it makes reference to the global environment.

One type of system whose operations cannot be fully expressed with a semaphore program is a system in which the processes do not execute within a single, global environment. If the system consists of processors connected together by a communication network, the processes execute within a number of local environments and hence cannot access global variables or semaphores. The notion of a global environment does not reflect the architecture of such a system. For example, in the airline reservation system, one cannot cause information to be transferred between the remote terminals and the central computer except by calling on the operating system to perform these operations.

The semaphore concept was a major step forward in making programs involving process synchronization easier to understand, but it still has several flaws as a programming tool. The first is the primitiveness of the semaphore operations. Semaphores provide a very simple form of process synchronization. It is left to the programmer to develop conventions about how semaphores will be used to provide the desired behavior. Complex forms of process synchronization, in which different processes have different priorities, such as the various solutions to the readers—writer's problem [10], typically have very obscure semaphore programs. Unless the conventions are carefully documented, the programs may be difficult to modify at a later date. Moreover, if just one process fails to obey the conventions as to how resources are to be accessed, the system may deadlock or in some other way behave improperly.

The second flaw is a total lack of modularity in the programs. Information about how a shared resource is utilized and how the synchronization is provided is distributed throughout the programs for the individual processes. For example, it is difficult to locate all sources of nondeterminacy in the system. The processes in the input/output buffer system would have the same programs if there were only one input process and one output process as it does with several input and several output processes. In the first case, the system is determinate, whereas it is not in the second. This lack of modularity, coupled with the primitiveness of semaphore operations, makes it very difficult for someone looking at a semaphore program to determine whether a resource is being accessed properly.

Regarding implementation, semaphores and their corresponding synchronization operations can be implemented without great difficulty on any system whose architecture reflects the idea of a global state, such as a multiprogramming system. The THE system of Dijkstra [14] is an example of a simple but elegant operating system which uses semaphores to synchronize processes.

3.2. Process Synchronization by Monitors

Monitors were developed to allow a more structured format for concurrent programs than is possible with semaphores. Unlike semaphore programs, all information about a set of shared resources and how they are used is contained in a single area of the program: the declaration of a monitor. The declaration of a monitor includes a number of procedures which define operations on the shared resources. These procedures are available to all processes in the system. When a process wishes to access a shared resource, such as a global variable or a shared hardware resource, it must do so by executing one of the procedures of the corresponding monitor. It should be emphasized that a monitor does not itself cause any action in the system. Instead, it is merely a collection of procedures which can be executed by the processes in the system. This idea of limiting the ways in which a shared resource can be accessed to the operations performed by a small set of procedures was originally proposed in conjunction with conditional critical sections [5,18].

Monitors are implemented in such a way that the execution of the procedures of a particular monitor are mutually exclusive. Hence, a process retains exclusive control of the resources of a monitor while executing one of the monitor procedures, until it surrenders its control. A process can surrender its control of the monitor in one of several ways. First, it can complete execution of the monitor procedure, at which time some other process can begin execution of one of the monitor procedures. This form of control-passing is sufficient to implement mutual exclusion of processes. The airline reservation system, for example, utilizes only this form of control-passing. Other forms of control-passing are provide by <u>condition</u> <u>variables</u> along with the operations delay and continue (Hoare calls these wait and signal). A condition variable has no visible value, although it does have an initially empty queue associated with it. When a process executes the statement delay(cond) in the body of a monitor procedure, the process name is placed on the queue for cond, the process is blocked from executing further, and control of the monitor is released. When a process executes the statement continue(cond), this process is temporarily blocked (unless the queue for cond is empty), and one of the processes on the queue for cond is resumed. Once this reawakened process leaves the monitor procedure, the process which executed the continue(cond) statement is resumed.

In the airline reservation system, accesses to the database would be controlled by a monitor database with procedures reserve and info as follows:

```
monitor database;
var available:array[1..limit] of integer; i:integer;

procedure entry reserve(f,n:integer; success:boolean);
begin
    if available[f] <= n
    then begin
        success:= true;
        available[f]:= available[f] - n;
    end
    else success:= false
end reserve;

procedure entry info(f,n:integer);
begin n:= available[f]
end info;

begin
    for i = 1 to limit do available[i]:= 100
end.
```

The monitor database controls all accesses to the array available, where available[f] is the number of seats available on flight f. During system operation, some process initializes the monitor by executing the statement init database. This causes the body of the monitor program to be executed, setting all elements of available to 100.   Then, to reserve n seats on flight f, a process executes the statement:

$$database.reserve(f,n,success),$$

and to find out how many seats are available, it executes:

$$database.info(f,n).$$

For the input/output buffer system, the buffer would be controlled by a monitor I/O_buffer with procedures deliver and retrieve as follows:

```
monitor I/O_buffer;
var buffer:block; inuse:boolean; free,loaded:condition;

procedure entry deliver(in:block);
begin
    if inuse then delay(free);
    buffer:= in;
    inuse:= true;
    continue(loaded)
end deliver;

procedure entry retrieve(out:block);
begin
    if not inuse then delay(loaded);
    out:= buffer;
    inuse:= false;
    continue(free)
end retrieve;

begin
    inuse:= false
end.
```

During system operation some process must initialize the monitor by executing the statement init I/O_buffer. This causes the variable inuse to be set to false. Thereafter, the input and output processes execute programs as follows:

Input[j]

Output[k]

```
while true do
begin
    read(inj,infilej);
    I/O_buffer.deliver(inj)
end
```

```
while true do
begin
    I/O_buffer.retrieve(outk);
    write(outk,outfilek)
end
```

The expressive power of monitors is equivalent to that of semaphores in the sense that one can write a program for a monitor semaphore with procedures wait and signal which models the behavior of a semaphore, and conversely one can write a semaphore program which models the behavior of a monitor. However, if one wishes to follow the convention that a shared resource in the system can be accessed only by calling a procedure of the corresponding monitor, then all accesses to that resource must be mutually exclusive. For example, in the airline reservation system several processes cannot execute the procedure database.info concurrently. Only by relaxing the restrictions so that the database could be accessed directly by the processes could the full concurrency in the system be realized. This, however, would compromise the goal of collecting together all information about how a resource is utilized into one section of the system specification.

The monitor construct provides more modularity than semaphores, and this yields more understandable programs. The ways in which a resource may be accessed are contained in a single section of the system specification, rather than in the programs for each process. This modularity also makes the system easier to modify. For example, if we wish to modify the input/output buffer system so that several blocks could be buffered at once, we need only modify the monitor procedures. The change would not affect the process programs.

The mutual exclusion of procedure calls, while it is a restriction in terms of expressive power, helps make monitor procedures easier to write than the equivalent semaphore programs. Monitor procedures are less susceptible to subtle timing errors than they would be if several processes could access the resources controlled by the monitor simultaneously. Perhaps a carefully designed extension to the monitor construct could be developed which allows procedure calls to proceed concurrently under some circumstances, while retaining the modularity and clarity of the monitor concept.

As with semaphores, monitors can be implemented without major difficulties on a multiprogramming system. The Solo operating system of Brinch Hansen [8] is written mainly in Concurrent Pascal [7], an extended version of Pascal which supports monitors. The programming language Modula [28] also provides a synchronization construct similar to the monitor. The ability to write an operating system in a high level language, including the communication and synchronization between processes, is an important advance in concurrent programming.

. **Processes Communicating by Message Passing**

In one more modular view of concurrent systems each process executes within a local environment that cannot be accessed or altered by any other process. For two processes to interact with each other, one process must send a message to the other, and the receiving process must accept the message. One of the first system designs which followed this approach was the Regnecentralen RC4000 computer system [4] in which the system contained a single CPU yet supported a number of independent message-passing processes.

To illustrate how message-passing semantics might be supported by a programming language, we shall define a language extension in which a message is a triple (destination,source,contents), where destination is the name of the receiving process, source is the name of the sending process, and contents is the information which the message is to convey. Messages in this language are of type record. Thus, for example, the contents field of a message m is referenced by the expression m.contents. Execution of the command send(m) by process P, where m is of type message, will cause a message (m.destination,P,m.contents) to be sent to the process m.destination. Each process has a single input queue into which all incoming messages are placed. Execution of the function receive will first cause the process to wait until a message is placed in its input queue, if one is not already present. Then the first message is removed from the queue and returned as the value of the function.

These two message-passing operations are sufficient to express the airline reservation system. Whereas in the global environment approach, the database is a global variable accessed by a number of different processes, with the message-passing approach we shall define a process transact which has sole access to the database. All transactions are initiated by sending messages to transact. The contents fields of these messages can have one of two formats:

('reserve',flight,number),

and

('info',flight)

The program for the process transact is as follows:

```
process transact;
var available:array[1..limit] of integer;
    request,reply:message; f,n:integer;

begin
    for n = 1 to limit do available[n]:= 100;
    while true do
    begin
        request:= receive;
        case request.contents.type of
            'reserve':
                begin
                    f:= request.contents.flight;
                    n:= request.contents.number;
                    if available[f] <= n
                    then begin
                        reply.contents:= true;
                        available[f]:= available[f] - n;
                    end
                    else reply.contents:= false
                end;
            'info':
                reply.contents:=
                    available[request.contents.flight]
        end;
        reply.destination:= request.source;
        send(reply)
    end
end.
```

Notice that this program does not realize all potential concurrencies in the system. The database transactions are processed sequentially, much as they were in the monitor program, because the process transact has exclusive access to the database, and it is a sequential process.

For the I/O buffer example, we shall use a process buffer_control to control the buffering between input and output processes. An input process will send a message containing the input block to buffer_control which in turn will send this block to one of the output processes. Each output process must notify buffer_control when it is ready to receive a block, or else buffer_control would have no way of knowing what output processes are free. This can be accomplished by sending a 'ready' message. Hence, the contents field of messages sent to buffer_control can have one of two formats:

$$('data', inblock),$$

and

$$('ready').$$

Unlike the processes in the airline reservation system, the process buffer_control cannot always service its input messages in the order received. For example, it may receive several 'ready' messages before receiving any 'data' messages. Hence, some means of storing messages in internal queues is required. For this reason we will use a data type **queue** on which the operations enqueue and dequeue are defined, as well as the boolean-valued function empty. The program for buffer_control is as follows:

```
process buffer_control;
var dataq,readyq:queue of message;
    inputm,outputm,datam,readym:message;

begin
    while true do
    begin
        inputm:= receive;
        case inputm.contents.type of
            'data':
                if empty(readyq) then enqueue(inputm,dataq)
                else begin
                    readym:= dequeue(readyq);
                    outputm.contents:= inputm.contents.inblock;
                    outputm.destination:= readym.source;
                    send(outputm)
                end;
            'ready':
                if empty(dataq) then enqueue(inputm,readyq)
                else begin
                    datam:= dequeue(dataq);
                    outputm.contents:= datam.contents.inblock;
                    outputm.destination:= inputm.source;
                    send(outputm)
                end
        end
    end
end.
```

The input and output processes execute the following codes:

```
Input[j]                              Output[k]

begin                                 begin
    m.destination:=                       m.destination:=
        'buffer_control';                     'buffer_control';
    m.contents.type:= 'data';             m.contents.type:= 'ready';
    while true do                         while true do
    begin                                 begin
        read(in,infilej);                     send(m);
        m.contents.inblock:= in;              outm:= receive;
        send(m)                               write(outm.contents,
                                                  outfilek)
    end                                   end
end.                                  end.
```

Note that in the above set of programs, there is no means of limiting the number of blocks buffered by buffer_control. If the input processes send blocks to buffer_control at a higher rate than buffer_control sends them to the output processes, the number of blocks stored in the queue dataq will grow without limit.

In order to limit this buffering, additional control messages could be sent between the input processes and buffer_control. For example, an input process may send a message 'ready_to_send' to buffer_control which, when it has sufficient space, sends a reply 'send'. Only when an input process receives permission would it send a block. Thus, message-passing can accomplish synchronization as well as communication between processes.

This view of processes as independent entities which can interact only by sending messages to one another is certainly more modular than the view of processes executing within a global environment. As a result, it is much clearer to the programmer exactly how the processes can affect one another. Furthermore, this view corresponds more closely to the way in which processes are implemented on a distributed computer system. For example, the program for the airline reservation system very naturally expresses the way in which such systems are implemented. In a typical system, remote "intelligent" terminals assemble messages requesting operations on the database. These messages are then sent to a central computer, which performs the operations and sends back reply messages. Control messages such as the ones sent between processes in the input/output buffer system correspond closely to the control signalling between the components of a distributed system. When the programming language reflects the underlying system design, a programmer can understand more fully how the program will be executed and hence can design programs which run efficiently on the system. Both the modularity and the closeness to the implementation make this approach to concurrent programming attractive for many important applications

The message-passing operations described so far are clearly too primitive for a high level programming language. Like semaphores, they provide only a simple form of process communication and synchronization, leaving the programmer to determine what types of processes are required, what types of control and data messages must be sent between processes, and at what points in the programs the messages should be sent.

Several languages have been proposed to express the operation of message-passing processes utilizing somewhat different conventions than the constructs shown here. Perhaps best known is the Communicating Sequential Processes language (CSP) of Hoare [20]. In this language, both the send and the receive operations specify the name of the process to send to or receive from. This eliminates the need for the internal queues shown in our buffer control program, because the process need accept 'data' messages only when the buffer is free, and 'ready' messages only when the buffer is filled. However, this explicit naming of processes has adverse effects on the modularity of the programs and makes it impossible to dynamically alter the process interconnections. Hoare's language also adopts a convention in which there is no queuing of messages. Instead the sender must wait until the receiver is ready to accept the message into its own local storage. While this convention limits some of the asynchrony between processes, it eliminates the need to store a potentially unbounded number of messages in the queues. Nondeterminacy is expressed in CSP by an alternative command in which the process can choose one command to execute from a set of commands subject to a set of enabling conditions. Unlike our illustrative language in which nondeterminacy was provided implicitly by the single input queue for each process, CSP programs must specify nondeterminacy explicitly with alternative commands. Given that unintentional nondeterminacy is a common form of error in concurrent programs, this feature seems quite desirable. The programming language Ada [21] has a tasking and communication model very similar to CSP, with the addition of constructs to express time-outs, polling, and interrupts.

A language presented by Kahn and MacQueen [24] allows a somewhat more modular process specification than either our illustrative language or CSP. In their language, a process is invoked with a set of parameters including the queues it uses for sending and receiving messages, much like the parameter passing mechanisms in conventional procedure calls. The message-passing operations in the process programs are written in terms of the formal queue parameters rather than the processes to which they will ultimately be connected. This permits a set of identical processes operating on different message queues to be created by invoking many instances of a single process program with different parameters. Furthermore, processes and the connections between them can be dynamically created and terminated.

Hewitt and Atkinson [16] have proposed a program structure called a serializer to provide a more structured and higher level view of concurrent programming in a message-passing environment. The purpose of the serializer construct is to provide the programmer with a general framework for resource controllers which is then customized to fit a particular application, much as the monitor construct provides a general framework for a resource controller operating in a global environment. In addition the serializer design tries to correct some of the weaknesses in monitors, such as the complexity of the operations delay and continue, and the limited amount of concurrency. The behavior of a serializer is defined in terms of the actor model of computation [15,17], a model in which message-passing is viewed as the fundamental operation. In this model every action is performed by an actor, where each actor behaves like a message-passing process. That is, it receives input messages, performs an operation on the input, generates output messages, and possibly changes its internal state. Unlike processes, however, actors can be dynamically created and abandoned. With this model a wide variety of activities can be expressed, such as concurrent operations, dynamic system creation and reconfiguration, and nondeterminacy. Furthermore, the actor model allows highly concurrent computations to be expressed more naturally than the sequential process model does, because the only sequencing constraints between actor activities are those imposed by the messages. This great expressive power of the actor model allows a serializer to have a much more sophisticated behavior than can be expressed in a programming language such as PASCAL extended with message-passing commands. Furthermore, since the designers of the serializer were not constrained by the limited types of behavior exhibited by sequential, message-passing processes, they could develop a cleaner structure with greater potential for concurrency. Serializers as well as the actor model are still in an early stage of development, and no existing architectures support this style of computation. Their influence on future language design and programming practice remains to be seen.

Sequential processes that communicate by message passing can be implemented without great difficulty. The processes can be carried out by a number of independent processors, such as one typically finds in a distributed computer system, or even by a more traditional multiprogramming system, such as the RC4000 computer system. By extending the RC4000 system with semaphore operations, Lauesen [26] was able to develop an operating system which is provably free of deadlocks. Few operating systems which use machine synchronization instructions can claim this achievement.

A system consisting of a small number of sequential, message-passing processes can achieve only a limited amount of concurrency, as was seen in the airline reservation example. Since a resource can be accessed by only one process, and this process operates sequentially, concurrent accesses to a single resource cannot be expressed. In some cases, a large resource can be partitioned into a number of parts, and each part managed by a separate process. For example, the information about each flight in the airline reservation system could be maintained by a separate process. However, if we want to add new flights to the database or remove old ones, some method of dynamically creating and abandoning processes is required. When the system is divided into many small parts which can be dynamically created and abandoned, it no longer seems justified to call these parts processes; rather they are more like actors. Exactly where the dividing line between the process model and the actor model lies is a matter of debate, as are many other issues in developing highly concurrent systems which operate in a message-passing environment.

5. Data-Driven Program Execution

The programming languages discussed so far (with the exception of those based on actor semantics) have been based on the concept of communicating, sequential processes. That is, a system is viewed as a number of processes which can proceed concurrently, but within each process only one action is performed at a time. Programming languages designed to express the behavior of these systems are similar to traditional languages, with constructs added to express process communication and synchronization. An alternative to sequential processes is to view a program as an unordered set of instructions, each of which defines how a set of values is to be computed and what identifier is to be associated with each value. Within an environment, an identifier must refer to a unique value. Rather than executing in strict sequential order, instructions can be executed as soon as their input operands are ready, i.e. as soon as the values required to compute the expressions have themselves been computed. This form of program execution is said to be data-driven, since the arrival of the operands, rather than the indication of a program counter, determines when an instruction will be executed. Languages which express programs for data-driven execution are often called data flow languages [1,2,11,25,27].

To express an unambiguous computation, instructions in a data flow language must be free of side effects. That is, the effect of executing an instruction can only be to compute a set of values for a set of identifiers. It cannot alter the definition of any other identifier in the program. Furthermore, the program must obey the "single assignment rule", meaning that each identifier is defined only once within an environment. Considering the importance of side-effects and multiple assignments to variables in traditional programming languages, one naturally wonders how a language could eliminate both of these properties and yet be able to express useful computations. Data flow languages can make up for these restrictions with recursive procedures and with data streams [23,27]. Recursion eliminates the need for iteration, a control structure which relies heavily on side effects and multiple assignments.[1] Streams allow the programmer to view a sequence of elementary data values as a single entity. Thus, by writing a procedure that accepts inputs that are data streams, one can express program units which perform operations on entire sequences of input values. Procedures which have streams as inputs and return streams as results will be called modules to differentiate them from procedures which operate on individual data values. For the airline reservation system

---

1. The "iteration" constructs of data flow languages such as Id and Val [1] can be viewed as syntactic sugarings for a simple form of recursion known as tail recursion.

example, we shall define a module transact with inputs request_stream:**stream of message** and available:**array**[1..limit] **of integer**, which will compute an output reply_stream:**stream of message**. That is, the module will receive a sequence of requests from the remote terminals and an initial state of the data base, and it will produce a sequence of replies.

To make use of streams, we must define some operations on them. To extract the values from a stream s, we define two functions: first(s) which returns the first value in the sequence, and rest(s) which returns the stream consisting of all elements in s except for the first one. To construct a stream, we define a function cons where the value of cons(x,s) is the stream consisting of x (which cannot be a stream) followed by the elements of stream s. Furthermore, we must define a rule for procedure invocation in data flow. In the earlier definitions for data flow languages [11], a procedure P(x,y,z) cannot be invoked until all input arguments x, y, and z are ready. With streams, however, this rule is modified somewhat. If, for example, x is a stream, then P could be invoked as soon as the first element of stream x is ready. Hence the module transact can be invoked as soon as the first request has arrived.

With a few modifications to the PASCAL syntax, we can arrive at a language which is suitable for expressing data flow programs. Most importantly, to emphasize the idea that an instruction is a definition of how a set of values is to be computed, assignment statements

$$\langle id \rangle := \langle exp \rangle$$

will be replaced by identifier definitions

$$\text{let } \langle id \rangle = \langle exp \rangle.$$

Furthermore, a side-effect free analogy to "updating" the array available is required. We will define the function modify(A,i,v)) which returns an array which is identical to A, except that the ith element is equal to v. Despite the syntactic similarities, however, the semantics of the data flow language are entirely different from PASCAL. In particular, the order in which statements are listed does not dictate the order in which they are executed.

The program for transact is as follows:

```
module transact(request_stream: stream of message;
        available: array[1..limit] of integer);

    returns reply_stream: stream of message;

var request,reply:message; f,n:integer;
    newstate: array[1..limit] of integer;

begin
    let request = first(request_stream);
    case request.contents.type of
        'reserve':
            begin
                let f = request.contents.flight;
                let n = request.contents.number;
                if available[f] <= n
                then begin
                    let reply.contents = true;
                    let newstate =
                        modify(available,f,available[f]-n)
                end
                else begin
                    let reply.contents = false;
                    let newstate = available
                end
            end;
        'info':
            begin
                let f = request.contents.flight;
                let reply.contents = available[f];
                let newstate = available
            end
    end;
    let reply.destination = request.source;
    let reply_stream =
        cons(reply, transact(rest(request_stream, newstate)))
end.
```

The module transact receives its input requests in the form of a single stream. This stream is composed of elements produced by a number of separate modules that transmit request messages from agent terminals. So far, no means for generating such a stream has been discussed. In fact, the data flow language which has been presented can express only determinate computations: the result of program execution depends only on the values of the inputs, and not on the order in which they are received. The airline reservation system, however, behaves nondeterminately, and hence some means of expressing nondeterminate operations in the language is required. For this purpose, we will define a primitive operation merge, where the value of merge(s1,s2) is a stream containing all elements of streams s1 and s2, such that the ordering of elements from s1 is preserved, as is the ordering of elements from s2, but the order in which an element from s1 and an element from s2 occur is arbitrary. This operation is sufficient to express a wide variety of nondeterminate computations. For example, suppose the airline reservation system contains three terminal modules which produce streams requests1, requests2, and requests3. We ca write the program which computes the three output streams as follows:

```
module system(request1,request2,request3: stream of message;
       available: array[1..limit] of integer);

   returns replies1,replies2,replies3: stream of message;

begin
   let r1 = tag(request1,1);
   let r2 = tag(request2,2);
   let r3 = tag(request3,3);
   let requests = merge(r1, merge(r2,r3));
   let replies = transact(requests,available);
   let replies1,replies2,replies3 = sort(replies)
end.
```

In this program the messages in the three streams of input requests are first tagged with the stream number. These three tagged streams are merged together into a single stream which serves as the input stream to transact. The output stream from transact is sorted according to the tag values into three streams of replies -- one for each terminal module.

A data flow program for the input/output buffer system will not be given here, because it does not demonstrate any new concepts.

Data flow languages seem very promising for expressing computations for concurrent execution, since the only restrictions on the concurrency are those imposed by data dependencies. Although side-effects and identifier redefinition are excluded, the combination of recursive procedures and data streams yields a surprisingly rich language. Furthermore, the single, nondeterminate operator merge is sufficient to express numerous types of nondeterminate system behavior. Not enough experience has been gained, however, to fully evaluate the expressive power of the language. Suggestions for extensions have been made [2], for example, which allow communication links between modules to be created dynamically. Just how necessary such a feature is, and how important other features may be, are open questions.

Data flow languages permit programs to be written which are far more modular than is possible with traditional languages. Each module of a program can be described fully in terms of its input/output behavior. Due to the absence of side-effects, sections of the program can interact only in limited and well-defined ways. In fact, each instruction executes in its own local environment: it computes a result based only on its operands. This high degree of modularity leads to programs which more clearly describe what computations the system is to perform. In addition, data flow languages allow the programmer to explicitly limit the sources of nondeterminacy in the system. Nondeterminacy can occur only where it is explicitly allowed through the use of the merge operator. Considering that unwanted nondeterminacy is a major source of errors in concurrent systems, a means of controlling it is of great significance.

The implementation of data flow languages is currently at a rather primitive state. Due to the high degree of concurrency and the asynchronous nature of instruction execution, these languages may require totally new forms of computer architecture. Several designs have been proposed [12,3], but numerous problems remain to be solved before practical data flow machines can be realized. The state of the art for data flow language design is well ahead of the state of the art for architectures which support these languages.

6. Conclusion

The three major approaches to concurrent programming discussed here differ greatly in their fundamental views of how a computer system operates. With the global environment approach, one views a system as a number of processes which execute "under one roof" and communicate with one another by altering the surrounding environment. With message-passing processes, one views a system as a number of processes which execute under their own roofs and send telegrams to one another. With data-driven program execution, the system is viewed as a network of operators, each of which receives data values, computes new data values, and sends these output values to the next operator in the network. Furthermore, this network dynamically expands as recursive procedures are invoked and contracts as they are completed. The three approaches differ in the amount of concurrency which they can achieve, the clarity of the programs, and the ease with which they can be implemented given the current state of computer system design.

No system composed of communicating, sequential processes can realize the full degree of concurrency latent in high level programs. However, a number of processes can often proceed concurrently. With semaphore-based programs, the number of active, concurrent processes is limited only by the cleverness of the programmer subject to the need to maintain a consistent global state. With monitor-based programs, one must choose between completely protecting each resource with a monitor and hence precluding concurrent accesses to this resource, or allowing processes to access a resource directly, thereby compromising the modularity provided by the monitor concept. With message-passing processes a resource can be directly accessed by only a single process. Hence, unless the resource can be partitioned into a number of parts each managed by a separate process, concurrency in the system is restricted. In contrast to programming languages based on sequential processes, data flow languages and actor-based systems can express all forms of concurrency allowed by the algorithm, although no existing machine architectures can fully exploit their benefits.

Evaluating how clearly each approach can express the operations of a system is a subjective judgment. However, such features as modularity, limited sources of nondeterminacy, and high-level language constructs are clearly desirable goals. In terms of modularity, the approaches to concurrent programming have been presented in order of increasing modularity. First, a semaphore-based language allows little modularity -- the processes can affect each other in numerous and often subtle ways. Next, monitors provide more modularity by restricting the ways in which each process can access global resources. Languages based on message-passing processes carry the modularity one step further by eliminating the global environment altogether. Finally, data flow languages, by eliminating all side effects, achieve a degree of modularity in which each program module can be viewed as defining a function from input values to output values. As for limiting the sources of nondeterminacy, only some of the message-passing languages and data flow languages provide a means of stating explicitly where nondeterminacy is allowed in the system. Operations on semaphores, global variable accesses, monitor procedure calls, and messages sent to a single queue from different sources, on the other hand, are all potential sources of nondeterminacy. When nondeterminacy is not wanted, the programmer must be careful to use these operations in a way which will not allow nondeterminate behavior.

High-level language support for concurrent programming has only recently become a major priority among language designers. With both semaphore-based systems and message-passing systems, the language constructs presented express very elementary forms of process communication and synchronization. The programmer must devise conventions for using these constructs to achieve the desired behavior. Data flow languages would also benefit from more sophisticated constructs. For example, a construct similar to a monitor has been proposed for data flow languages [2] which eliminates the need for the programmer to construct a tagged stream from several input streams and then to sort the output stream into its constituent parts. Designing high level programming tools which are sufficiently general and modular yet do not restrict the concurrency exploitable in their implementation is one of the most difficult challenges to the designer of future high-level languages.

Given the current state of computer design, one has little choice of which programming approach to use if a practical implementation is required. Both approaches which assume a global environment fit most naturally on a multiprogramming system consisting of processors sharing memory. Such systems are common, and as a result a large proportion of the work in concurrent programming has been directed toward this global environment approach. Message-passing processes, on the other hand, describe most naturally the operation of a system of independent processors connected by communication channels. Such systems are becoming increasingly common, due largely to a desire to distribute the processors geographically, and also to the availability of small, low-priced processors. Most programming of these systems is still done at the machine language level. No machine-independent languages for message-passing processes have come into accepted use. Finally, languages which express higher degrees of concurrency than can be achieved by communicating sequential processes, such as actor-based and data flow languages, have not yet been implemented to take advantage of this greater concurrency. Whereas the other approaches could be implemented by modifying existing machine designs, these high concurrency languages appear to require totally new approaches to computer design if the latent concurrency is to be realized. While the design of languages for concurrent programming is an interesting field of study in its own right, a language is of little use unless it can be effectively implemented. Hence, the design of computer systems to support languages which express high degrees of concurrency is also an important field of study.

7. References

1. Ackerman, W. B., "Data Flow Languages", IEEE Computer, 15-2, IEEE, New York, (February, 1982), pp. 15-25.
2. Arvind, K. P. Gostelow, and W. Plouffe, "Indeterminacy, Monitors, and Dataflow," Proceedings of the Sixth ACM Symposium on Operating Systems Principles, Operating Systems Review, 11-5, ACM, New York (November, 1977), pp. 159-169.
3. Arvind, and V. Kathail, "A Multiple Processor Dataflow Machine that Supports Generalized Procedures", Proceedings of the Eighth Annual Symposium on Computer Architecture, IEEE, New York, (May, 1981), pp. 291-302.

4. Brinch Hansen, P., "The Nucleus of a Multiprogramming System," Communications of the ACM, 13-4, ACM, New York (April, 1970), pp. 238-241, 250.
5. Brinch Hansen, P., "Structured Multiprogramming," Communications of the ACM, 15-7, ACM, New York (July, 1972), pp. 574-578.
6. Brinch Hansen, P. Operating System Principles, Prentice Hall, Englewood Cliffs, N. J. (July, 1973).
7. Brinch Hansen, P. "The Programming Language Concurrent Pascal," IEEE Transactions on Software Engineering, SE1-2, IEEE, New York (June, 1975), pp. 199-207.
8. Brinch Hansen, P., The Architecture of Concurrent Programs, Prentice-Hall, Englewood Cliffs, N. J. (July, 1977).
9. Campbell, and Habermann, "The Specification of Process Synchronization by Path Expressions," Lecture Notes in Computer Science, Volume 16, Springer Verlag, New York (1974).
10. Courtois, P. J., F. Heymans, and D. L. Parnas, "Concurrent Control with Readers and Writers," Communications of the ACM, 14-10, ACM, New York (October, 1971), pp. 667-668.
11. Dennis, J. B., "First Version of a Data Flow Procedure Language," Lecture Notes in Computer Science 19, G. Goos and J. Hartmanis, eds., Springer-Verlag, New York (1974), pp. 362-376.
12. Dennis, J. B., and D. P. Misunas, "A Preliminary Architecture for a Basic Data-Flow Processor," Proceedings of the Second Annual Symposium on Computer Architecture, IEEE, New York (January, 1975), pp. 126-132.

13. Dijkstra, E., "Co-operating Sequential Processes", Programming Languages, ed. F. Genuys, Academic Press, New York (1968), pp. 43-112.
14. Dijkstra, E., "The Structure of the THE Multiprogramming System," Communications of the ACM, 11-5, ACM, New York (May, 1968), pp. 341-346.
15. Greif, I., Semantics of Communicating Parallel Processes, Technical Report TR-154, MIT Laboratory for Computer Science, Cambridge, Mass. (September, 1975).
16. Hewitt, C., and R. Atkinson, "Parallelism and Synchronization in Actor Systems," Principles of Programming Languages, ACM, New York (January, 1977), pp. 267-280.
17. Hewitt, C., and H. Baker, "Laws for Communicating Parallel Processes," Information Processing 77, IFIP, North Holland Publishing Company, Amsterdam (1977), pp. 987-992.
18. Hoare, C. A. R., "Towards a Theory of Parallel Programming," Operating Systems Techniques, ed. C. A. R. Hoare, Academic Press, New York (1972).
19. Hoare, C. A. R., "Monitors: an Operating System Structuring," Communications of the ACM, 17-10, ACM, New York (October, 1974), pp. 549-557.
20. Hoare, C. A. R., "Communicating Sequential Processes", Communications of the ACM, 21-8 (August, 1978) pp. 666-677.
21. Ichbiah, J. D., et al, "Preliminary Ada Reference Manual", Sigplan Notices, 14-6, ACM, New York (June, 1979).
22. Jensen, K., and N. Wirth, PASCAL: User Manual and Report, 2nd ed., Springer Verlag, New York (1974).
23. Kahn, G., "Semantics of a Simple Language for Parallel Programming," Information Processing 74, IFIP, North Holland Publishing Company, Amsterdam, (1974), pp.471-475.
24. Kahn, G., and D. MacQueen, Coroutines and Networks of Parallel Processes, Information Processing 77, IFIP, North Holland Publishing Company, Amsterdam (1977), pp. 993-998.
25. Kessels, J. L. W., "A Conceptual Framework for a Nonprocedural Programming Language," Communications of the ACM, 20-12, ACM, New York (December, 1977), pp. 906-913.
26. Lauesen, S., "A Large Semaphore Based Operating System," Communications of the ACM, 18-7, ACM, New York (July, 1975), pp. 377-389.
27. Weng, K., Stream-Oriented Computations in Recursive Data Flow Schemas, Technical Memo TM-68, MIT Laboratory for Computer Science, Cambridge, Mass. (October, 1975).
28. Wirth, N., "Modula: A Programming Language for Modular Multiprogramming", Software Practice and Experience, 7-1 (January, 1977), pp. 3-35.

Streams and Managers

Arvind
J. Dean Brock

Laboratory for Computer Science
Massachusetts Institute of Technology
Cambridge, Massachusetts 02139
U. S. A.

Abstract

The sole effect of expression evaluation in a functional programming language is the production of a resultant value. This absence of side–effects greatly facilitates both the formal characterization and the concurrent execution of functional programs. Unfortunately, the absence of side–effects also conflicts with conventional means of achieving input/output, inter–process communication, and resource allocation. By incorporating the history of communication into a *stream*, functional programs can be written for I/O and communication. Using the stream concept, *managers* may be written to control access to resources shared by several processes.

1. I/O and Side–effects

In a side–effect free language, disjoint expressions may be evaluated concurrently without danger of interference. This freedom from interference, or locality of effect, is largely responsible for the parallelism obtained when applicative languages are evaluated using the dataflow graph model. Purists may differentiate between many classes of side–effect free languages: applicative, functional, dataflow, etc. We use the terms interchangeably. The important concept is the absence of side–effects.

Although many of the side–effects considered "necessary" by most programmers are easily foregone [1] (for example, by creating updated arrays instead of modifying arrays), one very important type of side effect, namely I/O, seems truly necessary. Consider a program to manage a video terminal. Such a program, among other things, echoes input characters for display on the screen and responds to the *delete* key by sending signals to reposition the cursor on the screen and erase the last input character. In a conventional non–functional language the input and output for the program is represented by files, which are explicitly mutated (changed) by the reading and writing of characters. In addition the program contains state, generally a buffer of the most recently received characters. An attempt to write the video terminal handler in a functional language immediately poses problems because without side–effects terminal interaction seems impossible to describe: two successive *delete*'s may have different effects. Also, the handler cannot be viewed as a function all of whose inputs are available before any answers are produced. Thus it would appear that I/O is anathema to functional languages. However, by changing our viewpoint of I/O, the "conflict" is resolved. In functional languages the I/O *channel* must be viewed as a special data value produced, or examined, by programs, not as a medium to be written, or read, by programs. The special I/O data value is

* This research was supported by the Advanced Research Projects Agency of the Department of Defense under Office of Naval Research contract N00014–75–C–0661 and by the Department of Energy under contract DE–AC02–79ER10473.

the *stream*, a sequence consisting of all the individual items written to, or read from, the channel. From this viewpoint, a terminal is a function whose input and output are streams of characters. Other elementary I/O devices, such as printers, may be similarly represented.

Streams, introduced in Section 2, solve a number of problems associated with input/output in a functional language context. Streams can be used to write functional programs that appear to have local state: the response of a program may depend on the order in which data items are input. However, functional languages, even with streams, lack the power to express indeterminate computation such as programs to serve several video terminals, and in Section 3 we introduce *merge*, an indeterminate stream operator. Unfortunately, certain classes of problems, specifically resource allocation among several competing processes, cannot be solved with *merge*'s alone, and in Section 4 the *manager* construct is developed for this purpose.

2. Streams

Weng [19] introduced the data structure *stream* into dataflow languages along with four primitive operators *first*, *rest*, *cons*, and *empty* for manipulating them. These operators were chosen to resemble the list operators of LISP. The operation *first* yields the first element of the stream, while *rest* yields the remainder. The operation *cons*, when applied to an elementary value and a stream, produces the stream consisting of the elementary value followed by the argument stream. Thus, for non–empty streams S, S equals *cons(first(S), rest(S))*. The emptiness of streams may be tested with the remaining stream operator *empty*. The functionality of these four operators is summarized below:

$$first([\,]) = error$$
$$first([x1, ...]) = x1$$

$$rest([\,]) = error$$
$$rest([x1, x2, ...]) = [x2, ...]$$

$$cons(x, [x1, ...]) = [x, x1, ...]$$

$$empty([\,]) = true$$
$$empty([x1, ...]) = false$$

Weng's language had three major constructs for writing stream programs: acyclic blocks, conditional expressions, and recursive procedures.

It is important to note that the stream operators are *non–strict*, that is, they can, and must, be applied to their stream arguments incrementally before the entire argument stream has been computed. For example, *rest(S)* can produce its result as soon as the first element of S is available — it need not wait until the computation of S is completed. The key to non–strictness is the implementation of the stream constructor *cons*. The output of *cons(x, S)* must be produced incrementally so that x, the first element of its result, may be accessed before the entire resultant stream has been computed. Weng chose the obvious incremental implementation of streams by representing them as a series of tokens passed through the arcs of a dataflow graph. Weng's implementation limits stream elements to simple (*i. e.* non–stream) value. Other implementations in which streams are represented by pointers into a "structure memory" are possible. It is not difficult to make such an implementation non–strict. A *cons* cell can be allocated and "used" before its components are available, if the components are tagged to indicate whether or not they have yet been computed. Within the structure memory, the elements of the stream may themselves be pointers to other streams, thus yielding a more general implementation of streams than possible with Weng's original proposal.

With these LISP–like stream operators, recursion is the natural programming style. Consider the problem of writing an elementary terminal line editor EditLine which collects the characters produced by a terminal into lines. Abstractly, EditLine may be considered a function which maps the elements of its domain, the streams of characters, into elements of its range, the streams of strings. For example:

EditLine(['I', 'd', 'EOL', 'I', 'd', 's', 'y', 's', 'EOL']) = ["Id", "Idsys"],
    where 'EOL' is the end–of–line character.

Using recursion, the function EditLine is written in an Weng–like language, having the syntax of Id, the dataflow programming language developed by Arvind, Gostelow, and Plouffe [3], as:

```
procedure EditLine (InStream)
( BuildLines(InStream, "") )

procedure BuildLines (InStream, LineBuff)
( if empty(InStream) then
    [ ]
  else
    ( let CharIn ← first(InStream) ;
          RestIn ← rest(InStream) ;
      in
          if CharIn = 'EOL' then
            cons( LineBuff, BuildLines(RestIn, "") )
          else
            BuildLines( RestIn, string–append(LineBuff, CharIn) ) ) ))
```

The "work" of this program is done by the procedure BuildLines. First, BuildLines tests for the termination of its input stream. If more characters remain to be processed, it gets the next (i.e., *first*) stream element and tests whether or not it is the end–of–line character. If it is end–of–line, the line buffer is *cons*'ed onto the beginning of the output stream and BuildLines is recursively invoked with a new, empty line buffer; otherwise the next character is appended to the line buffer and passed on to the next invocation of BuildLines. These programs illustrate well the most common form of recursive stream computation. On each step of the recursion, the next input value is obtained by use of *first* and the next output, if any, is *cons*'ed onto the front of an the stream produced by recursively processing the *rest* of the input. Here, the variable LineBuffer serves as the state for procedure BuildLines and is passed to all the stages of the recursion.

Id supports an iterative stream processing construct in addition to the four elementary stream operators. The iterative construct for reading streams is the *for–each* loop. On each iteration the loop header clause "*for each* x *in* S" causes the identifier x to be bound to the next element of the stream S. The iterative construct for producing streams is the *return–all* loop trailer. If "*return all* x" ends an Id loop, an output stream is generated which contains the values of x on each iteration as its elements. [Incidentally, arbitrary expressions may follow the *return–all*.] One final, and very useful, embellishment of the *return–all* is the *but* clause. The *but* clause may be used to disable the *return–all* for certain stream values, and thus may be used to "filter" streams. If the clause "*return all* x *but* a" follows a loop, the output stream will contain all the values of x *except* those with value a. Generally, the iterative specification of stream functions is much more succinct than the recursive specification. For example, the procedure EditLine (illustrated in Figure 1) may be written as:

```
procedure EditLine (InStream)
    ( initial LineBuff ← ""
    for each CharIn in InStream do
        new LineBuff, LineOut ←
        ( if CharIn = 'EOL' then
            "", LineBuff
        else
            string-append(LineBuff, CharIn), λ)
    return all LineOut but λ)
```

Note how the *but* clause ensures that lines are placed on the output stream only when the next input character is 'EOL'. In all other instances LineOut is bound to the value λ and then removed from the output stream.

Although we have discussed streams only in the context of dataflow languages, they have proven to be useful in other contexts, even in the formal description of non-applicative languages. In 1965 Landin [16] defined a lambda calculus based semantics for ALGOL-60 by representing the values of a loop variable as a stream. This was probably the first use of a non-strict data structure. Later, Burge [6] incorporated these ideas into the design of a functional language. In 1974 Kahn [13] recognized that the input and output channels of processes written with GET and PUT, the conventional I/O primitives for which side-effects are so important, can be viewed as streams and that, when processes are viewed as stream functions, the semantics of networks of parallel processes may be derived using a simple fixpoint theory. Friedman and Wise [9] have suggested making the list constructor *cons* of LISP non-strict. This makes LISP lists an even

Figure 1.

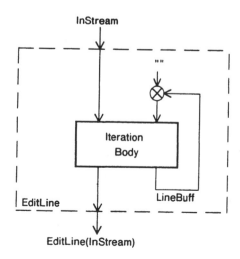

Iterative implementation of EditLine

more general data structure than the streams of Landin, Kahn, or Weng.

The EditLine example illustrates a stream function with a "conventional" subroutine relationship to its caller. However, stream functions can also be used to specify co-routines or even networks of processes. Figure 2 gives a rather simple interconnection of two stream procedures, P and Q. There are many ways in which this interconnection could be implemented. Generally the implementation will be determined by the specific area of application. For example, P could be a program and Q, a file server, executing inside a small single-user computer. On the other hand, this interconnection could be adapted to our video terminal example. P could be a terminal and Q, the computer system to which it is attached. In addition, the interconnection need not represent two closely-coupled systems. It could represent a widely-dispersed network: P could be the account management system for a bank in London, and Q could be a similar system for a bank in Tokyo, and the arcs between the systems could be underwater cables or satellites. In Id this cyclic interconnection can be quite naturally specified as:

> Pout, PtoQ ← P (Pin, QtoP) ;
> Qout, QtoP ← Q (Qin, PtoQ)

The four stream operators previously described and Id's iterative *for-each* construct are all *determinate*, that is, for each possible set of input stream arguments there is only one possible set of output stream results. Determinacy has some very important consequences. First, any program written with determinate operators or any network composed from determinate modules is itself determinate. Second, all determinate modules are time-independent: inputs for a determinate module can be arbitrarily delayed without affecting that module's eventual results. These two properties of determinacy combine to reduce the difficulty of debugging stream programs, for they insure that any stream computation is repeatable. However, they also prevent the writing of either time-dependent or non-determinate computation, and thus it is reasonable to ask whether or not there are any inherently non-determinate applications of sufficient importance to justify the incorporation of non-determinate operators or constructs into a dataflow programming language. It should be noted that, except for machine languages in which indeterminacy results from interrupt processing, almost all conventional programming languages (including FORTRAN, Algol, Pascal, LISP, Cobol, and PL/I) are

Figure 2.

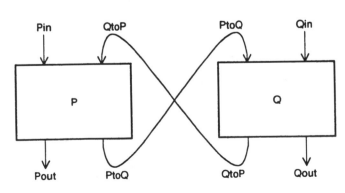

Interconnected network of P and Q

determinate. Concurrent Pascal and Ada are perhaps the only widely-known programming languages in which non-determinate computation can be expressed.

3. Non-determinate Computation

Resource allocators are part of many interesting application areas, such as transaction systems or operating systems. To see the necessity of non-determinate computation, let us consider a simple one-account, two-teller bank. The bank's accounting system processes streams of requests from and sends streams of replies to the two tellers. The tellers are competing for resources, in this case the dollars of the banks accounts, just as processes in a multi-user computer systems compete for resources such as tape drives. Suppose the tellers entered separate requests for the last dollar. We expect one teller to be granted the dollar, and the other to be denied it; however, we certainly do *not* expect, or want, that arbitration to be determinate. For if it were determinate, and consequently totally time-independent, the same teller would always "win" that particular race for the last dollar, even if the loser's request preceded his by hours or even by years. In reality the cost of determinacy is even higher: since the account management system is not prescient, it cannot know whether or not the preordained winner will ever wish to request the dollar, and thus the losing teller must always lose, even if the winner never enters the race. It is for these reasons, that determinate computation is inadequate for resource allocation problems.[1]

The smallest extension for obtaining non-determinism is the addition of a single non-deterministic stream operator, the *merge*. The *merge* receives two input streams and non-deterministically interleaves them into one output stream. The intended implementation of *merge* is an operator which waits for a value to appear on either of its input ports and then produces the received value at its output port and returns to its waiting state. Thus, there are three possible output stream responses when *merge* is applied to the input streams [5, 6] and [7]:

merge([5, 6], [7]) = [5, 6, 7] or [5, 7, 6] or [7, 5, 6]

Obviously, *merge* is not a function. In the presence of feedback, the choices of the *merge* may be further constrained, and Brock and Ackerman [5] have proven that the *merge* cannot even be formally represented as a relation on input and output streams. Given two terminal input streams TTY1 and TTY2, the *merge* operator and EditLine, our previously written stream program, can be used in the expression:

merge(EditLine(TTY1), EditLine(TTY2))

to interleave the commands (lines) typed on the two terminals into one. Within a operating system, this combined command stream could then be passed to stream-based resource allocators, often written with only determinate operators, and acted upon without the very serious problems encountered using totally determinate resource allocators.

---

[1]. Admittedly, there are imaginative schemes for restoring determinacy; but, all such schemes involve imposing somewhat troublesome (and ridiculous) prerequisites on system users. For example, the system would require that every user produce a (possibly null) output character every milli-second, and then it could poll its users in a round-robin fashion.

The two teller bank system can be written using *merge*'s to resemble the network of Figure 3. This network is composed of four types of modules, only one of which need be indeterminate. Each Tag–*i* module receives one input request stream, and tags each of its values with the number *i*. In Id this is simply written as:

```
procedure Tag–i(X)
  ( for each x in X do
    return all ⟨i, x⟩ )
```

The tagged requests are then interleaved by a *merge* operator to form a single, combined stream of requests. This stream is next sent to the resource controller, Money–control, a stream procedure "containing" the resource. This procedure examines the tagged request stream and produces a stream of tagged responses. Suppose this trusting bank does nothing but maintain account balances, without even checking for account overdrafts. All requests to the bank are integers. Positive integers represent deposits. Negative integers represent withdrawals (negative deposits). Each transaction is confirmed by giving the new account balance. Then the resource allocator is:

```
procedure Money–control(REQ)
  ( initial account–balance ← 0
    for each req in REQ do
      new account–balance ← account–balance + req[2] ;
      confirmation ← new account–balance
    return all ⟨req[1], confirmation⟩ )
```

Distribute, the remaining module of the two teller bank system, is a determinate module which removes the tags and routes untagged responses to the appropriate recipients. With this "template" many resource allocation system may be programmed merely by replacing the resource controller module. The applicative

Figure 3.

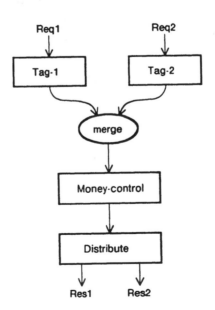

Res1, Res2 ← Distribute(Money–control(*merge*(Tag–1(Req1),Tag–2(Req2))))

Two teller bank system

airline reservation system of Dennis [8] is constructed in this way.

While, in theory, the *merge* satisfies our requirements for non–determinism; in practice, it is clumsy to use because of the difficulties of connecting a resource allocator to its users. Interconnection with *merge*'s alone requires of each user an input–output stream pair for each resource it uses, and of each allocator an input–output stream pair for each user it services, and that requirement is a difficult, if not impossible, to satisfy in a flexible system. For while it is straightforward to extend this bank account system to service any fixed number N of tellers; it would be difficult, if not impossible, to extend it to arbitrary N or varying N. For this reason the language Id has managers [2, 3]: a high–level program construct, encompassing the previously presented allocator template, for specifying non–determinate computation. A related data construct has been proposed by Jayaraman and Keller [12] to solve the same problem.

From the viewpoint of its users, an Id manager resembles a normal (i. e. non–stream) function. The manager is "invoked" with single requests and yields single replies. This is very different from the resource allocator described in the previous example which was applied to streams of requests to yield streams of replies. In its calling sequence, the Id manager is quite conventional — resembling the calling sequence of Hoare's [11] monitors.

Linguistically, the manager is one or more Id assignments surrounded by an *entry–exit* pair. The assignment specifies a stream computation, the *entry* clause specifies how manager requests are formed into the input streams of the assignment, and the *exit* clause specifies how manager replies are formed from the output streams of the assignment. Below is the Id manager (illustrated in Figure 4) for the trusting bank account system.

```
bank ← manager(initial–deposit)
        ( entry TRANSACTION do
    CONFIRMATION ← ( initial account–balance ← initial–deposit
                    for each transaction in TRANSACTION do
                        new account–balance ← account–balance + transaction ;
                        confirmation ← new account–balance
                    return all confirmation )
        exit CONFIRMATION )
```

The *entry* clause of the bank manager causes all manager requests to be merged into a stream TRANSACTION, while the *exit* clause causes the values of the stream CONFIRMATION to be distributed as responses to the requests. To insure that each requester receives the proper response, it is very important that one response is produced for each request and that the i'th element of the response stream be, in fact, the intended response to the i'th request. Detailed implementations, at the dataflow machine level, for exit–entry have been described by Arvind, Gostelow, and Plouffe [3] and by Catto and Gurd [7].

In a computation there may be several instances of a manager. Each instance is created with, naturally enough, the *create* operator, so that *create*(M, V) makes an new instance of M with initial state V. Once created, a manager may be passed to many computations which then share it and thusly share the resource it protects. To send a request X to a manager M, the operation *use*(M, X) is performed. The operation returns the manager response.

Figure 4.

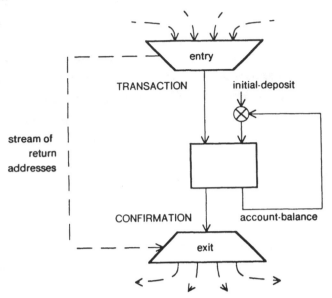

entry

TRANSACTION   initial-deposit

stream of
return
addresses

CONFIRMATION   account-balance

exit

Manager implementation of the bank system

When the manager is used by many independent computations (or processes) the order in which requests arrive at the manager are unpredictable, and the *entry* clause serves as a non-deterministic *merge* of several "streams" of user requests. Often the indeterminism implicit within the *entry* will be the only indeterminism occurring within managers, although for sophisticated scheduling strategies use of the *merge* operator may be required within the manager body.

4. Scheduling with Managers

Unlike the simple bank system, many resource allocation problems require the scheduling of resource utilization according to request type, user priority, or resource state. In these situations, a resource scheduler is needed. The scheduler is a stream procedure which receives streams derived from two sources: the requests to the manager and the responses of the protected resource. The scheduler produces streams which enable resource access.

A manager using a scheduler is shown in Figure 5. This manager controls a printer. Messages of the form <size-of-file, file> are sent to the manager. Short print jobs, those less than ten pages, are rewarded absolute priority in printing. The stream procedure Classify examines the stream of manager requests and produces an output stream whose i'th element is 1 if the i'th request is short and 2 if the i'th request is long.

Figure 5.

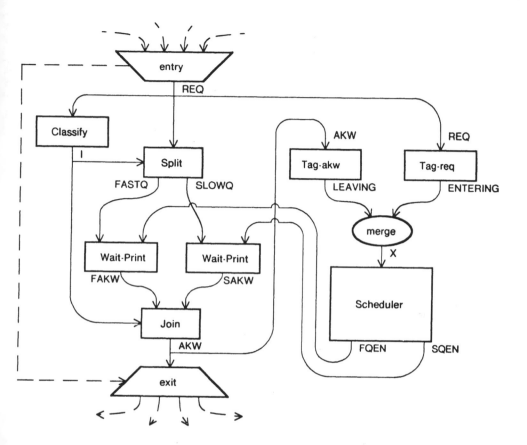

Priority printer manager

procedure Classify(REQ)
   (*for each* req in REQ *do*
      i ← (*if* req[1] < 10 *then* 1 *else* 2)
     return all i) ;

he stream procedure Split uses the output of Classify to divide the input request stream into one stream of
ort requests and another of long requests.

procedure Split (I, X)
   (*for each* i *in* I ; x *in* X *do*
     x1, x2 ← (*if* i = 1 *then* x, λ *else* λ, x)
     return all x1 *but* λ, *all* x2 *but* λ)

ie split request streams are examined by separate resource controllers which we will examine in more detail
ortly. The responses of the controllers are joined by the procedure Join. The output of Split is used to
sure that the responses are joined in the same manner in which they were split.

```
procedure Join (I, X1, X2)
  ( if first(I) = 1 then cons(first(X1), Join(rest(I), rest(X1), X2))
                 else cons(first(X2), Join(rest(I), X1, rest(X2))) )
```

It may be the case that an $i+1$'th request is short and processed before a long i'th request. An implementation of cons which is non-strict in both arguments is needed if the response for the short request is allowed to "leave" the manager before the response to the long request. This degree of non-strictness does not occur in the Weng implementation of streams in which individual stream values are produced strictly in order of their position within the stream, but can be obtained using the U-interpreter [3] implementation of streams where individual stream values are tagged with their position in the stream and then produced in an arbitrary order. The U-interpreter also allows stream producing iterations to be overlapped. This same degree of non-strictness is also available when streams are implemented using the demand-driven interpreters for the functional languages LISP[9, 10, 14], Lucid [4], and SASL [17].

Actual resource allocation occurs within the Wait-f procedures. These procedures, one for each request class, simply delay the application of a procedure f until an enabling value is available on an associated enabling stream.

```
procedure Wait-f(Q, QEN)
  ( for each req in Q ; enable in QEN do
       result ← f(req)
    return all result )
```

The protected procedure f may itself be a "call to" (i.e., use of) another manager, and in this manner managers may be recursive and arbitrarily nested.

The enabling streams are produced by Scheduler which generates them using as its input stream the merged tagged streams of requests to the manager and responses from the protected resource. Momentarily assuming the existence of the scheduler, the manager of Figure 5 can be programming in Id as:

```
manager Printer
  ( entry REQ do
      I ← Classify(REQ) ;

      FASTQ, SLOWQ ← Split(I, REQ) ;

      FAKW ← Wait-print(FASTQ, FQEN) ;
      SAKW ← Wait-print(SLOWQ, SQEN) ;

      AKW ← Join(I, FAKW, SAKW) ;

      ENTERING ← Tag-req(REQ) ;
      LEAVING ← Tag-akw(AKW) ;

      X ← merge(ENTERING, LEAVING) ;
      FQEN, SQEN ← Scheduler(X)
    exit AKW )
```

The guts of the manager lie in its scheduler: the remainder is simply a highly structured interconnection of trivial stream procedures. Obviously, more syntax could be developed to aid the manager programmer.

The Scheduler receives a stream of tagged values. Inputs of the form <"req", <file-size, file>> are requests to the manager. Other inputs are acknowledgments from the controlled printer resource. The first field of other inputs is "akw". The scheduler is generating two output enabling streams (FQEN and SQEN) which are routed to the fast and slow queues of the printer. The task of the scheduler is to make sure that fast jobs are printed before slow ones. It does this by watching the printer acknowledge stream to determine when previously enabled requests have been serviced. The scheduler needs a state of three internal variables to accomplish its task:

busy — is true if the printer is servicing a request,
nfq — is the number of queued (waiting) fast jobs, and
nsq — is the number of queued slow jobs.

The Scheduler itself is nothing but a seven case analysis of the state of the printer and of the requests.

```
FQEN, SQEN ← procedure Scheduler(X)
  ( initial nfq, nsq ← 0, 0 ;
          busy ← false

  for each x in X do
    fqen, sqen, new nfq, new nsq, new busy ←
      ( if x[1] = "akw" then
          ( if nfq = 0 ∧ nsq = 0 then λ, λ, 0, 0, false
          elseif nfq = 0 ∧ nsq > 0 then λ, "go", 0, nsq-1, true
          !!! nfq > 0 !!! else "go", λ, nfq-1, nsq, true )

        !!! x is a request !!! else
          ( if busy then ( if x[2,1] < 10 then λ, λ, nfq + 1, nsq, true
                                      else λ, λ, nfq, nsq + 1, true )
            else ( if x[2,1] < 10 then "go", λ, 0, 0, true
                              else λ, "go", 0, 0, true )))

  return all fqen but λ, all sqen but λ )
```

Let us consider one of the cases. Suppose the fast queue is empty (nfq = 0), the slow queue is not (nsq ≠ 0), and the next tagged input is a printer acknowledgment. In this situation, the second case of Scheduler, a queued slow request is enabled (with the string "go") and the slow queue counter is decremented. The other cases are similar.

Obviously, the scheduler is the most difficult part of writing the printer manager. It is here that possibility of semantic error is greatest. For example, suppose we had initialized the variable busy to true (and originally we had). In that case the manager would appear to deadlock. It would always queue its requests without ever sending them to the printer and, consequently, without ever receiving any acknowledgments from the printer. The construction of good invariants can significantly reduce the number of programming errors. Our invariants for the scheduler, written using the internal variables busy, nfq, and nsq of Scheduler and stream variables FASTQ, SLOWQ, FQEN, SQEN, and X of the Printer manager, are:

number-of-fast-requests-in(X) = size-of(FASTQ) = size-of(FQEN) + nfq
number-of-slow-requests-in(X) = size-of(SLOWQ) = size-of(SQEN) + nsq
number-of-acknowledgments-in(X) = size-of(FQEN) + size-of(SQEN), if ~busy
                                = size-of(FQEN) + size-of(SQEN) - 1, if busy

Id managers are not a syntactic solution to all the pitfalls seen in many resource allocation systems. In particular, it is possible to write "bad" managers which deadlock. However, Wadge [18] has developed criterion for determining the existence of potential deadlock which are applicable to a wide class of determinate systems.

5. Conclusions and Scope for Further Research

Thus far we have presented the reader with a discussion of the problems that the incorporation of history sensitive and non–determinate computation into applicative languages posed, and have advanced streams and managers as solutions to those problems. However, we must include one caveat (or perhaps one challenge for the ambitious reader): Managers are not completely functional and can introduce some of the same problems found in object–oriented programming. For example, because a manager may be passed a reference to itself, it is possible to form a cycle in the manager's machine–level representation and to, thus, complicate reference count garbage collection. Managers even allow us to simulate our old nemesis, the memory cell: In particular, the following manager is a memory cell receiving read requests of the form ⟨"read", V⟩ and write requests of the form ⟨"write", V⟩:

```
cell ← manager (InitV)
     ( entry REQ do

   RES ← ( initial V ← InitV
              for each req in REQ do
                new V, res ←
                   ( if req[1] = "read" then
                       V, V
                    !!! req[1] = "write" !!! else
                       req[2], V )
              return all res) )

     exit RES )
```

> "We have met the enemy, and he is us!"
> *Pogo*, Walt Kelley

With this manager, memory cell address may be created merely by the call *create*(cell, initial–V).

Research must be directed toward the development of methodologies for reasoning about the correctness of managers or, for that matter, any of the "less applicative" constructs for specifying inter–process communication and sharing of resources. We believe our emphasis on streams will enable us to develop more successful strategies than are possible with totally object–oriented constructs. For example, we can write invariants on the *history* of communication by *direct* use of the variables of our program as opposed to using unguaranteed encodings of program history into non–stream variables. We also believe that streams will prove to be a more natural basis for developing formal semantics for that very difficult domain of indeterminate communication. Already, Brock and Ackerman [5] have developed *scenarios* and Kosinski [15] has developed *tagged sequences* to represent dataflow streams. Such formalisms should, in turn, prove useful in developing a bases for formal reasoning about the correctness of programs using streams and managers.

6. References

[1] Ackerman, W. B., "Data Flow Languages", *Computer 15*, 2(February 1982), 15–25.

[2] Arvind, K. P. Gostelow, and W. Plouffe, "Indeterminacy, Monitors and Dataflow", *Proceedings of the Sixth ACM Symposium on Operating Systems Principles, Operating Systems Review 11*, 5(November 1977), 159–169.

[3] Arvind, K. P. Gostelow, and W. Plouffe, *An Asynchronous Programming Language and Computing Machine*, Department of Information and Computer Science (TR 114a), University of California – Irvine, Irvine, California, September 1978.

[4] Ashcroft, E. A., and W. W. Wadge, "Lucid, a Nonprocedural Language with Iteration", *Communications of the ACM 20*, 7(July 1977), 519–526.

[5] Brock, J. D., and W. B. Ackerman, "Scenarios: A Model of Non–determinate Computation", *International Colloquium on Formalization of Programming Concepts, Lecture Notes in Computer Science 107*, April 1981, 252–259.

[6] Burge, W. H., *Recursive Programming Techniques*, Addison–Wesley Publishing Co., Reading, Massachusetts, 1975.

[7] Catto, A. J., and J. R. Gurd, "Resource Management in Dataflow", *Proceedings of the 1981 Conference on Functional Programming Languages and Computer Architecture*, October 1981, 77–84.

[8] Dennis, J. B., "A Language Design for Structured Concurrency", *Design and Implementation of Programming Languages: Proceedings of a DoD Sponsored Workshop, Lecture Notes in Computer Science 54*, October 1976, 231–242.

[9] Friedman, D. P., and D. S. Wise, "CONS Should Not Evaluate its Arguments", *Automata, Languages, and Programming: Third International Colloquim* (S. Michaelson and R. Milner, Eds.), July 1976, 257–284.

[10] Henderson, P., *Functional Programming: Application and Implementation*, Prentice/Hall International, Englewood Cliffs, New Jersey, 1980.

[11] Hoare, C. A. R., "Monitors: An Operating System Structuring Concept", *Communications of the ACM 17*, 10(October 1975), 549–557.

[12] Jayaraman, B., and R. M. Keller, "Resource Control in a Demand–driven Data–flow Model", *Proceedings of the 1980 International Conference on Parallel Processing*, August 1980, 118–127.

[13] Kahn, G., "The Semantics of a Simple Language for Parallel Programming", *Information Processing 74: Proceedings of IFIP Congress 74*, August 1974, 471–475.

[14] Keller, R. M., G. Lindstrom, and S. S. Patil, "A Loosely–Coupled Applicative Multi–processing System", *Proceedings of the 1979 National Computer Conference, AFIPS Conference Proceedings 48*, June 1979, 613–622.

[15] Kosinski, P. R., "A Straightforward Denotational Semantics for Non–Determinate Data Flow Programs", *Conference Record of the Fifth ACM Symposium on Principles of Programming Languages*, January 1978, 214–221.

[16] Landin, P. J., "A Correspondence between ALGOL 60 and Church's Lambda Notation: Part I", *Communications of the ACM 8*, 2(February 1965), 89–101.

[17] Turner, D. A., "A New Implementation Technique for Applicative Languages", *Software – Practice and Experience 9*, 1(January 1979), 31–49.

[18] Wadge, W. W., "An Extensional Treatment of Dataflow Deadlock", *Theoretical Computer Science 13*, 1(January 1981), 3–15.

[19] Weng, K.-S., *Stream–Oriented Computation in Recursive Data Flow Schemas*, Laboratory for Computer Science (TM–68), MIT, Cambridge, Massachusetts, October 1975.